Level
4

AIM HIGH 에임하이

Active Curriculum for Successful Listening

LISTENING 리스닝

In-Depth Lab

We're
위아북스

AIM HIGH LISTENING • Level 4

지은이 In-Depth Lab
펴낸곳 (주)위아북스
펴낸이 전수용·조상현

등록번호 제300-2007-164호
주소 서울특별시 마포구 합정동 359-1 정촌빌딩 1층
전화 02-725-9988 ● **팩스** 02-725-9863
홈페이지 www.wearebooks.co.kr

북디자인 나인플럭스

ISBN 978-89-93258-37-0 54740

AIM HIGH 에임하이

Active Curriculum for Successful Listening

LISTENING 리스닝

In-Depth Lab

We're
위아북스

Prologue

청해 Listening Comprehension 란 내용을 듣고 이해하는 것을 말한다. 이는 단순히 영어를 얼마나 들을 수 있는가가 아니라 들은 내용을 얼마나 이해할 수 있는가를 뜻하는 것이다. 그러나 영어를 모국어로 하지 않는 사람들에게는 영어 자체가 잘 들리지 않는 경우가 많기 때문에 청해의 수준까지 도달하는 데에는 많은 어려움이 있다.

따라서 청취 실력을 향상시키기 위해서는 속도에 적응하는 것이 최우선 과제다. 빠른 속도로 지나가는 단어 하나하나를 들으려 하지 말고, 들리는 대로 덩어리째 듣고 이해할 수 있도록 많은 연습을 해야 한다. 듣는 것은 귀가 하지만 이해하는 것은 머리가 하는 일이므로, 영어의 빠른 속도에 적응하고 덩어리로 듣는 훈련과 동시에 들은 내용을 이해하는 훈련을 해야 한다.

이를 위해 본 교재에서는 청취한 내용을 머릿속에서 어떻게 정리해야 하는지 훈련시키는 Guided Listening 코너를 마련하였다. 이 코너에 포함된 Listening Notes를 이용해 들은 내용을 메모하면서 머릿속에 정리해라.

많은 교재들이 '들었는지 못 들었는지' 만 평가하는 문제들을 주로 다루고 있다. 하지만 실질적으로 청해 능력을 평가하기 위해 사용되는 문제의 형태는 좀 더 다양하다. 본 교재는 주제 및 목적 Main Idea/Purpose, 소재 Main Topic, 세부 정보 Detail, 기본 이해 Comprehension, 정보간의 관계 Relationship of Ideas, 세부 추론 Inference I, 전체 추론 Inference II, 화자의 입장 또는 목적 Stance/Function 등 8가지 문제 유형을 통해 청해 능력을 훈련하도록 구성하였다.

최근의 청취 시험들은 속도가 점점 빨라지고 있으며 내용도 길어지고 있다. 주제 또한 어려운 것들이 많아지는 추세이며 그 종류 또한 다양해지고 있다. 이러한 추세에 따라 본 교재에서는 다양한 주제의 대화 및 담화를 엄선하여 수록하였으며, 각종 시험의 청취 영역에 대비할 수 있도록 내용의 길이를 조절하였다.

청취 시험들이 변별력을 높이기 위해 시도 중인 것들 가운데 하나가 완벽한 이해를 요구하는 문제수를 늘리는 것이다. 세부 사항을 들었는지 묻는 문제보다는 내용을 완벽하게 이해했는가를 묻거나 전체를 이해했는지를 묻는 문제들이 늘고 있으며, 선택지들의 난이도 또한 높아지고 있다. 이에 대비하기 위해 본 교재에는 다양한 문제 유형은 물론 내용에 대한 완벽한 이해도를 묻는 문제들을 많이 수록하였다.

청취 훈련의 가장 기본은 '많이 듣는 것'이다. 따라서 듣고 문제를 푸는 데 그치지 않고 들은 내용을 충분히 반복 청취하여 완벽한 훈련이 될 수 있도록 각 section 뒤에 Dictation을 마련하였다. 본 교재의 모든 독자들이 영어의 속도에 완벽하게 적응하고 들리는 순서대로 덩어리째 이해할 수 있을 때까지 부단한 노력을 하기 바란다.

In-Depth Lab

Features

1 청취의 8가지 핵심 Question Types

토플, 텝스 등 각종 청취 테스트의 핵심적인 문제 유형을 면밀히 분석하여 세분하였다. 모든 유형의 청취 시험에 완벽하게 대비할 수 있도록 다양하고도 근본적인 listening skill들을 연습하도록 구성하였다.

▶ Main Idea/Purpose, Main Topic, Detail, Comprehension, Relationship of Ideas, Inference I, Inference II, Stance/Function

2 다양한 형태 및 주제에 대한 청취

여러 유형의 테스트에서 접할 수 있는 강의, 연구 결과, 방송, 연설 등의 다양한 담화문과, 일상생활에서 일어날 수 있는 실질적인 대화를 청취함으로써 다양한 청취 형태와 주제에 익숙해지도록 하였다.

3 소리로 익히는 청취 훈련

청취 훈련을 위해서는 눈으로 읽고 손으로 쓰는 훈련보다는 소리를 듣고 익히며 그 표현을 소리로 인식하고, 같은 뜻이나 비슷한 표현 또한 소리로 인식하는 것이 중요하다. 따라서 읽거나 쓰는 방식이 아닌, sound로 익히고 sound로 확인하는 다양한 청취 훈련을 하도록 구성하였다.

▶ 영어 설명을 듣고 해당 단어 쓰기
▶ 우리말 문장을 읽은 후 같은 뜻의 영어 문장을 듣고 찾기
▶ 세 덩어리의 영어를 듣고 하나의 완성된 영어 문장으로 만들기
▶ 영어 문장을 읽은 후 같은 뜻의 영어 문장을 듣고 찾기

4 Guided Listening 훈련

Listening Notes를 통해 청취하는 내용의 핵심 정보를 메모하는 것은 물론 내용의 전체적인 흐름을 머리로 이해하는 훈련이 되도록 하였다. 청취 지문의 전형적인 구조에 익숙해짐으로써 '예측 청취'를 가능케 하여 전반적인 청해 실력을 향상시킬 수 있다.

▶ Cause and Effect, Problem and Solution, Exemplifying, Classifying, Process or Sequence 등

Listening Skill Building **Question Types**

1 Main Idea/Purpose
전체적인 내용의 이해를 통해 직·간접적으로 드러난 대화의 목적 및 담화의 주제를 파악하는 능력

2 Main Topic
핵심어(key word) 및 대화와 담화에서 주로 이야기되고 있는 소재를 파악하는 능력

3 Detail
중요한 세부 정보에 대한 청취 능력

4 Comprehension
청취한 내용에 대한 이해 능력

5 Relationship of Ideas
언급된 정보들간의 관계 파악 능력

6 Inference I
세부적인 내용에 근거한 추론 능력

7 Inference II
전체 또는 다양한 정보에 근거한 추론 능력

8 Stance/Function
화자의 입장 및 목적 파악 능력

Topics

LEVEL 2

대화의 주제		총 56
의사전달	● ●	2
여행	● ● ● ● ● ●	6
계획/약속	● ● ● ● ● ● ● ●	8
교통	● ● ● ● ●	5
회사와 업무	● ● ● ● ● ●	6
쇼핑/상점/수리점	● ● ● ● ● ●	6
여가/취미생활	● ● ● ● ●	5
식사/식당	● ●	2
건강/병원/약국	● ● ● ●	4
학교	● ● ● ● ●	5
전화 통화	● ● ●	3
부동산 및 가정생활	● ● ● ●	4

담화의 주제		총 56
강의 및 조사 결과	● ● ● ● ● ● ● ● ● ● ● ● ● ● ● ● ● ● ● ●	20
연설	● ● ●	3
보도/방송	● ● ● ● ● ● ● ● ● ● ● ●	12
전화 메시지	●	1
안내 방송 및 공지 사항	● ● ● ● ● ●	6
광고	● ● ● ● ●	5
의견 제시 및 주장	● ● ● ● ●	5
기타	● ● ● ●	4

Topics

LEVEL 4

대화의 주제		총 48
의사전달	● ● ● ● ● ●	6
여행	● ● ● ●	4
계획/약속	● ● ● ●	4
교통	● ●	2
회사와 업무	● ● ● ●	4
쇼핑/상점/수리점	●	1
여가/취미생활	● ● ● ● ●	5
감정 표현	● ●	2
식사/식당	●	1
건강/병원/약국	● ● ● ● ●	5
인사/소개/칭찬/축하/감사	● ●	2
학교	● ● ● ● ●	5
전화 통화	●	1
부동산 및 가정생활	● ● ● ● ●	5
은행과 우체국	●	1

담화의 주제		총 64
강의 및 조사 결과	● ●	28
연설	● ● ● ● ● ● ●	7
보도/방송	● ● ● ● ● ● ● ● ● ● ● ● ● ● ●	15
전화 메시지	●	1
안내 방송 및 공지 사항	● ● ● ● ●	5
광고	● ●	2
의견 제시 및 주장	●	1
교육/소개 및 조언	● ● ● ● ●	5

How To Use This Book

VOCABULARY PREVIEW

몰라서 안 들릴 수 있는 어휘와 표현을 선행 학습함으로써 학습 효과를 높인다.

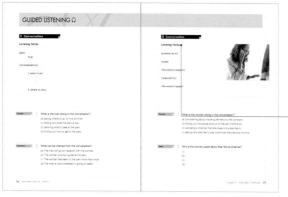

GUIDED LISTENING

Conversation 2개, Monologue 2개로 구성되었으며, 각 2문제씩 달려 있다. 하나의 Script를 들은 뒤 그 Chapter에 해당하는 유형의 문제 1과 추가적인 문제 2를 풀어 봄으로써 들은 것을 잘 이해했는지 확인한다. 선택지도 모두 영문으로 되어 있다.

Listening Notes

주어진 clues를 참고하여 들으면서 내용을 메모해 머릿속에 정리할 수 있도록 한다.

DICTATION GUIDED LISTENING

GUIDED LISTENING에 대한 받아쓰기 코너. 듣기 어려운 단어, 연어, 중요한 표현 등이 빈칸으로 제시되어 들은 것을 재확인하며 학습할 수 있다. 본문의 문제를 그대로 보여 주기 때문에 2차 학습까지 용이하며 중요한 어휘도 학습할 수 있다.

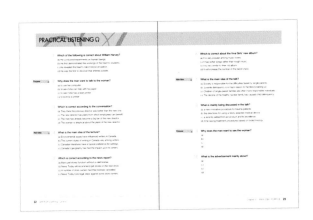

PRACTICAL LISTENING

Chapter마다 10문제씩으로 구성되어 있다. 다양한 문제 유형을 풀어 볼 수 있으며, 그 Chapter에 해당하는 문제에는 유형이 제시되어 있다.

DICTATION PRACTICAL LISTENING

PRACTICAL LISTENING 10문제에 대한 받아쓰기 코너다. 듣기 어려운 단어, 연어, 중요한 표현 등이 빈칸으로 제시되어 들은 것을 다시 한 번 확인하며 학습할 수 있다. 본문의 문제를 그대로 보여 주기 때문에 2차 학습까지 용이하며 중요한 어휘도 학습할 수 있다. 선택지의 내용도 녹음하여 들려 줌으로써 자칫 놓치기 쉬운 부분까지 추가 학습이 가능하다.

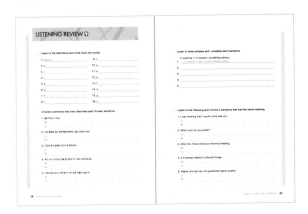

LISTENING REVIEW

소리로 익히는 훈련을 위한 테스트다. 4가지 방식의 훈련법으로 청취 연습을 할 수 있다.

A 영어 설명을 듣고 그에 해당하는 영단어를 써 보는 훈련이다.

B 영어 문장 2개를 들은 후 주어진 우리말과 같은 뜻의 문장을 찾는 훈련이다.

C 세 덩어리의 chunk를 듣고 하나의 완전한 문장이 되도록 배열한다.

D 영어 문장 2개를 들은 후 주어진 영어 문장과 같은 의미가 되는 문장을 찾는 훈련이다.

Contents

Prologue
Features
Listening Skill Building Question Types
Topics _ LEVEL 1~4
How To Use This Book

AIM HIGH

Active Curriculum for Successful Listening

LISTENING

CHAPTER 01

MAIN IDEA/ PURPOSE

VOCABULARY PREVIEW 🎧

Write down the meanings of the words.

01	sanctuary	13	skeptical
02	accountable	14	ethnic
03	mold	15	sparsely
04	tolerable	16	sprawling
05	repairable	17	terrain
06	ailment	18	draw upon
07	acupuncture	19	pathetic
08	pulsation	20	footage
09	circulate	21	revoke
10	conduit	22	rampant
11	bring about	23	saturate
12	implement	24	blood clotting

GUIDED LISTENING 🎧

1 Conversation

Listening Notes

(plan)

    to go

(recommendation)

    1. (what to do)

        •

        •

    2. (where to stay)

Purpose

1 What is the man doing in the conversation?

    (a) asking where to go for the summer

    (b) finding out what the park is like

    (c) planning what to see at the park

    (d) finding out how to get to the park

Inference I

2 What can be inferred from the conversation?

    (a) The man will go on vacation with the woman.

    (b) The woman is a tour guide at the park.

    (c) The woman has been to the park more than once.

    (d) The man is now interested in going on safari.

2 Conversation

Listening Notes

(problem) my bill

(cause)

(the woman's complaint)

(responsibility)

(the woman's request)

Purpose

1 What is the woman doing in the conversation?

(a) complaining about insulting remarks by the company

(b) finding out the actual amount of the last month's bill

(c) canceling a channel that she does not subscribe to

(d) asking why she has to pay more than the previous months.

Detail

2 Why is the woman upset about Star Movie Channel?

(a)

(b)

(c)

(d)

3 Monologue

Listening Notes

(Main Idea) Let's discuss

Culture

Cultural differences

Body languages

(Possible consequences)

    damage

Main Idea

1   What is the main idea of the talk?

(a) Cultural differences are due to narrow attitudes.

(b) Every society has a different culture that should be respected.

(c) Serious misunderstandings may arise due to cultural differences.

(d) Business should be done outside cultural limits.

Detail

2   Which is NOT mentioned as an influence that culture has on a person?

(a) the way the person talks

(b) the way the person acts

(c) the way the person interacts with others

(d) the way the person perceives things

4 Monologue

Listening Notes

(Main Idea)
    known as
    each having its

(Example 1): Navaho
(Example 2): Europeans
(Example 3): Chinese
These forms of healing
        sustained through
        preserved

(Many people's belief)

Main Idea

1 What is the main idea of the lecture?

(a) Every culture has unique types of traditional forms of healing.

(b) Some cultures were more advanced in treatment of sick people.

(c) Alternative medicine today is derived from the ancient world.

(d) Alternative medicine in some cultures has proved to be effective.

Detail

2 What did the Navaho Indians use to heal people?

(a)

(b)

(c)

(d)

1 Conversation

1 What is the man doing in the conversation?
(a) asking where to go for the summer
(b) finding out what the park is like
(c) planning what to see at the park
(d) finding out how to get to the park

2 What can be inferred from the conversation?
(a) The man will go on vacation with the woman.
(b) The woman is a tour guide at the park.
(c) The woman has been to the park more than once.
(d) The man is now interested in going on safari.

M Hi, Stuart told me that you've been to Steven National Park. Is that so?

W Yeah, it's a very beautiful place. _____?

M No. My wife and I are planning to go there this summer. What could we do there?

W Well, there's so much to do there. _____, there's a bird sanctuary and deer grounds. _____ safaris?

M No, but my wife is.

W You _____. It's excellent.

M Do you know any good places _____?

W Yes, you could stay _____. We always stay there whenever we go. I can _____ if you want it.

M Thanks, I'd appreciate that.

in addition to ~외에도 | sanctuary 금렵구, 자연 보호구역 | deer 사슴 | safari 사파리 | whenever ~할 때마다

2 Conversation

1 What is the woman doing in the conversation?
(a) complaining about insulting remarks by the company
(b) finding out the actual amount of the last month's bill
(c) canceling a channel that she does not subscribe to
(d) asking why she has to pay more than the previous months

2 Why is the woman upset about Star Movie Channel?
(a) Because they changed the fee without asking her.
(b) Because they canceled her subscription to the channel.
(c) Because they didn't send her the bill directly.
(d) Because they didn't reflect the rate in the bill.

(Telephone rings.)

M I'm Mark from City Cable. How may I help you?

W Hi. I'm Miss Crawford. I see that my bill is a little higher than usual. Do you think this is _____?

M Miss Crawford, I can see your bill details on my computer screen and I see that your bill is _____. Do you subscribe to Star Movie Channel?

W Yes, I do.

M Actually, that channel _____, which is _____.

W But _____ about it earlier. How can you increase the bill _____?

M Well, that's the responsibility of the movie channel and we are _____.

W Okay, please do me a favor and cancel my subscription to the channel.

M Sure, Miss Crawford.

bill 청구서, 계산서 | than usual 여느 때보다 | subscribe 신청하다, 예약 구독하다 | monthly rate 한 달 이용료 | permission 허가, 허용 | accountable 책임 있는, 해명할 의무가 있는 | insulting 모욕적인, 무례한

1 What is the main idea of the talk?
  (a) Cultural differences are due to narrow attitudes.
  (b) Every society has a different culture that should be respected.
  (c) Serious misunderstandings may arise due to cultural differences.
  (d) Business should be done outside cultural limits.

2 Which is NOT mentioned as an influence that culture has on a person?
  (a) the way the person talks
  (b) the way the person acts
  (c) the way the person interacts with others
  (d) the way the person perceives things

W Let's discuss the impact of cultural differences on our lives. Culture usually molds a person in the way he talks, behaves, interacts with other people, and largely _____ _____. Cultural differences may _____ _____ if two people _____ _____ of each other. Body languages, along with social and cultural codes, differ from culture to culture, and _____ _____ are very high. The difference seems to be _____; however, during business meetings or diplomatic situations, a small misinterpretation may lead to serious consequences: damage done may be far from repairable.

mold 형성하다 | perceive 지각하다, 인식하다 | give rise to ~을 일으키다, 생기게 하다 | misunderstanding 오해 | misinterpret 잘못 해석하다, 오해하다 | tolerable 참을 수 있는, 용인될 수 있는 | diplomatic 외교의 | consequence 결과, 결말 | repairable 돌이킬 수 있는

1 What is the main idea of the lecture?
  (a) Every culture has unique types of traditional forms of healing.
  (b) Some cultures were more advanced in treatment of sick people.
  (c) Alternative medicine today is derived from the ancient world.
  (d) Alternative medicine in some cultures has proved to be effective.

2 What did the Navaho Indians use to heal people?
  (a) herbs
  (b) acupuncture
  (c) sand painting
  (d) Western medicine

M In earlier times, people _____ in different ways, some of which are even practiced up to now. All these practices are collectively known as _____, each having _____. One Native American tribe from the southwest, called the Navaho, believes in sand painting _____. Europeans _____ for all kinds of diseases. _____, which has been in practice among Chinese people for centuries. These forms of healing have been sustained through all types of modernization and have preserved their traditional values. Many people who believe in alternative forms of healing find them as effective as Western medicine.

treat (질병을) 치료하다 | ailment 질병 | practice 실행하다, 관행, 관례 | up to now 지금까지, 현재까지 | alternative medicine 대체 의학 | sand painting 모래 그림 (여러 가지로 착색한 모래로 그리는 주술적인 그림) | remedy 치료, 의료 | healing 치유, 치료 | acupuncture 침술

1   Which of the following is correct about William Harvey?

(a) He conducted experiments on human beings.

(b) He first demonstrated the workings of the heart to students.

(c) He revealed the heart's role in blood circulation.

(d) He was the first to discover that arteries pulsate.

Purpose

2   Why does the man want to talk to the woman?

(a) to use her computer

(b) to ask if she can help with his paper

(c) to see if she has a laser printer

(d) to borrow a printer

3   Which is correct according to the conversation?

(a) They think the previous director was better than the new one.

(b) The new director has plans from which employees can benefit.

(c) The man has already become a big fan of the new director.

(d) The woman is skeptical about the plans of the new director.

Main Idea

4   What is the main idea of the lecture?

(a) Environmental issues have influenced writers in Canada.

(b) The current styles of writing in Canada vary among writers.

(c) Canadian literatures have a typical preference for settings.

(d) Canada's geography has had the impact upon its writers.

5   Which is correct according to the news report?

(a) Many pet stores function without a valid license.

(b) News Today will recommend pet stores on the next show.

(c) A number of store owners had their licenses cancelled.

(d) News Today took legal steps against some store owners.

6 Which is correct about the Viva Girls' new album?

   (a) It is very popular among music lovers.

   (b) It has softer songs rather than rough music.

   (c) It is very similar to their old album.

   (d) It will increase the number of the band's fans.

Main Idea 7 What is the main idea of the talk?

   (a) Society is responsible for the difficulties faced by single parents.

   (b) Juvenile delinquency is a major reason for families breaking up.

   (c) Children of single-parent families are often more responsible individuals.

   (d) The decline of the healthy nuclear family has caused child delinquency.

8 What is mainly being discussed in the talk?

   (a) a new innovative procedure for trauma patients

   (b) the directions for using a newly adopted medical device

   (c) a recently added first aid product and its excellence

   (d) time-saving treatment procedures based on biotechnology

Purpose 9 Why does the man want to see the woman?

   (a)

   (b)

   (c)

   (d)

10 What is the advertisement mainly about?

   (a)

   (b)

   (c)

   (d)

1 Monologue

Which of the following is correct about William Harvey?
(a) He conducted experiments on human beings.
(b) He first demonstrated the workings of the heart to students.
(c) He revealed the heart's role in blood circulation.
(d) He was the first to discover that arteries pulsate.

M Today's lecture deals with William Harvey, the 17th century English physiologist. Harvey discovered that _____ _____ by the heart, and not by the rhythmic pulsation of the arteries as believed. It was through his work that we came to understand that _____ _____, a muscle _____ _____. _____ _____, but merely act as conduits through which blood flows. He came to this conclusion _____ of patients and experiments with animals. These included observing pulsation of _____, or animals in which the heart was removed and continued to pulse for a time. He published his findings on the workings of the heart in 1628.

rhythmic 리드미컬한 | pulsation 박동 | artery 동맥 | vein 정맥 | circulate 순환하다 | merely 단순히 | conduit 수로, 도랑 | extensive 광범위한

2 Conversation

Why does the man want to talk to the woman?
(a) to use her computer
(b) to ask if she can help with his paper
(c) to see if she has a laser printer
(d) to borrow a printer

M Can I come in for seconds?
W Hi, Mark. Come in. _____
M Well, I'm working on my paper and _____ _____. But...
W Isn't your computer connected to the Internet or anything?
M It is not the Internet. I need to print some pages, but it doesn't seem to be working from this morning.
W Oh! _____. So you can use my computer. Or do you want to take the printer to your room?
M I don't know how long it would take, so, if you don't mind, _____ the first thing tomorrow.
W That's okay. By the way, how many pages are you going to print?
M About seventy.
W Oh, then you should use Jenny's printer.
M _____?
W It is, but Jenny's is a laser printer and is much faster.

for seconds 잠깐만, 잠깐 동안 | connect 연결하다 | bring ~ back ~을 돌려주다 | borrow 빌리다

3 Conversation

Which is correct according to the conversation?

(a) They think the previous director was better than the new one.

(b) The new director has plans from which employees can benefit.

(c) The man has already become a big fan of the new director.

(d) The woman is skeptical about the plans of the new director.

W I heard that a new director has joined your company. How's he?

M Well, he's a strict person but very knowledgeable. He's very different _____.

W Is he _____ or shareholder-friendly?

M He says he's on our side. He wants _____ _____ in the company.

W Sounds good. It seems like he has big plans.

M Maybe. Let's _____. A lot of directors usually talk a lot but _____ _____.

W I hope he is different _____ _____.

director 이사, 국장, 지도자, 관리자 | strict 엄격한, 엄밀한 | knowledgeable 많이 아는, 박식한, 정보통의 | different from ~와 다른 | previous 앞의, 이전의 | shareholder 주주 | friendly ~에 우호(친화)적인 | bring about 초래하다, 불러일으키다 | significant 중요한, 의미 있는 | implement 이행하다, 수행하다 | be poor at ~에 서투르다 | skeptical 회의적인

4 Monologue

What is the main idea of the lecture?

(a) Environmental issues have influenced writers in Canada.

(b) The current styles of writing in Canada vary among writers.

(c) Canadian literatures have a typical preference for settings.

(d) Canada's geography has had the impact upon its writers.

W Writers from various nations have often been influenced _____ _____. This _____ _____ Canada as well. I'm going to discuss _____ _____ on Canadian literature: its natural environment. Though sparsely populated, Canada is the second-largest country in the world. The country's _____ _____ has inspired various themes in writers _____ _____ Margaret Atwood, who is known for scholarly fiction, and Douglas Coupland, whose work draws upon pop culture. Both would agree that the geography of Canada has greatly influenced _____, although their styles are completely different. This means that various Canadian artists perceive the nation's geography in different ways, and that is _____.

ethnic 민족의 | surroundings (주위) 환경 | hold true for ~에도 사실이다, 적용되다 | long-standing 오래 계속되는, 오랜 | sparsely 성기게, 듬성듬성하게 | populate ~에 살다, 거주하다 | sprawling 불규칙하게 퍼져 있는 | terrain 지형, 지세 | inspire 영감을 불어넣다 | diverse 다양한 | scholarly 학자다운, 학문적인 | draw upon ~에 의존하다 | geography 지리, 지세, 지형 | perceive 인식하다 | preference 선호

5 Monologue

Which is correct according to the news report?
(a) Many pet stores function without a valid license.
(b) News Today will recommend pet stores on the next show.
(c) A number of store owners had their licenses cancelled.
(d) News Today took legal steps against some store owners.

M News Today brings you _____ _____ in 35 of the 100 pet stores we shopped at with a hidden camera while investigating _____ _____ among pet store owners. What we saw there was shocking, and we'll have a look at some of that footage later on. _____. The photos may not be _____. Because what we saw there was so disturbing, we felt that we had to take immediate action, and not just report what we uncovered. Therefore, the news network, _____ and legal staff, has lodged _____ against the store owners to have their business licenses revoked. Conditions in the remaining 65 stores _____ _____. If you are considering buying a pet, here's a list of outstanding stores as rated by our experts.

expose 폭로, 적발 | **pathetic** 형편없는, 아주 불충분한 | **footage** 비디오 자료 화면 | **appropriate** 적당한, 적절한 | **disturbing** 교란시키는, 불온한 | **take action** 조치를 취하다 | **legal staff** 법률 자문단 | **lodge~against** …에 대해 (고소장, 신고서 등을) 제출하다, (반대, 항의 등을) 제기하다 | **complaint** (민사의) 고소 | **revoke** 철회하다, 무효로 하다 | **valid** 유효한 | **take legal steps against** ~를 고소하다

6 Conversation

Which is correct about the Viva Girls' new album?
(a) It is very popular among music lovers.
(b) It has softer songs rather than rough music.
(c) It is very similar to their old album.
(d) It will increase the number of the band's fans.

W Hey, I bought the Viva Girls' new album.
M You mean _____ "Precious Love"?
W Yeah. Have you heard any of the songs on the album?
M Some of them, yes. I didn't buy the CD, though. I heard them on the radio.
W So, _____?
M I thought the album's _____.
W Yeah, the music is _____.
M It's more like pop than rock music. I don't think many people expected that kind of music from them.
W It's quite possible that they'll lose their popularity because of that.
M Will you buy their next album?
W Maybe not, _____.

precious 소중한, 귀중한 **not as good as** ~만큼 좋지 않은, ~만 못한 **previous** 이전의, 앞선 **appealing** 매력적인, 사람을 끄는, 호소하는 듯한
rather than ~라기보다는 **similar to** ~와 유사한, 비슷한

7 Monologue

What is the main idea of the talk?

(a) Society is responsible for the difficulties faced by single parents.

(b) Juvenile delinquency is a major reason for families breaking up.

(c) Children of single-parent families are often more responsible individuals.

(d) The decline of the healthy nuclear family has caused child delinquency.

M Most people _____ between the growing number of households _____ _____ and _____ _____. Increasing numbers of children are _____ _____ as single parents _____ _____. This causes children to grow up _____ from outside the home. It is true that there are many single-parent families — most often headed by women — that are doing well. All evidence points to the fact that on average, though, children raised by single parents have _____ _____ and getting involved in crime. My fear is that until society fights to reestablish the traditional nuclear family, the issue of juvenile delinquency can only get worse.

rampant 만연하는, 유행하는 juvenile delinquency 미성년(청소년) 범죄 dubious 모호한, 애매한 on average 일반적으로 probability 확률, 가망성
drop out of ~을 중퇴하다, 도중에 그만두다 get involved in ~에 연루되다 nuclear family 핵가족 (부부와 미혼 자녀로만 구성된 가족)

8 Monologue

What is mainly being discussed in the talk?

(a) a new innovative procedure for trauma patients

(b) the directions for using a newly adopted medical device

(c) a recently added first aid product and its excellence

(d) time-saving treatment procedures based on biotechnology

W The latest product to be included in _____ _____ is the Blue Algae bandage. _____ _____ for trauma situations, it stops bleeding almost instantly. More interestingly, the bandage works based on biotechnology that is simply amazing. The bandage _____ _____ complex carbohydrate solution derived from single-cell algae. The algae in this solution accelerate _____ _____, and do so much faster than _____ _____ used in traditional bandages. Use of this product reduces bleeding time by 75%. While the new bandages are currently being used only for emergencies, they could be more widely used in the future. This is one more example of how the cutting-edge world of biotechnology _____ _____ to everyday life.

emergency first aid kit 응급처치용 상자 alga 해조, 조류 (pl. algae) trauma 외상(성 증상) instantly 즉시 based on ~에 근거한
biotechnology 생명공학 saturate 적시다, 배어들게 하다 carbohydrate 탄수화물 solution 용액, 용제, 해결책 derive 끌어내다, 얻다
blood clotting 혈액 응고 artificial 인공의 chemical 화학 compound 혼합물 cutting-edge 최첨단 innovative 혁신적인

9 Conversation

Why does the man want to see the woman?
(a) to thank her for the grade
(b) to promise to attend all the classes
(c) to obtain permission to audit a class
(d) to ask what the requirements are for History 203

M Good morning, Professor Presley.

W Good morning. How may I help you?

M My name is Steve. I was in your history class last semester, 'The Rise and Fall of Rome.'

W Oh, now I remember you. _____ _____.

M I really appreciated that.

W No, you _____. _____ _____ on that paper.

M Thanks a lot. By the way, Professor Presley, I was wondering ____ _____, History 203.

W Well, I don't usually _____ since most of them who did before didn't attend class regularly.

M Oh, that's not a big deal. I promise that I'll attend all the classes. If I have to do assignments or papers, _____ _____. But if it is just the attendance, then _____.

W Okay, you can come from tomorrow.

M Thank you. I'll see you then.

semester 학기 deserve ~할 만하다 | audit (대학 강의를) 청강하다 assignment 숙제, 할당된 일 | attendance 출석 | permission 허락, 허가

10 Monologue

What is the advertisement mainly about?
(a) getting discounted fares with airlines
(b) receiving air miles through hotel room reservations
(c) making credit card payments for hotel rooms
(d) saving money on hotel rooms through advance booking

M Are you traveling? Now, here's a chance to _____ both on the planes you take and the hotels you stay at. How? _____ _____ on your High Saver Miles card all this month while enjoying the comfort of a Starlux Hotel! Starlux Hotels, located in over 300 locations around the world, are _____ _____, _____ _____. To take advantage of this offer, _____ with your credit card and receive up to 500 miles on any Transoceanic, Interstate Combine or Westward flight. That means that _____ _____! For reservations, contact your local travel agent or call us at 888-5000.

discount 할인 affordable (가격이) 알맞은 take advantage of ~을 이용하다 | qualifying 한정된 | advance booking 사전 예약

LISTENING REVIEW 🎧

A Listen to the definitions and write down the words.

1. perceive _____
2. s _____
3. s _____
4. r _____
5. s _____
6. f _____
7. p _____
8. r _____

9. v _____
10. c _____
11. s _____
12. t _____
13. a _____
14. a _____
15. d _____
16. p _____

B Choose a sentence that best describes each Korean sentence.

1. 이 새로운 밴드는 앞으로 좀 더 광범위하게 사용될 수 있을 것입니다.
   (a) _____
   (b) _____

2. 많은 이사들이 대개 말은 많지만, 말한 것을 실천하는 데는 서투르니까 말이야.
   (a) _____
   (b) _____

3. 그것은 호텔에 머무르면 항공가격이 할인된다는 것을 의미합니다!
   (a) _____
   (b) _____

4. 유럽 사람들은 모든 질병에 허브 치료법을 사용하는 것으로 유명합니다.
   (a) _____
   (b) _____

5. 이것은 아이들이 집 밖에서 이중적인 가치체계를 가지고 자라게 합니다.
   (a) _____
   (b) _____

C Listen to three phrases and complete each sentence.

any good places / do you know / to stay there
1. ➡ Do you know any good places to stay there? _____

2. _____

3. _____

4. _____

5. _____

D Listen to the following and choose a sentence that has the same meaning.

1. Be sure and go to the safari there.
   (a) _____
   (b) _____

2. The heart is responsible for pumping blood throughout the body.
   (a) _____
   (b) _____

3. It is likely that children should not see the photos.
   (a) _____
   (b) _____

4. Serious misunderstandings may arise due to cultural differences.
   (a) _____
   (b) _____

5. The geography of Canada has greatly influenced writers' writings.
   (a) _____
   (b) _____

CHAPTER 02

MAIN TOPIC

VOCABULARY PREVIEW 🎧   Write down the meanings of the words.

01	diploma	13	manhood
02	diabetic	14	status
03	declaration	15	tenet
04	articulation	16	convert
05	Genesis	17	sacred
06	fable	18	orthodox
07	deposit	19	rigorous
08	physiotherapy	20	addictive
09	tattooing	21	legible
10	scar	22	emit
11	ritual	23	blast
12	induction	24	attribute

GUIDED LISTENING 🎧

1 Conversation

Listening Notes

(Purpose of visit) I want to

(requirement 1):
    (What to do)
    remember to

(requirement 2):
    (What to do)
    Make sure

Main Topic   1   What is mainly being discussed?

    (a) what to bring to the admission office

    (b) where to join the French Literature course

    (c) how to complete the course registration form

    (d) what to take before the literature course

Detail   2   What will the man have to do later on?

    (a) fill out his telephone number in the form

    (b) bring his proof of address and phone number

    (c) make three copies of his high school diploma

    (d) have his telephone repaired in his room

2 Conversation

Listening Notes

(Purpose of talk) Do you have

I'm carrying

(purpose):

you should have

(how often)

Main Topic **1** What is mainly being discussed in the conversation?

(a) a treatment with herbs for his disease

(b) the prescription that the man made up for the woman

(c) the declaration of what the man has purchased abroad

(d) the procedure of declaring herbs imported from a foreign country

Inference I **2** What can be inferred from the conversation?

(a)

(b)

(c)

(d)

3 Monologue

Listening Notes

(Written language)

(major role)

(African languages)

(reason 1)

(reason 2)

Main Topic

1 What is the best title for this lecture?

(a) African Languages in Former British Colonies

(b) The Impact of Colonization on African Languages

(c) The Advancement of African Literature

(d) Two Major Barriers to African Literature

Comprehension

2 Which of the following is correct according to the lecture?

(a) Most of the African literatures are written in English.

(b) Former French colonists created a new language for Africans.

(c) French colonists allowed the use of African languages.

(d) A huge variation among African spoken languages exists.

4 Monologue

Listening Notes

(Topic)
       (several types)
       (reason) having
       dealing with

(Popular story 1)
       (example)
(Popular story 2)
       (example)
(Popular story 3)
       (example)

Main Topic

1 What is the lecture about?

(a) different characters in a famous story

(b) types of messages in old fables

(c) translating stories from Greek into different languages

(d) some common types of popular stories

Detail

2 Which is mentioned as a reason for a fondness for fables among children?

(a)

(b)

(c)

(d)

1 Conversation

1 What is mainly being discussed?
(a) what to bring to the admission office
(b) where to join the French Literature course
(c) how to complete the course registration form
(d) what to take before the literature course

2 What will the man have to do later on?
(a) fill out his telephone number in the form
(b) bring his proof of address and phone number
(c) make three copies of his high school diploma
(d) have his telephone repaired in his room

M Hi, I want to join the French Literature course.

W Okay. Please _____.

M Well, the form requires a telephone number. I don't have one yet; we just moved in.

W Fine, you may _____, but please remember _____.

M Sure.

W Do you have personal photographs now?

M No, but I can get them by tomorrow. _____ ?

W Three copies. _____ _____. It starts at 10:00 a.m.

M Sure. See you tomorrow then.

fill out (양식 따위를) 써넣다, 채우다 | personal 본인의, 개인의 | registration 등록 | diploma 졸업증서

2 Conversation

1 What is mainly being discussed in the conversation?
(a) a treatment with herbs for his disease
(b) the prescription that the man made up for the woman
(c) the declaration of what the man has purchased abroad
(d) the procedure of declaring herbs imported from a foreign country

2 What can be inferred from the conversation?
(a) The woman is interested in herbs.
(b) The man goes abroad once in a while.
(c) The man is working at a hospital.
(d) The woman will not allow the herbs.

W Do you have anything in your bags which you would like us to know about, sir?

M Yeah, I'm carrying 4 kg of _____.

W Are they _____ ?

M Yes, I'm _____.

W Well, you should have _____ _____, then. Could I have a look at it?

M Sure, here it is.

W Okay, this is fine. Do you go every month _____ _____ ?

M Not exactly, but _____.

W Fine, please step through and sign here before you go.

herb 약초 | medicinal 의약의, 약용의 | diabetic 당뇨병 환자 | treatment 치료, 치료법 | prescription 처방전 | whenever ~할 때마다 | short 부족한, 모자라는 | declaration 세관 신고

3 Monologue

1 What is the best title for this lecture?
   (a) African Languages in Former British Colonies
   (b) The Impact of Colonization on African Languages
   (c) The Advancement of African Literature
   (d) Two Major Barriers to African Literature

2 Which of the following is correct according to the lecture?
   (a) Most of the African literatures are written in English.
   (b) Former French colonists created a new language for Africans.
   (c) French colonists allowed the use of African languages.
   (d) A huge variation among African spoken languages exists.

W Written language is _____.
It has a major role in _____ like poems and stories. Surprisingly, African languages did not _____ _____ for centuries. Even today, only about _____ African languages have written forms of expression. One of the reasons could be that there is vast variation among African languages. A basic African language may remain the same; however, its words, spelling and articulation may differ from one culture to another. _____ _____ present in African languages has its origin in South Africa and other former British colonies. People in former French and Portuguese colonies _____ _____ African languages, which blocked their development and limited their reach.

written language 문자 언어, 성문 언어 poem 시 vast 막대한, 광대한 variation 변화, 변동 spelling 철자법 articulation 발음법 colony 식민지 block 막다, 저해하다

4 Monologue

1 What is the lecture about?
   (a) different characters in a famous story
   (b) types of messages in old fables
   (c) translating stories from Greek into different languages
   (d) some common types of popular stories

2 Which is mentioned as a reason for a fondness for fables among children?
   (a) They are fascinated by animals that can talk.
   (b) They love the imaginary animals introduced in the stories.
   (c) They like fascinating images of animals in the books.
   (d) They love to read and listen to stories about great heroes.

W Everyone, especially children, is fond of stories. There are several types of stories, having _____, _____ and _____ _____. Some types of stories are more popular than others. Some might have originated thousands of years ago, but _____. Some stories are common to all people across the world. One such story is *Genesis* in the Bible. Children often love reading and hearing _____ _____. *The Iliad* and *The Odyssey* are two such stories written by Homer that describe ancient Greek heroes. Another very popular form of story is fables where animals talk to each other. Aesop's fables are very popular among children _____ _____.

be fond of ~을 좋아하다 subject 주제 originate 생기다, 유래하다 Genesis 창세기 fable 우화 translate 번역하다

1 Which is correct about the man according to the conversation?

(a) He wants to live in the southern suburbs.

(b) He thinks the place is too far from the station.

(c) He is looking for a quiet place to live in.

(d) He wants to live near public transportation.

Main Topic

2 What is mainly being discussed?

(a) coffee helps avert gallstone formation

(b) the questionable health benefits of coffee

(c) coffee being used to dissolve gallstones

(d) caffeinated beverages that should be avoided

3 What is correct about Steve according to the conversation?

(a) He hurt his right elbow after playing tennis.

(b) He started treatment a long time ago.

(c) He delayed treatment on his elbow.

(d) He plays tennis with his left arm.

Main Topic

4 What is the topic of the talk?

(a) the reasons for body scarring in Africa

(b) a comparison of tattooing and scarification

(c) how scarification came to Africa

(d) the diverse tattooing traditions in Africa

5 Which is correct according to the report?

(a) Astronaut Yi So-yeon has developed several space technologies.

(b) Korea may join multinational space efforts.

(c) Male and female astronauts will enter space separately.

(d) Korean space technologies are aboard the ISS.

6 What is mainly taking place in the conversation?

(a) The woman is doing some house chores.

(b) The woman is asking the man for help.

(c) The man is holding a chair for the woman.

(d) The couple is deciding where to hang the picture.

7 What is the lecturer's main point about Islam?

(a) It has many points similar to Orthodox Judaism.

(b) It is easy to join but has daily rules to follow.

(c) A person must read the Koran before becoming a Muslim.

(d) Muslims are strict about the foods which they shouldn't eat.

8 What is the speaker's main point?

(a) Smoking can worsen your health severely.

(b) Weight can be reduced by exercising.

(c) Be sure to exercise after you quit smoking.

(d) Don't get an addictive personality.

9 What is the woman mainly doing in the conversation?

(a)

(b)

(c)

(d)

10 What is the speaker's view on American responsibility toward global warming?

(a)

(b)

(c)

(d)

1 Conversation

Which is correct about the man according to the conversation?

(a) He wants to live in the southern suburbs.

(b) He thinks the place is too far from the station.

(c) He is looking for a quiet place to live in.

(d) He wants to live near public transportation.

M Hi, I'm looking for an apartment to rent. Could you help me?

W Certainly. Are you _____?

M Not really, but I'd prefer a place near convenient public transportation.

W Would you mind one in the southern suburbs?

M Not at all. But is it near to any public transportation?

W It is _____ to the bus stop.

M That's not bad. How long will it take to the subway?

W It _____
from the bus stop. It is a little far to walk, but, if you ride a bicycle, it wouldn't take long.

M Well, I have a bicycle, but I think taking a walk to the station would not be a bad idea. How much is the rent?

W $700 per month with _____.

M That's a little _____.

W _____?

M About $500 per month.

W That's _____ I can show for now. Would you like to take a look before making your decision?

M Sure, I'd love to.

look for ~을 찾다 | rent 임대하다, 임대(료) | prefer ~을 선호하다, 더 좋아하다 convenient 편리한, ~에 가까운 | public transportation 대중교통 | suburb 교외, 근교 | deposit 보증금 budget 예산, 경비, 비용

2 Monologue

What is mainly being discussed?

(a) coffee helps avert gallstone formation

(b) the questionable health benefits of coffee

(c) coffee being used to dissolve gallstones

(d) caffeinated beverages that should be avoided

W You may have _____
recently: perhaps you've heard that many health problems have been _____ drinking coffee. Coffee has been blamed for a number of health problems, especially _____
_____. Now, those claims are being proven false. Researchers now say that a few cups of coffee a day may actually prevent gallstones. _____
who drank two to three cups of coffee a day were seen to have _____ gallstones _____
_____. Apparently the chemicals in coffee lower those levels of cholesterol in bile that are responsible for causing gallstones, thus reducing the risk of their formation in coffee drinkers.

attribute ~의 탓으로 돌리다 | high blood pressure 고혈압 | false 그릇된, 거짓의 | gallstone 담석 | subject 실험 참가자 | apparently 명백하게 | bile 담즙 | formation 형성 avert 막다 dissolve 용해시키다, 분해시키다 beverage 음료

3 Conversation

What is correct about Steve according to the conversation?

(a) He hurt his right elbow after playing tennis.
(b) He started treatment a long time ago.
(c) He delayed treatment on his elbow.
(d) He plays tennis with his left arm.

W _____, Steve?
M Well, _____.
W Aren't you _____?
M Yeah, I just started physiotherapy last week. I'm also _____
_____.
W Oh, I guess you had gone a long time without treating it.
M Yes. I didn't _____ for two weeks. And I think that's why it has become worse.
W Try not to use your elbow, or it will get even worse.
M I know.
W But you still play tennis every morning.
M It is my left elbow _____ when playing tennis.
W You know you're still using your left elbow a lot when you're playing.
M I guess you're right. I thought it is just my right arm that I'm using, but I do actually use my left arm _____
_____.
W Exactly.

elbow 팔꿈치 | hurt 아프다, 다치다 | treat 치료하다, 처치하다 | physiotherapy 물리치료 | painkiller 진통제 | go without ~없이 지내다 | grab 움켜잡다 | delay 늦추다, 미루다, 연기하다

4 Monologue

What is the topic of the talk?

(a) the reasons for body scarring in Africa
(b) a comparison of tattooing and scarification
(c) how scarification came to Africa
(d) the diverse tattooing traditions in Africa

M After the history of _____, let me now tell you something about _____ known as "scarification" or body scarring. While tattooing involves _____, scarification involves _____ and the creation of scars. This practice has been followed for centuries by African tribes, for many reasons. In Mozambique, for instance, _____ _____ in life like a boy's induction _____. Some kinds of scarification might also indicate a person's social status or special accomplishments. An accomplished warrior might have several types of scarification done, to indicate his heroic deeds on the battlefield. _____
_____, scarification might be prohibited to younger males who have never experienced any fighting.

tattooing 문신술 | scarification 스캐러피케이션, 난절법 | scar ~에 상처를 남기다, 상처, 자국 | practice 풍습, 습관, 관행 | ritual 의식의, 제식의 | induction 도입, 취임 | manhood (남자의) 성년, 성인 | status 지위, 신분 | vein 기질, 특질, 맥락 | diverse 다양한

5 Monologue

Which is correct according to the report?

(a) Astronaut Yi So-yeon has developed several space technologies.
(b) Korea may join multinational space efforts.
(c) Male and female astronauts will enter space separately.
(d) Korean space technologies are aboard the ISS.

W Koreans are _____

_____. Everyone watched as Astronaut Yi So-yeon

_____. Our country has plans _____

_____, male and female, into space

_____. _____,

engineers, and scientists. They may also participate in international

space programs designed to _____

like the International Space Station, or ISS. We can be proud of our

nation's great advances _____

_____.

---

enthusiastic 열성적인, 열광적인 | astronaut 우주비행사 | blast (로켓 등을) 분사하여 발진시키다 | participate in ~에 참가하다 | be proud of ~을 자랑스러워하다 | advance 진보 | multinational 다국적인 | separately 따로따로 | aboard ~을 타고 있는

---

6 Conversation

What is mainly taking place in the conversation?

(a) The woman is doing some house chores.
(b) The woman is asking the man for help.
(c) The man is holding a chair for the woman.
(d) The couple is deciding where to hang the picture.

W Justin, could you please come here and help me?

M Not now. I'm quite busy.

W You don't seem to be. You're just watching TV.

M You know _____. I don't want to miss

the game for even a second.

W It won't take much time. Just hold this chair while I _____

_____ on the wall.

M Can't you do that after the match?

W No, I'm going out in the evening.

M Then, leave it there. I will _____.

W I really want to see _____ before

I go out. Can't you just _____ the

chair for a few seconds?

M There are _____. Hold on.

W If you don't come right away, you are not getting the video game I

was going to buy you for your birthday.

M Okay, fine. Why don't you hold the chair? _____

_____.

---

semifinal 준결승 | miss 놓치다, 빠뜨리다, 빼놓다 | for a second 1초 동안, 잠깐 동안 | hang ~을 걸다, 달아매다 | house chore 집안일

---

7 Monologue

What is the lecturer's main point about Islam?
(a) It has many points similar to Orthodox Judaism.
(b) It is easy to join but has daily rules to follow.
(c) A person must read the Koran before becoming a Muslim.
(d) Muslims are strict about the foods which they shouldn't eat.

W I'm going to talk today about some of the basic tenets of Islam. It may surprise you to know that Islam is _____ _____. All you need to do is agree to submit to the will of God, or "Allah." _____ _____, you are a Muslim: meaning "one who submits to Allah." Of course, as with any other religion, a believer has to study Islam's sacred texts, specifically the Koran, and _____ _____. _____ _____ Christianity, but somewhat like Orthodox Judaism, Islam has many rules that _____ _____, such as avoiding specific foods like pork.

tenet 교의, 주의 convert 전환하다, 전향하다 submit 복종하다 will 의지 sacred 신성한 Koran 코란(이슬람교 성전) prescription 규정, 법규 mainstream 주류를 이루는 Christianity 기독교 orthodox 정통의 Judaism 유대교 pork 돼지고기 similar to ~과 비슷한

8 Monologue

What is the speaker's main point?
(a) Smoking can worsen your health severely.
(b) Weight can be reduced by exercising.
(c) Be sure to exercise after you quit smoking.
(d) Don't get an addictive personality.

M If you are trying to quit smoking, it is a good idea _____ _____. This will have _____, including avoiding gaining weight. Many smokers have "_____." If they _____, they may take up another, such as eating or, worse, drinking more heavily. These will _____ _____ smoking does. Exercise will also _____, give you more energy, and make you feel better about yourself.

quit 그만두다 rigorous 엄격한, 매우 혹독한 addictive 중독성의, 습관성인 impact 영향을 미치다 worsen 악화시키다 severely 심각하게

9 Conversation

What is the woman mainly doing in the conversation?

(a) checking on her class schedule for next week
(b) confirming if she has prepared the right materials
(c) finding out important things that she has to do
(d) asking the man to help her study for an exam

W Hey, Robert. I've been looking for you around campus.
M Well, _____. Tell me, what's the matter?
W You know I've been away since my father was sick.
M Right. How is he doing now?
W He's still in the hospital. But the surgery went well and the doctor said he will _____.
M Thank God he will be okay.
W So, I could come back to school. And I have a lot of things to catch up. Since we are taking the same classes, I thought it might be helpful to talk to you.
M Sure. Well, we _____ this Friday.
W Oh, I _____ about that.
M Have you _____?
W Not at all.
M You should talk to the professor and _____. And another important thing. We have an exam in Chemistry 201 next week.
W We do? Oh, no. _____? Should I go talk to the professor, too?
M Well, we didn't do much while you're away. We just finished up the last experiment. You can just study a few chapters in the textbook.
W Can I borrow your notes?
M Sure. But I'm not sure if you'll find my handwriting legible enough.
W Don't worry. _____.

now that ~이므로 surgery 수술 catch up 따라잡다, 보충하다 extension 연장, 연기 chemistry 화학 experiment 실험 handwriting 필적, 필체 legible 읽기 쉬운, 알아볼 수 있는

10 Monologue

What is the speaker's view on American responsibility toward global warming?

(a) America needs to avoid conforming to the Kyoto Treaty.
(b) Americans are preparing to assist China and India with clean technologies.
(c) America has failed to act responsibly on the environment.
(d) Americans have polluted the world during their late industrialization.

M We need to do more to stop _____ _____. Many Americans blame China and India for pollution. Because of these countries' industrializations they are _____. However, the fact is India and China have agreed to environmental agreements like the Kyoto Protocol, while the United States has not. The U.S. needs to conform to the Kyoto Treaty, as a responsible country. It also must _____ _____. Americans should remember that their country _____ a lot during its early industrialization.

deadly 치명적인 spread 확산, 퍼짐 global warming 지구온난화 industrialization 산업화 emit 방출하다, 발산하다 greenhouse gas 온실 가스 environmental 환경의 agreement 의정서, 협약 conform to ~을 따르다, 지키다 developing country 개발도상국 assist 돕다, 조력하다

A Listen to the definitions and write down the words.

1. sacred _____

2. d_____

3. s_____

4. d_____

5. t_____

6. a_____

7. s_____

8. p_____

9. c_____

10. t_____

11. a_____

12. r_____

13. b_____

14. o_____

15. s_____

16. l_____

B Choose a sentence that best describes each Korean sentence.

1. 2주 동안 팔꿈치 진찰을 받지 않았다.

(a) _____

(b) _____

2. 저는 이 경기를 1초도 놓치고 싶지 않아요.

(a) _____

(b) _____

3. 내 필체를 네가 알아볼 수 있을지 모르겠다.

(a) _____

(b) _____

4. 지구온난화의 치명적인 확산을 막기 위해 더 많을 것을 해야 할 필요가 있다.

(a) _____

(b) _____

5. 놀랍게도 이슬람은 가장 개종하기 쉬운 종교 중의 하나이다.

(a) _____

(b) _____

C Listen to three phrases and complete each sentence.

it has become worse / why / that's
1. ➡ That's why it has become worse.

2. _____

3. _____

4. _____

5. _____

D Listen to the following and choose a sentence that has the same meaning.

1. It has been said that coffee is not good for health.
   (a) _____
   (b) _____

2. Do you have anything to declare?
   (a) _____
   (b) _____

3. A huge variation among African languages exists.
   (a) _____
   (b) _____

4. Children are fascinated by animals that can talk.
   (a) _____
   (b) _____

5. I want to live near public transportation.
   (a) _____
   (b) _____

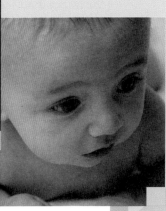

VOCABULARY PREVIEW 🎧

Write down the meanings of the words.

01 irritated	13 prolonged
02 authority	14 equip
03 species	15 avert
04 on the verge of	16 sober
05 habitat	17 Republican
06 encroach	18 immense
07 tremendous	19 tax burden
08 take measures	20 undermine
09 awareness	21 solitude
10 inanimate	22 droop
11 cuddle	23 embezzlement
12 hostility	24 lapse

GUIDED LISTENING 🎧

1 Conversation

Listening Notes

(problem)

(the woman's advice)

(the man's decision)

Detail

1 What does the woman advise the man to do?

(a) to ask the manager for overtime pay

(b) to report it to a supervisor

(c) to tell the employee union

(d) to try to get the manager fired

Detail

2 What is the man afraid of?

(a) not getting paid for overtime work

(b) working overtime

(c) losing his job

(d) refusing to work overtime

2 Conversation

Listening Notes

(vacation)

      the first time

(appreciation)

        for

        for

(the woman's apology)

(the man's opinion)

Detail

1   Why does the woman apologize?

  (a) for not watering the plants

  (b) for not picking up the mail

  (c) for going on vacation

  (d) for letting the daisies die

Comprehension

2   Which of the following is correct according to the conversation?

  (a)

  (b)

  (c)

  (d)

3 Monologue

Listening Notes

(Leatherback sea turtles)

      found

(Concern):

      (estimation)

(Cause 1):

(Cause 2):

(The speaker's assertion)

Detail

1 What is destroying the natural habitat of the turtles?

(a) commercial fishing industries

(b) careless authorities

(c) development on their mating grounds

(d) growing tourism

Main Topic

2 What is the issue addressed here?

(a) the sea as an important source of fish

(b) the age of leatherback sea turtles

(c) the rapid growth of coastal properties

(d) the possible extinction of an animal species

4 Monologue

Listening Notes

(Topic) we will discuss

(The first hint)

(Reaction to an object)

(Reaction to human)

Detail

1 Why do babies cuddle up to you according to the lecture?

(a) Because they try to balance their body instinctively.

(b) Because they instinctively like to hug.

(c) Because they want to interact with anything they see.

(d) Because they are aware of human beings.

Comprehension

2 Which is correct according to the lecture?

(a)

(b)

(c)

(d)

1 Conversation

1 What does the woman advise the man to do?
(a) to ask the manager for overtime pay
(b) to report it to a supervisor
(c) to tell the employee union
(d) to try to get the manager fired

2 What is the man afraid of?
(a) not getting paid for overtime work
(b) working overtime
(c) losing his job
(d) refusing to work overtime

W What's the matter? You _____ .

M The manager _____ . I'm so annoyed with him.

W What did he say to you?

M Well, he wants me _____ but says that _____ ! Can you believe that?

W He can't do that. He has to pay for overtime work. Why don't you tell him directly?

M Actually, _____ if I spoke like that.

W He doesn't have the authority to fire you. I think you should go ahead and tell him. If he doesn't agree to pay, you should refuse to do the overtime.

M Well then, _____ . Wish me luck!

W All the best!

irritated 화가 난 overtime 시간외로, 시간외 노동, 초과근무 fire 해고하다 authority 권한, 권능, 직권 | supervisor 감독관

2 Conversation

1 Why does the woman apologize?
(a) for not watering the plants
(b) for not picking up the mail
(c) for going on vacation
(d) for letting the daisies die

2 Which of the following is correct according to the conversation?
(a) The woman forgot to take care of the bugs.
(b) The man forgot to tell the woman to kill the bugs.
(c) The woman didn't know the man's vacation would be this long.
(d) The man does not want her to feel guilty about the plants.

W Hey, good to see you back. How was your vacation?

M Great! We enjoyed it a lot. It was the first time _____ _____ .

W I can understand. I'm sure you must have had lots of fun.

M Yeah. I'm so grateful to you _____ _____ .

W It wasn't a problem at all. But I'm feeling bad about the daisies. Even though I watered them every day, they _____ _____ .

M Please don't worry about them. They probably wouldn't have survived anyway _____ .

W Is that true? If I had known, I could have done something to kill them.

M Actually there was nothing that could have been done about the bugs. So, please _____ .

W I'm glad that you told me that.

grateful 감사하고 있는, 고마워하는 | take care of ~을 돌보다 | even though 비록 ~할지라도, ~하지만 | water 물을 주다 bug 벌레, 곤충

3 Monologue

1 What is destroying the natural habitat of the turtles?
   (a) commercial fishing industries
   (b) careless authorities
   (c) development on their mating grounds
   (d) growing tourism

2 What is the issue addressed here?
   (a) the sea as an important source of fish
   (b) the age of leatherback sea turtles
   (c) the rapid growth of coastal properties
   (d) the possible extinction of an animal species

W Leatherback sea turtles are one of the oldest species on Earth. They are usually found in coastal regions of Mexico, Costa Rica and Malaysia. _____ these turtles are _____ has raised concerns among environmentalists. It is estimated that worldwide only 40,000 turtles are left from the hundreds of thousands that existed 13 years ago. Coastal areas are the _____ _____. However, rapidly growing _____ have encroached upon these natural habitats of the turtles. Also, the development of coastal property has been tremendous over the last few years, _____ of the turtles. If _____ to check this, leatherback sea turtles may become extinct one day.

leatherback sea turtle 장수바다거북 species (생물) 종(種) coastal 해안의, 해변의 region 지역 on the verge of (파멸 등에) 직면하여 extinction 멸종 environmentalist 환경론자 habitat 서식지 lay (알을) 낳다 encroach 침해하다, 침입하다 tremendous 엄청난, 거대한 mating 짝짓기, 교미 take measures 조치를 취하다

4 Monologue

1 Why do babies cuddle up to you according to the lecture?
   (a) Because they try to balance their body instinctively.
   (b) Because they instinctively like to hug.
   (c) Because they want to interact with anything they see.
   (d) Because they are aware of human beings.

2 Which is correct according to the lecture?
   (a) Babies don't like social interaction.
   (b) Babies can distinguish humans from other objects.
   (c) Babies try to cuddle up to any objects and hold them.
   (d) Babies react toward humans more often.

W Today, we will discuss the development of social awareness in babies. _____ of other human beings is the first hint of social interaction in a baby. You may have noticed how babies _____ in their environments. However, their reaction to human faces is different from their reaction to _____. You may try _____ in front of a baby and note how the baby reacts to it. The baby usually tries _____ _____. _____, when you pick up a baby, the baby usually cuddles up to you. This reaction _____ in babies and indicates their level of awareness of human beings.

awareness 인지, 인식 be aware of ~을 인식하다 hint 힌트, 징후 interaction 상호작용 react to ~에 반응하다 inanimate 무생물의 object 물건, 물체 on the contrary 반대로 cuddle 꼭 껴안다, 바짝 붙다 instinctive 본능적인 indicate 나타내다, 표시하다

1 Which is correct according to the news report?

(a) Yugoslavia welcomes the UN's presence.

(b) Yugoslavia promises to improve the security situation.

(c) The UN will reduce the number of peacekeepers in Yugoslavia.

(d) The UN peacekeepers averted social problems in Yugoslavia.

Detail

2 Why did the man come home late?

(a) Because he had to take colleagues out for a drink.

(b) Because he couldn't finish the work on time.

(c) Because his co-worker didn't let him go early.

(d) Because his colleague forgot to bring his presentation files.

3 What are the man and woman mainly discussing?

(a) what kind of music they enjoy

(b) what music they'd like to perform with the band

(c) getting free tickets to a show

(d) going out for live music

Detail

4 Why are the Republicans opposed to the President's proposed tax plan?

(a) Because it will only benefit upper-income citizens.

(b) Because it will only burden ordinary citizens.

(c) Because it is impossible to carry it into effect.

(d) Because it will damage the overall economy.

5 What can be inferred from the conversation?

(a) The woman uses the computer too often.

(b) The man has lots of work to do on the computer.

(c) The man is unlikely to change his habits.

(d) The woman had been sick because of a computer.

Detail

6 What has affected the artists' style?

(a) the environment
(b) development of the city
(c) individualized society
(d) various fields of art

7 What is the speaker mainly doing in the announcement?

(a) receiving visitors on a warship
(b) giving commands to sailors at sea
(c) describing war exhibits in a museum
(d) explaining the history of a fleet

Detail

8 What is the man worried about?

(a) being late for the appointment
(b) cold weather at night
(c) meeting Jenny's teacher
(d) visiting a friend's house

9 What will the speaker probably talk about next?

(a)
(b)
(c)
(d)

10 Which is correct according to the lecture?

(a)
(b)
(c)
(d)

1 Monologue

Which is correct according to the news report?

(a) Yugoslavia welcomes the UN's presence.

(b) Yugoslavia promises to improve the security situation.

(c) The UN will reduce the number of peacekeepers in Yugoslavia.

(d) The UN peacekeepers averted social problems in Yugoslavia.

M Coming to international news, the United Nations will call back some of its peacekeeping personnel in Yugoslavia because of _____ to its _____ _____ in the area. In recent months some UN forces have come under fire, and two UN soldiers from the Netherlands were killed. UN representatives in Yugoslavia added that the reduction in forces _____ in the security situation of the region. Officials from UN headquarters in New York say that _____ _____.

This comes as a relief to leaders in Western Europe, whose countries had supplied most of the troops to the UN peacekeeping forces in Yugoslavia.

call back 소환하다, 불러들이다 **peacekeeping** 평화유지의 **hostility** 적대 행위, 반항 **prolonged** 장기의, 오래 끄는 **under fire** 공격을 받는, 포화를 받는 **representative** 대표자 **reduction** 축소, 삭감 **security** 보안, 안보 **region** 지역 **headquarter** 본부 **equip** 장비를 갖추다 **avert** 피하다, 막다

2 Conversation

Why did the man come home late?

(a) Because he had to take his colleagues out for a drink.

(b) Because he couldn't finish the work on time.

(c) Because his co-worker didn't let him go early.

(d) Because his colleague forgot to bring his presentation files.

W What have you been doing? Do you know that it's one in the morning?

M I'm sorry, dear. Didn't you go to sleep?

W No, I was so worried. _____?

M Actually, one of our colleagues got promoted, so he took everybody out for drinks.

W That means _____?

M Well, I got out of the office late since I had to finish _____ _____ tomorrow. And I was going to come home since it was almost 10 when I was done.

W You should've.

M But John, the one who got promoted, _____ and I couldn't refuse. So, I thought I would just show up and stay there for 30 minutes or so, but he _____ everybody stay, even when it got late.

W At least you could have called to let me know. Go to bed for now. We will talk about this tomorrow _____.

hold up 정지하다, 지체시키다 **colleague** 동료 **get promoted** 승진하다 **keep on -ing** 계속 ~하다 **show up** 나타나다 **at least** 적어도, 최소한 **could have p.p.** ~할 수 있었을 텐데 **sober** 술 취하지 않은, 맑은 정신의

3 Conversation

What are the man and woman mainly discussing?
(a) what kind of music they enjoy
(b) what music they'd like to perform with the band
(c) getting free tickets to a show
(d) going out for live music

M Would you like to go to Fusion 9 tonight?

W Is _____ there?

M Yeah, one of my friends is _____.
I think you'll enjoy it.

W What kind of music do they play? If it is a rock, _____
_____. You know it's too loud.

M Well, they play jazz, but it's Latin jazz. So _____
_____, but _____ rock music.

W I love Latin jazz. Well, what's the entry fee?

M We've got free tickets, so there's nothing to worry about!

W Sounds perfect!

M Okay then, I'll _____ at 8:00 p.m.

---

perform 공연하다, 연주하다 | **as much as** ~만큼 …한 | **entry fee** 입장료, 참가비 | **pick up** ~을 마중 나가다, 태우러 가다

4 Monologue

Why are the Republicans opposed to the President's proposed tax plan?
(a) Because it will only benefit upper-income citizens.
(b) Because it will only burden ordinary citizens.
(c) Because it is impossible to carry it into effect.
(d) Because it will damage the overall economy.

W Coming to political news, Republicans reacted sharply to the president's _____
_____ to pay for Social Security, saying it would create an immense tax burden for ordinary citizens. They added that this plan amounted to wild populism, and merely served _____
_____. They asserted that the tax increase, instead of falling on the wealthy, would in truth _____. The Republicans have demanded an alternative that would not cause a tax increase for anyone. _____ that the Republicans have _____ and are quoting erroneous data. He insisted that the tax increase was _____
_____.

Republican 공화당(의) | **react** 대응하다, 반응하다, 반대하다 | **sharply** 민첩하게, 날카롭게 | **upper-income** 고소득의 | **Social Security** 사회 보장 (제도) |
immense 거대한, 막대한 | **tax burden** 조세 부담 | **amount to** 결과적으로 ~이 되다 | **populism** 대중의 칭찬 | **undermine** 손상시키다 | **credibility** 신용, 진실성 |
alternative 대안, 다른 방도 | **erroneous** 잘못된, 틀린

5 Conversation

What can be inferred from the conversation?
(a) The woman uses the computer too often.
(b) The man has lots of work to do on the computer.
(c) The man is unlikely to change his habits.
(d) The woman had been sick because of a computer.

W　Have you finished working on the computer?

M　Well, I'm almost done. Do you want to use it?

W　No. Actually _____ in front of the computer _____ .

M　It's only two hours a day. I don't think that's too much.

W　But these two hours are _____ _____ on the computer.

M　Well, _____ . It actually _____ _____ .

W　I'm sure _____ , but you're wrong.

in front of ~의 앞에 | **healthy** 건강한, 건강에 좋은 | **in addition to** ~에 더하여, ~일뿐 아니라, ~외에 또 | **at work** 직장에서, 일하는 | **bother** ~을 귀찮게 하다, ~에게 폐를 끼치다 | **unwind** 긴장을 풀다, 편한 마음을 갖게 하다 | **convince** 확신시키다, 납득시키다 | **be unlikely to** ~할 것 같지 않다

6 Monologue

What has affected the artists' styles?
(a) the environment
(b) development of the city
(c) individualized society
(d) various fields of art

M　Today I want to talk about something _____ _____ Washington State art. Washington's _____ , _____ , heavy rains and _____ has _____ _____ in many art forms. Dave Tobey is a famous Washington modern artist who has painted dark, forbidding themes of pain and suffering. Dale Chihuly is likewise internationally known for his drooping, sad glassworks. Although the two artists work in very different fields, it is clear _____ _____ .

impact 충돌, 영향 | **forest** 숲 | **abundant** 풍부한, 많은 | **foggy** 안개가 자욱한 | **solitude** 고독 | **forbidding** 기분 나쁜, 무서운 | **theme** 주제
droop 축 늘어지다, 처지다 | **glasswork** 유리공예

7 Monologue

What is the speaker mainly doing in the announcement?
(a) receiving visitors on a warship
(b) giving commands to sailors at sea
(c) describing war exhibits in a museum
(d) explaining the history of a fleet

M _____ the USS Garvin. This is a Class 7 _____ in 1997 at Norfolk, Virginia. The ship has _____, including the most advanced command and control combat management equipment in the world. The Minerva radar and fire-control system it has enables the ship to _____ _____ at once. It thus has the weapons' capability to fight an entire enemy fleet on its own. The ship also has 2 helicopters for reconnaissance, _____ _____, or _____ _____. Today, we are open to the public. You are free to look around selected areas of the ship and ask any questions you have. Thank you.

destroyer 구축함, 파괴자 domestically 국내에서, 국내 문제에 관해서 state-of-the-art 첨단 기술을 사용한, 최신식의 | combat 전투, 투쟁
management 관리, 처리, 감독 equipment 장비 | fire-control system 사격 통제 시스템 | engage (적군과) 교전하다, (군대를) 교전시키다 fleet 함대, 선박
reconnaissance 정찰(대) | antisubmarine 대(對)잠수함의

8 Conversation

What is the man worried about?
(a) being late for the appointment
(b) cold weather at night
(c) meeting Jenny's teacher
(d) visiting a friend's house

W Oh no, have you heard the weather forecast?
M No, what did it say?
W There'll be heavy snow this evening. That means it's going to be _____.
M You'd better _____.
W I will just take this jacket with me.
M And _____. You know we have a dinner appointment at 7 with Jenny's teacher.
W I know. I will try to come as soon as possible.
M I mean _____. Last time when it was raining hard, it took you more than an hour to get home, remember?
W Yeah, we were supposed to go to a friend's house for dinner, but we _____ because I was late. I'll try to leave the office as soon as my boss leaves.
M _____. I can't make Ms. Johnson wait at the restaurant for a long time.

weather forecast 일기예보 heavy snow 큰 눈, 폭설 | freezing 어는, 몹시 추운 bundle up 따뜻하게 옷을 껴 입다 | heavy traffic 극심한 교통량
get home 귀가하다 | be supposed to ~하기로 되어 있다 | make it 약속을 지키다, 해내다

9 Monologue

What will the speaker probably talk about next?

(a) the importance of leadership in business
(b) a specific example of unethical practices
(c) the issue of falling standards in business education
(d) course credits needed for a business degree

W In my career as business educator, I have seen some dramatic changes in business education. In the past 5 years, for example, we've introduced Web business courses, _____ _____ and inserted trendy corporate valuations and analyses into the curriculum. We also take _____, although the concept of ethics has not gained _____. If current reports are true, it seems that business graduates are more interested in _____ _____! One only has to open the daily papers to read about tales of CEOs _____ _____, stock manipulation, embezzlement, or other _____. One of the most infamous of these was the case of the company Enron.

incorporate 짜 넣다, 만들다, (회사를) 법인 조직으로 만들다 ┃ insert 끼워 넣다, 삽입하다 ┃ valuation 평가, 사정 ┃ analysis 분석 (pl. analyses) ┃ ethics 윤리학, 도덕론 ┃ deserve ~을 받을 만하다, ~의 가치가 있다 ┃ credit 학점 ┃ accounting 회계 ┃ fraud 사기, 기만 ┃ stock manipulation 주가 조작 ┃ embezzlement 횡령, 착복 ┃ lapse 잘못, 실수, 타락

10 Monologue

Which is correct according to the lecture?

(a) France turned to colonialism before the 16th century.
(b) French colonies sometimes rebelled against French authorities.
(c) France won a military campaign in Vietnam in the early 1950s.
(d) French colonies were ruled by armies comprised of natives.

W Today, I'll continue with French colonialism, one of the most important elements in French history. From the 16th century forward, France dedicated much of its military strength to _____ _____ and _____ _____. Its colonial decline began in the early 1950s with a failed attempt to overcome a Vietnamese nationalist or communist movement. The French suffered _____ _____ to the Vietnamese forces in the northern part of the country, after _____ _____ for an extended period. Trouble continued through that decade, with France losing the last of its major colonies, Algeria, as the decade closed. Despite this, several former French colonies, especially those in Africa, _____ _____ from France.

colonialism 식민주의 ┃ dedicate A to B B에 A를 바치다 ┃ possession 재산, 부 ┃ quell 억누르다, 진압하다 ┃ rebellion 반란, 폭동 ┃ colonial 식민지의 ┃ decline 쇠퇴, 하락 ┃ communist 공산주의 ┃ humiliating 치욕이 되는, 굴욕적인 ┃ defeat 패배 ┃ surrender 항복 ┃ shell 포격하다

LISTENING REVIEW 🎧

A Listen to the definitions and write down the words.

1. habitat _____
2. h_____
3. s_____
4. a_____
5. d_____
6. c_____
7. e_____
8. u_____

9. d_____
10. s_____
11. s_____
12. e_____
13. f_____
14. p_____
15. h_____
16. r_____

B Choose a sentence that best describes each Korean sentence.

1. 적어도 전화해서 알려 줄 수 있었잖아요.
(a) _____
(b) _____

2. 함대의 공개된 부분을 자유롭게 둘러보세요.
(a) _____
(b) _____

3. 프랑스는 해외에서 부를 취득하는 데 군사적 힘을 쏟았다.
(a) _____
(b) _____

4. 윤리 개념이 그 중대성을 제대로 인정받지 못해 왔다.
(a) _____
(b) _____

5. 세금 인상이 부유층에 돌아가지 않고, 실제로는 중산층에게 돌아갈 것이다.
(a) _____
(b) _____

C **Listen to three phrases and complete each sentence.**

the one / kept on calling / who got promoted
1. ➡ The one who got promoted kept on calling.

2. _____

3. _____

4. _____

5. _____

D **Listen to the following and choose a sentence that has the same meaning.**

1. These turtles may become extinct one day.
   (a) _____
   (b) _____

2. Because I didn't know, I could not do anything to kill them.
   (a) _____
   (b) _____

3. His co-worker didn't let anybody go early.
   (a) _____
   (b) _____

4. Babies can distinguish humans from other objects.
   (a) _____
   (b) _____

5. The UN will reduce the number of peacekeepers in Yugoslavia.
   (a) _____
   (b) _____

COMPREHENSION

VOCABULARY PREVIEW 🎧

Write down the meanings of the words.

01	conclusive	13	glamorize
02	substantial	14	conceive
03	fake-looking	15	venue
04	kidney	16	mingle
05	transplant	17	acclaim
06	prognosis	18	span
07	magnificent	19	marvel
08	prominent	20	by leaps and bounds
09	intimate	21	obese
10	glimpse	22	console
11	delve into	23	compelling
12	aptly	24	custody

GUIDED LISTENING 🎧

1 Conversation

Listening Notes

(Derek)

    (appearance)

    He wants to

(everyone's opinion)

    (reason) I heard that

Comprehension

1 What does NOT match the information in the conversation?

(a) They have never met Derek before.

(b) Derek is known to have a bad temper.

(c) The man and the woman are going hiking.

(d) The man does not have a good opinion of Derek.

Inference II

2 What can be inferred about the man?

(a) He is not comfortable with Derek.

(b) He doesn't know who Derek is.

(c) He doesn't want others to join.

(d) He is not familiar with the other friends.

2 Conversation

Listening Notes

(in the newspaper)

(the woman's opinion)

    (about photo)

    (about hair samples)

    (about people who have seen)

Comprehension

1 Which of the following is correct according to the conversation?

(a) The man and other people have seen Bigfoot.

(b) The woman thinks the photos are real.

(c) The hair samples belong to Bigfoot.

(d) The woman thinks there is lack of proof.

Inference II

2 What can be inferred from the conversation?

(a)

(b)

(c)

(d)

3 Monologue

Listening Notes

(William Wright)

    surgery to receive

    (his condition)

    All three organs

    The surgery went on

    (doctor's comment)

    (doctor's expectation)

Comprehension

1 Which is correct about William Wright?

(a) He doesn't have heart surgery.

(b) He has been in critical condition for a week.

(c) He's in stable condition presently.

(d) His surgery was finished within an hour.

Inference II

2 What can be inferred from the news?

(a) William will be given permission to leave the hospital after a week.

(b) The doctors are hesitant to announce the positive result.

(c) William will need a great deal of care for a certain period of time.

(d) It was the biggest surgery that the team has performed.

4 Monologue

Listening Notes

(pharaohs)
    buried in
(Tutankhamen)
    (who)
    buried
    contained
    mask represented
(Tutankhamen's tomb)
    evidence to
    no mention
        suggesting that

Comprehension

1 Which is correct about Tutankhamen, according to the lecture?

(a) He was known for his long life.

(b) He was one of the most influential kings.

(c) His achievements were not documented.

(d) His tomb was found outside a pyramid.

Detail

2 What can we learn from the treasures in the tomb?

(a)

(b)

(c)

(d)

1 Conversation

1 What does NOT match the information in the conversation?
(a) They have never met Derek before.
(b) Derek is known to have a bad temper.
(c) The man and the woman are going hiking.
(d) The man does not have a good opinion of Derek.

2 What can be inferred about the man?
(a) He is not comfortable with Derek.
(b) He doesn't know who Derek is.
(c) He doesn't want others to join.
(d) He is not familiar with the other friends.

W Do you know Derek?

M The guy _____ and _____ _____?

W Yeah. He wants to join us for our hiking trip.

M Sounds strange! I've never seen him talking to anybody. What did you say to him?

W Well, I told him that _____ _____. What do you think?

M Is everybody okay with it?

W No, actually nobody liked _____. I just don't understand why.

M Well, I heard that _____ and _____ _____.

W Maybe that's the reason he's always alone.

ponytail 포니테일(뒤에서 묶어 아래로 드리운 머리) take along ~을 가지고[데리고] 가다 familiar 친한, 익숙한

2 Conversation

1 Which of the following is correct according to the conversation?
(a) The man and other people have seen Bigfoot.
(b) The woman thinks the photos are real.
(c) The hair samples belong to Bigfoot.
(d) The woman thinks there is lack of proof.

2 What can be inferred from the conversation?
(a) They have seen the photo of Bigfoot before.
(b) They have some proof that Bigfoot exists.
(c) The man thinks that gorilla suits are too widely available.
(d) The woman believes that the hair samples prove Bigfoot's existence.

W Can you believe this? There's another photo of Bigfoot in the newspaper. They're _____.

M Let me see. This one looks like a real picture.

W Don't you think it could just be _____?

M Not likely. The report also says that they've found _____ _____.

W The results of the hair samples are never conclusive. Don't you remember the mammoth case? They _____ _____.

M You're right, but I'm sure this time they'll be able to find _____.

W But they _____ that Bigfoot exists, except for some fake-looking photographs and some odd hair samples.

M Well, there are people who say that they have seen Bigfoot.

W I don't believe those jerks. They might have seen some ordinary animal in the dark.

trace 추적하다 suit 복장 conclusive 결정적인, 확실한 mammoth 매머드 belong to ~에 속하다 substantial 실질적인 fake-looking 가짜처럼 보이는 odd 단편적인, 우연한, 임시의 jerk 바보, 얼간이 ordinary 평범한, 보통의

3 Monologue

1 Which is correct about William Wright?
(a) He doesn't have heart surgery.
(b) He has been in critical condition for a week.
(c) He's in stable condition presently.
(d) His surgery was finished within an hour.

2 What can be inferred from the news?
(a) William will be given permission to leave the hospital after a week.
(b) The doctors are hesitant to announce the positive result.
(c) William will need a great deal of care for a certain period of time.
(d) It was the biggest surgery that the team has performed.

M William Wright underwent surgery to receive liver, heart and kidney transplants yesterday, and _____ _____ his condition seems to be stable. His condition was initially critical but has now dramatically improved. He is being taken care of _____ of Boston General Hospital. All three organs of Mr. Wright were diseased and had to be removed. The surgery went on for about 16 hours and 20 minutes. The doctor who _____ that performed the surgery said that the coming few days will be important _____. Considering the present condition of Mr. Wright, the doctors are _____ _____. Mr. Wright is expected to remain in the intensive care unit for another week.

surgery 수술 liver 간 kidney 신장 transplant 이식 stable 안정된 initially 처음에는 take care of ~을 돌보다, 보살피다
intensive care unit 중환자실, 집중 치료부 병동 organ 기관, 장기 prognosis 예후

4 Monologue

1 Which is correct about Tutankhamen, according to the lecture?
(a) He was known for his long life.
(b) He was one of the most influential kings.
(c) His achievements were not documented.
(d) His tomb was found outside a pyramid.

2 What can we learn from the treasures in the tomb?
(a) his age of death
(b) how prominent he was
(c) the era he lived in
(d) his artistic taste

W Kings or "pharaohs" in ancient Egypt used to be buried _____ _____. An example worth citing is that of Tutankhamen's. Tutankhamen was a teenage pharaoh, who died when he was just 18 years of age. He was _____ _____. In addition to the gold, it also _____ _____ of Egypt _____. His funeral mask looked magnificent, and well represented the artistry of Egypt of in earlier times. Tutankhamen's tomb was first opened in 1922, many centuries after he was buried. There is _____ _____ the era of Egyptian history to which he belonged. But, there is no mention of Tutankhamen in Egyptian writings, suggesting that he may have not been _____ _____.

pharaoh (고대 이집트의) 왕, 파라오 funeral 장례식의 Tutankhamen 투탕카멘 (기원전 14세기 이집트 제18왕조의 젊은 왕; 1922년에 그 분묘가 발견되었음.)
grand 웅대한, 장엄한 be made out of ~으로 만들어지다 solid gold 순금 magnificent 장대한, 굉장한 artistry 예술적 기교(수완) era 시대, 시기

1   Which is correct about Montagne according to the lecture?

(a) His sense of detachment kept him from pursuing fame.

(b) His largely autobiographical writing aptly captured human nature.

(c) He glamorized himself in order to comment on humanity.

(d) He detailed common people's everyday lives with great accuracy.

2   What are the man and woman mainly discussing?

(a) whether they can buy a second car or not

(b) how highly-priced cars are

(c) what kind of car they will buy

(d) where they will get a loan from

3   What can be inferred about the festival?

(a) It launches new film-makers.

(b) It helped its founders earn international fame.

(c) It is dedicated to preserving Western cultural identity.

(d) It features both Western and Asian films.

4   What is mainly being discussed?

(a) the deadline of the article

(b) the burden of meeting deadlines

(c) the scope of journalism

(d) the man's career as a journalist

5   What is mainly being introduced here?

(a) surgeons endorsing technology

(b) Paris as a leader in medical science

(c) the latest robot-assisted surgery

(d) the risks in remote control surgery

6 What is the main topic of the talk?

(a) what behaviors parents should avoid

(b) which diets are unsuitable for young children

(c) why young children become overweight

(d) how parents can help overweight children

Comprehension 7 Which is correct according to the conversation?

(a) The subway train arrived late at the station.

(b) The subway train had an accident.

(c) The man does not want to wait for a taxi.

(d) The woman is unsure why the subway train is late.

8 What is the speaker mainly doing in the talk?

(a) introducing an artist's new work

(b) paying tribute to an employee

(c) announcing an honor won by an employee

(d) telling colleagues to complete a window display

Comprehension 9 What is correct about the constable's position according to the lecture?

(a)

(b)

(c)

(d)

Comprehension 10 Which is correct about the woman according to the conversation?

(a)

(b)

(c)

(d)

1 Monologue

Which is correct about Montagne according to the lecture?

(a) His sense of detachment kept him from pursuing fame.

(b) His largely autobiographical writing aptly captured human nature.

(c) He glamorized himself in order to comment on humanity.

(d) He detailed common people's everyday lives with great accuracy.

M   Today's lecture deals with one of the greatest figures in French Literature, Michel De Montagne. His essays during the Renaissance _____ and _____. He wrote of his failing memory, _____ and his wish to detach himself from all things worldly. Even as he wrote about himself, Montagne was in fact _____ _____. His true genius lies in this achievement.

intimate 깊은, 심오한 | glimpse 일별, 힐끗 봄 | delve into ~을 탐구하다 | failing 약해 가는 | scorn 경멸, 냉소
detach oneself from ~로부터 이탈하다, 떨어지다 | chronicle 연대순으로 기록하다 | aptly 적절히, 교묘히 | glamorize 낭만적으로 다루다, 미화하다 |
detachment 분리, 초연함

2 Conversation

What are the man and woman mainly discussing?

(a) whether they can buy a second car or not

(b) how highly-priced cars are

(c) what kind of car they will buy

(d) where they will get a loan from

M   I think we should _____ now.

W   Yes. The office is quite far. Going by car would _____ _____. But I'm not sure if we can afford it.

M   How about getting a loan?

W   _____ will be really high. I don't think we can afford that.

M   How about _____?

W   Buying a used car wouldn't solve the problem completely. You know those reliable used cars are still expensive, and we will still need some money.

M   We can _____. How about that?

W   Maybe. But what about the cost of insurance and gas?

M   Well, if we get a small car, we could _____.

W   Fine, let's go ahead with it.

flexibility 유연성, 융통성 | loan 대출, 융자 | insurance 보험 | manage 어떻게든 ~하다, ~을 경영하다, 꾸려나가다 | go ahead with ~을 진행하다, 자, 어서 ~하세요
highly-priced 고가의, 비싼

3 Monologue

What can be inferred about the festival?
(a) It launches new film-makers.
(b) It helped its founders earn international fame.
(c) It is dedicated to preserving Western cultural identity.
(d) It features both Western and Asian films.

W   As founders of the United Film Festival, we are proud to see it enter its 20th year. We _____ _____ and look forward to its great future. We're proud to say that many young directors _____ _____ here, such as Ming Li Pao, who released his first film, "Shades of Autumn" at the festival, and later became one of the greatest directors in the world. The festival was conceived as a platform to bring together Western and Eastern cultures _____ _____. It is one of the best venues for directors, actors, and producers from two different cultures _____ _____. We never imagined it would become an _____ event _____ _____.

founder 창시자 look forward to ~을 기대하다, 기다리다 release 개봉하다, 공개하다 conceive 생각하다, 고안하다 venue 장소, 현장
mingle 어울리다, 섞이다 acclaim 갈채하다, 환호하다 span (짧은) 기간, 거리

4 Conversation

What is mainly being discussed?
(a) the deadline of the article
(b) the burden of meeting deadlines
(c) the scope of journalism
(d) the man's career as a journalist

W   Oh, tomorrow is _____ ! I hate deadlines.
M   But as a journalist _____.
W   If I'd had few more hours, _____ _____.
M   It's not only you, all journalists feel the need for more time.
W   Do you also think that way?
M   Yes. I _____ working under deadlines.
W   I'm surprised to know that. I mean you always look relaxed and seem to have a lot of time.
M   Do I? Well, that's not true at all. _____ when I have to.

deadline 원고 마감 시간, 마감 시한 submit ~을 제출하다 journalist 기자, 언론인 stressed out 스트레스로 지친, 스트레스가 쌓인 relaxed 느긋한
work one's head off 뼈 빠지게 일하다, 몰두해서 일하다 burden 짐, 의무, 부담, 괴로움 scope 범위, 영역

5 Monologue

What is mainly being introduced here?
(a) surgeons endorsing technology
(b) Paris as a leader in medical science
(c) the latest robot-assisted surgery
(d) the risks in remote control surgery

W   Welcome to TechWatch, where we show you scientific marvels from around the world. This week's edition of TechWatch takes you to Europe as we _____ in medical technology. As we know, that's _____ — with new advances that allow doctors _____ _____ and safer than ever. Through the use of these technologies, medicine is being truly _____ _____. First, we go to Paris to watch a robot helping with an open heart surgery. The chief surgeon is not _____ for this procedure. Instead you can watch him directing it from the far side of the room by using a remote control device. It promises to be _____ _____. Let's watch right now!

marvel 놀라운 일, 경이로움 by leaps and bounds 급속도로 advance 진척, 향상 chief surgeon 집도의 fascinating 놀라운 endorse 보증하다, (어음 따위에) 배서하다 assist 돕다

6 Monologue

What is the main topic of the talk?
(a) what behaviors parents should avoid
(b) which diets are unsuitable for young children
(c) why young children become overweight
(d) how parents can help overweight children

M   If your child has _____, it's time to begin establishing healthy eating habits. Waiting could have terrible health consequences. Obese children _____ _____, including heart disease and diabetes. It's important to establish healthy habits and _____ _____ to avoid that. Don't overemphasize physical appearance, though, because that rarely works. Indeed, it could sometimes cause the opposite to happen, with a child who is depressed about his appearance eating more _____ _____. Instead, _____ _____ and a schedule of physical exercise _____. Most importantly, you need to avoid bad eating habits so they do not ruin your child's health. Make sure that you cook healthy meals at home for the child. _____ too by eating right yourself.

obesity 비만 | consequence 결과 | obese 살찐, 뚱뚱한 | be prone to ~하는 경향이 있다 | diabetes 당뇨 | rarely 거의 ~하지 않는 | console 위로하다 | enforce 집행하다, 강요하다 | boost 끌어올리다, 증대시키다 | ruin 망치다 | positive 긍정적인

7 Conversation

Which is correct according to the conversation?

(a) The subway train arrived late at the station.
(b) The subway train had an accident.
(c) The man does not want to wait for a taxi.
(d) The woman is unsure why the subway train is late.

M There are so many people on the platform. What's the matter?

W I'm not sure. I think the subway is late for some reason.

M Was there an accident on the line?

W That's quite possible. At least they should _____ _____, though.

M Yeah, how long can we _____?

W I bet it'll take some time. I don't think we should wait here _____ _____. Why don't we take a taxi?

M Well, _____. But what about _____?

W I'm sure we can get our money back.

M Well, let's just go find out.

for some reason 어떠한 이유로 | at least 적어도 | inform 사람 of ~에게 ~을 알리다, 통지하다 | keep -ing 계속해서 ~하다 | I bet 틀림없이 ~이다
fare 운임, 요금 | unsure 확신이 없는, 불안한, 모르는

8 Monologue

What is the speaker mainly doing in the talk?

(a) introducing an artist's new work
(b) paying tribute to an employee
(c) announcing an honor won by an employee
(d) telling colleagues to complete a window display

W Elaine's Jewelry owes a great deal to Frank Parks, who helped _____. His window displays have been as scintillating and compelling as any artist's. For 40 years, these displays, numbering over 7,000, _____ _____ in town. He has always known just _____ _____ in any window, making them true works of art that have made it onto the pages of _____ _____ like USA Style and Milan Elegance. Today we, the employees of Elaine's, honor him as he retires. Here's to Frank. It's safe to say that _____ _____ without his contribution to our store over the decades.

jewelry 보석(류) | scintillating 번쩍이는, 재치가 넘치는 | compelling 강력한, 감탄하지 않을 수 없는 | stunning effect 뛰어난 효과 | retire 은퇴하다
Here's to ~에게 건배 (~에게 행운이 있기를) | It's safe to say that ~라 해도 괜찮다, 과언이 아니다 | contribution 공헌 | colleague 동료

9 Monologue

What is correct about the constable's position according to the lecture?
(a) It involved giving up regular work.
(b) People appointed to it enjoyed high status.
(c) People often volunteered for it.
(d) It entailed operating as an informant.

M Towns in the North American colonies of the 15th century usually appointed constables _____.
Constables earned no salary and had no uniform. _____ while doing their duty. These men were never very popular, since their jobs entailed reporting neighbors' behavior to the courts, arresting criminal offenders and being responsible for their _____. Constables were usually chosen because they had _____ of a town and their activities. Constables rarely had to _____. Knowing the "town bad guys" and the activities they engaged in, they could usually quickly _____ within days or even hours of a crime. On the downside, it also meant that they were _____, always asking about the goings-on of the innocent as well.

appoint 지명하다, 임명하다 | constable 보안관, 치안관, 경관 | uphold 지키다 | exempt 면제된 | entail ~을 필요로 하다, 수반하다 | arrest 체포하다 | offender 범죄자, 위반자 | custody 구류 | trial 재판 | perpetrator 범죄자, 가해자 | downside 부정적인 면 | perpetually 끊임없이 | nosy 캐묻기 좋아하는 | informant 정보 제공자, 밀고자

10 Conversation

Which is correct about the woman according to the conversation?
(a) Her credit card limit has been exceeded.
(b) Her credit card application was rejected.
(c) She turned down a credit card offer.
(d) She has a bad credit record for not paying off her bills.

M What happened to the new credit card _____? Did you get it?
W No, I didn't.
M Why? Did you _____?
W No. _____. They found my credit history to be too short. It should be a minimum of six months. I didn't know that I have to have a credit history.
M Well, I think _____ if you get somebody to co-sign.
W Well, I thought about that, but they don't allow it. I mean if I don't get a credit card, how am I going to ever have a history? I would have understood _____.
M Maybe you should try some other banks. They might be less rigid. Once you get one and use it for several months, then you will have your history.
W You're right. I definitely need a credit card so that I don't have to go to an ATM _____.

apply for 신청하다, 지원하다 | fail to ~하지 못하다(않다) | submit 제출하다, 제시하다 | document 서류, 문서 | co-sign 공동 서명하다, 연대 보증인으로 서명하다 | rigid 엄격한, 완고한 | ATM 현금 자동 지급기(automated-teller machine) | run out of ~을 다 쓰다, ~이 다 떨어지다

LISTENING REVIEW 🎧

A Listen to the definitions and write down the words.

1. obese _____
2. e _____
3. k _____
4. c _____
5. a _____
6. c _____
7. p _____
8. p _____

9. c _____
10. c _____
11. g _____
12. m _____
13. t _____
14. d _____
15. d _____
16. s _____

B Choose a sentence that best describes each Korean sentence.

1. 그것이 그가 사람들과 잘 지내지 못하는 이유이다.

(a) _____
(b) _____

2. 내가 신용 기록이 있어야 한다는 것을 몰랐어.

(a) _____
(b) _____

3. 비만 아이들은 다양한 질병을 앓기 쉽습니다.

(a) _____
(b) _____

4. 또한 임무를 수행하면서, 그들은 본업을 안 가질 수도 없었다.

(a) _____
(b) _____

5. 그의 공헌이 없었다면 오늘의 우리도 없었을 것이다.

(a) _____
(b) _____

C Listen to three phrases and complete each sentence.

nobody / of taking him along / liked the idea

1. ➡ Nobody liked the idea of taking him along.

2. _____

3. _____

4. _____

5. _____

D Listen to the following and choose a sentence that has the same meaning.

1. Some people say they seemed to see Bigfoot.

(a) _____

(b) _____

2. The Constable's position entailed operating as an informant.

(a) _____

(b) _____

3. The festival features both Western and Asian cultures.

(a) _____

(b) _____

4. Mr. Wright will need a great deal of care for a week.

(a) _____

(b) _____

5. Tutankhamen's achievement was not documented in history.

(a) _____

(b) _____

CHAPTER 05

RELATIONSHIP OF IDEAS

VOCABULARY PREVIEW 🎧

Write down the meanings of the words.

01	avenue	13	relatively	
02	wire some money	14	emir	
03	starve to death	15	emissary	
04	reputation	16	ratification	
05	implementation	17	treaty	
06	boost	18	stretch	
07	tusk	19	kind of stifling	
08	dominance	20	tablet	
09	herd	21	congestion	
10	herbivorous	22	impending	
11	fossil	23	restoration	
12	brutal	24	shunt	

GUIDED LISTENING 🎧

1 Conversation

Listening Notes

(movie)

    starring

    got

(the man's opinion)

    better if

    It looked

Relationship of Ideas

1   What comparison do the speakers make between two movies?

    (a) the use of special effects

    (b) the appearance of famous stars

    (c) the creativity of storyline

    (d) the availability of films

Inference II

2   What can be inferred from the conversation?

    (a) The woman does not like superheroes.

    (b) The man does not like computer effects in movies.

    (c) The man is interested in making movies.

    (d) The woman likes to see movies with computer effects.

2 Conversation

Listening Notes

(the woman's favor)

(jobs to take care of)
1.

2.

3.

4.

Relationship of Ideas 1 In what order will he take care of the jobs?

(a) from the most private to the least private

(b) from the most time taking to the least time taking

(c) from the most difficult to the least difficult

(d) from the most urgent to the least urgent

Inference I 2 What can be inferred about the speakers?

(a)

(b)

(c)

(d)

3 Monologue

Listening Notes

(concern)

    about

(reason for training)

    The company has signed

    Managers

(suggestion)

    consider

(comparison)

Relationship of Ideas

1   What comparison does the speaker make between training and not training the managers?

    (a) chance of success abroad

    (b) length of employment

    (c) amount of loss and gain

    (d) degree of satisfactory service

Inference II

2   What can be inferred from the talk?

    (a) Training methods will boost a company's reputation.

    (b) There have been serious financial losses.

    (c) The speaker is going overseas soon.

    (d) The previous training was not effective for managers.

4 Monologue

Listening Notes

(Mastodons)

    (appearance)

(large tusks)

    used to

    (fossil evidence)

(fossils from a Midwestern site)

Relationship of Ideas

1 Which best explains the relationship between damaged tusks of Mastodons and its population?

(a) Severely damaged tusks mean the number of Mastodons decreased.

(b) Less damaged tusks mean the number of Mastodons increased.

(c) Severely damaged tusks mean there were a lot of Mastodons.

(d) Less damaged tusks mean there was much competition among Mastodons.

Main Topic

2 What is the main topic of the talk?

(a)

(b)

(c)

(d)

1 Conversation

1 What comparison do the speakers make between two movies?
(a) the use of special effects
(b) the appearance of famous stars
(c) the creativity of storyline
(d) the availability of films

2 What can be inferred from the conversation?
(a) The woman does not like superheroes.
(b) The man does not like computer effects in movies.
(c) The man is interested in making movies.
(d) The woman likes to see movies with computer effects.

M Yesterday I saw this movie "Amazing Man" _____ _____ and about his exciting adventures.

W Is it the movie that _____?

M Yes. Have you seen the movie?

W Yeah. It was _____.

M Uh... I think it could have been better, if the computer-generated imagery was used less often. It looked more _____ than a movie.

W No, I felt the effects were good. Well, have you seen the movie "Dark Night?" It is one of the old superhero movies _____ _____. I mean many famous actors and actress starred in the movie. And _____ _____. But I didn't feel it was very good.

M I've seen it. You're right. _____.

W Right. I think the technology has really _____ _____ for creativity.

M Yeah. I hope we get to see more such films in the future.

star 주연하다 | superhero 슈퍼 히어로, 초능력을 가진 영웅 | cartoon 만화 | awesome 최고의, 멋진 | appealing 매력적인, 흥미를 끄는 | avenue 수단, 방법 | special effect 특수 효과

2 Conversation

1 In what order will he take care of the jobs?
(a) from the most private to the least private
(b) from the most time taking to the least time taking
(c) from the most difficult to the least difficult
(d) from the most urgent to the least urgent

2 What can be inferred about the speakers?
(a) The woman is not going to wait for him.
(b) The man is going to have lunch alone.
(c) The woman is freer than the man.
(d) The man is going to withdraw some money.

W Are you going to the food court, Sam?

M Yes, I'm going to have lunch. Could I get you something?

W Yeah. Please get me a hotdog. _____.

M Sure. But you'll have to wait for an hour or so. I've got _____ _____ while I'm out.

W Really? What're you going to be doing?

M Well, I have to go to the bank. My sister asked me _____ _____ which has to be paid in 15 minutes, _____ _____.

W I see. Is there any other place you have to go?

M I will have to _____ . But it won't take that long since I just need to return this book _____ _____. _____. They charge $5 on all late returns.

W All right.

M On my way back I'll stop to have lunch at a food court and get the hotdog for you.

W Just don't make me starve to death.

too ~ to …하기에는 너무 ~하다 | odd 여분의, 나머지의, 단편적인 | wire some money 돈을 송금하다 | fee 요금, 수수료 | or else 그렇지 않으면 | drop by ~에 들르다 | due 마감 기한인 | charge 청구하다 | starve to death 굶어 죽다 | urgent 급한, 긴박한 | withdraw (돈을) 인출하다

1 What comparison does the speaker make between training and not training the managers?
   (a) chance of success abroad
   (b) length of employment
   (c) amount of loss and gain
   (d) degree of satisfactory service

2 What can be inferred from the talk?
   (a) Training methods will boost a company's reputation.
   (b) There have been serious financial losses.
   (c) The speaker is going overseas soon.
   (d) The previous training was not effective for managers.

M Many of you may be concerned about the time, cost and investment _____ preparing to work overseas. The company _____ with overseas clients which are very important _____. _____. Managers working with these clients need special training. I would suggest that you consider the financial aspects when a manager _____ _____ because of _____. It is a huge loss for the company because _____ _____ and we also lose the customer. This cost is much more than what we spend on the training of the managers. I am sure we all can understand what the implementation of this method could bring.

investment 투자 overseas 해외에서 | aspect 국면, 양상 reputation 명성 worsen 악화하다, 악화시키다 implementation 이행, 수행
boost 증가시키다, 높이다

---

1 Which best explains the relationship between damaged tusks of Mastodons and its population?
   (a) Severely damaged tusks mean the number of Mastodons decreased.
   (b) Less damaged tusks mean the number of Mastodons increased.
   (c) Severely damaged tusks mean there were a lot of Mastodons.
   (d) Less damaged tusks mean there was much competition among Mastodons.

2 What is the main topic of the talk?
   (a) the function of elephants' tusks
   (b) elephants and their violent behavior
   (c) Mastodons' tusk usage
   (d) mating rituals among elephants and Mastodons

M Mastodons were huge, hairy, elephant-like animals that lived between 10,000 and 4 million years ago. They had long tusks and trunks like elephants, but their tusks were bigger than _____ _____. Scientists suggest that large tusks in Mastodons were used _____ _____ and _____ _____, similar to the other herbivorous tusked species. _____ obtained in the American Northeast shows that Mastodons over the age of twenty _____ _____ during spring and summer, probably _____. The brutal fights caused _____, which is apparent in mastodon fossils. The fossils obtained from a Midwestern site reveal relatively less damage to the tusk. It is quite possible that due to hunting, Mastodons decreased in numbers, thereby decreasing the competition among the herd.

Mastodon 마스토돈 (코끼리 비슷한 고대 생물) tusk (코끼리 따위의) 엄니 | trunk (코끼리의) 코 territory 영토, 영역 dominance 우월함, 지배 herd 무리, 떼 |
herbivorous 초식성의 | fossil 화석 mating 짝짓기, 교미 brutal 잔인한 internal 내부의, 깊은 | ritual 의식, 제식

1   What is the news report mainly about?

(a) the value of an antique silver dollar

(b) rare coins discovered in the Middle East

(c) the auctioning of a special silver dollar

(d) a gift planned for the Emir of Yemen

Relationship of Ideas

2   What comparison does the woman make between the previous and the new apartments?

(a) the size and maintenance

(b) the price and size

(c) the distance to the office and cleanness

(d) the maintenance and distance to the office

3   Which is correct about Mr. Baylor according to the conversation?

(a) He has to come in for a checkup after a month.

(b) He must take a tablet after every meal.

(c) He needs to take two tablets a day.

(d) He needs to change his old prescription.

Relationship of Ideas

4   Which of the following is NOT mentioned as a process of boarding?

(a) to proceed to the gate

(b) to present a boarding pass

(c) to wait until the row is allowed to proceed

(d) to get the row confirmed by gate staff

5   What is the advertisement mainly about?

(a) a national holiday in Britain

(b) a nationwide carpooling day

(c) a special carpooling service

(d) a new public transport system

6 What is the speech mainly about?

(a) a review of American maintenance systems today

(b) paying for infrastructure restoration in older American cities

(c) American cities at risk from possible volcanic eruptions

(d) the threat of infrastructure failures in old American cities

7 What can be inferred about the woman from the conversation?

(a) She does not want to attend a meeting.

(b) She is usually late in her submissions.

(c) She has no experience in preparing reports.

(d) She doesn't get work from just one person.

Relationship of Ideas 8 What comparison does the woman make between the Le Carte and the Continental?

(a) the size of the rooms with night views and the price

(b) the number of rooms available and the bill

(c) the availability of rooms with a night view and the cost

(d) the distance to the city and the prices of the rooms

9 What is called into question by the speaker?

(a)

(b)

(c)

(d)

Relationship of Ideas 10 Which of the following best describes the relationship between feeling and logic?

(a)

(b)

(c)

(d)

1 Monologue

What is the news report mainly about?
(a) the value of an antique silver dollar
(b) rare coins discovered in the Middle East
(c) the auctioning of a special silver dollar
(d) a gift planned for the Emir of Yemen

M Monday's auction, _____ dated 1805 and _____ to the Emir of Yemen, was expected to receive record-breaking bids of almost three million dollars. The silver dollar was _____ _____ by an emissary of U.S. president Andrew Jackson as a present for the Emir _____ _____. The coin has special value because it _____ _____ between the young United States of America and a nation in the Middle East. Thus, prior to bidding opening, most analysts expected it would ultimately _____ _____. To the surprise of many, however, the silver dollar remained unsold after bids failed to meet the reserve price. The coin may be put on auction sometime again when conditions are more favorable.

silver dollar 1달러짜리 은화 | issue 발행하다 | emir (이슬람 국가의) 수장, 족장 | bid 입찰가 | emissary 사자, 밀사 | ratification 비준 | treaty 조약, 협약
analyst 분석 전문가 | fetch 가져오다, (~가격에) 팔리다 | meet 충족시키다 | reserve price 경매 최저 가격 | favorable 유리한, 알맞은

2 Conversation

What comparison does the woman make between the previous and the new apartments?
(a) the size and maintenance
(b) the price and size
(c) the distance to the office and cleanness
(d) the maintenance and distance to the office

M Your new apartment is quite spacious. It _____ _____.

W Well, I had to _____. I _____, too.

M Oh, do you think it was wise to spend money that way?

W It's my dream apartment, so I don't mind _____ _____.

M I thought your previous place was not that bad.

W Yeah, it was very close to my office and clean. But it was kind of stifling.

M But can you _____?

W That's exactly what I mean by dream apartment. It doesn't cost much for the maintenance. The apartment is huge but new, so it costs less. Remember? For the maintenance in the previous apartment, I had to _____.

M I see your point.

spacious 넓은 | fortune 재산, 거금, 큰돈 | stretch ~을 펴다, 한껏 사용하다 | finance 금융거래, 재정, 자금조달 | loan 대부, 대출, 융자 | kind of stifling 다소 갑갑한
sacrifice ~을 희생하다, 바치다, 단념하다

3 Conversation

Which is correct about Mr. Baylor according to the conversation?

(a) He has to come in for a checkup after a month.
(b) He must take a tablet after every meal.
(c) He needs to take two tablets a day.
(d) He needs to change his old prescription.

W   Mr. Baylor, here's your prescription.

M   Thank you. When should I take these?

W   It's _____. You should _____

_____.

M   It says here that I will have to take these for a week. Is that right?

W   Yeah, you'll have to _____,

as your doctor _____.

M   So, _____?

W   It depends on your doctor.

M   Okay. _____? Oh, do I pay here?

W   You can _____. It is $9.75

total.

M   Thank you.

---

prescription 처방, 처방약   tablet 정제, 알약   come in for ~을 받다   checkup 점검, 정밀검사, 건강진단   recommend 추천하다, 권하다, 충고하다
depend on ~에 달려 있다

---

4 Monologue

Which of the following is NOT mentioned as a process of boarding?

(a) to proceed to the gate
(b) to present a boarding pass
(c) to wait until the row is allowed to proceed
(d) to get the row confirmed by gate staff

W   Attention, passengers. Orient Air _____ from

Cape Town _____ Bangkok is now boarding.

Please listen carefully _____

before moving toward the entrance gate — this will serve _____

_____. Passengers

booked in First Class, _____ or

traveling with children are asked to board right now. We'll open boarding

to passengers in Rows 34 through 54 in a few minutes. We request

that you remain seated until that time. You will be asked to show your

boarding pass _____. You cannot

enter the plane _____, but you may

enter the aircraft any time after that. If you have any questions about

your seating, please ask the gate staff. Thank you; we will begin

boarding now.

---

passenger 승객   bound for ~행인, ~를 향한   board 탑승하다   move toward ~를 향해 움직이다   smooth 매끄럽게 하다, 수월하게 하다

5 Monologue

What is the advertisement mainly about?
(a) a national holiday in Britain
(b) a nationwide carpooling day
(c) a special carpooling service
(d) a new public transport system

M   June 14th is National Carpool Day! As responsible British citizens, show your concern for the environment and _____ _____ on our roads by sharing a car with family, friends, or colleagues. The more cars _____, the fewer total cars we'll have on the roads. That means that we'll have a cleaner Britain and _____ for everyone. National Carpool Day is a way that every citizen can join this effort. _____ — _____ of driving for a while! We're certain that once you carpool, you'll understand its lower price, ease and environmental benefits — and continue with it. Register at www.carpool.org to find other passengers traveling on your route and to know more about events _____ _____.

responsible 책임감 있는 congestion 혼잡, 붐빔 colleague 동료 take over 인계받다, 떠맡다 for a while 잠시 동안 route 도로, 노선
public transport 대중교통

6 Monologue

What is the speech mainly about?
(a) a review of American maintenance systems today
(b) paying for infrastructure restoration in older American cities
(c) American cities at risk from possible volcanic eruptions
(d) the threat of infrastructure failures in old American cities

W   A modern infrastructure is crucial to economic prosperity. We need modern roads and rail systems and ports to make sure that goods can _____ _____. When infrastructure is lacking, billions of dollars are wasted as cars, trucks, trains, and ships _____ _____, _____ — or _____ in various lines or traffic jams. Yet, the infrastructure in our country is aging and we don't seem to be doing much to either maintain or replace it. We have only _____ _____. After all, there is nothing politically exciting about maintaining a road system. _____ and a nationwide neglect of maintenance have left the country's transportation systems _____ _____. In terms of impending infrastructure failure, America's older cities are like volcanoes waiting to erupt.

infrastructure 기간시설 prosperity 번창, 융성 goods 화물, 상품 breakdown 고장, 파손, 붕괴, 와해 apathy 무관심 neglect 경시, 간과, 소홀함
incapable of ~할 수 없게 하는 in terms of ~에 관하여, ~의 점에서 (보아) impending 절박한 erupt 폭발하다 restoration 회복, 복구

7 Conversation

What can be inferred about the woman from the conversation?
(a) She does not want to attend a meeting.
(b) She is usually late in her submissions.
(c) She has no experience in preparing reports.
(d) She doesn't get work from just one person.

M   Jane, what's the status of the financial report I asked you to do?
W   Well, I'm almost _____.
M   I requested that report a week ago.
W   I'm really sorry for that, but I was busy with the reports _____ _____, assigned by Mr. Ford. I didn't even have much time _____ _____.
M   So when can I expect it?
W   I think I can have it done in about two hours _____ _____.
M   It's almost time to leave. Why don't you just _____ tomorrow morning?
W   That will give me some time to review before I give it to you. Thanks.
M   Well, I'm sorry that _____ _____.
W   That's okay.

status 지위, 신분, 상태 | financial 재정의, 회계의 | be busy with ~로 바쁘다 | annual 일년의, 해마다의 | provided 만일 ~라면 | submission 제출, 제안, 복종

8 Conversation

What comparison does the woman make between the Le Carte and the Continental?
(a) the size of the rooms with night views and the price
(b) the number of rooms available and the bill
(c) the availability of rooms with a night view and the cost
(d) the distance to the city and the prices of the rooms

W   Welcome to Sydney Visitors Bureau. How can I help you?
M   I just arrived from California and would like to reserve a hotel room.
W   Would you like _____?
M   Well, _____ and would like some place near Einstein Hall in the city.
W   In that case you have a choice between the Le Carte and the Continental. You can get a room that has a great night view in the Le Carte since most of the rooms are _____.
M   What about the other hotel?
W   You _____ a room with a nice night view.
M   I see. _____ the Le Carte is more expensive.
W   Well, the hotel bill in the Le Carte is a little higher but _____ _____. Meanwhile, the Continental is cheaper but you will have to pay the breakfast and sauna.
M   I'll take the Le Carte _____.
W   Sure. I'll make the reservation.

bureau (관청의) 국, 안내소 | reserve 예약하다 | suburbs 근교, 교외 | in that case 그 경우는, 그렇다면 | night view 야경 | free of charge 무료로 make a reservation 예약하다

9 Monologue

What is called into question by the speaker?

(a) the link between IQ and musical talent
(b) the subjects used in a renowned 1992 study
(c) the possible impact of music on intelligence
(d) the strategies of mind-enhancing recordings

M Do certain types of music really make you smarter ? This has been _____ and talk shows. I'm now going to speak about this _____ _____ regarding the influence of certain music on intelligence. Many commentators have suggested that classical music makes one smarter. Some mothers or even pregnant women have taken to playing classical music _____ _____. Two recent studies _____ that listening to a Schubert sonata will make you smarter. They say that audio inputs of classical music before an IQ test will not _____ _____. This finding overturns an influential 1992 study which claimed that subjects gained up to 10 IQ points, although temporarily, after listening to Schubert. The earlier study had generated an entire industry for soundtracks leading to so-called _____.

recurring 되풀이하는, 계속 나타나는 | psychology 심리학 | ongoing 계속되고 있는 | debate 토론, 논쟁 | regarding ~에 관한 | intelligence 지능, 지성 | commentator 논평가 | previous 이전의 | outcome 결과 | overturn 뒤집어엎다, 전복시키다 | subject (실험의) 대상자, 피실험자 | enhancement 강화, 증진

10 Monologue

Which of the following best describes the relationship between feeling and logic?

(a) disturbances of decision making
(b) basic qualities that should complement each other
(c) two basic things necessary when decision making
(d) disturbing quality and useful quality

W Of all the things we need to understand _____ _____ in this world, we think our feelings are the easiest to comprehend. This, sadly, is not the case. Many people in fact _____ to such an extent that they consequently don't know how to deal with them. Often they _____. The truth is that being _____ is a basic part of understanding oneself and the world around one. _____ _____, but its complement. If something seems right logically, but our feelings object to it, we shouldn't just shunt our feelings aside. They may be sending us _____ to make the correct decisions in our lives. The phrase "listen to your heart" has more than a bit of wisdom in it.

function 기능하다, 역할하다 | comprehend 이해하다 | to such an extent 어느 정도로는 | suppress 억누르다 | antithesis 정반대, 대조 | logic 논리 | complement 보충, 보완 | object to ~에 반대하다 | shunt 옆으로 돌리다, 회피하다 | vital 생명의, 절대적으로 필요한 | disturbance 혼란, 방해

LISTENING REVIEW 🎧

A Listen to the definitions and write down the words.

1. pregnant _____
2. w _____
3. c _____
4. a _____
5. s _____
6. t _____
7. s _____
8. a _____

9. e _____
10. i _____
11. t _____
12. d _____
13. h _____
14. a _____
15. e _____
16. s _____

B Choose a sentence that best describes each Korean sentence.

1. 당신이 다른 중요한 일로 바쁘다는 것을 잊고 있었어요.

(a) _____

(b) _____

2. 감정은 논리의 반대편에 있는 것이 아니라 논리를 보완해 주는 것입니다.

(a) _____

(b) _____

3. 야경이 좋은 객실을 얻을 가능성이 더 적죠.

(a) _____

(b) _____

4. 많은 논평가들이 말하기를 클래식 음악이 사람을 더 똑똑하게 만든다고 말합니다.

(a) _____

(b) _____

5. 우리가 더 많은 차를 나눠 탈수록, 도로에는 차량이 더 줄어들 것입니다.

(a) _____

(b) _____

C Listen to three phrases and complete each sentence.

that has a great night view / you can get / a room
1. ➡ You can get a room that has a great night view.

2. _____

3. _____

4. _____

5. _____

D Listen to the following and choose a sentence that has the same meaning.

1. You need to take two tablets a day.
(a) _____
(b) _____

2. You can enter the plane after your row is called.
(a) _____
(b) _____

3. It will take only a few minutes as I just have to return this book.
(a) _____
(b) _____

4. This cost is much less, if we spend money on the training of the managers.
(a) _____
(b) _____

5. Relatively less damaged tusks indicate that Mastodons decreased in numbers.
(a) _____
(b) _____

VOCABULARY PREVIEW 🎧   Write down the meanings of the words.

01	big-budget	13	inadequate
02	gadget	14	vital
03	sophisticated	15	swap
04	calamity	16	subjective
05	mishap	17	passive
06	landslide	18	seamlessly
07	exceptional	19	waddle
08	goaltending	20	inevitable
09	indicative	21	behold
10	oppression	22	eatery
11	stick to	23	agile
12	glucose	24	clumsy

GUIDED LISTENING 🎧

1 Conversation

Listening Notes

(Nina Forest)

     (who)

     working on

(movie)

     I'm playing

     sharing with

     (locales)

Inference I

1 What can be inferred about the actress?

(a) She is used to cold weather.

(b) She became successful through this film.

(c) She likes the weather of Hong Kong.

(d) She does not feel comfortable working with Tom.

Comprehension

2 Which of the following is correct according to the interview?

(a) Nina is working with a legendary movie director.

(b) The setting for the movie is an Asian city.

(c) The movie was released a couple of days ago.

(d) Nina was brought up in two families.

2 Conversation

Listening Notes

(book)

     about

(the woman's guess)

(the man's explanation)

     It imagines

     It's all about

     deals with

(the woman's opinion)

Inference I

1   What can be inferred about the speakers?

    (a) Both of them will buy the book.

    (b) The man has read the book before.

    (c) The woman is not going to buy the book.

    (d) The woman is not interested in fiction.

Comprehension

2   What could NOT be the source of the fictional future mentioned in the book?

    (a)

    (b)

    (c)

    (d)

3 Monologue

Listening Notes

(match)

(France vs Brazil)

(Brazil)

(France)

proud of

hopeful of

1 What can be inferred about the World Soccer Championship?

(a) The Brazilian team was weaker than people thought.

(b) The Brazilian team lacked good players.

(c) France won because of outstanding defense.

(d) France won because of its strong teamwork.

2 What can be inferred about Darius Brown?

(a) He scored many goals in the championship.

(b) He was not recognized much before the championship.

(c) He won the championship twice in a row.

(d) He will be playing at the Olympic games.

4 Monologue

Listening Notes

(sock hops)

because
(This phenomenon)
    indicative of

(Before rock and roll)
(After rock and roll)

    Gradually
    still called   even though

Inference I

1 What can be inferred about the term sock hops?

(a) The term lost currency after a while.

(b) The term was coined by high school students.

(c) The term was used by a variety of people.

(d) The term represents rock and roll music.

Relationship of Ideas

2 What are the causes for the emergence of sock hops?

(a)

(b)

(c)

(d)

1 Conversation

1 What can be inferred about the actress?
(a) She is used to cold weather.
(b) She became successful through this film.
(c) She likes the weather of Hong Kong.
(d) She does not feel comfortable working with Tom.

2 Which of the following is correct according to the interview?
(a) Nina is working with a legendary movie director.
(b) The setting for the movie is an Asian city.
(c) The movie was released a couple of days ago.
(d) Nina was brought up in two families.

M _____ the superstar of the year, Miss Nina Forest! How have you been doing, Nina?

W Fine, George. Thank you.

M Currently you are _____, *The Seasons*. Would you like to tell us something about that?

W Yeah, the movie is an emotional drama and I'm playing _____ _____ caught between two families. And for the first time I'm sharing the screen with the legendary Tom McKenzie.

M How is it, working with such an experienced actor?

W Oh, I'm so lucky to be working with him. There is so much to learn from him.

M We heard that the movie is _____ around Hong Kong. Do you like the place?

W Well, Hong Kong is a beautiful city; however, I found it to be too warm. You know where I grew up, right? I mean I'm from Maine. Anyways, it took me some time to adjust to it. Overall, it was great fun, though!

M Well, we wish you the best for _____ _____. Thank you for coming to the show.

currently 현재, 지금 | big-budget 큰 자본을 들인 | for the first time 처음으로 | legendary 전설적인 | locale 현장, 장소 | Maine 메인 주 (미국 북동쪽에 있는 주) | adjust to ~에 적응하다, 순응하다 | overall 전반적으로, 총체적으로

2 Conversation

1 What can be inferred about the speakers?
(a) Both of them will buy the book.
(b) The man has read the book before.
(c) The woman is not going to buy the book.
(d) The woman is not interested in fiction.

2 What could NOT be the source of the fictional future mentioned in the book?
(a) a nuclear war
(b) a massive landslide
(c) a sudden ice age
(d) sophisticated robots

M I'm going to the bookstore. _____?

W Sure. Are you looking for a specific book?

M Yeah. There was a program on TV about a fiction writer, who usually writes about _____. What they showed on TV was quite interesting.

W You mean a science fiction story _____? I can guess what it's going to be about: robots, machinery, and gadgets.

M Well, the book is quite different. It imagines a future without describing any sophisticated machinery or hi-tech computers. It's _____.

W Sounds interesting! Does the book deal with _____ _____ or _____ occurring in the future?

M Yes. That's what makes the book so exciting.

W In that case, I might be interested in reading it after you finish it.

fiction 소설, 허구 | machinery 기계류 | gadget 장치, 도구 | sophisticated 복잡한 | humanity 인간성, 인류애 | calamity 재해, 재난 | man-made 인간이 만든, 인조의 | mishap 불행한 일, 불운 | nuclear 핵의 | massive 대량의 | landslide 산사태 | ice age 빙하기

3 Monologue

1 What can be inferred about the World Soccer Championship?
   (a) The Brazilian team was weaker than people thought.
   (b) The Brazilian team lacked good players.
   (c) France won because of outstanding defense.
   (d) France won because of its strong teamwork.

2 What can be inferred about Darius Brown?
   (a) He scored many goals in the championship.
   (b) He was not recognized much before the championship.
   (c) He won the championship twice in a row.
   (d) He will be playing at the Olympic games.

W   Today was the last day of the World Soccer Championship. _____ _____, played in Stevens Outdoor Stadium, was another important match that _____ _____ every moment of the game. France won the match, despite the fact that Brazil was stronger, with many well-known players. Worth mentioning was _____ _____ of Darius Brown, who did not _____ _____ even a single goal. France is proud of winning the title _____ _____. With Darius Brown on the team, France is hopeful of winning an Olympic gold medal as well. The Olympic games will be held in September, two months from now.

spectator 관중 despite ~에도 불구하고 | mention 언급하다 exceptional 특별히 뛰어난, 비범한 goaltending (스포츠의) 골 방어, 골 수비 | opponent (경기·논쟁 따위의) 적, 상대 in a row 일렬로, 연속적으로 | outstanding 눈에 띄는, 현저한 defense 수비, 방어

4 Monologue

1 What can be inferred about the term sock hops?
   (a) The term lost currency after a while.
   (b) The term was coined by high school students.
   (c) The term was used by a variety of people.
   (d) The term represents rock and roll music.

2 What are the causes for the emergence of sock hops?
   (a) the oppression of high schools and the students' desire for freedom
   (b) a change in trendy music and the wooden courts
   (c) the acceptance and popularity of new dancing fashion
   (d) the unpopularity and decline of leather-soled shoes

W   High school dances in the 1950s were called sock hops because the dances were performed without shoes. This _____ _____ was indicative of the changing cultural practices at the time. High school dances, during those days, used to be held on gyms' basketball courts — which were _____. Before _____ _____, the dances were of a slow, smooth nature and were performed _____ _____. However, leather-soled shoes were _____ rock and roll music: active rock music dancing could damage wooden floors. Gradually, the leather-soled dress shoe _____. High school dances were still called sock hops for a while even though the kids were dancing with their casual shoes on.

phenomenon 현상 | indicative ~을 나타내는, ~의 표시인 | leather-soled shoes 바닥이 가죽으로 된 신발 | misfit 부적합, 맞지 않는 것 | currency 통용, 유통 | represent 대표하다, 상징하다 | oppression 억압, 중압감 | trendy 유행하는

Inference I

1 What can be inferred about the man?

(a) He had been successful in his previous company.

(b) He is regretting having started his business.

(c) He wants the woman to help him with the business.

(d) He is thinking of closing his own business.

2 Which is correct according to the lecture?

(a) Insulin impedes the absorption of glucose.

(b) Insulin causes blood sugar levels to go up.

(c) High blood sugar levels can damage nerves.

(d) Type-2 diabetes is rarer than Type-1.

3 Which is correct according to the conversation?

(a) The man is going to go to Egypt next vacation.

(b) The man's schedule in Egypt is very tight.

(c) The woman has been to Egypt once before.

(d) The woman has saved enough money for a vacation.

4 What should students do before the end of the week?

(a) take the final oral test

(b) select a time to be tested

(c) decide on an assignment topic

(d) hand in their final assignment

Inference I

5 What can be inferred about the novel *Mrs. Dalloway* from the lecture?

(a) Its characters tend to resemble Woolf herself.

(b) Woolf's personal consciousness is absent from it.

(c) It reveals Woolf's awareness of contemporary philosophy.

(d) The story deals with the past and memory of its characters.

6 Which is correct according to the conversation?

(a) They forgot to pay the man's mother's medical bills.

(b) They are going to visit the landlord soon.

(c) They didn't know the rent was to be paid on Sunday.

(d) They are going to send the rent to the landlord.

7 Which is correct about humpbacks according to the talk?

(a) They have short flippers.

(b) They continue to dwindle in number.

(c) They are protected by law.

(d) They are mainly white in color.

Inference I 8 What can be inferred about the man?

(a) He wanted to have some pizza for lunch.

(b) He does not enjoy fast food very much.

(c) He does not mind what he eats for lunch.

(d) He is irritated with the woman.

9 Which is correct about Tree Kangaroos according to the lecture?

(a)

(b)

(c)

(d)

Inference I 10 What can be inferred about the airline from the talk?

(a)

(b)

(c)

(d)

1 Conversation

What can be inferred about the man?
(a) He had been successful in his previous company.
(b) He is regretting having started his business.
(c) He wants the woman to help him with the business.
(d) He is thinking of closing his own business.

M I've started _____. Did I do the right thing by starting my own business?

W Yes, indeed. Why would you think otherwise?

M There's _____. I'm even unable _____ to start the business.

W Don't worry. Once your business is up and running, money will eventually flow in.

M I don't know. I wouldn't be worried about these things if I stuck to the company I worked for. Plus, I didn't have to take out the loan that _____.

W Well, true, but you wouldn't be enjoying the flexible working hours. You always complained that you didn't have time for yourself since you had to go to work very early almost every day.

M Yeah, but everything's going very slowly at the moment and doesn't seem to be picking up.

W It will. You need to have patience _____ _____.

eventually 결국에는 flow in 흘러 들어오다 stick to ~을 고수하다, ~에 달라붙다 take out a loan 빚을 내다, 대출 받다 burden ~에게 짐을 지우다, ~을 괴롭히다 | flexible 탄력적인, 융통성이 있는 | at the moment 바로 지금 pick up (장사 따위가) 잘되다 patience 참을성 long-term 장기적인

2 Monologue

Which is correct according to the lecture?
(a) Insulin impedes the absorption of glucose.
(b) Insulin causes blood sugar levels to go up.
(c) High blood sugar levels can damage nerves.
(d) Type-2 diabetes is rarer than Type-1.

M Today I've come _____, more specifically Type-2 diabetes, the most common kind. Type-2 occurs when the body is _____. Insulin is a hormone _____. It is necessary _____ from our food into the body's cells so as to provide them with energy. So when insulin is absent or is inadequate, glucose is not absorbed by cells. _____ _____. A person with this condition is a Type-2 diabetic. If not detected in time, or left untreated, diabetes can seriously affect the brain, nerves, heart, and other critical parts of the body. Type-2 diabetes can most easily be treated by proper diet and exercise, _____ _____.

diabetes 당뇨병 absorb 흡수하다 insulin 인슐린 (췌장에서 분비되는 단백질 호르몬; 당뇨병 치료제) | transfer 옮기다, 건네다 | glucose 포도당 | cell 세포 | inadequate 불충분한 diabetic 당뇨병 환자, 당뇨병의

3 Conversation

Which is correct according to the conversation?
(a) The man is going to go to Egypt next vacation.
(b) The man's schedule in Egypt is very tight.
(c) The woman has been to Egypt once before.
(d) The woman has saved enough money for a vacation.

W What are your plans for summer vacation?

M I'm going to Egypt.

W Wow, it will be really nice. I heard Egypt has many historical places. What are you going to do there?

M I plan to go sightseeing and visit all the Pyramids.

W _____?

M For five days.

W And you think you can _____?

M I know there are a lot of things to see, but if you find out _____ _____, you will understand.

W I think a vacation _____. If I were you, I wouldn't be very excited.

M It's not like I can go to Egypt every vacation. _____ when I have a chance.

W Well, I hope you have a wonderful time there. Gee, I wish I could go somewhere for my vacation.

M _____.

W I will have to try to do that before my next vacation.

historical 역사의, 역사적인 go sightseeing 관광을 가다 packed 꽉 찬, 빡빡한 relaxing 여유 있는

4 Monologue

What should students do before the end of the week?
(a) take the final oral test
(b) select a time to be tested
(c) decide on an assignment topic
(d) hand in their final assignment

W I have an important announcement to make before completing this class. Your _____ is scheduled for next week. I have posted a blank schedule on my office door. By 9:00 a.m. this Friday morning, you are required to write your name _____ _____, to show when you'd like to be tested. It is vital that _____. If you want to get the slot of your choice, I suggest picking one early. I will not allow any student to take another student's slot, _____ _____ once they have posted. My suggestion to you is that if you know the slot you want, _____. Also, please check the class webpage for instructions regarding your final assignment.

complete 완성하다, 마치다 oral 구술의, 입의 post 게시하다, 공시하다 vital 절대로 필요한, 지극히 중요한 due date 마감 날짜 swap 교환하다, 바꾸다
assignment 과제, 숙제 hand in ~을 제출하다

5 Monologue

What can be inferred about the novel *Mrs. Dalloway* from the lecture?

(a) Its characters tend to resemble Woolf herself.
(b) Woolf's personal consciousness is absent from it.
(c) It reveals Woolf's awareness of contemporary philosophy.
(d) The story deals with the past and memory of its characters.

M   Like a true modernist, Virginia Woolf approached reality differently. When she described _____, she sought to make them authentic, hold them up as being relative and show how they were constantly changing. Her characters were not "flat," with _____. They were constantly changing, constantly reflecting on where they were, where they had been, and where they were going. Reading Woolf, the reader _____, and so moves beyond being a passive observer. Her novel *Mrs. Dalloway* is a fine expression of the style referred to as stream-of-consciousness, with its rich texture _____ _____. The narrative _____ between the conscious and the unconscious, the real and the fantastic and from memory to the present moment.

subjective 주관적인 character 등장인물 flat 평면적인 steady 꾸준한 passive 수동적인 observer 관찰자 referred to as ~이라고 일컬어지는 stream-of-consciousness 의식의 흐름 texture 조직, 구성 seamlessly 이음매 없이, 구분 없이

6 Conversation

Which is correct according to the conversation?

(a) They forgot to pay the man's mother's medical bills.
(b) They are going to visit the landlord soon.
(c) They didn't know the rent was to be paid on Sunday.
(d) They are going to send the rent to the landlord.

M   I will be ready in 5 minutes. What about you?
W   I've just _____. I'm ready.
M   Please check if there is anything you should do before we leave.
W   Oh, I just remembered. _____ _____ yet.
M   But last Sunday you told me that you'd pay it.
W   Yeah. I was _____, but we had to visit your mother.
M   Oh, yes, I remember, she was ill and we became very busy helping her.
W   And after that I forgot to pay the rent. What should we do now? Should we just visit the landlord now and pay?
M   I think we should _____ to explain this situation.
W   _____.

rent 임대(료) be supposed to ~하기로 되어 있다 landlord 집주인 wire (돈을) 송금하다 medical bill 의료비

7 Monologue

Which is correct about humpbacks according to the talk?
(a) They have short flippers.
(b) They continue to dwindle in number.
(c) They are protected by law.
(d) They are mainly white in color.

W On today's outing we're going to see humpback whales, named _____. They are largely black, _____ and long wing-shaped flippers. They are a sight to behold as they break the surface of the water and _____ before diving deep again. As they generally swim close to the shore, whalers once found it easy to target them, causing _____ _____ in their numbers. It was once feared that the whales would be made extinct through excessive hunting, and only the concern of environmentalists and legal action _____ _____. A law prohibiting the hunting of humpbacks, passed in 1972, has since helped them recover. It is unclear, however, whether we will ever see humpbacks return to the large populations which once dotted the American coasts.

outing 소풍 humpback whale 혹등고래 | distinctive 독특한, 분명한 throat 목 flipper 지느러미 모양의 발 behold 보다 surface 표면 expel 내뿜다 blowhole (고래의) 분수 구멍 drastic 급격한, 과격한 extinct 멸종된, 절멸한 dwindle 줄다, 적어지다

8 Conversation

What can be inferred about the man?
(a) He wanted to have some pizza for lunch.
(b) He does not enjoy fast food very much.
(c) He does not mind what he eats for lunch.
(d) He is irritated with the woman.

W This pizza place is too crowded. Can we go somewhere else?
M But _____. We will have to wait anywhere we go around this time.
W I know, but I don't like standing and waiting like this. And the line is not getting shorter. I'm starving.
M Fine, do you know any other place?
W Yeah, there's _____.
M What do they serve there? _____?
W Yes. They have _____.
M I thought that you wanted to have pizza.
W Not any more.
M Okay, let's have lunch there. We can't waste any more time searching for other places.
W I know. And I have no more energy to move around.
M Let's _____ and go back to the office.

crowded 붐비는, 혼잡한 starve 굶주리다, 배고프다 eatery 간이식당 | outlet 소매점, 판매점 | variety 변화, 다양성 search for ~을 찾다

9 Monologue

Which is correct about Tree Kangaroos according to the lecture?
(a) They resemble small bears.
(b) They live mainly on the forest floor.
(c) They move swiftly on the ground.
(d) They have short and thick tails.

M _____ on Earth, many can be found in the tropical rain forests of Northern Queensland in Australia. One of them is the Tree Kangaroo which, _____ _____, lives high up in the trees and feeds on leaves and fruit. By living there high above the ground, it avoids ground-based predators and also is able to _____ _____ that it would be unable to reach from the ground. As in all nature, however, there are the inevitable trade-offs. The Tree Kangaroo is _____ _____ as it moves among the treetops, but is _____ _____, waddling around back and forth uncertainly. The Tree Kangaroo looks more like a small bear with a long tail than a kangaroo, but the two kangaroo species actually have the same ancestors.

numerous 다수의, 많은 | species 종, 종류 | predator 육식동물 | inevitable 피할 수 없는 | trade-offs 타협점, (교섭에서의) 교환 조건 | agile 기민한, 날쌘 | clumsy 서투른, 솜씨 없는 | waddle 비틀거리다, 뒤뚱거리다 | back and forth 앞뒤로 | uncertainly 불안정하게

10 Monologue

What can be inferred about the airline from the talk?
(a) It has long considered changing its name.
(b) It will reduce the number of its aircraft.
(c) It will operate new routes outside the nation.
(d) It seeks to benefit from a higher volume of customers.

W I've called this meeting of executives to make an important announcement. You all know that our airline's operating costs _____, primarily because of fuel costs which continue to rise. During this same time, _____. The result of this has been that _____. We have to change this situation before things become truly serious and _____ _____. At yesterday's board meeting we decided that we would start offering low-cost flights to attract more customers. It is something we've wanted to do for a long time. Our new service will be called "BudJet" and we plan to launch it across the nation. "BudJet" will offer no free services on flights — even meals and beverages will be charged to customers. All luggage _____ will also be charged.

executive 중역, 간부, 경영진 | shoot up 하늘 높이 치솟다, (물가가) 급등하다 | quarter 4분의 1, (1년의) 사분기 | revenue 수익, 수입 | profit margin 이윤 마진 | squeeze 짜내다 | jeopardy 위험 | attract 끌다, ~의 마음을 끌다 | beverage 음료 | charge 부담시키다, 청구하다 | luggage 화물 | stow 싣다, 실어 넣다

A Listen to the definitions and write down the words.

1. spectator _____

2. g_____

3. o_____

4. g_____

5. o_____

6. e_____

7. m_____

8. p_____

9. s_____

10. w_____

11. s_____

12. c_____

13. f_____

14. s_____

15. a_____

16. d_____

B Choose a sentence that best describes each Korean sentence.

1. 임대료는 그날 내기로 되어 있었다.
   (a) _____
   (b) _____

2. 고등학교 댄스는 여전히 한동안은 sock hops라고 불렸다.
   (a) _____
   (b) _____

3. 그것은 음식물에 들어 있는 당분이나 포도당을 우리 몸속 세포로 나르는 데에 필요하다.
   (a) _____
   (b) _____

4. 혹등고래들의 수가 다시 원상복구 되는 것을 볼 수 있을 것인지는 미지수이다.
   (a) _____
   (b) _____

5. 독자들은 Woolf의 소설을 읽을 때, 등장인물의 마음으로 바로 들어가게 된다.
   (a) _____
   (b) _____

C Listen to three phrases and complete each sentence.

it / I found / to be too warm

1. ➡ I found it to be too warm. _____

2. _____

3. _____

4. _____

5. _____

D Listen to the following and choose a sentence that has the same meaning.

1. The brain, nerves, and heart can be damaged by diabetes.

(a) _____

(b) _____

2. Humpbacks are protected by law to prevent their extinction.

(a) _____

(b) _____

3. The opponents didn't get a single goal because of the exceptional goaltender.

(a) _____

(b) _____

4. We have decided to benefit from a higher volume of customers by offering low-cost flights.

(a) _____

(b) _____

5. You have to write your name in a blank of the schedule before the end of the week.

(a) _____

(b) _____

CHAPTER 07

INFERENCE II

VOCABULARY PREVIEW 🎧

Write down the meanings of the words.

01	censor	13	endorse
02	snatch	14	accuse
03	perspective	15	pharmaceutical
04	offend	16	willful
05	prevalent	17	attic
06	patrol	18	untidiness
07	drastic	19	tribe
08	take the initiative	20	barbaric
09	personnel	21	sanction
10	reportedly	22	feasibly
11	gender-neutral	23	pictograph
12	counterpart	24	juxtapose

GUIDED LISTENING 🎧

1 Conversation

Listening Notes

(Topic)

(the woman's opinion)

(the man's opinion)

(this movie)

      about

Inference II

1   What can be inferred from the conversation?

    (a) They both are not interested in violent movies.

    (b) The man has seen the movie recently.

    (c) The new Bond movie will be released soon.

    (d) The woman likes action movies.

Detail

2   What are the speakers doing in the conversation?

    (a) asking what kinds of movies each other likes

    (b) exchanging opinions about Bond movies

    (c) deciding which movie to watch

    (d) talking about what the movie was like

2 Conversation

Listening Notes

(purpose of talk) can you

(the man's problem)

(the woman's advice)

(the man's schedule)

(the woman's offer) Can I get you

Inference II

1 What can be inferred from the conversation?

(a) Neither of them will go to the concert.

(b) The man's toothache is severe.

(c) The woman will get a refund for the tickets.

(d) Today is the last day of the concert.

Comprehension

2 Which is correct according to the conversation?

(a)

(b)

(c)

(d)

3 Monologue

Listening Notes

(Democracy)

    all about

(Censoring literature)

    is like

    (for writers) we are limiting

        1.

        2.

    (for ourselves)

        we are restricting

(content)

(teacher)

If we censor

Inference II

1 What can be inferred from the talk?

  (a) Censorship for young people is necessary in some sense.

  (b) Censorship is not beneficial for writers and readers.

  (c) All democracies around the world censor sometimes.

  (d) Teachers should have the right to censor literature for their students.

Relationship of Ideas

2 What are the two reasons that support the speaker's opinion on censorship?

  (a) It interferes with our thoughts and confuses our perspectives.

  (b) It violates the right to express ourselves and limits our thought.

  (c) It is disrespectful of the writers and restricts their creativity.

  (d) It violates the right to read and limits the development of literature.

Listening Notes

(Topic)

(surprising facts)

> *crime prevention programs*
> *public vs private*
> > *business groups*
> > *citizens*

(result)

examples indicate

Inference II

1 What can be inferred from the speech?

(a) Citizens are taking their own initiatives to prevent crime.

(b) People consider the police useless.

(c) Private security firms are replacing public police.

(d) Public police departments need more personnel.

Comprehension

2 Which of the following is correct according to the speech?

(a)

(b)

(c)

(d)

1 Conversation

1 What can be inferred from the conversation?
   (a) They both are not interested in violent movies.
   (b) The man has seen the movie recently.
   (c) The new Bond movie will be released soon.
   (d) The woman likes action movies.

2 What are the speakers doing in the conversation?
   (a) asking what kinds of movies each other likes
   (b) exchanging opinions about Bond movies
   (c) deciding which movie to watch
   (d) talking about what the movie was like

M _____ James Bond?

W Well, no. Why do you ask?

M Have you seen his latest movie *Secret Underwater*?

W No. Actually I don't like those kinds of movies filled with action and unreal gadgets.

M Yeah, _____.
   But I heard it is quite different from typical Bond movies.

W Oh, really? What is it about?

M The movie is about _____, but doesn't have those action-packed scenes. It's all about strategy.

W Oh, _____.

M So what do you say?

W Let's _____.

latest 최신의, 최근의 | gadget 기계 장치 | typical 전형적인 | strategy 전략, 작전

2 Conversation

1 What can be inferred from the conversation?
   (a) Neither of them will go to the concert.
   (b) The man's toothache is severe.
   (c) The woman will get a refund for the tickets.
   (d) Today is the last day of the concert.

2 Which is correct according to the conversation?
   (a) The man made an appointment at the dental clinic.
   (b) The man postponed the meeting until the afternoon.
   (c) They will go to the concert after work.
   (d) The woman is expecting some clients in the afternoon.

M Stella, can you manage to go to the concert alone?

W Why? Aren't you coming?

M I've got _____. Luckily, I have an appointment with my dentist in the evening.

W Oh no. Why don't you go home and take a rest?

M _____. I have some important clients coming over in the afternoon; I need to see them.

W Okay, I understand. Can I _____
   _____?

M Thanks, I've already _____. That's why I'm able to talk now.

W Good. As soon as I finish my work, I'll leave for the concert.

have an appointment 예약하다, 약속하다 | dentist 치과의사 | take a rest 쉬다

3 Monologue

1 What can be inferred from the talk?
- (a) Censorship for young people is necessary in some sense.
- (b) Censorship is not beneficial for writers and readers.
- (c) All democracies around the world censor sometimes.
- (d) Teachers should have the right to censor literature for their students.

2 What the two reasons that support the speaker's opinion on censorship?
- (a) It interferes with our thoughts and confuses our perspectives.
- (b) It violates the right to express ourselves and limits our thought.
- (c) It is disrespectful of the writers and restricts their creativity.
- (d) It violates the right to read and limits the development of literature.

M Democracy is all about the right to freedom of expression. _____, in other words, is like snatching away one's basic human rights. By censoring certain literature, we are limiting a writer's _____ and disrespecting his or her talent. We are also restricting ourselves _____ rather than broadening our perspectives. Content which may be offending to one person may not be offending to another. Therefore, _____ to decide which content is suitable for him or her. Moreover, teachers who teach literature _____ but also connect literature to prevalent social attitudes. If we censor their content, we refuse to learn and _____.

democracy 민주주의 | censor 검열하다, 검열하여 삭제하다 | snatch 앗아가다 | flow 흐름 | disrespect 경시하다, 무시하다 | restrict 제한하다, 한정하다 | broaden 넓히다, 확장하다 | perspective 견해, 시야 | content 내용 | offend ~의 감정을 상하게 하다, 불쾌하게 하다 | prevalent 널리 보급된, 우세한 | trend 경향, 추세

4 Monologue

1 What can be inferred from the speech?
- (a) Citizens are taking their own initiatives to prevent crime.
- (b) People consider the police useless.
- (c) Private security firms are replacing public police.
- (d) Public police departments need more personnel.

2 Which of the following is correct according to the speech?
- (a) The crime rate has been increasing recently.
- (b) Security forces hired by many businesses patrol the city.
- (c) Many people volunteer to patrol the city when necessary.
- (d) The number of public police officers has decreased.

W Dealing with the increasing crime rate is _____. I must point out some surprising facts about it. Many crime _____ are being managed by the people themselves, including individuals, business groups and communities. It is quite astonishing to know that the public police force is _____. Many business groups have hired private security forces for their safety. Many citizens have _____ that patrol the city when required. As a result, there has been _____ in the city. These examples indicate the level of awareness and sense of responsibility among common citizens.

deal with ~을 다루다, ~에 대처하다 | debate 토론, 논쟁 | prevention 예방 | security 보안, 안전 | volunteer 자원봉사자, 지원자 | patrol 순찰하다 | drastic 급격한, 격렬한 | awareness 인지도 | take the initiative 솔선하다 | personnel 전직원, 인원

1 Which is correct according to the news report?

(a) China plans to send women into space by 2010.

(b) China has trained thirty five male pilots to be astronauts.

(c) China's next space program has fewer women than South Korea's.

(d) China's air force gives more advanced training to female astronauts.

Inference II

2 What can be inferred from the conversation?

(a) They have a habit of keeping a fan on while sleeping.

(b) They agree that keeping a fan on is bad for their health.

(c) They are not going to use a fan while sleeping.

(d) They prefer fans to air conditioners.

3 Which of the following is true according to the news report?

(a) Eazy Diet pills can actually cause people to gain weight.

(b) Henry maintains he was unaware they were ineffective.

(c) Glindia received bad publicity over similar harmful drugs.

(d) Researchers used outdated methods to test their effectiveness.

4 Which is correct according to the conversation?

(a) The woman wants to take either English or Spanish.

(b) The woman will be graduating next semester.

(c) The man advises the woman to drop one of the classes.

(d) The man can't help the woman when the class is full.

5 What is the conversation mainly about?

(a) the cleaning up of the attic

(b) the untidiness of the attic

(c) the contents of the boxes

(d) the work of the man's father

6 What can be inferred from the lecture?

(a) The Aztecs taught their skills to neighboring tribes.

(b) The Aztecs were pervasive and powerful even as nomads.

(c) The Aztecs were not leaders in cultural innovation.

(d) The Aztecs moved to central Mexico to cultivate crops.

7 Which is correct according to the announcement?

(a) The WFDA receives little support outside Asia.

(b) Internet news organizations founded the WFDA.

(c) The WFDA is a website run from Singapore.

(d) The WFDA is hosting a conference in India.

8 What can be inferred from the conversation?

(a) The attorney will meet Mr. Kingsley immediately.

(b) Mr. Kingsley doesn't like being interrupted during a meeting.

(c) The man is one of Mr. Kingsley's several attorneys.

(d) The attorney thinks Mr. Kingsley will see him now if it's urgent.

9 What is the speaker's view of present international climate negotiations?

(a)

(b)

(c)

(d)

10 What can be inferred from the lecture?

(a)

(b)

(c)

(d)

1 Monologue

Which is correct according to the news report?

(a) China plans to send women into space by 2010.

(b) China has trained thirty five male pilots to be astronauts.

(c) China's next space program has fewer women than South Korea's.

(d) China's air force gives more advanced training to female astronauts.

M An official from China's space program announced last night that the nation's first team of female astronauts will _____ _____ before 2010. They will join their male colleagues as mission commanders and flight engineers. The chief of the space program has reportedly said that four female astronauts will be sent on the mission. China's air force has already _____ _____ to be given training as astronauts. China has _____ to ensure that its space program is _____, and that women astronauts _____ _____. Nevertheless, South Korea remains the only nation so far whose first astronaut was a woman.

colleague 동료 commander 지휘관, 사령관 | reportedly 보도에 따르면, 들리는 바에 의하면 | determined 확실한, 결심한, 단호한 | ensure 확실시하다 | gender-neutral 남녀 구별이 없는, 남녀에게 균등한 | counterpart 상대방, 짝의 한 쪽 | nevertheless 그럼에도 불구하고, 그렇지만

2 Conversation

What can be inferred from the conversation?

(a) They have a habit of keeping a fan on while sleeping.

(b) They agree that keeping a fan on is bad for their health.

(c) They are not going to use a fan while sleeping.

(d) They prefer fans to air conditioners.

M I feel so tired.

W Maybe because it is the first day of the workshop.

M Maybe. I'd better _____ before any night activities.

W Yeah. I think I'm going to _____, too.

M You can have the bed. I'll sleep on the couch.

W Thanks. By the way, are you going to keep the fan running while you sleep?

M Yes. Why not?

W _____ can make you sick.

M I've never heard that before. If it is an air conditioner, it might not be that healthy, but it's a fan.

W I heard it spreads dust, increasing your risk of getting sick.

M Well, _____ and have never had any problem.

W You mean you've never had any problem yet. You know it's always good _____.

M Well, I guess turning off the fan wouldn't hurt me, either.

get some sleep 조금 자두다 get some shut-eye 눈을 붙이다, 잠깐 자다 | couch 침상, 소파 | keep ~ -ing ~을 계속 …하게 하다 | fan 선풍기 spread 퍼뜨리다, 뿌리다, 퍼지게 하다 dust 먼지 be on the safe side 조심하다, 신중을 기하다 turn off 끄다 | prefer A to B B보다 A를 더 좋아하다

3 Monologue

Which of the following is true according to the news report?

(a) Eazy Diet pills can actually cause people to gain weight.

(b) Henry maintains he was unaware they were ineffective.

(c) Glindia received bad publicity over similar harmful drugs.

(d) Researchers used outdated methods to test their effectiveness.

W   Leading baseball player Patrick Henry is being sued by a consumer rights group for misrepresenting facts about the weight loss pills he endorsed. The group has _____ Henry _____ about the effectiveness of Eazy Diet pills, manufactured by the Glindia Pharmaceutical Company. Independent research has repeatedly shown that pills like Eazy Diet _____. Glindia is accused of knowing this fact, and yet marketing the pills as useful anyway — a form of _____. Henry, who is on a 4-year contract with Glindia, _____. He says that Glindia told him repeatedly that the pills were effective in losing weight. Henry admits, however, that he never used the pills himself, _____ in his ads.

sue 고소하다, 소송을 제기하다   misrepresent 잘못 전하다, 거짓 전하다   pill 알약   endorse 보증하다, (어음 따위에) 배서하다   manufacture 제조하다   pharmaceutical 제약의   have little impact on ~에 거의 영향을 미치지 않다   fraud 사기   willful 계획적인, 고의의   admit 인정하다   contrary to ~와는 반대로

4 Conversation

Which is correct according to the conversation?

(a) The woman wants to take either English or Spanish.

(b) The woman will be graduating next semester.

(c) The man advises the woman to drop one of the classes.

(d) The man can't help the woman when the class is full.

W   I'd like to _____, please.
M   Which section would you like to join?
W   The 8:30 class, please.
M   I'm sorry, it's already full. You can enroll in the 10:30.
W   That's not possible. I have another class at the same time.
M   _____?
W   English Literature 302.
M   English Literature 302? Let me see. Well, _____ _____ English Literature 302 at 8:30. Why don't you take it in the morning and take Spanish at 10:30?
W   Can I do that?
M   _____. I'm really sorry. English Literature 302 at 8:30 is also full.
W   _____. They are important for my graduation.
M   _____ if you spoke to the course supervisor. He may be able to help you.
W   Okay, thank you. I'll do that.

enroll in ~에 등록하다   graduation 졸업   supervisor 감독(자), 관리자, 지도주임   semester 학기

5 Conversation

What is the conversation mainly about?
(a) the cleaning up of the attic
(b) the untidiness of the attic
(c) the contents of the boxes
(d) the work of the man's father

M I'm really grateful that you _____.

W Hey, you're always welcome. Moreover, _____
_____ are so interesting.

M Yeah, he used to collect anything that had unusual colors or
shapes.

W He must be a very creative person.

M Yeah, but it will take us a long time _____
_____.

W I can't wait to open these things and look into the contents.

M Well, let's move _____ and then we
can open them one by one.

W Okay, should we take these boxes first?

M Well, let's take those cabinets; they _____.

grateful 고맙게 여기는, 감사하는 | **moreover** 게다가, 더구나 **attic** 다락방 | **can't wait to** ~하는 것을 기다릴 수 없다 **contents** 속에 든 것, 내용물, 목차
downstairs 아래층에(으로) **one by one** 하나씩, 차례로 | **cabinet** 수납장, 진열장 | **untidiness** 지저분함

6 Monologue

What can be inferred from the lecture?
(a) The Aztecs taught their skills to neighboring
tribes.
(b) The Aztecs were pervasive and powerful even
as nomads.
(c) The Aztecs were not leaders in cultural
innovation.
(d) The Aztecs moved to central Mexico to
cultivate crops.

M The Aztecs are said to have had one of the most advanced cultures
among ancient South American tribes, but we must remember that
_____. The Aztecs
were a people who easily absorbed the best elements of foreign
cultures, and this was a decided strength for them. For centuries, ____
_____ limited to northern Mexico,
where they struggled to survive. In the 12th century they migrated to
central Mexico and built their capital city. From then on, they began
_____ of existing cultures and
expand their power _____. The dominant
position they made for themselves by the 14th century was entirely
_____.

tribe 부족 **absorb** 흡수하다 **barbaric** 미개한, 야만인 같은 | **nomad** 유목민 **survive** 살아남다 **migrate** 이주하다 | **adopt** 채택하다, 채용하다 | **conquest** 정복
dominant 우세한, 지배적인 **absorption** 흡수, 병합 **acquisition** 습득, 획득 **pervasive** 널리 퍼져 있는 | **innovation** 쇄신, 혁명 **cultivate** 경작하다

7 Monologue ▮

Which is correct according to the announcement?

(a) The WFDA receives little support outside Asia.
(b) Internet news organizations founded the WFDA.
(c) The WFDA is a website run from Singapore.
(d) The WFDA is hosting a conference in India.

W Students, _____ Web for Democracy in Asia, or WFDA, is meeting this week. You probably didn't know this, but the WFDA _____ in 1997 at a conference of Internet news organizations in Singapore. Its aim was to promote independent Web journalism, human rights and democratic participation _____. The WFDA maintains that democracy in the modern era is _____ _____, and the Web is ideal for that. Online gatherings and discussions, political movements, _____, and other activities help grow democracy across the Pacific and Indian Oceans. I hope you will all make time _____, because it combines your interest _____ with your passion for democracy.

democracy 민주주의 | launch 착수하다, 진출시키다 organization 조직, 구성, 단체 promote 활성화하다, 진행시키다 participation 참여, 관여 region 지역 maintain 주장하다, 지지하다 be dependent on ~에 의존하다 mass 대중, 다수 gathering 모임 voter 유권자 awareness 인식, 깨달음 combine 결합하다, 화합하다 passion 열정

8 Conversation ▮

What can be inferred from the conversation?

(a) The attorney will meet Mr. Kingsley immediately.
(b) Mr. Kingsley doesn't like being interrupted during a meeting.
(c) The man is one of Mr. Kingsley's several attorneys.
(d) The attorney thinks Mr. Kingsley will see him now if it's urgent.

M Hi, I would like to meet Mr. Kingsley. _____.
W Well, he's in a company meeting. Did you make an appointment?
M No, but I want to speak to him urgently.
W I'm sorry, sir. _____ Mr. Kingsley now.
M Okay, when will the meeting be over?
W It may take about an hour or so. Would you like to wait here?
M _____ since I have an appointment with another client in 30 minutes. Well, can you just _____ _____ and give him these papers? I'm sure he will understand. And I will wait here _____ _____.
W All right.
M Oh, let me just write something on the paper.
W Sure. Take your time.
M If he can't come out, please tell him that I will call him later _____. Thanks a lot.
W No problem.

attorney 변호사 make an appointment 선약하다 | urgently 다급하게 | disturb 방해하다 be over 끝나다 arrange 정하다, 준비하다 immediately 즉시 interrupt 방해하다

9 Monologue

What is the speaker's view of present international climate negotiations?
(a) They are of no value and produce insubstantial results.
(b) They create more discord than peace among nations.
(c) They pressure major polluters to make overnight changes.
(d) They are of interest only to climate experts.

M _____ about the world climate issue than just negotiating agreements. International agreements like the Kyoto Treaty are meaningless until the major polluters of the world like North America, Japan, and Europe make substantial cuts in their _____. These treaties also need empowered international monitors who can _____. Most importantly, major polluting countries must _____ _____ in their citizens and corporations. In the end, this is what will reduce pollution, since monitors _____ _____ every factory within a large country. Treaties and agreements amount to nothing more than _____ _____, and achieve very little in concrete terms — unless polluting countries truly move to enforce them.

negotiate 협상하다, 협의하다 | substantial 실질적인, 주요한 | greenhouse gas 온실 가스 | emission 방출 | empowered 권한을 가진
sanction 인가하다, 규정을 설정하다 | instill 주입시키다, 조금씩 가르치다 | feasibly 실행할 수 있도록, 그럴듯하게 | amount to ~이나 매한가지이다, 결국 ~이 되다 |
grandstanding 유리한 입지를 얻으려는 행동 | enforce 집행하다, 강제하다 | of no value 가치가 없는 | discord 불일치, 알력

10 Monologue

What can be inferred from the lecture?
(a) Pictographs from ancient Egypt can be confusing.
(b) Pictography is an inherently rigid system of writing.
(c) Egyptian writing has remained the same since ancient times.
(d) Egyptian pictographs represented more than just real objects.

W You all know that the Egyptians began using pictographs _____ _____, most commonly for the purpose of trade. These pictographs were _____ _____, and made ancient Egypt quite advanced compared to earlier civilizations which lacked a written language of any type. Today I will tell you about the more complex pictography that the Egyptians' pictographs _____ _____. In this system, they juxtaposed existing pictographs _____. For example, if they wanted to refer to the human soul, the custom was to draw an eagle above a man's head. This shows that Egyptian pictographs were sophisticated enough _____ _____, not just physical acts and items.

pictograph 상형문자 | represent 나타내다 | concrete 구체적인 | object 대상, 물체 | trade 거래, 교환 | advanced 진보한, 진보적인 | lack ~이 없다, 모자라다 |
evolve 발달시키다 | juxtapose 병렬하다, 병치하다 | intangible 손으로 만질 수 없는 | sophisticated 정교한, 매우 복잡한

LISTENING REVIEW 🎧

A   Listen to the definitions and write down the words.

1. patrol _____   9. c _____

2. e _____   10. e _____

3. a _____   11. c _____

4. c _____   12. i _____

5. i _____   13. s _____

6. p _____   14. n _____

7. i _____   15. n _____

8. b _____   16. j _____

B   Choose a sentence that best describes each Korean sentence.

1. 그들은 이미 존재하던 문화로부터 선진기술을 받아들이기 시작했다.

   (a) _____

   (b) _____

2. 훨씬 더 많은 것들이 세계 기후 문제와 관련하여 처리되어야 한다.

   (a) _____

   (b) _____

3. 감시단들이 큰 국가 안의 모든 공장을 일일이 방문할 수 있을 것 같지 않다.

   (a) _____

   (b) _____

4. 이집트의 상형문자는 철학적인 개념들을 표현할 만큼 충분히 정교했다.

   (a) _____

   (b) _____

5. 그린디아는 이 사실을 알면서도 이 약이 좋다고 홍보했기 때문에 고소되었다.

   (a) _____

   (b) _____

C   Listen to three phrases and complete each sentence.

that the WFDA is meeting this week / remind you / let me

1. ➡ Let me remind you that the WFDA is meeting this week.

2. _____

3. _____

4. _____

5. _____

D   Listen to the following and choose a sentence that has the same meaning.

1. The Aztecs moved to central Mexico to build their capital city.
   (a) _____
   (b) _____

2. Many people volunteer to patrol the city when necessary.
   (a) _____
   (b) _____

3. Internet news organizations founded the WFDA.
   (a) _____
   (b) _____

4. China plans to send women into space by 2010.
   (a) _____
   (b) _____

5. Censoring certain literature is disrespectful of the writers and restricts their creativity.
   (a) _____
   (b) _____

VOCABULARY PREVIEW 🎧

Write down the meanings of the words.

01	puerile	13	urine
02	skeptical	14	lead
03	manageable	15	mercury
04	dispose of	16	pesticide
05	constitute	17	brood
06	satellite	18	merciless
07	discard ·	19	glow
08	collide	20	weary
09	inflict	21	desolation
10	artificial	22	synopsis
11	striking	23	subdue
12	hazard	24	predecessor

GUIDED LISTENING 🎧

1 Conversation

Listening Notes

(problem)

    (reason)

(What happened)

(the woman's suggestion)

Function 1 Why does the man say he noticed the rip in the subway?

(a) to imply that he is not sure how the shirt got the rip

(b) to explain where he got the rip on his shirt

(c) to emphasize how embarrassing he was in the morning

(d) to explain how the shirt got ripped in the subway

Comprehension 2 Which of the following is correct according to the conversation?

(a) The man's clock stopped this morning.

(b) The woman noticed the rip as soon as she saw him.

(c) The man doesn't know where the store is.

(d) The woman thinks the man is ridiculous.

2 Conversation

Listening Notes

(mail)

(the man's opinion)

(the woman's opinion)

(what is required)

(the man's advice)

Stance

1 Which describes the sequence of emotions that the man undergoes?

(a) irritated → curious → skeptical

(b) irritated → skeptical → curious

(c) skeptical → curious → irritated

(d) curious → irritated → skeptical

Detail

2 What does the woman have to do to win the prize?

(a)

(b)

(c)

(d)

3 Monologue

Listening Notes

(Pollution)

    on Earth   *in space*

(Space trash)

    constituted of

    is a result of

    (difficulty of tracking)

        1.

        2.

    (danger)

trying to find a solution

    because

Stance

1 What can be inferred about the speaker?

(a) She is very concerned about pollution on Earth that is not disposable.

(b) She anguishes over the damage caused by space trash

(c) She is worried about the consequence that space trash can bring.

(d) She is optimistic about the missions to dispose space trash.

Inference I

2 What does the speaker imply about space trash?

(a) It is formed by spaceship emissions.

(b) It is made of relatively harmless objects in space.

(c) It is harder to manage than pollution on Earth.

(d) It sometimes destroys human life.

4 Monologue

Listening Notes

(An average American)

has about

(fact)

Americans have

revealed

(the research)

(participant)

The results indicated

(chemicals)

Among them were

Researchers say that

Function   1   Why does the speaker say that more information is necessary to understand the long-term effects?

(a) to imply that there is no concrete evidence that the chemicals are harmful

(b) to show the researchers are not sure what diseases the chemicals may cause

(c) to explain the research was important and it needs to be continued

(d) to point out the research was incomplete and has not proved anything yet

Detail   2   Which is NOT mentioned as a possible reason for the chemicals in the body?

(a)

(b)

(c)

(d)

1 Conversation

1 Why does the man say he noticed the rip in the subway?
   (a) to imply that he is not sure how the shirt got the rip
   (b) to explain where he got the rip on his shirt
   (c) to emphasize how embarrassed he was in the morning
   (d) to explain how the shirt got ripped in the subway

2 Which of the following is correct according to the conversation?
   (a) The man's clock stopped this morning.
   (b) The woman noticed the rip as soon as she saw him.
   (c) The man doesn't know where the store is.
   (d) The woman thinks the man is ridiculous.

W Hey, your shirt has got a big rip. What happened?
M It's _____.
W Did the alarm clock rip your shirt? Sounds ridiculous!
M Oh no. _____ this morning, so I got up too late! I quickly took my clothes from the drawer, dressed myself and rushed to the subway.
W But then who tore your shirt?
M Well, it was in the subway that I noticed that _____ _____. So I took a look down and _____. As I was already running late, I decided to go ahead to the office.
W _____; why don't you get a shirt from a nearby store?
M That's a good idea. I'll get it right now _____ _____.
W Good! Go ahead, but don't take too much time.

rip 쪼개다, 찢다, 찢음 | due to ~ 때문에 | ridiculous 어리석은, 우스운, 엉뚱한 | drawer 서랍 | rush to ~로 돌진하다 | stare at ~를 쳐다보다
obvious 분명해 보이는, 확실하게 보이는

2 Conversation

1 Which describes the sequence of emotions that the man undergoes?
   (a) irritated ➡ curious ➡ skeptical
   (b) irritated ➡ skeptical ➡ curious
   (c) skeptical ➡ curious ➡ irritated
   (d) curious ➡ irritated ➡ skeptical

2 What does the woman have to do to win the prize?
   (a) build up a big pile of magazines
   (b) read as many magazines as possible
   (c) subscribe to the magazines at least for a year
   (d) invest money in subscribing to the magazines

M Hey, there's a piece of mail for you. It says that _____ _____! Do you think it's real?
W It could be. Give it to me.
M I thought you'd tell me to throw it out. Do you _____ _____?
W Well, yes. I know people who have really won prizes.
M I can't believe that. Do they want you to do something to win the prize?
W Not exactly; however, you'd need to _____ _____ first.
M Now, I see why _____. I don't want you to subscribe to any more of them!
W Don't tell me that nobody else reads the magazines. I'm sure dad and mom do.
M _____ all of your mail and magazines if you don't listen to me.

throw ~ out ~을 버리다 | subscribe 정기구독하다 | irritated 화가 난 | curious 호기심이 있는, 캐묻는 | skeptical 의심하는

3 Monologue

1 What can be inferred about the speaker?
   (a) She is very concerned about pollution on Earth that is not disposable.
   (b) She anguishes over the damage caused by space trash
   (c) She is worried about the consequence that space trash can bring.
   (d) She is optimistic about the missions to dispose of space trash.

2 What does the speaker imply about space trash?
   (a) It is formed by spaceship emissions.
   (b) It is made of relatively harmless objects in space.
   (c) It is harder to manage than pollution on Earth.
   (d) It sometimes destroys human life.

W Pollution on Earth is quite manageable but trash in space is _____. Space trash is constituted of pieces of satellites or other objects sent to space that have broken into pieces, fallen off larger spaceships or satellites or _____ _____ for some reason. Space trash is a result of the 4,000 satellites that have been launched over the last 60 years. There are around 13,000 such objects being tracked by NASA, while _____ _____. Although sometimes small, space trash travels at very high speeds and is _____ if it _____ in space. The government and private agencies are trying to find a solution to space trash, because every time a space shuttle comes back from its mission, it usually _____ by space trash.

manageable 처리할 수 있는 dispose of ~을 처분하다 constitute 구성하다 satellite 위성 fall off (이탈하여) 떨어지다 discard 버리다, 폐기하다 track 추적하다 countless 수없이 많은 collide 충돌하다 inflict (타격·상처·고통 따위를) 주다, 입히다 emission 발사 relatively 비교적

4 Monologue

1 Why does the speaker say that more information is necessary to understand the long-term effects?
   (a) to imply that there is no concrete evidence that the chemicals are harmful
   (b) to show the researchers are not sure what diseases the chemicals may cause
   (c) to explain the research was important and it needs to be continued
   (d) to point out the research was incomplete and has not proved anything yet

2 Which is NOT mentioned as a possible reason for the chemicals in the body?
   (a) industrial lead
   (b) mercury
   (c) tobacco smoke
   (d) exhaust gas

M An average American has about 27 different _____ _____ in his or her body — this striking fact was reported on Thursday by U.S. health researchers. This report is the first scientific evidence of the fact that Americans have measurable levels of artificial chemicals in their bodies which may be _____. The researchers revealed that, although the artificial chemicals do not _____ _____, their impact on the human body could be harmful if they remain in the body for a long time. Americans' _____ such as pollutants may be a possible cause of this finding. As a part of the research, 5,600 people were tested in 12 U.S. regions. The results indicated the presence of 27 different artificial chemicals _____ of the study participants. Among them were _____, tobacco smoke and pesticides. Researchers say that more information is necessary to understand _____ of these chemicals.

artificial 인공의 chemicals 화학물질 striking 놀라운 measurable 측정할 수 있는 over the long term 장기간에 걸쳐 reveal 밝히다, 드러내다 pose (문제 등을) 제기하다 hazard 위험 impact 영향, 충격 exposure 노출 pollutant 오염물질 region 지역 presence 존재, 현존 urine 소변 participant 참여자, 참가자 lead 납 mercury 수은 pesticide 살충제

PRACTICAL LISTENING 🎧

1　What can be inferred from the talk?

(a) Hopper's *Nighthawks* is the first ever 'modern' work.

(b) Cafes and diners feature prominently in Hopper's paintings.

(c) Hopper's work is fairly unknown and easily misunderstood.

(d) Modern art typically illustrates themes of isolation.

Stance

2　What does the man think about playing bingo?

(a) It is wasteful.

(b) It is complicated.

(c) It is risky.

(d) It is puerile.

3　What are the man and woman mainly discussing?

(a) finding places to stay in Paris

(b) staying in Paris on vacation

(c) landing in Paris late at night

(d) booking seats on a flight to Paris

4　Which is correct according to the weather report?

(a) Tampa will have clear skies this evening.

(b) Stormy weather will continue over the next few days.

(c) Temperatures may fall below 60°F tonight.

(d) Humidity is expected tomorrow afternoon.

Function

5　Why does the professor mention his web site?

(a) to explain why he has opened his web site

(b) to imply that students who visit there have advantages

(c) to indicate where the details of the assignment are

(d) to recommend that the students visit the web site often

6 Which is correct about the conversation?

(a) The woman does not think the man will win the marathon.

(b) The man's knee was recently operated on.

(c) The man does not want to run the marathon.

(d) The woman is going to participate in the marathon.

Stance

7 Which best describes the man's attitude towards Naomi?

(a) hostile

(b) critical

(c) amicable

(d) outraged

8 Which is correct about sarcoidosis, according to the lecture?

(a) It causes damage by attacking the body's skin.

(b) Corticosteroids are known to be an effective cure.

(c) About 2.8% of the population is affected by it.

(d) It could prove to be fatal in some cases.

Function

9 Why does the woman mention her father?

(a)

(b)

(c)

(d)

10 What will the speaker probably do following this talk?

(a)

(b)

(c)

(d)

1 Monologue

What can be inferred from the talk?

(a) Hopper's *Nighthawks* is the first ever 'modern' work.

(b) Cafes and diners feature prominently in Hopper's paintings.

(c) Hopper's work is fairly unknown and easily misunderstood.

(d) Modern art typically illustrates themes of isolation.

W Today's gallery walk includes a viewing of one of Edward Hopper's best known paintings, titled *Nighthawks*. In it, you will see _____ _____ at a 24-hour cafe. They are _____ _____ strong electric lights. Each of the characters in the painting looks _____ _____. The painting also implies the characters either work during the night, or work so late that it carries them into the night. There is also _____ and hopelessness about the characters. The atmosphere in the painting conveys a sense of _____, making it typically modern, and one of Hopper's greatest works. This same mood can be captured in _____ by different artists that we'll be going on to view in just a few moments.

brood 곰곰이 생각하다 | merciless 무자비한, 냉혹한 | glow 타오르는 듯한 밝음 | weary 피로한, 지쳐 있는 | seediness 초라함, 기분이 좋지 않음 | convey 전달하다, 옮기다 | extreme 극도의 | desolation 쓸쓸함, 황폐함 | feature ~의 특징을 이루다 | prominently 두드러지게

2 Conversation

What does the man think about playing bingo?

(a) It is wasteful.

(b) It is complicated.

(c) It is risky.

(d) It is puerile.

W Jonathan, why didn't you come to bingo night? We missed you a lot.

M _____ from the hospital and had to be there.

W We have another session next week. Make sure that you come.

M I don't know about bingo.

W What do you mean?

M I mean the game looks simple, but _____.

W Well, listen. You know what bingo cards look like, right? _____ has a number, except for the center square, which is considered filled. The letters B, I, N, G, O are pre-printed above _____, with one letter appearing above each column.

M I know that part.

W All right. The printed numbers on the card _____ _____: 1 to 15 in the B column; 16 to 30 in the I column; 31 to 45 in the N column; 46 to 60 in the G column and 61 to 75 in the O column.

M This is exactly what I mean. I mean what is the point of the game?

W It's fun, and if you're lucky, you can win some money, too.

M I don't want to be sitting there for hours _____ _____. And I don't think it is fun.

W Come on, Jonathan! Go there once. I'm sure you'll find it interesting.

emergency 응급, 위급 | grid 격자 (모양) | except for ~을 제외한 | square 네모 칸 | vertical 수직의 | correspond to 대응하다, (~에) 해당하다 | puerile 철없는, 미숙한

3 Conversation

What are the man and woman mainly discussing?
(a) finding places to stay in Paris
(b) staying in Paris on vacation
(c) landing in Paris late at night
(d) booking seats on a flight to Paris

M   What time is it?

W   Aren't you sleeping? It's one in the morning.

M   So, we will be arriving in Paris _____, right?

W   Yeah!

M   Will it be possible _____?

W   There are a few hotels near the airport. I usually stay there

_____.

M   They'll be quite expensive, I guess.

W   Yes, they are. But it's okay _____.

M   Well, if you don't mind, you can come with me to my friend's apartment. He is coming to the airport to pick me up.

W   Seriously? Well...

M   There are many rooms. I'm sure you will find it comfortable. Plus, you don't want _____.

W   If your friend allows, I think it is not bad at all.

layover (여행할 때의) 도중 하차, 잠깐 머물기   pick ~ up ~를 데리러 오다   plus 게다가, 더하여

4 Monologue

Which is correct according to the weather report?
(a) Tampa will have clear skies this evening.
(b) Stormy weather will continue over the next few days.
(c) Temperatures may fall below 60°F tonight.
(d) Humidity is expected tomorrow afternoon.

W   Hope you enjoyed our last hour of country music: I know I did! And now, here's the weather in Tampa with me, Susan. _____! It's going to be a wet one today! The forecast indicates _____ in the afternoon, followed by heavy showers this evening. We could _____ _____ by 9:00 p.m. We're going to _____ following that rain, hotter than usual even for July. Expect a low of 64°F and a high of 88°F tomorrow, with clear skies and dry heat in the morning. A lot of humidity _____ by tomorrow afternoon, so you're probably going to feel hot, _____. We won't be able to expect cooler weather anytime before the end of the month, I'm afraid.

raincoat 우비   up to 최고 ~까지   string 일련, 한 차례   humidity 습기, 습도   sticky 끈적끈적한, 불쾌한

5 Monologue

Why does the professor mention his web site?

(a) to explain why he has opened his web site

(b) to imply that students who visit there have advantages

(c) to indicate where the details of the assignment are

(d) to recommend that the students visit the web site often

M Your quarterly assignment this time is writing _____ _____. Those who have visited my web site recently may already know the process. That is, you will _____ _____ that has been done on today's topic, summarize it, and then "critique the critics," so to speak. After that, you will then _____. It will be one of your first steps in learning to become a serious and trained person of literature. For this, you will need to refer to articles, books, web sites and other material _____ _____. You are required to summarize and evaluate each of the works you have consulted. In effect, you will be giving me _____ _____ published on this subject. Please note that the assignment is _____.

assignment 과제, 숙제 | review 비평, 평론 | critical 비판적인 | summarize 요약하다 | critique 비평하다 | critics 비평, 비판 | so to speak 말하자면, 이를테면
inject 삽입하다, 도입하다 | refer to 언급하다, 인용하다 | evaluate 평가하다 | consult 참고하다, 참조하다 | synopsis 개요, 개관 | due 만기인, 기한인

6 Conversation

Which is correct about the conversation?

(a) The woman does not think the man will win the marathon.

(b) The man's knee was recently operated on.

(c) The man does not want to run the marathon.

(d) The woman is going to participate in the marathon.

W Do you remember that there's a marathon this weekend?

M Yes, how could I forget? I'm _____.

W Are you really serious about it?

M Of course I am. You know that I've been planning for it for a long time.

W That's true, but _____. You've just _____.

M My knee is alright now.

W I think you should reconsider going.

M I've been running for a couple days for practice. And _____ _____.

W Well, at least, _____ before you participate, would you?

M I already did, and she said _____.

participate in ~에 참가하다, 참여하다 | stress ~에 압력을 가하다 | knee 무릎 | recover (from) (~에서) 낫다, 회복하다 | surgery 수술
reconsider 재고하다, 다시 생각하다 | fit 적당한, 꼭 맞는, 건강한 | operate on ~을 수술하다

7 Monologue

Which best describes the man's attitude towards Naomi?

(a) hostile
(b) critical
(c) amicable
(d) outraged

M Hey Naomi, this is Ben. We were supposed to meet to go to Brian and Nicole's _____ on Stratford, remember? I hope you remember. All the guests are _____ _____, but it'll take at least an hour or so to get there from Burlington Avenue. It's 8:00 p.m. and I've been waiting for you on Burlington in front of Dixon's for the past half hour. You should _____ as soon as you receive this message. If I don't get your call by 8:15, I'll go to the party without you. You _____ _____ last time. I can't wait any longer when you're not calling me. And I don't want to be late for this event because I promised Brian that I'd be there on time. Even if you can't _____ _____, still call me. You could also _____ _____ my PDA. So, call or text me soon, bye.

be supposed to ~하기로 되어 있다 | housewarming party 집들이 파티 | at least 적어도 | in vain 헛되이, 무익하게 | make it 약속을 지키다, 성공하다

8 Monologue

Which is correct about sarcoidosis, according to the lecture?

(a) It causes damage by attacking the body's skin.
(b) Corticosteroids are known to be an effective cure.
(c) About 2.8% of the population is affected by it.
(d) It could prove to be fatal in some cases.

W Sarcoidosis is _____ mainly affecting the lungs, eyes, or skin. Generally the patient suffers no more than severe physical discomfort, although there are _____ _____, and even death in an estimated 2.8% of patients. There is _____ for the condition and very few treatment options. Corticosteroids offer slight relief to some patients, but for a majority of them even _____ _____. Research continues _____ _____, but they have yielded nothing positive yet, mainly because we still understand so little about the human immune system. This means that, for the most part, a person with this illness will exist _____ _____ for the remainder of his or her life.

sarcoidosis [병리] 유육종증(類肉腫症) (림프절·폐·뼈·피부에 육종 같은 것이 생김) | disorder 장애 | immune system 면역체계 | lung 폐 no more than 단지, 겨우 (=only) | severe 극심한, 호된 | discomfort 불쾌, 불편 | organ 기관, 장기 | corticosteroid 코르티코스테로이드 (부신피질 호르몬 및 그 비슷한 화학 물질) | relief 완화, 안정 | remainder 나머지, 잔여

9 Conversation

Why does the woman mention her father?
(a) to imply that he is a very strict person
(b) to explain why she lived in many places
(c) to suggest he liked to travel a lot
(d) to indicate where she is from

M Where are you from, Angelina?
W Well, I _____ .
M Seems that you've travelled a lot, then.
W I lived in many places. My dad was _____ .
M That sounds exciting! You must have lived in many interesting countries.
W That's true. I enjoyed it a lot but could not make many friends.
M That's _____ when you keep moving.
W You're right. _____ , everything was great. What about you? Where are you from?
M I'm from Canada.
W You know what? I've never been to Canada.
M That's good. I mean _____ I know better than you.
W I really wanted to visit some of my best friends in Ottawa. But I never had a chance.
M _____ . Well, if you plan to visit your friends there, I really want _____ .
W Great!

navy 해군 | make a friend 친구를 사귀다, 친해지다 disadvantage 불리한 조건, 불편, 손해

10 Monologue

What will the speaker probably do following this talk?
(a) present a powerful empire that lasted for a long time
(b) discuss the empire founded by Rome
(c) point out Greek, Macedonian, and other empires on a map
(d) list the ancient empires by order on a chart

M Let's _____ . Ancient Greece was a powerful kingdom that was conquered by Macedonia, which _____ by Rome. This is the general pattern in ancient history: one kingdom wins battles, becomes powerful and _____ . It manages _____ , and often has a much larger and more powerful economic and cultural system as well. These factors combine _____ _____ both large and small. It lasts until another empire comes along that is stronger, bigger and lasts longer. The new empire's military, economic and cultural power is usually _____ . Now, I'm going to tell you about an empire that grew even bigger and mightier than that of Rome.

in turn 번갈아, 차례차례 | subdue 정복하다, 진압시키다 | might 힘, 세력, 권력 | as well 또한 | overcome 극복하다 | predecessor 전임자, 이전에 있었던 것

LISTENING REVIEW 🎧

A   Listen to the definitions and write down the words.

1. might_____

2. s_____

3. d_____

4. p_____

5. p_____

6. c_____

7. s_____

8. e_____

9. d_____

10. v_____

11. m_____

12. e_____

13. d_____

14. p_____

15. b_____

16. y_____

B   Choose a sentence that best describes each Korean sentence.

1. 나는 지난번에도 너를 기다렸었지만 쓸모없는 일이었잖아.
   (a) _____
   (b) _____

2. 그들은 강한 전깃불에 가차 없이 노출되어 선명하게 포착되어 있다.
   (a) _____
   (b) _____

3. 틀림없이 재미있는 많은 나라에서 살았겠네요.
   (a) _____
   (b) _____

4. 우리는 아직 인간의 면역 체계에 대하여 거의 아무것도 이해하고 있지 못하다.
   (a) _____
   (b) _____

5. 이 왕국보다 더 힘세고 크고 오래 지속할 제국이 나타날 때까지 계속된다.
   (a) _____
   (b) _____

C Listen to three phrases and complete each sentence.

a big pile of magazines / I see / why you've built up

1. ➡ I see why you've built up a big pile of magazines.

2. _____

3. _____

4. _____

5. _____

D Listen to the following and choose a sentence that has the same meaning.

1. Humidity is expected tomorrow afternoon.
   (a) _____
   (b) _____

2. I noticed in the subway that people were staring at me.
   (a) _____
   (b) _____

3. Space trash is harder to manage than pollution on Earth.
   (a) _____
   (b) _____

4. The researchers are not sure what diseases these chemicals may cause.
   (a) _____
   (b) _____

5. You will need to give a synopsis and estimate each of the materials you have referred to.
   (a) _____
   (b) _____

MEMO

CHAPTER 01 MAIN IDEA / PURPOSE

VOCABULARY PREVIEW

01. sanctuary 금렵구, 자연 보호구역
02. accountable 책임 있는, 해명할 의무가 있는
03. mold 형성하다
04. tolerable 참을 수 있는, 용인될 수 있는
05. repairable 돌이킬 수 있는
06. ailment 질병
07. acupuncture 침술
08. pulsation 박동
09. circulate 순환하다
10. conduit 수로, 도랑
11. bring about 초래하다, 불러일으키다
12. implement 이행하다, 수행하다
13. skeptical 회의적인
14. ethnic 민족의
15. sparsely 성기게, 듬성듬성하게
16. sprawling 불규칙하게 퍼져 있는
17. terrain 지형, 지세
18. draw upon ~에 의존하다
19. pathetic 형편없는, 아주 불충분한
20. footage 비디오 자료화면
21. revoke 철회하다, 무효로 하다
22. rampant 만연하는, 유행하는
23. saturate 적시다, 배어들게 하다
24. blood clotting 혈액 응고

GUIDED LISTENING

1	1. b	2. c	2	1. d	2. a
3	1. c	2. d	4	1. a	2. c

1 Conversation

M: Hi, Stuart told me that you've been to Steven National Park. Is that so?

W: Yeah, it's a very beautiful place. <u>Have you been there</u>?

M: No. My wife and I are planning to go there this summer. What could we do there?

W: Well, there's so much to do there. <u>In addition to the park</u>, there's a bird sanctuary and deer grounds. <u>Are you interested in</u> safaris?

M: No, but my wife is.

W: You <u>must not miss the safari there</u>. It's excellent.

M: Do you know any good places <u>to stay there</u>?

W: Yes, you could stay <u>at a bed & breakfast</u>. We always stay there whenever we go. I can <u>give you the number</u> if you want it.

M: Thanks, I'd appreciate that.

M: 안녕, Stuart가 그러는데, 당신 Steven National Park에 다녀왔다면서요. 그래요?

W: 네, 정말 아름다운 곳이더군요. 그곳에 가본 적 있나요?

M: 아니요, 아내와 저는 이번 여름에 거기 갈 계획이에요. 거기서 무엇을 할 수 있나요?

W: 음, 할 것이 아주 많아요. 그 공원 외에도, 조류 보호구역과 사슴 서식지가 있죠. 사파리에 관심이 있나요?

M: 아니요, 하지만 제 아내는 관심이 있어요.

W: 거기 사파리는 놓치지 마세요. 정말 굉장해요.

M: 거기 숙박하기 괜찮은 곳 좀 아시나요?

W: 네, bed & breakfast에 묵을 수 있어요. 우리는 갈 때마다 거기 묵죠. 원한다면, 전화번호를 드릴 수 있어요.

M: 고마워요, 그러면 감사하겠어요.

Purpose

1 What is the man doing in the conversation?
   (a) asking where to go for the summer
   (b) finding out what the park is like
   (c) planning what to see at the park
   (d) finding out how to get to the park

이 대화에서 남자가 하고 있는 것은?
(a) 여름에 가야 할 장소 묻기
(b) 그 공원이 어떤지 알아보기
(c) 그 공원에서 무엇을 볼지 계획하기
(d) 그 공원에 어떻게 가는지 알아보기

Answer Key

Level 4

에임하이

AIM HIGH

Active Curriculum for Successful Listening

LISTENING 리스닝

In-Depth Lab

We're
위아북스

Answer Key

AIM HIGH

Active Curriculum for Successful Listening

LISTENING 리스닝

In-Depth Lab

We're
위아북스

해설 여자가 다녀온 Steven National Park에 관한 정보를 묻는 남자와의 대화이다. 거기서 무엇을 할 수 있는지, 묵을 만한 장소는 있는지 묻는 것으로 보아, 남자는 그 공원이 어떤지 알아보고 있는 것이므로 정답은 (b)이다.

Inference I

2 What can be inferred from the conversation?

(a) The man will go on vacation with the woman.

(b) The woman is a tour guide at the park.

(c) The woman has been to the park more than once.

(d) The man is now interested in going on safari.

이 대화에서 추론할 수 있는 것은 무엇인가?

(a) 남자는 여자와 함께 휴가를 갈 것이다.

(b) 여자는 공원의 관광 안내원이다.

(c) 여자는 그 공원에 한 번 이상 다녀왔다.

(d) 남자는 이제 사파리에 가는 데 관심이 있다.

해설 여자가 다녀온 Steven National Park에 관한 정보를 묻는 남자와의 대화이다. 여자는 다른 볼 것들이나 숙소에 관한 정보를 주고 있다. bed & breakfast(아침식사를 제공하는 숙소)라는 곳의 전화번호를 주겠다는 여자의 말에 남자가 고맙다고 답하는 것으로 보아, (c)의 내용을 추론할 수 있다. 또한 여자의 마지막 말 중에서 whenever we go라는 말로 정답을 확인할 수 있다.

함정 사파리는 남자가 아니라 남자의 아내가 관심이 있다고 했다.

어휘 in addition to ~외에도 sanctuary 금렵구, 자연 보호구역 deer 사슴 safari 사파리 whenever ~할 때마다

2 Conversation

(Telephone rings.)

M: I'm Mark from City Cable. How may I help you?

W: Hi. I'm Miss Crawford. I see that my bill is a little higher than usual. Do you think this is <u>a billing error</u>?

M: Miss Crawford, I can see your bill details on my computer screen and I see that your bill is <u>four dollars higher than usual</u>. Do you subscribe to Star Movie Channel?

W: Yes, I do.

M: Actually, that channel <u>has raised its monthly rates,</u> which is <u>reflected in your bill</u>.

W: But <u>we were not informed</u> about it earlier. How can you increase the bill <u>without our permission</u>?

M: Well, that's the responsibility of the movie channel

and we are <u>in no way accountable for it</u>.

W: Okay, please do me a favor and cancel my subscription to the channel.

M: Sure, Miss Crawford.

(전화벨이 울린다.)

M: City Cable의 Mark입니다. 어떻게 도와드릴까요?

W: 안녕하세요. 저는 Miss Crawford입니다. 청구서가 보통 때보다 약간 더 많이 나와서요. 청구서에 오류가 있는 걸까요?

M: Miss Crawford, 컴퓨터 화면으로 청구 세부사항을 볼 수 있는데, 보통 때보다 4달러 더 많이 나왔네요. 스타 영화 채널을 신청하셨죠?

W: 예, 그랬어요.

M: 사실, 그 채널이 한 달 사용료를 높여서, 청구서에 반영된 거예요.

W: 하지만 우리에게 미리 알려 주지 않았잖아요. 어떻게 우리의 허락 없이 요금을 높일 수 있는 거죠?

M: 음, 그건 그 영화 채널의 책임이고, 저희는 그걸 해명할 책임이 없습니다.

W: 알겠습니다. 부탁 하나만 들어 주세요, 그 채널 신청을 취소해 주세요.

M: 그러겠습니다. Miss Crawford.

Purpose

1 What is the woman doing in the conversation?

(a) complaining about insulting remarks by the company

(b) finding out the actual amount of the last month's bill

(c) canceling a channel that she does not subscribe to

(d) asking why she has to pay more than the previous months

이 대화에서 여자는 무엇을 하고 있는가?

(a) 그 회사의 모욕적인 언사에 대한 불평하기

(b) 지난달 청구서의 실제 금액 알아보기

(c) 그녀가 신청하지 않은 채널 취소하기

(d) 이전 달들보다 더 많은 요금을 내야 하는 이유 묻기

해설 청구서가 여느 때보다 더 많이 나와서 전화한 여자와 직원인 남자와의 대화이다. 신청한 영화 채널에서 요금을 높였다는 남자의 설명을 듣고, 다시 취소하고 있다. 그러므로 이 대화에서 여자가 하고 있는 것은 이전 달들보다 요금이 더 많이 나온 이유를 묻는 것이다.

함정 신청했던 영화 채널을 결국 다시 취소하고 있으나, 채널을 취소하기 위해 전화를 건 것은 아니다.

Detail

2 Why is the woman upset about Star Movie Channel?

(a) Because they changed the fee without asking her.

(b) Because they canceled her subscription to the

channel.

(c) Because they didn't send her the bill directly.

(d) Because they didn't reflect the rate in the bill.

(b) Every society has a different culture that should be respected.

(c) Serious misunderstandings may arise due to cultural differences.

(d) Business should be done outside cultural limits.

여자는 스타 영화 채널에 대해 왜 화가 나 있는가?

(a) 그들이 그녀에게 묻지도 않고 요금을 바꾸었기 때문이다.

(b) 그들이 그 채널에 대한 신청을 취소시켰기 때문이다.

(c) 그들이 그녀에게 바로 청구서를 보내지 않았기 때문이다.

(d) 그들이 청구서에 요금을 반영하지 않았기 때문이다.

해설 여자의 말 How can you increase the bill without our permission?(어떻게 우리의 허락 없이 요금을 높일 수 있는 거죠?)에서 여자가 화난 이유를 알 수 있다. 그러므로 정답은 (a)이다.

어휘 bill 청구서, 계산서 | than usual 여느 때보다 | subscribe 신청하다, 예약 구독하다 | monthly rate 한 달 이용료 | permission 허가, 허용 | accountable 책임 있는, 해명할 의무가 있는 | insulting 모욕적인, 무례한

이 이야기의 요지는 무엇인가?

(a) 문화의 차이는 편협한 태도 때문이다.

(b) 모든 사회는 존중되어야 하는 다른 문화를 가지고 있다.

(c) 문화의 차이 때문에 심각한 오해가 생길 수 있다.

(d) 사업은 문화적 테두리 밖에서 이루어져야 한다.

해설 사회에 따라 문화가 다르고, 문화가 다르기 때문에 오해가 생길 수 있다는 내용이다. 마지막에는 그러한 오해를 막기 위해, 타문화에 대한 이해가 필요하다는 언급도 되어 있다. 그러므로 이 담화의 주제는 (c)이다

함정 (b)는 담화의 내용을 너무 확대 해석한 것으로, 답이 될 수 없다.

3 Monologue

W: Let's discuss the impact of cultural differences on our lives. Culture usually molds a person in the way he talks, behaves, interacts with other people, and largely <u>the way he perceives other people</u>. Cultural differences may <u>give rise to misunderstandings</u> if two people <u>are not aware of the cultural backgrounds</u> of each other. Body languages, along with social and cultural codes, differ from culture to culture, and <u>the chances of these getting misinterpreted</u> are very high. The difference seems to be <u>tolerable generally</u>; however, during business meetings or diplomatic situations, a small misinterpretation may lead to serious consequences: damage done may be far from repairable.

W: 문화의 차이가 우리의 삶에 미치는 영향에 대해 이야기해 보도록 하죠. 문화는 일반적으로 사람이 말하고 행동하고 다른 사람들과 상호작용하는 방식을 형성하고, 주로 사람이 다른 사람들을 인식하는 방식을 형성합니다. 두 사람이 서로의 문화적 배경을 알지 못하면, 문화의 차이는 오해를 불러일으킬 수 있습니다. 사회적 문화적 코드에 따라 몸짓 언어는 문화마다 달라서, 잘못 해석될 가능성이 매우 높습니다. 그 차이는 일반적으로 용인될 수 있을 것처럼 보이지만, 사업상의 회의나 외교 상황에서는 작은 오해가 심각한 결과를 낳을 수도 있습니다. 그리고 이렇게 생긴 손해는 돌이킬 수 없을지도 모릅니다.

Main Idea

1   What is the main idea of the talk?

(a) Cultural differences are due to narrow attitudes.

Detail

2   Which is NOT mentioned as an influence that culture has on a person?

(a) the way the person talks

(b) the way the person acts

(c) the way the person interacts with others

(d) the way the person perceives things

문화가 사람에게 미칠 수 있는 영향으로 언급되지 않은 것은?

(a) 사람이 말하는 방식

(b) 사람이 행동하는 방식

(c) 사람이 다른 사람과 상호작용하는 방식

(d) 사람이 사물을 인식하는 방식

해설 문화는 사람이 말하고 행동하고 다른 사람들과 상호작용하는 방식과 다른 사람들을 인식하는 방식을 형성한다고 했으므로, 이와 다른 것은 (d) 사람이 사물을 인식하는 방식이다.

어휘 mold 형성하다 | perceive 지각하다, 인식하다 | give rise to ~을 일으키다, 생기게 하다 | misunderstanding 오해 | misinterpret 잘못 해석하다, 오해하다 | tolerable 참을 수 있는, 용인될 수 있는 | diplomatic 외교의 | consequence 결과, 결말 | repairable 돌이킬 수 있는

4 Monologue

M: In earlier times, people <u>used to treat ailments</u> in different ways, some of which are even practiced up to now. All these practices are collectively known as <u>traditional and alternative medicine</u>, each having <u>its own principles of practice</u>. One Native American tribe from the southwest, called the Navaho, believes in sand painting <u>to treat sick people</u>. Europeans <u>are known for using herbal remedies</u> for all kinds of diseases. <u>Another form of traditional healing is acupuncture</u>, which has been in practice among Chinese people for centuries. These forms of healing have been sustained through all types of modernization and have preserved their traditional values. Many people who believe in alternative forms of healing find them as effective as Western medicine.

M: 예전에 사람들은 다양한 방법으로 질병을 치료하곤 했습니다. 그것들 중 몇몇은 지금까지도 행해지고 있습니다. 이 모든 관행들은 총괄하여 전통 대체의학이라고 알려져 있는데, 각각의 것들에는 고유한 원칙이 있습니다. 나바호라고 불리는 미국 남서부의 한 인디언 부족은 아픈 사람들을 치료하는 데에 모래 그림의 효과를 믿고 있습니다. 유럽 사람들은 모든 질병에 허브 치료법을 사용하는 것으로 알려져 있습니다. 전통적인 치유법의 또 다른 형태는 침인데, 중국인들 사이에서 오랫동안 행해져 왔습니다. 이런 치유 방법들은 현대화 과정을 거쳐 오면서도 전통적인 가치를 보존하고 있습니다. 대체 치유법을 믿는 많은 사람들은 그것이 서양의 의학만큼 효과적이라는 것을 알고 있습니다.

Main Idea

1 What is the main idea of the lecture?

(a) **Every culture has unique types of traditional forms of healing.**

(b) Some cultures were more advanced in treatment of sick people.

(c) Alternative medicine today is derived from the ancient world.

(d) Alternative medicine in some cultures has proved to be effective.

이 강의의 요지는 무엇인가?

(a) 모든 문화에는 독특한 전통적인 치유 방법이 있다.

(b) 어떤 문화는 병든 사람들을 치료하는 데 좀 더 앞서 있었다.

(c) 오늘날 대체의학은 고대 세계에서 시작된 것이다.

(d) 몇몇 문화의 대체의학은 효과가 있는 것으로 증명되었다.

해설 세계 각국의 대체의학에 관한 내용이다. 그 예로 나바호 인디언의 모래 그림, 유럽 사람들의 허브, 중국 사람들의 침술을 들고 있다. 그러므로 이 강의의 요지는 모든 문화마다 독특한 전통적인 치유 방법이 있다는 것이다.

함정 (c) 대체의학은 고대 세계에서부터 시작되었다는 언급은 있으나, 그것 자체가 주제는 아니다. (d) 대체의학이 효과가 있다는 말도 언급되기는 하였으나, 그것이 주제는 아니다.

Detail

2 What did the Navaho Indians use to heal people?

(a) herbs

(b) acupuncture

(c) **sand painting**

(d) Western medicine

나바호 인디언들이 사람들을 치유하기 위해 사용하는 것은 무엇인가?

(a) 허브

(b) 침

(c) 모래 그림

(d) 서양 의학

해설 the Navaho, believes in sand painting to treat sick people에서 나바호 인디언이 사람들을 치유하기 위해 사용하는 것은 모래 그림임을 알 수 있다.

어휘 treat (질병을) 치료하다 | ailment 질병 | practice 실행하다, 관행, 관례 | up to now 지금까지, 현재까지 | alternative medicine 대체 의학 | sand painting 모래 그림 (여러 가지로 착색한 모래로 그리는 주술적인 그림) | remedy 치료, 의료 | healing 치유, 치료 | acupuncture 침술 | sustain 유지하다, 계속하다 | preserve 보존하다, 보호하다 | effective 효과적인

PRACTICAL LISTENING

1. c	2. d	3. b	4. d	5. d
6. b	7. d	8. c	9. c	10. b

1

M: Today's lecture deals with William Harvey, the 17th century English physiologist. Harvey discovered that <u>blood was pumped through the body</u> by the heart, and not by the rhythmic pulsation of the arteries as believed. It was through his work that we came to understand that <u>the heart was a muscle</u>, a muscle <u>responsible for pumping blood throughout the body.</u> <u>The veins were discovered not to circulate blood</u>, but merely act as conduits through which blood flows. He came to this conclusion <u>through extensive observation</u> of patients and experiments with animals. These included observing pulsation of <u>the heart in live animals</u>, or animals in which the heart was removed and continued to pulse for a time. He published his findings on the workings of the heart in 1628.

M: 오늘 강의는 17세기 영국인 생리학자 William Harvey에 대한 것입니다. Harvey는 심장에 의해서 몸의 혈액이 순환된다는 사실을 밝혔습니다. 이전에는 대동맥의 리드미컬한 박동으로 혈액 순환이 이뤄진다고 믿었었습니다. 그의 연구로 인하여 우리는 심장이 우리 몸의 구석구석에 혈액을 보낼 책임이 있는 근육들로 이루어진 사실을 알게 되었습니다. 정맥은 혈액 순환을 시키는 것이 아니라, 단순히 혈액이 지나는 수로의 역할만을 한다는 것으로 밝혀졌습니다. 그는 대다수의 환자들을 관찰하고 동물들의 실험을 통하여 이러한 결론을 도출했습니다. 이 실험에는 살아 있는 동물의 심장 박동을 관찰하는 것이나, 심장이 제거된 뒤에도 일정 시간 동안 심장 박동이 지속되는 동물도 관찰하였습니다. 그는 1628년에 심장의 역할에 관한 자신의 연구 결과물을 책으로 발간했습니다.

Q Which of the following is correct about William Harvey?

(a) He conducted experiments on human beings.

(b) He first demonstrated the workings of the heart to students.

(c) He revealed the heart's role in blood circulation.

(d) He was the first to discover that arteries pulsate.

다음 중 William Harvey에 대하여 옳은 것은?

(a) 그는 인간을 대상으로 실험을 하였다.

(b) 그는 학생들에게 심장의 역할에 대하여 처음으로 설명하였다.

(c) 그는 혈액 순환에 있어 심장의 역할을 밝혀냈다.

(d) 그는 대동맥 박동을 처음 발견한 사람이다.

해설 심장이 혈액을 순환시키는 역할을 한다는 사실을 밝힌 것이 William Harvey라고 말하고 있으므로 정답은 (c)이다.

함정 그는 대다수의 환자들을 관찰하고 동물들의 실험을 통하여 이러한 결론을 도출했다고 했으므로 (a)는 답이 아니다. 그가 1628년에 심장에 관한 책을 발간했다는 언급은 있지만 (b)의 내용은 언급되지 않았다. 그가 대동맥 박동을 처음 발견한 것이 아니라 심장에 의해서 몸의 혈액이 순환된다는 사실을 밝힌 것이므로 (d) 또한 답이 될 수 없다.

어휘 rhythmic 리드미컬한 | pulsation 박동 | artery 동맥 | vein 정맥 | circulate 순환하다 | merely 단순히 | conduit 수로, 도랑 | extensive 광범위한

2 Purpose

M: Can I come in for seconds?

W: Hi, Mark. Come in. What brought you here?

M: Well, I'm working on my paper and I need to do some research on the Internet. But...

W: Isn't your computer connected to the Internet or anything?

M: It is not the Internet. I need to print some pages, but it doesn't seem to be working from this morning.

W: Oh! I have just finished my paper. So you can use my computer. Or do you want to take the printer to your room?

M: I don't know how long it would take, so, if you don't mind, I would like to take it and bring it back to you the first thing tomorrow.

W: That's okay. By the way, how many pages are you going to print?

M: About seventy.

W: Oh, then you should use Jenny's printer.

M: Isn't your printer working?

W: It is, but Jenny's is a laser printer and is much faster.

M: 잠깐 들어가도 될까?

W: 안녕, Mark. 들어와. 여기는 웬일이야?

M: 음, 보고서를 작성하고 있는데, 인터넷 검색을 좀 해야 해서. 그런데….

W: 네 컴퓨터는 인터넷 같은 데 연결되어 있지 않아?

M: 인터넷이 아니라. 프린트를 좀 해야 하는데 오늘 아침부터 작동하지 않더라고.

W: 아! 나는 이제 막 보고서 작성을 마쳤어. 그러니까 내 컴퓨터를 써도 돼. 아니면 프린터를 네 방으로 가져갈래?

M: 얼마나 걸릴지 잘 모르겠어. 그러니까 너만 괜찮다면, 가져갔다가 내일 일찍 가져다 줄게.

W: 좋아. 그런데, 몇 페이지나 프린트할 거야?

M: 70장 정도.

W: 아, 그러면 Jenny의 프린터를 사용해야겠다.

M: 네 프린터는 작동되지 않아?

W: 되기는 하는데, Jenny 프린터가 레이저라 훨씬 더 빠르거든.

Q Why does the man want to talk to the woman?

(a) to use her computer

(b) to ask if she can help with his paper

(c) to see if she has a laser printer

(d) to borrow a printer

남자가 여자와 얘기하기를 바라는 이유는?

(a) 여자의 컴퓨터를 사용하려고

(b) 여자가 보고서 작업을 도와줄 수 있는지 물어보려고

(c) 여자가 레이저 프린터를 가지고 있는지 알아보려고

(d) 프린터를 빌리려고

남자는 보고서를 출력해야 해서 여자의 프린터를 사용해도 되냐고 물어보고 있다. 남자가 여자를 찾아간 이유는 프린터를 빌리기 위해서이므로 (d)가 정답이다.

함정 대화 처음에 컴퓨터를 빌리려는 것인 줄 잘못 이해한 여자와의 대화만 듣고, (a)를 정답으로 고르면 안 된다.

어휘 for seconds 잠깐만, 잠깐 동안 | connect 연결하다 | bring ~ back ~을 돌려주다 | borrow 빌리다

3

W: I heard that a new director has joined your company. How's he?

M: Well, he's a strict person but very knowledgeable. He's very different <u>from our previous director</u>.

W: Is he <u>employee-friendly</u> or shareholder-friendly?

M: He says he's on our side. He wants <u>to bring about significant changes</u> in the company.

W: Sounds good. It seems like he has big plans.

M: Maybe. Let's <u>see if he actually implements them</u>. A lot of directors usually talk a lot but <u>are poor at doing what they say</u>.

W: I hope he is different <u>from those other directors that we had</u>.

W: 너희 회사에 이사가 새로 왔다고 들었는데, 어때?

M: 음, 엄격하지만 아는 게 많은 사람이야. 예전 이사하고는 아주 달라.

W: 직원 친화적이야, 주주 친화적이야?

M: 그가 말하길, 그는 우리 편이래. 그는 회사에 중대한 변화를 불러일으키고 싶어 해.

W: 좋은데. 큰 계획을 가지고 있는 것 같아서.

M: 아마 그럴지도. 실제로 실행에 옮기는지 두고 보자고. 많은 이사들이 대개 말은 많지만, 말한 것을 실천하는 데는 서투르니까 말이야.

W: 이전의 이사들과는 다르길 바래.

Q Which is correct according to the conversation?

(a) They think the previous director was better than the new one.

(b) The new director has plans from which employees can benefit.

(c) The man has already become a big fan of the new director.

(d) The woman is skeptical about the plans of the new director.

이 대화에 근거하여 옳은 것은?

(a) 그들은 예전의 이사가 새 이사보다 더 나았다고 생각한다.

(b) 새 이사는 직원들에게 이익이 될 수 있는 계획을 가지고 있다.

(c) 남자는 새 이사의 열렬한 팬이 되었다.

(d) 여자는 새 이사의 계획에 대해 회의적이다.

해설 회사에 새로 부임한 이사에 관해 두 사람이 이야기하고 있다. 여자가 어떤 사람이냐고 묻자, 엄격하지만 매우 박식하고 예전 이사하고 많이 다르다고 한다. 또한 주주들보다는 직원들에게 더 친화적이며, 회사에 중요한 변화를 가져오고 싶어 한다고 말하고 있다. 따라서 정답은 (b)가 된다.

함정 남자는 새 이사를 열렬히 믿고 좋아하는 것이 아니라, 엄격하면서도 아는 것이 많으며 직원 친화적인 데다가 회사에 중대한 변화를 꾀하려는 것에 대한 긍정적인 기대를 하면서도, 실행에 옮길지를 일단 지켜보고 있는 상황이다. 따라서 (c)는 정답이 될 수 없다.

어휘 director 이사, 국장, 지도자, 관리자 | strict 엄격한, 엄밀한 | knowledgeable 많이 아는, 박식한, 정보통의 | different from ~와 다른 | previous 앞의, 이전의 | shareholder 주주 | friendly ~에 우호(친화)적인 | bring about 초래하다, 불러일으키다 | significant 중요한, 의미 있는 | implement 이행하다, 수행하다 | be poor at ~에 서투르다 | skeptical 회의적인

4 Main Idea

W: Writers from various nations have often been influenced <u>by their cultural, economic, or ethnic surroundings</u>. This <u>holds true for</u> Canada as well. I'm going to discuss <u>a long-standing influence</u> on Canadian literature: its natural environment. Though sparsely populated, Canada is the second-largest country in the world. The country's <u>sprawling terrain</u> has inspired various themes in writers <u>as diverse as</u> Margaret Atwood, who is known for scholarly fiction, and Douglas Coupland, whose work draws upon pop culture. Both would agree that the geography of Canada has greatly influenced <u>their imaginations and writings</u>, although their styles are completely different. This means that various Canadian artists perceive the nation's geography in different ways, and that is <u>reflected in the works they create</u>.

W: 여러 국가의 작가들은 그들의 문화, 경제, 민족적인 환경에 의해 종종 영향을 받습니다. 이것은 캐나다도 역시 마찬가지입니다. 캐나다 문학에 오랫동안 영향을 미친 그 자연 환경에 대하여 이야기하려고 합니다. 비록 인구 밀도는 낮지만 캐나다는 세계에서 두 번째로 큰 나라입니다. 광활한 대지는 학구적 소설로 유명한 Margaret Atwood나 대중문화에 근거하여 소설을 쓰는 Douglas Coupland 같은 다양한 작가들에게 여러 가지 주제에 대한 영감을 제공하였습니다. 그들의 문체는 전혀 다르지만 캐나다의

지형이 그들의 상상력이나 글쓰기에 큰 영향을 미쳤다는 데 두 사람 다 동의할 것입니다. 즉 다양한 캐나다 예술가들은 각기 다른 방법으로 그 나라의 지형을 인식하며 이는 그들이 창조하는 작업에 반영되는 것입니다.

Q What is the main idea of the lecture?

(a) Environmental issues have influenced writers in Canada.

(b) The current styles of writing in Canada vary among writers.

(c) Canadian literatures have a typical preference for settings.

(d) Canada's geography has had the impact upon its writers.

이 강의의 요지는 무엇인가?

(a) 환경 문제가 캐나다 작가들에게 영향을 미쳤다.

(b) 캐나다의 현대 글쓰기 스타일은 작가들마다 다양하다.

(c) 캐나다 문학에서 선호하는 배경이 있다.

(d) 캐나다 지형이 작가들에게 영향을 미쳤다.

[해설] 환경이 캐나다 예술가들과 문학 주제에 미치는 영향을 이야기하며 또한 이곳의 지형이 작가들의 상상력이나 글쓰기를 자극한다는 내용으로 보아 정답은 (d)이다.

[함정] 환경문제가 아니라 지형적 특색이 캐나다 작가들에게 미친 영향에 대해 말하고 있으므로 (a)는 답이 아니다. (b)와 (c)는 다루어지지 않은 내용이다.

[어휘] ethnic 민족의 | surroundings (주위) 환경 |
hold true for ~에도 사실이다, 적용되다 |
long-standing 오래 계속되는, 오랜 | sparsely 성기게, 듬성듬성하게 |
populate ~에 살다, 거주하다 | sprawling 불규칙하게 퍼져 있는 |
terrain 지형, 지세 | inspire 영감을 불어넣다 | diverse 다양한 |
scholarly 학자다운, 학문적인 | draw upon ~에 의존하다 |
geography 지리, 지세, 지형 | perceive 인식하다 |
preference 선호

5

M: News Today brings you an expose of the pathetic conditions in 35 of the 100 pet stores we shopped at with a hidden camera while investigating charges of animal cruelty among pet store owners. What we saw there was shocking, and we'll have a look at some of that footage later on. Be warned. The photos may not be appropriate for all ages. Because what we saw there was so disturbing, we felt that we had to take immediate action, and not just report what we uncovered. Therefore, the news network, on the advice of its consultant veterinarians and legal staff, has lodged formal complaints against the store owners to have their business licenses revoked. Conditions in the remaining 65 stores ranged from excellent to satisfactory. If you are considering buying a pet, here's a list of outstanding stores as rated by our experts.

M: News Today는 몰래카메라를 이용하여 실시한 애완동물 가게의 주인들 사이에 행해지는 동물 학대 실태조사에서 100군데 중 35군데의 상황이 형편없다는 것을 밝혀냈습니다. 우리가 본 것은 충격 그 자체였으며 잠시 뒤 관련 영상을 보겠습니다. 조심하십시오. 본 내용은 모든 연령대가 다 볼 수 있는 내용이 아닐 수도 있습니다. 우리가 현장에서 목격한 것들이 너무 충격적이었기에 우리는 비단 밝혀낸 것을 알리는 것에 그칠 것이 아니라 지금 당장 어떤 특단의 조치를 마련해야 한다고 생각했습니다. 그러므로 본 방송사에서는 수의사와 법률 자문단의 조언에 따라 가게 주인들의 사업자 면허를 취소해 달라는 공식 고소장을 제출했습니다. 나머지 65군데의 환경은 만족할 만한 수준에서 최고에까지 이르렀습니다. 만약 애완동물을 사시길 원한다면, 여기 전문가에 의하여 평가된 좋은 가게들의 명단이 있습니다.

Q Which is correct according to the news report?

(a) Many pet stores function without a valid license.

(b) News Today will recommend pet stores on the next show.

(c) A number of store owners had their licenses cancelled.

(d) News Today took legal steps against some store owners.

뉴스 방송에 따르면 옳은 것은?

(a) 많은 애완동물 가게가 유효한 면허 없이 운영된다.

(b) News Today는 다음 방송에서 애완동물 가게를 추천할 것이다.

(c) 많은 가게 주인들의 면허가 취소되었다.

(d) News Today는 몇몇 가게 주인들을 고소했다.

[해설] 몰래 카메라를 이용한 조사에서 밝혀낸 35군데의 애완동물 가게의 형편없는 상황을 밝혀낸 뒤 그 가게 주인들에 대한 고소장을 제출했다는 내용이다. 따라서 정답은 (d)이다.

[함정] (a)는 언급된 바가 없고 (b)는 지금 바로 그 목록을 제시하고 있다. 또한 (c)는 이미 취소되었다는 것이 아니라 그렇게 하려고 고소했다는 내용이므로 오답이다.

[어휘] expose 폭로, 적발 | pathetic 형편없는, 아주 불충분한 |
charge 고발, 고소, 죄과 | footage 비디오 자료화면 |
appropriate 적당한, 적절한 | disturbing 교란시키는, 불온한 |
take action 조치를 취하다 | legal staff 법률 자문단 |
lodge~against …에 대해 (고소장, 신고서 등을) 제출하다, (반대, 항의 등을) 제기하다 | complaint (민사의) 고소

revoke 철회하다, 무효로 하다 | rate 평가하다, 등급을 매기다
function 기능하다, 작동하다 | valid 유효한
take legal steps against ~를 고소하다

6

W: Hey, I bought the Viva Girls' new album.

M: You mean <u>their second album</u> "Precious Love"?

W: Yeah. Have you heard any of the songs on the album?

M: Some of them, yes. I didn't buy the CD, though. I heard them on the radio.

W: So, <u>how did you like them</u>?

M: I thought the album's <u>not as good as their previous one</u>.

W: Yeah, the music is <u>not so appealing</u>.

M: It's more like pop than rock music. I don't think many people expected that kind of music from them.

W: It's quite possible that they'll lose their popularity because of that.

M: Will you buy their next album?

W: Maybe not, <u>if it's the same as this one</u>.

W: 있잖아, 비바 걸스의 새 앨범을 샀어.

M: 두 번째 앨범 "Precious Love"를 말하는 거야?

W: 응. 그 앨범에 수록된 노래를 들어 본 적 있어?

M: 응. 몇 곡 들어 봤지. 하지만 CD를 사지는 않았어. 라디오에서 들었거든.

W: 노래가 어땠니?

M: 지난번 것만 못한 것 같은데.

W: 그래, 음악이 그다지 끌리지 않더라.

M: 록 음악이라기보다는 오히려 팝 같아. 많은 사람들이 그들에게 그런 노래를 기대하지는 않을 거야.

W: 그것 때문에 인기가 떨어질지도 몰라.

M: 다음 앨범을 살 거니?

W: 이번 것과 똑같다면, 아마 안 살 거야.

Q Which is correct about the Viva Girls' new album?

(a) It is very popular among music lovers.

(b) It has softer songs rather than rough music.

(c) It is very similar to their old album.

(d) It will increase the number of the band's fans.

비바 걸스의 새 앨범에 대한 설명으로 옳은 것은?

(a) 음악 애호가들 사이에서 매우 인기 있다.

(b) 거친 음악보다는 오히려 부드러운 음악을 담고 있다.

(c) 지난번 앨범과 아주 비슷하다.

(d) 팬들의 수가 늘어날 것이다.

[해설] 비바 걸스의 새 앨범에 관한 두 사람의 대화이다. 지난번 앨범보다 음악이 별로 좋지 않으며, 록음악보다는 팝에 가까워서 사람들이 많이 좋아하지 않을 것 같아서, 인기가 떨어질지 모른다고 이야기하고 있다. 따라서 거친 음악이라기보다는 오히려 부드러운 음악들로 구성되었다는 (b)가 정답이다.

[어휘] precious 소중한, 귀중한 |
not as good as ~만큼 좋지 않은, ~만 못한 | previous 이전의, 앞선 |
appealing 매력적인, 사람을 끄는, 호소하는 듯한 |
rather than ~라기보다는 | similar to ~와 유사한, 비슷한

7 Main Idea

M: Most people <u>are aware of the link</u> between the growing number of households <u>headed by a single working parent</u> and <u>the rampant problem of juvenile delinquency</u>. Increasing numbers of children are <u>being left unsupervised</u> as single parents <u>struggle alone to survive</u>. This causes children to grow up <u>with dubious values</u> from outside the home. It is true that there are many single-parent families — most often headed by women — that are doing well. All evidence points to the fact that on average, though, children raised by single parents have <u>a higher probability of dropping out of school</u> and getting involved in crime. My fear is that until society fights to reestablish the traditional nuclear family, the issue of juvenile delinquency can only get worse.

M: 대부분의 사람들은 늘어나는 편부편모 가정의 수와 청소년 범죄율 급등의 상관관계에 대하여 잘 인식하고 있습니다. 편부편모가 생계를 꾸려가기 위하여 혼자 노력하는 동안 점점 더 많은 아이들이 통제되지 못하고 있습니다. 이로 인해 아이들이 집 밖에서 쌓은 모호한 가치관을 가지고 자라게 됩니다. 많은 편부편모 가정들이 — 특히 여성에 의하여 이끌어지는 가정들 — 문제가 없는 것도 사실입니다. 그러나 일반적으로 모든 증거들에 보이듯이 편부편모 가정의 아이들은 학교를 중퇴하거나 범죄에 연관이 될 확률이 높습니다. 제가 우려하는 것은 우리 사회가 전통적인 핵가족(정상 가족)을 재구성하는 데 고분군투할 때까지는 청소년 범죄가 더욱더 악화될 수 있다는 것입니다.

Q What is the main idea of the talk?

(a) Society is responsible for the difficulties faced by single parents.

(b) Juvenile delinquency is a major reason for families breaking up.

(c) Children of single-parent families are often more responsible individuals.

(d) The decline of the healthy nuclear family has caused child delinquency.

이 이야기의 요지는 무엇인가?

(a) 사회는 편부편모가 가지는 어려움에 책임이 있다.

(b) 청소년 비행은 가족 해체의 주된 이유이다.

(c) 편부편모 가정의 아이들은 종종 더 책임감 있는 개인들이다.

(d) 건강한 핵가족 감소가 청소년 범죄를 야기한다.

해설 첫 문장에서 제시하고 있듯이 편부편모 가정의 수와 늘어나는 청소년 범죄율의 상관관계가 전체 주제이다. 따라서 핵가족의 해체로 인한 편부편모 가정의 아이들에게 생길 수 있는 문제를 언급하고 있으므로 답은 (d)이다.

함정 (a) 사회가 편부편모가 가지는 어려움을 책임져야 한다는 말은 없다. 다만 정상적인 핵가족을 위해 노력해야 한다는 말이 있을 뿐이다. 또한 가족 해체가 청소년 범죄의 주요한 이유이지 그 반대는 아니므로, 원인과 결과가 뒤바뀐 (b)는 오답이다.

어휘 rampant 만연하는, 유행하는 |
juvenile delinquency 미성년(청소년) 범죄 |
dubious 모호한, 애매한 | on average 일반적으로 |
probability 확률, 가망성 |
drop out of ~을 중퇴하다, 도중에 그만두다 |
get involved in ~에 연루되다 |
nuclear family 핵가족 (부부와 미혼 자녀로만 구성된 가족)

8

W: The latest product to be included in the emergency first aid kit is the Blue Algae bandage. Intended primarily for trauma situations, it stops bleeding almost instantly. More interestingly, the bandage works based on biotechnology that is simply amazing. The bandage is saturated with complex carbohydrate solution derived from single-cell algae. The algae in this solution accelerate blood clotting, and do so much faster than the artificial chemical compounds used in traditional bandages. Use of this product reduces bleeding time by 75%. While the new bandages are currently being used only for emergencies, they could be more widely used in the future. This is one more example of how the cutting-edge world of biotechnology is bringing practical solutions to everyday life.

W: 응급 구호품 상자에 추가된 최신 제품은 Blue Algae(푸른 해조) 밴드입니다. 주로 외상의 경우에 사용되는데 거의 즉각적으로 출혈을 멈추게 합니다. 더욱 흥미로운 점으로는 이 밴드가 정말 놀라운 생명공학에 의거한다는 것입니다. 밴드에는 단세포 해조에서 추출한 합성 탄수화물 용해제가 스며들어 있습니다. 이 용해제 속의 해초는 혈액 응고를 가속시키는데, 어떠한 재래식 밴드에 사용된 인공 화학 혼합물보다 훨씬 더 빠릅니다. 이 제품을 사용함으로써 출혈 시간을 75% 줄일 수 있습니다. 이 새로운 밴드가 지금은 응급시에만 사용되지만 앞으로 좀 더 광범위하게 사용될 수 있을 것입니다. 이것은 최첨단 생명공학이 우리 일상 생활에 실제적인 해결책을 가져다 주고 있는 또 하나의 좋은 예입니다.

Q What is mainly being discussed in the talk?

(a) a new innovative procedure for trauma patients

(b) the directions for using a newly adopted medical device

(c) a recently added first aid product and its excellence

(d) time-saving treatment procedures based on biotechnology

이 이야기에서 주로 무엇이 논의되고 있나?

(a) 외상환자를 위한 새로운 혁신적인 처치법

(b) 새롭게 채택된 의료 기구를 사용하는 방법

(c) 최근 추가된 응급처치용품과 그 우수성

(d) 생명공학에 근거한 시간이 단축되는 치료 과정

해설 새로운 응급 구호품으로 추가된 해조 밴드의 장점과 우수성이 언급되고 있다. 생명공학에 근거하여 만들어진 이 제품은 거의 즉각적으로 출혈을 멈추게 한다는 내용이다. 그러므로 주로 언급되고 있는 것은 최근 추가된 해조 밴드와 그 우수성이므로 (c)가 정답이다.

어휘 emergency first aid kit 응급처치용 상자 |
alga 해조, 조류 (pl. algae) | trauma 외상(성 증상) | instantly 즉시 |
based on ~에 근거한 | biotechnology 생명공학 |
saturate 적시다, 배어들게 하다 | carbohydrate 탄수화물 |
solution 용액, 용제, 해결책 | derive 끌어내다, 얻다 |
blood clotting 혈액 응고 | artificial 인공의 | chemical 화학 |
compound 혼합물 | cutting-edge 최첨단 |
innovative 혁신적인

9 Purpose

M: Good morning, Professor Presley.

W: Good morning. How may I help you?

M: My name is Steve. I was in your history class last semester, 'The Rise and Fall of Rome.'

W: Oh, now I remember you. You're the one I gave an A to on the final essay.

M: I really appreciated that.

W: No, you <u>deserved that grade. I could tell you worked really hard</u> on that paper.

M: Thanks a lot. By the way, Professor Presley, I was wondering <u>if I could audit your class</u>, History 203.

W: Well, I don't usually <u>allow students to audit my class</u> since most of them who did before didn't attend class regularly.

M: Oh, that's not a big deal. I promise that I'll attend all the classes. If I have to do assignments or papers, <u>I can't be sure if I can do them all</u>. But if it is just the attendance, then <u>I won't let you down</u>.

W: Okay, you can come from tomorrow.

M: Thank you. I'll see you then.

M: 안녕하세요, Presley 교수님.

W: 안녕하세요? 뭘 도와줄까요?

M: 제 이름은 Steve예요. 저는 지난 학기에 선생님의 역사 수업, '로마의 흥망성쇠' 를 들었어요.

W: 아, 이제 기억나는군. 기말시험에서 내가 A를 줬던 학생이군.

M: 정말 감사했습니다.

W: 아니. 자네는 그 점수를 받을 만했네. 자네가 보고서를 정말 열심히 작성했다는 것을 알 수 있었어.

M: 정말 감사합니다. 그런데 Presley 교수님, 교수님의 수업 '역사 203' 을 청강할 수 있는지 궁금해서요.

W: 음, 일반적으로는 내 수업을 청강하도록 허락하지 않네, 왜냐하면 전에 그렇게 했던 학생들 대부분이 수업에 제대로 출석하지 않더군.

M: 아, 그건 문제없어요. 모든 수업에 출석하겠다고 약속드릴게요. 문제가 과제나 보고서를 해야 한다는 것이면 확신할 수 없지만, 출석에 관한 것이라면 실망시켜 드리지 않을 거예요.

W: 알았네, 그럼 내일부터 오게나.

M: 고맙습니다. 그때 뵙겠습니다.

Q Why does the man want to see the woman?

(a) to thank her for the grade

(b) to promise to attend all the classes

(c) to obtain permission to audit a class

(d) to ask what the requirements are for History 203

남자는 왜 여자를 만나기를 원하는가?

(a) 학점에 대해 감사하려고

(b) 모든 수업에 출석하겠다고 약속하려고

(c) 수업을 청강할 수 있는 허락을 얻으려고

(d) '역사 203' 을 듣는 데 필요한 자격이 무엇인지 물어 보려고

해설 청강에 관한 두 사람의 대화이다. 남학생이 강의를 청강해도 되는지

여자 교수에게 묻자, 여자는 수업에 빠지지 않는 조건만 잘 지킬 수 있다면, 청강을 해도 좋다고 허락하고 있다. 따라서 남자는 여자에게 수업을 청강해도 되는지 허락을 받고 있는 것이므로 정답은 (c)이다.

함정 (a)와 (b)에 관한 언급이 있기는 하지만 부수적인 대화에 불과하다는 데에 유의한다.

어휘 semester 학기 | deserve ~할 만하다, 받을 가치가 있다 | audit (대학 강의를) 청강하다 | assignment 숙제, 할당된 일 | attendance 출석 | obtain ~을 얻다, 획득하다 | permission 허락, 허가

10

M: Are you traveling? Now, here's a chance to <u>get discounts</u> both on the planes you take and the hotels you stay at. How? <u>Earn miles</u> on your High Saver Miles card all this month while enjoying the comfort of a Starlux Hotel! Starlux Hotels, located in over 300 locations around the world, are <u>the affordable choice for the frequent traveler</u>, <u>whether for business or pleasure</u>. To take advantage of this offer, <u>just pay for a qualifying room rate</u> with your credit card and receive up to 500 miles on any Transoceanic, Interstate Combine or Westward flight. That means that <u>your hotel stays earn you plane discounts</u>! For reservations, contact your local travel agent or call us at 888-5000.

M: 여행하고 계신가요? 지금 당신이 이용하는 비행기와 투숙한 호텔의 할인가격 기회를 잡으세요. 어떻게요? 이번 달 편안한 Starlux 호텔에 머무르면서 High Saver Miles 카드에 마일리지를 적립하세요. Starlux 호텔은 전 세계 300군데에 위치하며 사업상 혹은 관광 여행객들처럼 자주 여행을 하시는 분들에게 알맞은 곳입니다. 이 기회를 이용하시려면, 정해져 있는 객실 요금을 신용카드로 지불하시기만 하면 됩니다. 그러면 Transoceanic, Interstate Combine 또는 Westward 항공사 어디서든 500마일리지까지 적립해 드립니다. 즉 호텔에 머무르면 항공가격이 할인된다는 것입니다! 예약하시려면, 지역 여행사나 우리에게 전화를 주세요. 888-5000번입니다.

Q What is the advertisement mainly about?

(a) getting discounted fares with airlines

(b) receiving air miles through hotel room reservations

(c) making credit card payments for hotel rooms

(d) saving money on hotel rooms through advance booking

이 광고는 주로 무엇에 대한 것인가?

(a) 항공 요금 할인 받기

(b) 객실 예약을 통한 항공 마일리지 받기

LISTENING REVIEW

A

1. perceive	2. sustain
3. skeptical	4. remedy
5. sanctuary	6. footage
7. preserve	8. revoke
9. vein	10. conduit
11. subscribe	12. terrain
13. acupuncture	14. ailment
15. delinquency	16. pathetic

1. to see, notice, or realize something, especially when it is not obvious

2. to continue or maintain something for a period of time

3. having doubts about something

4. something that is intended to cure you when you are ill or in pain

5. a place where birds or animals are protected and allowed to live freely

6. a film of a particular event or the part of a film which shows this event

7. to take action to save or protect something from damage or decay

8. to cancel something such as a license, a law, or an agreement

9. the thin tubes in your body through which your blood flows towards your heart

10. a small tunnel, pipe, or channel through which water or electrical wires go

11. to pay to receive copies of a magazine or a newspaper regularly

12. an area of land or a type of land when you are considering its physical features

13. the treatment of a person's illness or pain by sticking small needles into their body at certain places

14. an illness, especially one that is not very serious

15. criminal behavior, especially that of young people

16. sad and weak or helpless, and making you feel very sorry

B

1. b	2. a	3. b	4. a	5. a

1. 이 새로운 밴드는 앞으로 좀 더 광범위하게 사용될 수 있을 것입니다.

(a) The new bandages are being used broadly for emergencies.

(b) The new bandages could be more widely used in the future.

2. 많은 이사들이 대개 말은 많지만, 말한 것을 실천하는 데는 서투르니까 말이야.

(a) A lot of directors usually talk a lot but are poor at doing what they say.

(b) Many directors usually talk a lot but don't do what others ask them to do.

3. 그것은 호텔에 머무르면 항공가격이 할인된다는 것을 의미합니다!

(a) That means that you earn miles on your card for the flight.

(b) That means that your hotel stays earn you plane discounts!

4. 유럽 사람들은 모든 질병에 허브 치료법을 사용하는 것으로 유명합니다.

(a) Europeans are known for using herbal remedies for all kinds of diseases.

(b) Europeans have known how to use herbal remedies for all kinds of diseases.

5. 이것은 아이들이 집 밖에서 이중적인 가치 체계를 가지고 자라게 합니다.

(a) This causes children to grow up with dubious values from outside the home.

(b) This allows children to grow up with various values in and out of the home.

C

1. Do you know any good places to stay there?

2. News Today brings you an expose of the pathetic conditions.

3. It was through his work that we came to understand it.

4. The bandage works based on biotechnology that is simply amazing.

5. Many people who believe in alternative forms of healing find them effective.

1. any good places / do you know / to stay there

2. you / an expose of the pathetic conditions / News Today brings

3. it was / that we came to understand it / through his work

4. based on biotechnology / that is simply amazing / the bandage works

5. who believe in alternative forms of healing / find them effective / many people

D

1. b	2. a	3. b	4. a	5. a

1. Be sure and go to the safari there.

   (a) Make sure if the safari is available there.

   (b) You must not miss the safari there.

2. The heart is responsible for pumping blood throughout the body.

   (a) Blood is pumped through the body by the heart.

   (b) Your body pumps blood to the heart and the arteries.

3. It is likely that children should not see the photos.

   (a) Children will have a look at the photos later on.

   (b) The photos may not be appropriate for all ages.

4. Serious misunderstandings may arise due to cultural differences.

   (a) Cultural differences may give rise to misunderstandings.

   (b) A serious misinterpretation may lead to cultural differences.

5. The geography of Canada has greatly influenced writers' writings.

   (a) Canada's sprawling terrain has inspired various themes in writers.

   (b) Canadian writers perceive the nation's geography in the same way.

CHAPTER 02 MAIN TOPIC

VOCABULARY PREVIEW

01. diploma 졸업증서
02. diabetic 당뇨병 환자
03. declaration 세관 신고
04. articulation 발음법, 명확한 발음
05. Genesis 창세기
06. fable 우화
07. deposit 보증금
08. physiotherapy 물리치료
09. tattooing 문신술
10. scar ~에 상처를 남기다
11. ritual 의식의, 제식의
12. induction 도입, 취임
13. manhood (남자의) 성년, 성인
14. status 지위, 신분
15. tenet 교의, 주의
16. convert 전환하다, 전향하다
17. sacred 신성한
18. orthodox 정통의
19. rigorous 엄격한, 매우 혹독한
20. addictive 중독성의, 습관성인
21. legible 읽기 쉬운, 알아볼 수 있는
22. emit 방출하다, 발산하다
23. blast (로켓 등을) 분사하여 발진시키다
24. attribute ~의 탓으로 돌리다

GUIDED LISTENING

1	1. c	2. a	**2**	1. c	2. b
3	1. d	2. d	**4**	1. d	2. a

1 Conversation

M: Hi, I want to join the French Literature course.

W: Okay. Please <u>fill out this form for our records</u>.

M: Well, the form requires a telephone number. I don't have one yet; we just moved in.

W: Fine, you may <u>leave it blank</u>, but please remember <u>to fill it out once you get it</u>.

M: Sure.

W: Do you have personal photographs now?

M: No, but I can get them by tomorrow. <u>How many copies would you need</u>?

W: Three copies. <u>Make sure you bring them before the class</u>. It starts at 10:00 a.m.

M: Sure. See you tomorrow then.

M: 안녕하세요, 프랑스 문학 강의를 듣고 싶은데요.

W: 좋습니다. 등록을 위해 이 신청서를 기입해 주세요.

M: 음, 신청서에 전화번호를 적어야 하네요. 하지만 저는 없는데요, 방금 이사를 와서요.

W: 좋아요. 그냥 빈칸으로 두세요. 하지만, 생기게 되면 꼭 적어 주셔야 해요.

M: 물론이죠.

W: 지금 본인의 사진을 가지고 계신가요?

M: 아뇨, 하지만 내일까지 가져올 수 있어요. 몇 장이나 필요하죠?

W: 세 장이요. 강의 전에 꼭 가져오세요. 강의는 오전 10시에 시작해요.

M: 그럼요. 내일 뵐게요.

Main Topic

1   What is mainly being discussed?

(a) what to bring to the admission office

(b) where to join the French Literature course

(c) how to complete the course registration form

(d) what to take before the literature course

주로 무슨 이야기를 나누고 있는 대화인가?

(a) 입학 사무소에 무엇을 가져가야 하는지

(b) 어디에서 프랑스 문학 강좌를 신청할 수 있는지

(c) 강의 등록 신청서를 어떻게 작성하는지

(d) 문학 수업을 듣기 전에 무엇을 수강해야 하는지

해설 프랑스어 강좌에 등록하는 대화이다. 등록 신청서를 기입해야 하는데, 전화번호와 사진이 필요하다는 내용이므로 주로 이루어지는 대화는 신청서를 작성하는 방법에 관한 것이다. 그러므로 정답은 (c)이다.

Detail

2 What will the man have to do later on?

(a) fill out his telephone number in the form

(b) bring his proof of address and phone number

(c) make three copies of his high school diploma

(d) have his telephone repaired in his room

남자는 나중에 무엇을 해야 할 것인가?

(a) 등록 신청서에 전화번호 기입하기

(b) 주소와 전화번호 증명서 가져오기

(c) 고등학교 졸업증서 세 부 가져오기

(d) 그의 방에 있는 전화 수리하기

해설 등록 신청서에 적어야 하는 전화번호는 전화번호가 생기면 적기로 하였고, 필요한 사진 세 장은 다음날 가져오기로 했다. 그러므로 선택지 중 (a)가 정답이다.

함정 (b)는 언급되지 않은 내용이며, (c)는 고등학교 졸업장이 아니라 사진 3장을 가져오겠다고 했다. (d) 전화는 수리해야 하는 것이 아니라 설치해야 하는 것이다.

어휘 fill out (양식 따위를) 써넣다, 채우다 | personal 본인의, 개인의 | registration 등록 | diploma 졸업증서

2 Conversation

W: Do you have anything in your bags which you would like us to know about, sir?

M: Yeah, I'm carrying 4 kg of Chinese herbs.

W: Are they for some medicinal purpose?

M: Yes, I'm a diabetic and take those herbs as a treatment.

W: Well, you should have some kind of prescription for them, then. Could I have a look at it?

M: Sure, here it is.

W: Okay, this is fine. Do you go every month to buy these herbs?

M: Not exactly, but whenever I'm short, I do.

W: Fine, please step through and sign here before you go.

W: 가방에 신고하실 품목이 있나요?

M: 예, 중국 약초가 4kg 있어요.

W: 의약용인가요?

M: 네, 당뇨병이 있어서, 치료약으로 약초를 가지고 가는 거예요.

W: 음, 그러면 처방전을 가지고 있겠군요. 볼 수 있을까요?

M: 그럼요, 여기 있어요.

W: 좋아요, 됐습니다. 그 약초를 사기 위해 매달 가나요?

M: 그런 건 아니고, 모자랄 때마다 가요.

W: 됐습니다. 절차를 밟고 가시기 전에 여기 사인해 주세요.

Main Topic

1 What is mainly being discussed in the conversation?

(a) a treatment with herbs for his disease

(b) the prescription that the man made up for the woman

(c) the declaration of what the man has purchased abroad

(d) the procedure of declaring herbs imported from a foreign country

---

이 대화에서 주로 이야기되는 것은 무엇인가?

(a) 약초로 하는 그의 병 치료

(b) 남자가 여자에게 내려 준 처방전

(c) 남자가 외국에서 구입한 물품 세관 신고

(d) 외국에서 수입된 약초를 세관 신고하는 과정

해설 신고할 물건이 있냐는 여자의 질문에, 남자는 중국 약초가 있다고 대답하고, 이따금씩 약초를 사러 외국에 나간다는 남자의 대화로 보아, 통관에서 세관 신고를 하는 장면임을 알 수 있다.

함정 외국에 나가서 약초를 구입해 오는 남자와의 대화이다. 그러므로 정확하게 말하면 (d) 수입된 약초를 세관 신고하는 과정이라고 할 수는 없다는 데에 유의한다.

Inference I

2 What can be inferred from the conversation?

(a) The woman is interested in herbs.

(b) The man goes abroad once in a while.

(c) The man is working at a hospital.

(d) The woman will not allow the herbs.

이 대화에서 추론할 수 있는 것은 무엇인가?

(a) 여자는 약초에 관심이 있다.

(b) 남자는 가끔씩 외국에 나간다.

(c) 남자는 병원에서 일한다.

(d) 여자는 약초 반입을 허용하지 않을 것이다.

해설 매달 약초를 사러 나가느냐는 여자의 질문에 떨어지면 사러 나간다는 남자의 대답으로 남자가 가끔씩 외국에 나간다는 것을 추론할 수 있다.

함정 문제가 직접적으로 드러나 있지 않으므로 상황을 잘 파악해야 한다.

어휘 herb 약초 | medicinal 의약의, 약용의 | diabetic 당뇨병 환자 | treatment 치료, 치료법 | prescription 처방전

whenever ~할 때마다 | short 부족한, 모자라는 |
declaration 세관 신고

3 Monologue

W: Written language is <u>an essential part of any culture</u>. It has a major role in <u>the development of literature</u> like poems and stories. Surprisingly, African languages did not <u>have any written alphabets</u> for centuries. Even today, only about <u>50 among the 700 to 1,000</u> African languages have written forms of expression. One of the reasons could be that there is vast variation among African languages. A basic African language may remain the same; however, its words, spelling and articulation may differ from one culture to another. <u>A majority of the literature</u> present in African languages has its origin in South Africa and other former British colonies. People in former French and Portuguese colonies <u>were not allowed to learn</u> African languages, which blocked their development and limited their reach.

W: 문자는 어떤 문화에서도 필수적인 부분입니다. 그것은 시와 소설 같은 문학의 발달에 중요한 역할을 합니다. 놀랍게도, 아프리카 언어는 몇 세기 동안 성문화된 문자가 없었습니다. 심지어 오늘날에도 700에서 1,000개에 이르는 아프리카 언어 중 약 50개만이 문자 표현 방식을 가지고 있습니다. 이런 이유들 중 하나는 아프리카 언어에 수많은 다양성이 있기 때문입니다. 기본적인 아프리카 언어는 그대로일지도 모르지만, 단어, 철자와 발음은 문화마다 다양합니다. 아프리카 언어로 표현된 대부분의 문학은 남아프리카 공화국과 이전의 다른 영국 식민지에 그 근거를 두고 있습니다. 이전에 프랑스와 포르투갈의 식민지였던 곳의 사람들은 아프리카 언어를 배우지 못하게 했고, 그것이 언어의 발달과 확산을 막았습니다.

Main Topic

1 What is the best title for this lecture?

(a) African Languages in Former British Colonies

(b) The Impact of Colonization on African Languages

(c) The Advancement of African Literature

(d) Two Major Barriers to African Literature

이 강의에 가장 적절한 제목은 무엇인가?

(a) 이전에 영국 식민지였던 곳의 아프리카 언어

(b) 아프리카 언어에 미친 식민지의 영향

(c) 아프리카 문학의 발전

(d) 아프리카 문학의 발전을 저해한 두 가지 주요 장벽

해설 아프리카 문학에 미친 아프리카 언어에 대한 강의이다. 문화나 문학에는 성문 언어가 필수적인데, 아프리카에서 성문 언어가 발달하지 못한 이유를 두 가지로 들고 있다. 첫째 언어가 너무 다양하기 때문이며, 둘째 여러 국가들의 식민지였기 때문에 아프리카 언어를 사용하지 못했기 때문이라는 내용이다. 그러므로 이 강의의 가장 적절한 제목은 (d)이다.

함정 (a), (b), (c)는 모두 (d)의 내용을 전달하기 위해 언급된 하나의 요소들일 뿐이다.

Comprehension

2 Which of the following is correct according to the lecture?

(a) Most of the African literatures are written in English.

(b) Former French colonists created a new language for Africans.

(c) French colonists allowed the use of African languages.

(d) A huge variation among African spoken languages exists.

이 강의에 따르면 다음 중 옳은 것은?

(a) 대부분의 아프리카 문학은 영어로 쓰여 있다.

(b) 이전의 프랑스 식민지 개척자들은 아프리카에 새로운 언어를 만들어 주었다.

(c) 프랑스 식민지 개척자들은 아프리카 언어의 사용을 허용했다.

(d) 아프리카의 구어에는 막대한 다양성이 존재한다.

해설 아프리카 문학의 발전을 저해한 요인이 언어의 막대한 다양성과 식민지 정책이라는 내용이므로, 내용상 옳은 것은 (d)이다.

함정 (a)와 (b)는 언급되지 않은 내용이며, (c)는 사실과 반대되는 내용이다.

어휘 written language 문자 언어, 성문 언어 | poem 시 | vast 막대한, 광대한 | variation 변화, 변동 | spelling 철자법 | articulation 발음법 | colony 식민지 | block 막다, 저해하다

4 Monologue

W: Everyone, especially children, is fond of stories. There are several types of stories, having <u>different lands of origin</u>, <u>dealing with different subjects</u> and <u>carrying different messages</u>. Some types of stories are more popular than others. Some might have originated thousands of years ago, but <u>are still read and told</u>. Some stories are common to all people across the world. One such story is *Genesis* in the Bible. Children often love reading and hearing <u>stories about great heroes</u>. *The Iliad* and *The Odyssey* are two such stories written by Homer that describe ancient Greek heroes.

Another very popular form of story is fables where animals talk to each other. Aesop's fables are very popular among children <u>who find it very fascinating to imagine animals talking</u>.

W: 누구나, 특히 아이들은 이야기를 좋아합니다. 여러 종류의 이야기들이 있는데, 유래한 국가가 다르고 다른 주제를 다루며 다른 교훈이 담겨 있습니다. 어떤 종류의 이야기들은 다른 것들보다 더 인기가 있습니다. 어떤 것들은 몇 천 년 전에 시작되었을지 모르지만, 아직도 여전히 읽혀지고 구전되고 있습니다. 어떤 이야기들은 전 세계를 통해 모든 사람들에게 알려져 있습니다. 그런 이야기 중 하나가 성경의 『창세기』입니다. 아이들은 위대한 영웅에 대한 이야기를 읽고 듣는 것을 좋아합니다. 호머에 의해 쓰인 『일리아드』와 『오디세이』는 고대 그리스 영웅들을 묘사하는 그런 두 가지 이야기입니다. 또 다른 정말 유명한 이야기는 동물들이 서로 이야기하는 우화입니다. 『이솝 우화』는 동물들이 말을 한다고 상상하는 것이 매우 재미있다는 것을 알게 된 아이들 사이에서 매우 인기가 있습니다.

Main Topic

1 What is the lecture about?

(a) different characters in a famous story

(b) types of messages in old fables

(c) translating stories from Greek into different languages

(d) some common types of popular stories

이 강의는 무엇에 관한 것인가?

(a) 유명한 이야기에 나오는 다양한 등장인물들

(b) 오래된 우화에 담겨 있는 여러 교훈들

(c) 그리스어에서 다른 언어로 이야기를 번역하기

(d) 인기 있는 이야기의 일반적인 몇몇 종류들

해설 세계적으로 인기 있고 대중화되어 있는 이야기에 관한 강의이다. 창세기와 영웅을 다루고 있는 그리스 고전들과 우화를 그 예로 들어 설명하고 있다. 그러므로 (d)가 정답이다.

함정 『일리아드』와 『오디세이』의 주인공은 영웅이며 『이솝 우화』의 주인공은 동물들이라는 내용이 있다고 (a)를 답으로 착각해서는 안 된다. 이러한 언급은 세계적으로 인기 있는 이야기들을 소개하기 위한 설명일 뿐임에 유의한다.

Detail

2 Which is mentioned as a reason for a fondness for fables among children?

(a) They are fascinated by animals that can talk.

(b) They love the imaginary animals introduced in the stories.

(c) They like fascinating images of animals in the books.

(d) They love to read and listen to stories about great heroes.

아이들 사이에서 우화가 인기 있는 이유로 언급된 것은?

(a) 아이들은 말을 할 수 있는 동물들에 매우 흥미를 느낀다.

(b) 아이들은 이야기에 소개된 상상의 동물들을 좋아한다.

(c) 아이들은 책에 나오는 동물의 매력적인 이미지를 좋아한다.

(d) 아이들은 위대한 영웅에 관한 이야기를 읽고 듣는 것을 좋아한다.

해설 마지막 문장에 그 답이 나와 있다. 아이들이 우화를 좋아하는 것은 동물들이 말을 한다고 상상하는 것이 매우 재미있다고 생각하기 때문이므로 정답은 (a)이다.

함정 (d)는 『일리아드』와 『오디세이』에 관한 내용이므로 정답이 될 수 없다.

어휘 be fond of ~을 좋아하다   subject 주제   originate 생기다, 유래하다   Genesis 창세기   fable 우화   translate 번역하다

PRACTICAL LISTENING

1. d	2. a	3. c	4. a	5. b
6. b	7. b	8. c	9. c	10. c

1

M: Hi, I'm looking for an apartment to rent. Could you help me?

W: Certainly. Are you <u>specific about the location</u>?

M: Not really, but I'd prefer a place near convenient public transportation.

W: Would you mind one in the southern suburbs?

M: Not at all. But is it near to any public transportation?

W: It is <u>about a 10-minute walk</u> to the bus stop.

M: That's not bad. How long will it take to the subway?

W: It <u>takes another 10 minutes to the subway station</u> from the bus stop. It is a little far to walk, but, if you ride a bicycle, it wouldn't take long.

M: Well, I have a bicycle, but I think taking a walk to the station would not be a bad idea. How much is the rent?

W: $700 per month with <u>a deposit of $1,400</u>.

M: That's a little <u>beyond my budget</u>.

W: What's your budget for the rent?

M: About $500 per month.

W: That's the nearest place I can show for now. Would you like to take a look before making your decision?

M: Sure, I'd love to.

M: 안녕하세요, 임대할 아파트를 찾고 있는데, 좀 도와주실 수 있나요?

W: 물론이죠. 특별히 생각하고 있는 위치라도 있나요?

M: 그렇진 않아요. 하지만 편리한 대중교통과 가까운 곳이면 더 좋겠어요.

W: 남쪽 근교는 괜찮으세요?

M: 네. 그런데 대중교통과 가까운가요?

W: 버스 정류장까지 걸어서 약 10분 정도 거리예요.

M: 나쁘지 않네요. 전철역까지는 얼마나 걸릴까요?

W: 버스 정류장에서 전철역까지는 또 10분이 더 걸려요. 걸어서는 약간 멀지만, 자전거를 타면 오래 걸리지 않아요.

M: 음, 자전거가 있기는 한데, 역까지 걸어 다니는 것도 나쁘지는 않을 것 같네요. 임대료는 얼마예요?

W: 보증금 1,400달러에 한 달에 700달러예요.

M: 제 예산보다는 약간 더 높네요.

W: 임대료를 얼마 정도로 예상하시는데요?

M: 한 달에 500달러 정도요.

W: 지금 당장은 그곳이 보여 드릴 수 있는 가장 가까운 곳이겠네요. 결정 하시기 전에 한 번 보시겠어요?

M: 물론, 그러고 싶어요.

Q Which is correct about the man according to the conversation?

(a) He wants to live in the southern suburbs.

(b) He thinks the place is too far from the station.

(c) He is looking for a quiet place to live in.

(d) He wants to live near public transportation.

대화에 따르면 남자에 대한 설명으로 옳은 것은?

(a) 남쪽 근교에서 살고 싶어 한다.

(b) 그곳이 역에서 너무 멀다고 생각하고 있다.

(c) 살기 조용한 곳을 찾고 있다.

(d) 대중교통 가까이에 살고 싶어 한다.

해설 월세 아파트를 구하고 있는 남자와 여자 부동산 중개인과의 대화이다. 특별히 생각한 위치라도 있느냐는 여자의 질문에, 단지 교통이 편리한 곳이면 좋겠다고 말하고 있으므로 정답은 (d)가 된다.

함정 대중교통과 가까운 곳을 원하는 남자에게 여자가 남쪽 근교를 추천한 것이지, 남자가 그곳에 살고 싶다고 말하는 장면은 어디에도 없다. 또한 남자가 조용한 곳에서 살고 싶어 해서 여자가 남쪽 근교를 추천한 것이 아니기 때문에, (a)와 (c)는 정답이 아니다.

어휘 look for ~을 찾다 | rent 임대하다, 임대(료) | prefer ~을 선호하다, 더 좋아하다 | convenient 편리한, ~에 가까운 | public transportation 대중교통 | suburb 교외, 근교 | deposit 보증금 | budget 예산, 경비, 비용

2 Main Topic

W: You may have cut down on your coffee drinking recently: perhaps you've heard that many health problems have been attributed to drinking coffee. Coffee has been blamed for a number of health problems, especially high blood pressure or heart disease. Now, those claims are being proven false. Researchers now say that a few cups of coffee a day may actually prevent gallstones. Subjects of a recent study who drank two to three cups of coffee a day were seen to have a 40% lower risk of gallstones as compared to non-coffee drinkers. Apparently the chemicals in coffee lower those levels of cholesterol in bile that are responsible for causing gallstones, thus reducing the risk of their formation in coffee drinkers.

W: 당신은 최근 들어 커피를 삼가고 있을지도 모릅니다. 아마도 그것은 건강 문제의 많은 부분이 커피 때문이라고 들어서 그런 것일 수 있습니다. 커피는 많은 질병을 유발한다고 비난받아 왔으며, 무엇보다도 고혈압과 심장질환을 야기한다고 알려져 왔습니다. 지금은 그러한 주장들이 잘못된 것이라고 밝혀지고 있습니다. 연구진들이 말하기를, 하루에 몇 잔의 커피를 마심으로써 담석을 예방할 수 있을지도 모른다고 합니다. 커피를 마시지 않는 사람들과 비교하면, 하루에 2-3잔을 마시는 연구 대상자들이 담석에 걸릴 확률이 40% 낮다는 최근 연구 결과를 발표하였습니다. 이것은 커피에 들어있는 화학물질이 담석을 유발하는 담즙의 콜레스테롤 수치를 낮추어 주어서, 커피를 마시는 이들에게 담석이 형성될 위험을 낮추어 주는 것으로 보입니다.

Q What is mainly being discussed?

(a) coffee helps avert gallstone formation

(b) the questionable health benefits of coffee

(c) coffee being used to dissolve gallstones

(d) caffeinated beverages that should be avoided

주로 논의되고 있는 것은 무엇인가?

(a) 담석 형성을 막는 데에 도움이 되는 커피

(b) 의심스러운 커피의 건강상의 이로움

(c) 담석을 용해시키는 데 사용된 커피

(d) 피해야 하는 카페인 음료

해설 커피를 마시는 사람들이 담석에 걸릴 확률이 적다는 것과 그 이유에 대한 설명이므로 정답은 (a)이다.

3

W: How's your elbow, Steve?

M: Well, it's hurting a lot.

W: Aren't you getting it treated?

M: Yeah, I just started physiotherapy last week. I'm also taking painkillers.

W: Oh, I guess you had gone a long time without treating it.

M: Yes. I didn't have it looked at for two weeks. And I think that's why it has become worse.

W: Try not to use your elbow, or it will get even worse.

M: I know.

W: But you still play tennis every morning.

M: It is my left elbow that hurts, and I use my right arm when playing tennis.

W: You know you're still using your left elbow a lot when you're playing.

M: I guess you're right. I thought it is just my right arm that I'm using, but I do actually use my left arm to grab the racket or balls.

W: Exactly.

W: 팔꿈치는 어때, Steve?

M: 많이 아파.

W: 치료 받고 있지 않니?

M: 받아. 바로 지난주에 물리치료를 시작했어. 진통제도 먹고 있고.

W: 아, 오랫동안 치료하지 않고 놔둔 것 같네.

M: 응. 2주 동안 진찰을 받지 않았어. 그래서 더 악화된 것 같아.

W: 팔꿈치를 쓰지 않도록 해, 그렇지 않으면 더 악화될 거야.

M: 알아.

W: 하지만 너는 여전히 매일 아침 테니스를 치잖아.

M: 아픈 건 왼쪽 팔꿈치이고, 테니스를 칠 때에는 오른쪽 팔을 사용하는 걸, 뭐.

W: 그래도 테니스를 치는 동안 여전히 왼쪽 팔꿈치를 많이 쓰게 될 거야.

M: 네 말이 맞을 것 같다. 내가 사용하는 건 오른쪽 팔일뿐이라고 생각했

었는데, 사실은 라켓이나 공을 집으려면 왼쪽 팔도 쓰게 되겠다.

W: 맞아.

Q What is correct about Steve according to the conversation?

(a) He hurt his right elbow after playing tennis.

(b) He started treatment a long time ago.

(c) He delayed treatment on his elbow.

(d) He plays tennis with his left arm.

대화에 근거하여 Steve에 대한 설명 중 옳은 것은?

(a) 테니스를 친 후에 오른쪽 팔꿈치를 다쳤다.

(b) 오래 전에 치료를 시작했다.

(c) 팔꿈치 치료를 미뤘었다.

(d) 왼쪽 팔로 테니스를 친다.

4 Main Topic

M: After the history of tattooing, let me now tell you something about another form of body decoration known as "scarification" or body scarring. While tattooing involves the use of ink on the body, scarification involves actual cutting of the body and the creation of scars. This practice has been followed for centuries by African tribes, for many reasons. In Mozambique, for instance, ritual scarring marks a special event in life like a boy's induction into manhood. Some kinds of scarification might also indicate a person's social status or special accomplishments. An accomplished warrior might have several types of scarification done, to indicate his heroic deeds on the battlefield. In a similar vein, scarification might be prohibited to younger males who have never experienced any fighting.

M: 문신의 역사에 이어, "스캐러피케이션(난절법)" 또는 신체에 흉터내기

로 알려진 신체 장식의 또 다른 방법에 대해 얘기하겠습니다. 문신은 신체에 잉크를 사용해서 모양을 나타내는 반면, 스캐러피케이션은 실제로 신체의 일부를 절개해서 흉터를 만들어내는 일입니다. 이런 풍습은 아프리카 부족들에 의해 수세기 동안 여러 가지 이유로 행해져 왔습니다. 예를 들어 모잠비크에서는 소년의 성인식 같은 인생에 있어 중요한 행사를 하는 데 제식의 일종으로 사용했습니다. 일부 스캐러피케이션은 또한 개인의 사회적 지위나 개인의 특별한 성취를 나타내기도 합니다. 유능한 전사라면 여러 형태의 스캐러피케이션을 했을 수도 있습니다. 전장에서의 자신의 영웅적인 행동을 표시하기 위해서 말입니다. 이와 유사한 맥락에서 한번도 싸워 보지 못한 젊은 남성들에게는 이러한 스캐러피케이션은 금지되었을 것입니다.

Q What is the topic of the talk?

(a) the reasons for body scarring in Africa

(b) a comparison of tattooing and scarification

(c) how scarification came to Africa

(d) the diverse tattooing traditions in Africa

이 이야기의 화제는?

(a) 아프리카에서 신체 흉터내기를 하는 이유

(b) 문신과 스캐러피케이션의 비교

(c) 스캐러피케이션이 아프리카에 도입된 방법

(d) 아프리카의 여러 다양한 문신의 전통들

해설 스캐러피케이션(난절법)의 정의, 사용자, 의미 등의 전체 개요를 설명하다가 중반 이후부터는 스캐러피케이션이 행해지는 이유에 대해 자세히 설명하고 있으므로 강의의 주제는 (a)가 된다.

함정 (b) "After the history of tattooing ~"이라고 말한 부분을 통해 문신에 관해서는 이미 이야기가 끝났음을 알 수 있다. 따라서 지금 들은 강의 내용에 국한해서 볼 때 문신은 이야기의 주제에서 벗어나 있음을 간파해야 한다. (c)와 (d)에 대한 언급은 없다.

어휘 tattooing 문신술 | scarification 스캐러피케이션, 난절법 | scar ~에 상처를 남기다, 상처, 자국 | practice 풍습, 습관, 관행 | ritual 의식의, 제식의 | induction 도입, 취임 | manhood (남자의) 성년, 성인 | status 지위, 신분 | vein 기질, 특질, 맥락 | diverse 다양한

---

proud of our nation's great advances <u>in technologies that have allowed us to do all of this.</u>

W: 한국 사람들은 우리나라의 우주 프로그램에 열성적입니다. 이소연 우주비행사가 우주로 발사되어 나갈 때 모든 사람이 지켜보았습니다. 우리나라는 앞으로 우주로 더 많은 남자와 여자 우주비행사를 보낼 계획입니다. 그들은 조종사, 엔지니어와 과학자로서 가게 될 것입니다. 그들은 또한 국제우주정거장, 즉 ISS 같은 모든 인류에게 이익이 되도록 고안된 국제 우주 프로그램에도 참여할 수 있습니다. 우리는 이 모든 것을 가능하게 해 준 기술에 있어서 우리나라가 많이 진보되어 있다는 것이 자랑스럽습니다.

Q Which is correct according to the report?

(a) Astronaut Yi So-yeon has developed several space technologies.

(b) Korea may join multinational space efforts.

(c) Male and female astronauts will enter space separately.

(d) Korean space technologies are aboard the ISS.

이 기사에 따르면 옳은 것은?

(a) 이소연 우주비행사는 인류를 위해 우주 기술을 몇 가지 개발했다.

(b) 한국은 다국적 우주 프로젝트에 참가할 수 있다.

(c) 남성과 여성 우주비행사들은 각각 따로 우주에 갈 것이다.

(d) 한국 우주 기술은 ISS에 탑재해 있다.

해설 한국이 우주 프로젝트에 관심이 많다고 하면서, 한국 최초의 우주비행사 이소연을 언급하고 있다. 더 많은 우주비행사들을 우주로 보낼 계획이며, 국제 우주 프로그램에도 참여할 수 있다고 말하고 있으므로 (b)가 정답이다.

함정 (c)에 대한 언급은 나타나지 않았다. ISS 같은 곳에 참여할 수도 있다는 언급이 있으므로 (d)는 오답이다.

어휘 enthusiastic 열성적인, 열광적인 | astronaut 우주비행사 | blast (로켓 등을) 분사하여 발진시키다 | participate in ~에 참가하다 | be proud of ~을 자랑스러워하다 | advance 진보 | multinational 다국적인 | separately 따로따로 | aboard ~을 타고 있는

5

W: Koreans are <u>enthusiastic about our nation's space program</u>. Everyone watched as Astronaut Yi So-yeon <u>blasted into space</u>. Our country has plans <u>to send more astronauts</u>, male and female, into space <u>in the coming years</u>. <u>They will go as pilots</u>, engineers, and scientists. They may also participate in international space programs designed to <u>benefit all humankind</u> like the International Space Station, or ISS. We can be

---

6 Main Topic

W: Justin, could you please come here and help me?

M: Not now. I'm quite busy.

W: You don't seem to be. You're just watching TV.

M: You know <u>it's the semifinals</u>. I don't want to miss the game for even a second.

W: It won't take much time. Just hold this chair while I <u>hang the picture</u> on the wall.

M: Can't you do that after the match?

W: No, I'm going out in the evening.

M: Then, leave it there. I will <u>hang it later</u>.

W: I really want to see <u>how it looks on the wall</u> before I go out. Can't you just <u>come over and hold</u> the chair for a few seconds?

M: There are <u>5 more minutes left until half time</u>. Hold on.

W: If you don't come right away, you are not getting the video game I was going to buy you for your birthday.

M: Okay, fine. Why don't you hold the chair? <u>I'll hang it for you.</u>

W: Justin, 여기 와서 나 좀 도와 줄래?

M: 지금은 안 돼요. 무척 바쁘거든요.

W: 안 그런 것 같은데. TV를 보고 있잖아.

M: 이건 준결승이란 말이에요. 저는 이 경기를 1초도 놓치고 싶지 않아요.

M: 시간이 많이 걸리지는 않을 거야. 벽에 그림을 거는 동안 이 의자만 좀 잡아 줘.

M: 시합이 다 끝난 다음에 하면 안 될까요?

W: 안 돼. 나는 저녁 때 외출할 거야.

M: 그러면 그냥 거기 두세요. 제가 나중에 걸게요.

W: 외출하기 전에 벽에 잘 어울리는지 보고 싶단다. 그냥 와서 잠깐만 의자를 좀 잡아 주면 안 되겠니?

M: 전반전이 5분 남았어요. 잠깐만 기다려 주세요.

W: 지금 당장 오지 않으면, 생일선물로 사 주기로 했던 비디오게임은 없을 줄 알거라.

M: 좋아요. 엄마가 의자를 잡고 있는 게 어때요? 제가 걸게요.

Q What is mainly taking place in the conversation?

(a) The woman is doing some house chores.

(b) The woman is asking the man for help.

(c) The man is holding a chair for the woman.

(d) The couple is deciding where to hang the picture.

대화에서 주로 벌어지고 있는 것은?

(a) 여자는 집안일을 하고 있다.

(b) 여자는 남자에게 도움을 청하고 있다.

(c) 남자는 여자를 위해 의자를 붙잡고 있다.

(d) 두 사람은 어디에 그림을 걸지 결정하고 있다.

해설 TV를 보고 있는 아들에게 엄마가 벽에 그림 거는 것을 도와달라고 하고 있는 장면이다. 남자는 준결승전 시합이기 때문에 1초도 안 보면 안 되니까 자꾸 이런저런 핑계를 대고 있다. 이에 엄마가 의자를 잡아 주지 않으

면 비디오게임은 없을 거라고 말하고 나서야, 아들은 다가가서 자기가 그림을 걸겠다고 하는 장면이다. 여자가 계속해서 남자에게 도움을 요청하고 있으므로 정답은 (b)이다.

어휘 semifinal 준결승 | miss 놓치다, 빠뜨리다, 빼놓다
for a second 1초 동안, 잠깐 동안 | hang ~을 걸다, 달아매다
house chore 집안일

7

W: I'm going to talk today about some of the basic tenets of Islam. It may surprise you to know that Islam is <u>one of the world's easiest religions to convert to</u>. All you need to do is agree to submit to the will of God, or "Allah." <u>From that point on</u>, you are a Muslim: meaning "one who submits to Allah." Of course, as with any other religion, a believer has to study Islam's sacred texts, specifically the Koran, and <u>follow the prescriptions found there</u>. <u>Unlike mainstream</u> Christianity, but somewhat like Orthodox Judaism, Islam has many rules that <u>a believer should follow on a daily basis</u>, such as avoiding specific foods like pork.

W: 오늘은 이슬람의 몇몇 기본 교의에 대해 이야기하겠습니다. 이슬람이 세계에서 가장 개종하기 쉬운 종교 중의 하나라는 것을 알게 되면, 놀랄지도 모릅니다. 신, 즉 "알라"의 뜻에 복종하겠다고 동의하기만 하면 됩니다. 그러는 순간부터 이슬람교도, 그러니까 "알라에게 복종하는 사람"이 되는 것입니다. 물론 여느 다른 종교에서처럼, 믿는 사람은 이슬람의 신성한 책, 특히 코란을 공부해야 하며 거기에서 습득한 규범을 따라야 합니다. 주류를 이루는 기독교와는 다르지만 정통 유대교와는 다소 비슷하게, 이슬람은 돼지고기와 같은 특별한 음식을 피해야 하는 것과 같은 매일매일 지켜야 하는 규범이 많습니다.

Q What is the lecturer's main point about Islam?

(a) It has many points similar to Orthodox Judaism.

(b) It is easy to join but has daily rules to follow.

(c) A person must read the Koran before becoming a Muslim.

(d) Muslims are strict about the foods which they shouldn't eat.

이슬람에 관한 강사의 주요 요점은?

(a) 정통 유대교와 비슷한 점이 많다.

(b) 교인이 되기는 쉬우나 날마다 지켜야 하는 규칙이 있다.

(c) 이슬람교도가 되기 전에 코란을 읽어야 한다.

(d) 이슬람교도는 절대 먹지 말아야 할 음식에 엄격하다.

해설 이슬람에 관한 강의이다. 개종하기는 쉬우나, 정통 유대교처럼 매일

지켜야 하는 규칙들이 많다는 내용이므로, 정답은 (b)이다.

(a) 따라야 할 규범이 많다는 것을 설명하기 위한 부분적 설명에 불과하다. (c) 이슬람교도가 되려면, 일단 "알라" 의 의지에 복종하겠다고 동의하기만 하면 된다고 했다. (d) 이슬람교도는 돼지고기를 먹지 말아야 한다는 언급은 있지만, 이것이 이 강의의 주요 요점이 될 수는 없다.

어휘 tenet 교의, 주의 | convert 전환하다, 전향하다 |
submit 복종하다 | will 의지 | sacred 신성한 |
Koran 코란(이슬람교 성전) | prescription 규정, 법규 |
mainstream 주류를 이루는 | Christianity 기독교 |
orthodox 정통의 | Judaism 유대교 | pork 돼지고기 |
similar to ~과 비슷한

8

M: If you are trying to quit smoking, it is a good idea <u>to start a rigorous exercise program</u>. This will have <u>many benefits</u>, including avoiding gaining weight. Many smokers have "<u>addictive personalities</u>." If they <u>drop one addiction</u>, they may take up another, such as eating or, worse, drinking more heavily. These will <u>impact your health as negatively as</u> smoking does. Exercise will also <u>keep you busy</u>, give you more energy, and make you feel better about yourself.

M: 담배를 끊고자 하면, 매우 혹독한 운동을 시작하는 것이 좋습니다. 이렇게 하면 몸무게가 느는 것을 피하는 것은 물론 많은 장점이 있습니다. 많은 흡연자들이 "중독성의 성격" 을 지니고 있습니다. 그들은 하나의 중독을 포기하면, 먹는 것, 더욱 나쁘게는 심한 과음과 같은 다른 중독을 갖게 될 수도 있습니다. 이러한 것들은 흡연만큼 부정적인 영향을 미칠 것입니다. 운동은 또한 사람을 바쁘게 만들고, 더 많은 에너지를 주며, 스스로에 대해 더 낫게 느끼게 만들 것입니다.

Q What is the speaker's main point?

(a) Smoking can worsen your health severely.

(b) Weight can be reduced by exercising.

(c) Be sure to exercise after you quit smoking.

(d) Don't get an addictive personality.

화자의 주요 요점은 무엇인가?

(a) 흡연은 건강을 심하게 악화시킬 수 있다.

(b) 몸무게는 운동에 의해 감소될 수 있다.

(c) 담배를 끊은 후에는 반드시 운동을 하도록 하라.

(d) 중독성의 성격을 갖지 마라.

해설 담배를 끊으려고 한다면, 운동을 시작하라는 조언이다. "중독성이 강한 사람" 은 담배 대신 운동에 심취할 수 있도록 하라는 것이며, 운동이 주는 많은 이로움을 설명하고 있다. 그러므로 정답은 (c)이다.

(a), (b)는 언급된 내용이기는 하지만, 화자가 이야기하려는 중심 내용은 아니다. (d) 중독성의 성격을 가진 사람들이 있다는 말은 있지만, 그러지 말라는 내용은 아니다.

어휘 quit 그만두다 | rigorous 엄격한, 매우 혹독한 |
addictive 중독성의, 습관성인 | impact 영향을 미치다 |
worsen 악화시키다 | severely 심각하게

9 Main Topic

W: Hey, Robert. I've been looking for you around campus.

M: Well, <u>now that you've found me</u>. Tell me, what's the matter?

W: You know I've been away since my father was sick.

M: Right. How is he doing now?

W: He's still in the hospital. But the surgery went well and the doctor said he will <u>get better soon</u>.

M: Thank God he will be okay.

W: So, I could come back to school. And I have a lot of things to catch up. Since we are taking the same classes, I thought it might be helpful to talk to you.

M: Sure. Well, we <u>have a history paper due</u> this Friday.

W: Oh, I <u>totally forgot</u> about that.

M: Have you <u>done some research</u>?

W: Not at all.

M: You should talk to the professor and <u>get an extension</u>. And another important thing. We have an exam in Chemistry 201 next week.

W: We do? Oh, no. <u>How am I going to study for that</u>? Should I go talk to the professor, too?

M: Well, we didn't do much while you're away. We just finished up the last experiment. You can just study a few chapters in the textbook.

W: Can I borrow your notes?

M: Sure. But I'm not sure if you'll find my handwriting legible enough.

W: Don't worry. <u>I'll manage</u>.

W: 아, Robert, 캠퍼스에서 계속 너를 찾고 있었어.

M: 음, 그럼 찾았으니까, 말해 봐. 무슨 일이야?

W: 우리 아버지가 편찮으셔서 학교에 못 나왔던 거 알지?

M: 그래. 지금은 어때서?

W: 아직 병원에 계셔. 하지만 수술이 잘 되어서 곧 회복되실 거라고 의사가 그러더라.

M: 괜찮으시다니 감사할 일이구나.

W: 그래서 이제 학교에 올 수 있었어. 보충해야 할 것이 많네. 우리가 같은 수업을 받고 있으니까, 너에게 말하면 도움이 될 거라고 생각했어.

M: 물론이지. 음. 이번 금요일이 제출 기한인 역사 보고서가 있어.

W: 아, 까맣게 잊고 있었어.

M: 자료를 좀 찾았어?

W: 전혀.

M: 교수님께 말해서 기한을 좀 연장해야겠다. 그리고 또 중요한 것. 다음 주에 화학 201 시험이 있어.

W: 그래? 아, 이런. 어떻게 공부해야 하지? 교수님을 또 찾아가서 말씀드려야 할까?

M: 음, 네가 없는 동안 진도가 많이 나가지는 않아서, 마지막 실험을 마쳤을 뿐이야. 교과서 몇 챕터만 공부하면 될 거야.

W: 네 공책을 빌릴 수 있을까?

M: 물론이야. 그런데 내 필체를 네가 알아볼 수 있을지 모르겠다.

W: 걱정 마. 어떻게든 알아서 해볼 테니까.

Q What is the woman mainly doing in the conversation?

(a) checking on her class schedule for next week

(b) confirming if she has prepared the right materials

(c) finding out important things that she has to do

(d) asking the man to help her study for an exam

대화에서 여자는 주로 무엇을 하고 있는가?

(a) 다음 주 수업 시간표 점검하기

(b) 준비물을 잘 챙겼는지 확인하기

(c) 해야 하는 중요한 일들 알아보기

(d) 시험 공부할 수 있도록 남자의 도움을 요청하기

해설 아버지가 편찮으셔서 학교에 빠졌던 여자는 남자를 만나 학업에 관해 이것저것 물어보고 있다. 역사 보고서를 제출해야 하고 화학 시험이 있다는 정보를 얻었고, 시험에 도움이 되도록 화학 공책을 빌리고 있으므로 정답은 (c)이다.

함정 시험에 대비해 공부할 수 있도록 도움을 요청하기 위해 남자를 찾은 것이 아니라, 여자가 없는 동안의 수업에 대해 묻다가 화학 시험에 관한 이야기까지 나온 것이므로, (d)를 정답으로 착각해서는 안 된다.

어휘 look for ~을 찾다 | now that ~이므로, ~이기 때문에 | surgery 수술 | get better 회복하다 | catch up 따라잡다, 보충하다 | due 마감인, 제출 기한인 | extension 연장, 연기 | chemistry 화학 | experiment 실험 | handwriting 필적, 필체 | legible 읽기 쉬운, 알아볼 수 있는

10

M: We need to do more to stop the deadly spread of global warming. Many Americans blame China and India for pollution. Because of these countries' industrializations they are emitting a lot of greenhouse gases. However, the fact is India and China have agreed to environmental agreements like the Kyoto Protocol, while the United States has not. The U.S. needs to conform to the Kyoto Treaty, as a responsible country. It also must provide clean production technologies to developing countries. Americans should remember that their country also polluted the world a lot during its early industrialization.

M: 우리는 지구온난화의 치명적인 확산을 막기 위해 더 많은 것을 해야 할 필요가 있습니다. 많은 미국인들이 오염에 대해 중국과 인도를 비난합니다. 산업화 때문에, 그 국가들은 온실 가스를 많이 방출하고 있습니다. 그러나 사실은 미국과는 달리, 인도와 중국은 교토 의정서 같은 환경 협약에 동의해 왔습니다. 미국은 책임을 지는 나라로서 도쿄 협약을 지켜야 할 필요가 있습니다. 미국은 또한 개발도상국들에게 청정 생산 기술을 제공해야 합니다. 미국인들은 자신들의 나라가 초기 산업화 시기 동안 세계를 많이 오염시켰다는 것을 기억해야 합니다.

Q What is the speaker's view on American responsibility toward global warming?

(a) America needs to avoid conforming to the Kyoto Treaty.

(b) Americans are preparing to assist China and India with clean technologies.

(c) America has failed to act responsibly on the environment.

(d) Americans have polluted the world during their late industrialization.

지구온난화에 관해 미국의 책임에 대한 화자의 견해는 무엇인가?

(a) 미국은 교토 협약을 따르는 것을 피할 필요가 있다.

(b) 미국인들은 청정 기술로 중국과 인도를 도울 준비를 하고 있다.

(c) 미국은 환경에 대해 책임 있게 행동하고 있지 않았다.

(d) 미국인들은 후기 산업화 동안 세계를 오염시켰다.

해설 미국은 인도나 중국이 지구온난화를 가속화시키는 오염물질을 방출하고 있다고 비난하고 있지만, 정작 미국도 초기 산업화 때 오염을 일으켰으며 지금은 교토 협약도 지키지 않는다고 비난하고 있다. 미국이 교토 협약을 지킬 것과 개발도상국에 청정 생산 기술을 전수해 줌으로써, 책임 있게 행동하라는 내용이므로 (c)가 정답임을 알 수 있다.

함정 미국 사람들은 청정 기술로 중국과 인도를 도와야 한다는 주장이므로 (b)는 오답이다. (d) 후기(late) 산업화 동안이 아니라 초기(early)임에 유의한다.

어휘 deadly 치명적인 | spread 확산, 퍼짐 | global warming 지구온난화 | because of ~ 때문에

industrialization 산업화 | emit 방출하다, 발산하다 |
greenhouse gas 온실 가스 | environmental 환경의 |
agreement 의정서, 협약 | conform to ~을 따르다, 지키다 |
developing country 개발도상국 | assist 돕다, 조력하다

13. a liquid produced by your liver which helps you to digest fat

14. holding the older and more traditional ideas of their religion or party

15. a smaller area which is part of the city or large town but is outside its center

16. clear enough to read

LISTENING REVIEW

A

1. sacred	2. deposit
3. submit	4. diploma
5. tattoo	6. avert
7. subject	8. physiotherapy
9. chores	10. tenet
11. articulation	12. rigorous
13. bile	14. orthodox
15. suburb	16. legible

1. believed to be holy and to have a special connection with God

2. a sum of money which you pay when you start renting something

3. to allow something to be done to you, or to do what someone wants, for example because you are not powerful enough to resist

4. a qualification which may be awarded to a student by a university or college

5. a design that is drawn on someone's skin using needles to make little holes and filling them with colored dye

6. to prevent something unpleasant from happening

7. the person or animal that is being tested or studied in an experiment or piece of research

8. a medical treatment for problems of the joints, muscles, or nerves, which involves doing exercises or having part of your body massaged or warmed

9. tasks such as cleaning, washing, and ironing that have to be done regularly at home

10. the main principles on which a theory or belief is based

11. the action of producing a sound or word clearly, in speech or music

12. very thorough and strict

B

1. a	2. b	3. b	4. a	5. b

1. 2주 동안 팔꿈치 진찰을 받지 않았다.

   (a) I didn't have my elbow looked at for two weeks.

   (b) I didn't have looked at my elbow for two weeks.

2. 저는 이 경기를 1초도 놓치고 싶지 않아요.

   (a) I don't want to miss even a second at the game.

   (b) I don't want to miss the game for even a second.

3. 내 필체를 네가 알아볼 수 있을지 모르겠다.

   (a) I don't know how you could find my handwriting legible before.

   (b) I'm not sure if you'll find my handwriting legible enough.

4. 지구온난화의 치명적인 확산을 막기 위해 더 많은 것을 해야 할 필요가 있다.

   (a) We need to do more to stop the deadly spread of global warming.

   (b) We need to know how to stop the fatal spread of global warming.

5. 놀랍게도 이슬람은 가장 개종하기 쉬운 종교 중의 하나이다.

   (a) Surprisingly, it is easy to convert Islam to one of the religions.

   (b) Surprisingly, Islam is one of the easiest religions to convert to.

C

1. That's why it has become worse.

2. It is a good idea to start a rigorous exercise program.

3. All you need to do is agree to submit to the will of God.

4. Scarification might be prohibited to younger males who have never experienced any fighting.

5. A majority of the literature present in African languages has its origin in South Africa.

1. it has become worse / why / that's

2. a rigorous exercise program / it is a good idea / to start

3. submit to the will of God / agree to / all you need to do is

4. who have never experienced any fighting / scarification / might be prohibited to younger males

5. a majority of the literature / has its origin in South Africa / present in African languages

D

1. a   **2.** b   **3.** a   **4.** b   **5.** b

1. It has been said that coffee is not good for health.

   (a) Coffee has been blamed for a number of health problems.

   (b) It is said that a few cups of coffee may prevent gallstones.

2. Do you have anything to declare?

   (a) Do you have anything which you would like to give us?

   (b) Do you have anything which you would like us to know about?

3. A huge variation among African languages exists.

   (a) There is vast variation among African languages.

   (b) Vast variation is an essential part of African languages.

4. Children are fascinated by animals that can talk.

   (a) Children love the imaginary animals introduced in the stories.

   (b) Children find it very fascinating to imagine animals talking.

5. I want to live near public transportation.

   (a) I think taking a walk to the station would not be a bad idea.

   (b) I'd prefer a place near convenient public transportation.

CHAPTER 03 DETAIL

VOCABULARY PREVIEW

01. irritated 화가 난
02. authority 권한, 권능, 직권
03. species (생물) 종(種)
04. on the verge of (파멸 등에) 직면하여
05. habitat 서식지
06. encroach 침해하다, 침입하다
07. tremendous 엄청난, 거대한
08. take measures 조치를 취하다
09. awareness 인지, 인식
10. inanimate 무생물의
11. cuddle 꼭 껴안다, 바짝 붙다
12. hostility 적대 행위, 반항
13. prolonged 장기의, 오래 끄는
14. equip 채비를 갖추다
15. avert 피하다, 막다
16. sober 술 취하지 않은, 맑은 정신의
17. Republican 공화당(의)
18. immense 거대한, 막대한
19. tax burden 조세 부담
20. undermine 손상시키다
21. solitude 고독
22. droop 축 늘어지다, 처지다
23. embezzlement 횡령, 착복
24. lapse 잘못, 실수, 타락

GUIDED LISTENING

1	1. a	2. c	2	1. d	2. d
3	1. a	2. d	4	1. d	2. b

1 Conversation

W: What's the matter? You <u>look irritated</u>.

M: The manager <u>called me into his office</u>. I'm so annoyed with him.

W: What did he say to you?

M: Well, he wants me <u>to work overtime</u> but says that <u>I won't be paid for it</u>! Can you believe that?

W: He can't do that. He has to pay for overtime work. Why don't you tell him directly?

M: Actually, <u>I'm scared that he would fire me</u> if I spoke like that.

W: He doesn't have the authority to fire you. I think you should go ahead and tell him. If he doesn't agree to pay, you should refuse to do the overtime.

M: Well then, <u>let me take a chance and tell him</u>. Wish me luck!

W: All the best!

W: 무슨 문제가 있어요? 기분이 안 좋아 보이네요.

M: 부장님이 자기 방으로 오라고 부르더라고요. 그에게 너무 화가 나요.

W: 그가 뭐라고 했는데요?

M: 음, 내가 초과근무를 좀 하기를 원한대요, 하지만 그에 대한 수당은 없을 거래요! 믿을 수 있어요?

W: 그는 그렇게 할 수 없어요. 초과근무에 대해 지불해야만 해요. 그에게 직접 말하지 그래요?

M: 사실, 그렇게 말하면, 그가 저를 해고할까봐 두려워요.

W: 그에게는 당신을 해고할 권리가 없어요. 저는 당신이 그에게 가서 말해야 한다고 생각해요. 그가 수당을 주지 않겠다고 하면, 추가근무를 거절해야 해요.

M: 음, 그러면 한번 가서 얘기해 볼게요. 행운을 빌어 줘요!

W: 행운을 빌어요!

Detail

1 What does the woman advise the man to do?

(a) to ask the manager for overtime pay

(b) to report it to a supervisor

(c) to tell the employee union

(d) to try to get the manager fired

여자가 남자에게 하라고 충고하는 것은 무엇인가?

(a) 부장님에게 초과근무 수당 요청하기

(b) 감독관에게 보고하기

(c) 직원 노조에 말하기

(d) 부장님이 해고당하게 하기

Detail

2   What is the man afraid of?

(a) not getting paid for overtime work

(b) working overtime

(c) losing his job

(d) refusing to work overtime

남자가 두려워하는 것은 무엇인가?

(a) 초과근무 수당을 받지 못하는 것

(b) 초과근무

(c) 직장을 잃는 것

(d) 초과근무를 거절하는 것

해설 남자의 말 Actually, I'm scared that he would fire me if I spoke like that.(사실, 그렇게 말하면, 그가 저를 해고할까봐 두려워요.)를 들었으면, 답을 금방 알 수 있다. 그러므로 (c)가 정답이다.

함정 나머지 (a), (b), (d)는 모두 언급되기는 하였으나, 남자가 두려워하는 것은 아니라는 데에 유의한다.

어휘 irritated 화가 난 | overtime 시간외로, 시간외 노동, 초과근무 | fire 해고하다 | authority 권한, 권능, 직권 | supervisor 감독관

2 Conversation

W: Hey, good to see you back. How was your vacation?

M: Great! We enjoyed it a lot. It was the first time <u>the whole family traveled together</u>.

W: I can understand. I'm sure you must have had lots of fun.

M: Yeah. I'm so grateful to you <u>for taking care of my plants and for collecting our mail</u>.

W: It wasn't a problem at all. But I'm feeling bad about the daisies. Even though I watered them every day, they <u>dried up and died</u>.

M: Please don't worry about them. They probably wouldn't have survived anyway <u>with all the bugs around</u>.

W: Is that true? If I had known, I could have done something to kill them.

M: Actually there was nothing that could have been done about the bugs. So, please <u>don't feel bad</u>

<u>about it</u>.

W: I'm glad that you told me that.

W: 돌아와서 기뻐요. 휴가는 어땠어요?

M: 좋았어요. 정말 재미있었죠. 가족 전체가 함께 여행한 것은 처음이었거든요.

W: 이해할 수 있어요. 정말 재미있었을 것이라고 생각해요.

M: 네. 우리 화초를 돌보아 주고 우편물을 받아 줘서 너무 고마워요.

W: 전혀 힘들지 않았어요. 하지만 데이지꽃 때문에 좀 속상해요. 매일 물을 주었지만, 말라버리더니 죽었어요.

M: 걱정하지 마세요. 온통 벌레 먹어서, 어떻게 해도 살아남지 못했을 거예요.

W: 정말이에요? 그걸 알았더라면, 벌레를 죽이기 위해 뭔가를 했을 텐데요.

M: 사실 벌레에 대해서 할 수 있는 일은 없었어요. 그러니, 속상하지 마세요.

W: 그렇게 말해 주니 고맙네요.

Detail

1   Why does the woman apologize?

(a) for not watering the plants

(b) for not picking up the mail

(c) for going on vacation

(d) for letting the daisies die

여자는 왜 사과하고 있는가?

(a) 화초에 물을 주지 않아서

(b) 우편물을 챙겨 주지 않아서

(c) 휴가를 가서

(d) 데이지꽃들을 죽게 해서

해설 남자가 가족 휴가를 간 사이, 여자가 이런저런 일을 봐 주었다. 화초에 물을 주고 우편물을 챙겨 주었지만, 데이지가 죽어버려서 미안해 하는 여자에게, 남자는 걱정하지 말라고 하고 있다. 그러므로 여자가 미안해 하는 일은 (d)이다.

함정 데이지가 죽은 것은 화초에 물을 주지 않아서 그런 게 아니라 벌레 때문이었으므로 (a)는 오답이다.

Comprehension

2   Which of the following is correct according to the conversation?

(a) The woman forgot to take care of the bugs.

(b) The man forgot to tell the woman to kill the bugs.

(c) The woman didn't know the man's vacation would be this long.

(d) The man does not want her to feel guilty about the plants.

대화에 따르면 다음 중 옳은 것은?

(a) 여자는 벌레를 돌보아 주는 것을 잊었다.

(b) 남자는 여자에게 벌레를 없애라고 말하는 것을 잊었다.

(c) 여자는 남자의 휴가가 이렇게 길 줄은 몰랐다.

(d) 남자는 여자가 화초들에 대해 죄책감을 느끼기를 바라지 않는다.

해설 휴가를 떠났던 남자 대신 화초를 돌본 여자는 데이지가 죽은 것에 대해 미안해 하고 있다. 남자는 그게 여자의 잘못이 아니라, 원래 벌레를 먹어서 어쩔 수 없었을 테니, 걱정하지 말라고 위로한다. 그러므로 정답은 (d)이다.

함정 벌레 때문이었다는 말을 듣고, 여자는 알았더라면 벌레를 없애려고 했을 것이라고 말하지만, 남자는 그래도 할 수 있는 일이 없었을 거라고 말하고 있으므로 (b)는 오답이다.

어휘 grateful 감사하고 있는, 고마워하는 | take care of ~을 돌보다 | even though 비록 ~할지라도, ~하지만 | water 물을 주다 | bug 벌레, 곤충

3 Monologue

W: Leatherback sea turtles are one of the oldest species on Earth. They are usually found in coastal regions of Mexico, Costa Rica and Malaysia. A recent report suggesting that these turtles are on the verge of extinction has raised concerns among environmentalists. It is estimated that worldwide only 40,000 turtles are left from the hundreds of thousands that existed 13 years ago. Coastal areas are the natural habitat where the turtles usually lay their eggs. However, rapidly growing commercial fishing industries have encroached upon these natural habitats of the turtles. Also, the development of coastal property has been tremendous over the last few years, destroying the mating grounds of the turtles. If the authorities don't take any measures to check this, leatherback sea turtles may become extinct one day.

W: 장수바다거북은 지구상에서 가장 오래된 종들 중 하나입니다. 이 거북들은 주로 멕시코, 코스타리카, 말레이시아의 해안 지역에서 발견됩니다. 이 거북들이 멸종의 위기에 처해 있다는 최근의 한 보고서가 환경론자들 사이에서 관심을 불러일으켰습니다. 13년 전에는 수십만 마리였던 거북들이 이제는 세계적으로 4만 마리만이 남아 있다고 추정됩니다. 해안 지역은 거북들이 일반적으로 알을 낳는 자연 서식지입니다. 그러나 순식간에 커지고 있는 상업적인 낚시 산업이 거북의 이러한 자연 서식지를 침해했습니다. 또한, 해안 지역은 지난 몇 년 동안 개발이 엄청나게 일어나서, 거북들의 짝짓기 장소를 파괴했습니다. 당국이 이것을 조사하기 위한 조치를 취

하지 않는다면, 장수바다거북은 언젠가 멸종될 것입니다.

Detail

1   What is destroying the natural habitat of the turtles?

(a) commercial fishing industries

(b) careless authorities

(c) development on their mating grounds

(d) growing tourism

거북들의 자연 서식지를 파괴하는 것은?

(a) 상업적인 낚시 산업

(b) 부주의한 당국

(c) 짝짓기를 하는 장소의 개발

(d) 성장하는 관광 산업

해설 멸종 위기에 처해 있는 장수바다거북에 관한 내용이다. 해안 지역은 거북들이 알을 낳는 자연 서식지인데, 상업적인 낚시 산업과 해안 지역의 개발이 거북의 자연 서식지를 침해해서 멸종 위기에 처해 있다는 내용이다. 그러므로 정답은 (a)이다.

함정 정부가 거북의 자연 서식지를 침해하는 요소들에 대해 어떤 조치를 내려야 한다는 주장은 있지만, 정부의 부주의가 거북의 자연 서식지를 침해한다고는 볼 수 없으므로 (b)는 오답이다. (c)는 짝짓기 장소가 아니라 알을 낳은 해안 지역의 개발이다. (d)의 관광 산업에 관한 언급은 없다.

Main Topic

2   What is the issue addressed here?

(a) the sea as an important source of fish

(b) the age of leatherback sea turtles

(c) the rapid growth of coastal properties

(d) the possible extinction of an animal species

여기서 다루어지고 있는 이슈는 무엇인가?

(a) 물고기의 중요한 원천으로서의 바다

(b) 장수바다거북의 나이

(c) 해안 지역의 빠른 성장

(d) 한 동물 종의 멸종 가능성

해설 멸종 위기에 처해 있는 장수바다거북에 관한 내용이다. 낚시 산업의 발달과 해안 지역 개발이 그 주된 원인일 수 있고, 당국의 조치를 촉구하고 있다. 그러므로 정답은 (d)이다.

어휘 leatherback sea turtle 장수바다거북 | species (생물) 종(種) | coastal 해안의, 해변의 | region 지역 | on the verge of (파멸 등에) 직면하여 | extinction 멸종 | environmentalist 환경론자 | habitat 서식지 | lay (알을) 낳다 | encroach 침해하다, 침입하다 | tremendous 엄청난, 거대한 | mating 짝짓기, 교미 | take measures 조치를 취하다

4 Monologue

W: Today, we will discuss the development of social awareness in babies. <u>Being aware</u> of other human beings is the first hint of social interaction in a baby. You may have noticed how babies <u>react to different things</u> in their environments. However, their reaction to human faces is different from their reaction to <u>inanimate objects</u>. You may try <u>holding up a doll</u> in front of a baby and note how the baby reacts to it. The baby usually tries <u>to reach the object and hold it</u>. <u>On the contrary</u>, when you pick up a baby, the baby usually cuddles up to you. This reaction <u>is instinctive</u> in babies and indicates their level of awareness of human beings.

W: 오늘 우리는 갓난아이들의 사회 인지 발달에 대해 논할 것입니다. 다른 사람의 존재를 인식한다는 것이 아기에게 있어서 사회적 상호작용의 첫 번째 징조입니다. 여러분은 아기들이 환경에서 서로 다른 사물들에 어떻게 반응하는지 보았을 수도 있습니다. 그러나 사람의 얼굴에 대한 반응은 생명이 없는 물체들에 대한 반응과는 다릅니다. 아기 앞에 인형을 하나 들고 있으면서 아기가 그것에 어떻게 반응하는지 볼 수 있을 것입니다. 일반적으로 아기는 그 물건에 손을 뻗쳐서 잡으려고 할 것입니다. 반대로, 여러분이 아기를 안을 때는, 일반적으로 아기는 여러분을 꼭 껴안습니다. 이 반응은 아기에게 있어 본능적인 것이며 사람들을 인식한다는 점을 보여 주는 것입니다.

Detail

1 Why do babies cuddle up to you according to the lecture?

(a) Because they try to balance their body instinctively.

(b) Because they instinctively like to hug.

(c) Because they want to interact with anything they see.

(d) Because they are aware of human beings.

이 강의에 따르면 아기들이 사람을 꼭 껴안는 이유는 무엇인가?

(a) 아기들이 본능적으로 몸의 균형을 맞추려고 하기 때문이다.

(b) 아기들이 본능적으로 껴안는 것을 좋아하기 때문이다.

(c) 아기들은 보이는 모든 것에 반응을 하고 싶어 하기 때문이다.

(d) 아기들이 사람을 인식하기 때문이다.

해설 갓난아이들의 사회 인지 발달에 대한 강의이다. 아기들은 환경에 반응하는데, 일반적으로 사물은 잡으려고 하지만, 사람에 대해서는 꼭 껴안는 반응을 보이는 것으로 보아, 아기들도 사람을 인지한다는 내용이다. 이렇게 서로 다른 반응을 보이는 것은 아기들이 사람을 인식하기 때문이므로, (d)가 정답이다.

Comprehension

2 Which is correct according to the lecture?

(a) Babies don't like social interaction.

(b) Babies can distinguish humans from other objects.

(c) Babies try to cuddle up to any objects and hold them.

(d) Babies react toward humans more often.

이 강의에 따르면, 옳은 것은?

(a) 아기들은 사회적 상호작용을 좋아하지 않는다.

(b) 아기들은 사람과 사물을 구분할 수 있다.

(c) 아기들은 어떤 물건이든지 껴안고 잡으려고 한다.

(d) 아기들은 사람에게 더 자주 반응한다.

해설 아기들은 사물 잡으려고 하고 사람은 꼭 껴안으려고 하는 반응으로 보아, 아기들이 사람과 사물을 구분할 수 있다는 것을 알 수 있으므로, (b)가 정답이다.

어휘 awareness 인지, 인식 | be aware of ~을 인식하다 | hint 힌트, 징후 | interaction 상호작용 | react to ~에 반응하다 | inanimate 무생물의 | object 물건, 물체 | on the contrary 반대로 | cuddle 꼭 껴안다, 바짝 붙다 | instinctive 본능적인 | indicate 나타내다, 표시하다

PRACTICAL LISTENING				
1. c	2. c	3. d	4. b	5. c
6. a	7. a	8. a	9. b	10. b

1

M: Coming to international news, the United Nations will call back some of its peacekeeping personnel in Yugoslavia because of <u>social concerns and growing hostility</u> to its <u>prolonged military presence</u> in the area. In recent months some UN forces have come under fire, and two UN soldiers from the Netherlands were killed. UN representatives in Yugoslavia added that the reduction in forces <u>is related to the improvement</u> in the security situation of the region. Officials from UN headquarters in New York say that <u>local forces are now equipped enough to handle the security situation on their own</u>. This comes as a relief to leaders in Western Europe, whose countries had supplied most of the troops to the UN peacekeeping forces in Yugoslavia.

M: 다음은 국제 뉴스입니다. UN은 유고슬라비아에 장기 주둔하고 있는 군에 대한 사회적인 염려와 (군에 대한) 반감이 증대되고 있음을 이유로 평화유지단 일부를 소환하기로 했습니다. 최근 몇 달간 일부 UN 군대가 공격을 받았으며 네덜란드 출신의 두 명의 유엔군이 사망했습니다. 유고슬라비아 유엔 대표는 군 감축은 이 지역의 안보 상황이 개선된 것과 관련이 있다고 덧붙였습니다. 뉴욕에 있는 유엔 본부 관리들은 유고슬라비아의 군 병력이 이제 자국의 안보를 담당할 만큼 충분한 장비를 갖추고 있다고 말합니다. 이는 유고슬라비아 내 유엔 평화유지군에게 대부분의 병력을 공급했던 서유럽 지도자들에게는 좋은 소식입니다.

Q Which is correct according to the news report?

(a) Yugoslavia welcomes the UN's presence.

(b) Yugoslavia promises to improve the security situation.

(c) The UN will reduce the number of peacekeepers in Yugoslavia.

(d) The UN peacekeepers averted social problems in Yugoslavia.

뉴스에 따르면 다음 중 옳은 것은?

(a) 유고슬라비아는 유엔의 주둔을 환영한다.

(b) 유고슬라비아는 안보상황을 개선시키겠다고 약속한다.

(c) 유엔은 유고슬라비아 내 평화유지군의 수를 감축할 것이다.

(d) 유엔 평화유지군이 유고슬라비아 내 사회 문제를 막았다.

해설 유고슬라비아 내 평화유지군에 관한 뉴스이다. 유엔이 이들 평화유지군에 대한 사회적 염려와 이들에 대한 적대감 증가를 이유로 평화유지군 일부를 자국으로 불러들일 것이라는 뉴스를 전하고 있다. 따라서 뉴스의 내용에 해당하는 것은 (c)이다.

함정 유고슬라비아가 자국의 안전을 책임질 만큼 장비를 갖추었고, 국내 상황도 개선되었다는 내용은 있지만, 대외적으로 '안보상황을 개선시키겠다고 약속한다(b)'는 내용은 없다.

어휘 call back 소환하다, 불러들이다 | peacekeeping 평화유지의 | hostility 적대 행위, 반항 | prolonged 장기의, 오래 끄는 | under fire 공격을 받는, 포화를 받는 | representative 대표자 | reduction 축소, 삭감 | security 보안, 안보 | region 지역 | headquarter 본부 | equip 장비를 갖추다 | avert 피하다, 막다

2 Detail

W: What have you been doing? Do you know that it's one in the morning?

M: I'm sorry, dear. Didn't you go to sleep?

W: No, I was so worried. <u>What held you up at work</u>?

M: Actually, one of our colleagues got promoted, so he took everybody out for drinks.

W: That means <u>you've been drinking</u>?

M: Well, I got out of the office late since I had to finish <u>this file for the presentation</u> tomorrow. And I was going to come home since it was almost 10 when I was done.

W: You should've.

M: But John, the one who got promoted, <u>kept on calling</u> and I couldn't refuse. So, I thought I would just show up and stay there for 30 minutes or so, but he <u>kept on insisting</u> everybody stay, even when it got late.

W: At least you could have called to let me know. Go to bed for now. We will talk about this tomorrow <u>when you're sober</u>.

W: 뭐하고 있었던 거예요? 새벽 1시인 거 알아요?

M: 미안해요, 여보. 안 잤어요?

W: 아니, 너무 걱정했어요. 회사에서 무엇 때문에 그렇게 늦은 거예요?

M: 실은, 동료 한 명이 승진을 해서, 모두를 데리고 나와서 술을 샀거든요.

W: 그럼 여태 술을 마신 거예요?

M: 음, 내일 있을 프레젠테이션 파일 작업을 마무리하느라 사무실에서 늦게 나왔어요. 일을 마쳤을 때가 거의 10시가 다 되었기 때문에 집으로 향하고 있었죠.

W: 그래야죠.

M: 하지만 John이, 그 승진한 사람이, 계속 전화를 했고 거절할 수가 없었어요. 그래서 그냥 잠시 들러서 30분 정도만 있다가 오려고 했는데, 그 친구가 다들 못 가게 계속 붙잡는 바람에, 이렇게까지 늦었네요.

W: 적어도 전화해서 알려 줄 수 있었잖아요. 이제 주무세요, 이것에 대한 이야기는 내일 맑은 정신일 때 해요.

Q Why did the man come home late?

(a) Because he had to take his colleagues out for a drink.

(b) Because he couldn't finish the work on time.

(c) Because his co-worker didn't let him go early.

(d) Because his colleague forgot to bring his presentation files.

남자가 집에 늦게 온 이유는?

(a) 남자가 동료들에게 술을 사야 했기 때문이다.

(b) 남자가 제 시간에 일을 마무리하지 못했기 때문이다.

(c) 남자의 동료가 그를 일찍 보내지 않았기 때문이다.

(d) 남자의 동료가 그의 프레젠테이션 파일을 가져오는 것을 잊었기 때문이다.

해설 밤늦게 집에 돌아온 남편과 안 자고 기다리고 있던 아내와의 대화이

다. 왜 늦었냐는 아내의 물음에, 남편은 일이 늦게 끝났고 회사동료가 승진
턱으로 술을 샀는데, 그 친구가 못 가게 해서 일찍 나올 수 없었다고 그 이
유를 설명하고 있다. 따라서 정답은 (c)이다.

[어휘] hold up 정지하다, 지체시키다 │ colleague 동료 │
get promoted 승진하다 │ keep on -ing 계속 ~하다 │
show up 나타나다 │ at least 적어도, 최소한 │
could have p.p. ~할 수 있었을 텐데 │
sober 술 취하지 않은, 맑은 정신의

3

M: Would you like to go to Fusion 9 tonight?

W: Is <u>something special happening</u> there?

M: Yeah, one of my friends is <u>performing with the
band</u>. I think you'll enjoy it.

W: What kind of music do they play? If it is a rock, <u>I
wouldn't be very interested</u>. You know it's too loud.

M: Well, they play jazz, but it's Latin jazz. So <u>it might
be still loud</u>, but <u>not as much as</u> rock music.

W: I love Latin jazz. Well, what's the entry fee?

M: We've got free tickets, so there's nothing to worry
about!

W: Sounds perfect!

M: Okay then, I'll <u>pick you up</u> at 8:00 p.m.

M: 오늘 밤에 Fusion 9 바에 갈래?

W: 무슨 특별한 거라도 하니?

M: 응. 친구 하나가 밴드랑 공연하거든. 네가 좋아할 것 같아서.

W: 어떤 종류의 음악을 연주하는데? 록이라면, 별로 관심이 없는데. 너무
시끄럽잖아.

M: 음, 재즈를 연주할 거야. 그런데 라틴 재즈라서 록 음악만큼은 아니겠
지만, 그래도 좀 소리가 크기는 할 거야.

W: 난 라틴 재즈를 좋아해. 음, 입장료는 얼마야?

M: 공짜표가 있으니까, 걱정할 거 없어!

W: 잘 됐다!

M: 알았어, 그럼 저녁 8시에 데리러 갈게.

Q What are the man and woman mainly discussing?

(a) what kind of music they enjoy

(b) what music they'd like to perform with the band

(c) getting free tickets to a show

(d) going out for live music

남자와 여자는 주로 무슨 이야기를 하고 있는가?

(a) 그들이 즐겨 듣는 음악의 종류에 대해 이야기하기

(b) 밴드와 연주하고 싶어 하는 음악 정하기

(c) 쇼를 볼 수 있는 공짜표 얻기

(d) 라이브 음악 들으러 나가기

[해설] 남자는 여자에게 친구의 밴드 공연을 보러 가자고 하고 있다. 여자는
록음악은 싫다고 했지만, 공연될 음악은 재즈이며, 남자에게 공짜 티켓이
있어서 입장료는 무료이다. 또 남자가 8시에 여자를 데리러 가겠다고 한
다. 따라서 두 사람은 지금 친구의 밴드 공연, 즉 라이브 음악을 들으러 가
는 것에 대해 이야기하고 있으므로, 정답은 (d)가 된다.

[함정] 록음악은 싫고 재즈 중에서 라틴 재즈를 좋아한다는 부분만 듣고 (a)
를 정답으로 고르면 안 된다.

[어휘] perform 공연하다, 연주하다 │ as much as ~만큼 …한 │
entry fee 입장료, 참가비 │ pick up ~을 마중 나가다, 태우러 가다

4 Detail

W: Coming to political news, Republicans reacted
sharply to the president's <u>proposed tax increases on
upper-income citizens</u> to pay for Social Security,
saying it would create an immense tax burden for
ordinary citizens. They added that this plan amounted
to wild populism, and merely served <u>to undermine the
president's credibility</u>. They asserted that the tax
increase, instead of falling on the wealthy, would in
truth <u>fall mainly on the middle class</u>. The Republicans
have demanded an·alternative that would not cause a
tax increase for anyone. <u>The president for his part
asserted</u> that the Republicans have <u>got their figures all
wrong</u> and are quoting erroneous data. He insisted that
the tax increase was <u>both necessary and just</u>.

W: 정치 뉴스입니다. 공화당은 사회 보장 제도 비용과 관련, 고소득 시민
들에게 세금 부담을 높이겠다는 대통령의 제안에 날카롭게 대응했습니다.
공화당은 그것이 일반 시민들에게 막대한 조세 부담을 안겨 줄 것이라고
말했습니다. 그들은 이번 안은 무모한 대중 인기주의나 다름없으며, 대통
령의 신용만 손상시킬 뿐이라고 덧붙였습니다. 그들은 세금 인상이 부유층
에 돌아가지 않고, 실제로는 중산층에게 돌아갈 것이라고 단언했습니다.
공화당은 누구에게도 세금 인상을 지우지 않을 다른 대안을 요구했습니다.
그러나 대통령은 공화당이 그릇된 수치를 가지고 있으며 잘못된 데이터를
인용하고 있다고 주장했습니다. 대통령은 세금 인상은 필요할 뿐만 아니라
정당한 조치였다고 강조했습니다.

Q Why are the Republicans opposed to the President's
proposed tax plan?

(a) Because it will only benefit upper-income citizens.

(b) Because it will only burden ordinary citizens.

(c) Because it is impossible to carry it into effect.

(d) Because it will damage the overall economy.

공화당은 대통령의 세금 법안에 왜 반대하는가?

(a) 고소득 시민들에게만 이로울 것이기 때문이다.

(b) 보통 시민들에게 부담만 될 뿐이기 때문이다.

(c) 실효를 거두기 불가능하기 때문이다.

(d) 전반적으로 경제에 해가 될 것이기 때문이다.

해설 대통령의 고소득층 세금 인상 제안에 대해 공화당이 반대를 제기하고 있다는 내용의 뉴스이다. 공화당은 이 안이 결국 고소득층이 아니라 일반 시민들에게 세금 부담을 가중시키게 될 것이라는 이유로 반대를 표명하고 있으므로 정답은 (b)이다.

어휘 Republican 공화당(의) | react 대응하다, 반응하다, 반대하다 | sharply 민첩하게, 날카롭게 | upper-income 고소득의 | Social Security 사회 보장 (제도) | immense 거대한, 막대한 | tax burden 조세 부담 | amount to 결과적으로 ~이 되다 | populism 대중의 칭찬 | undermine 손상시키다 | credibility 신용, 진실성 | alternative 대안, 다른 방도 | erroneous 잘못된, 틀린

5

W: Have you finished working on the computer?

M: Well, I'm almost done. Do you want to use it?

W: No. Actually spending so much time in front of the computer may not be healthy for you.

M: It's only two hours a day. I don't think that's too much.

W: But these two hours are in addition to the time you spend at work on the computer.

M: Well, that doesn't bother me. It actually helps me to unwind.

W: I'm sure I can't convince you otherwise, but you're wrong.

W: 컴퓨터 사용 다 했니?

M: 음, 거의 다 했어. 컴퓨터 쓰고 싶어서 그래?

W: 아니. 사실 컴퓨터 앞에서 너무 많은 시간을 보내는 것은 네 건강에 좋지 않을 거야.

M: 하루에 단 2시간인데, 뭘. 난 그게 너무 많은 시간이라고 생각하지 않아.

W: 하지만 직장에서 컴퓨터 쓰는 시간을 뺀 두 시간이잖아.

M: 나는 괜찮아. 실제로 긴장을 푸는 데 도움이 된다고.

W: 달리 너를 납득시키지 못하겠지만, 아무튼 네가 틀린 거야.

Q   What can be inferred from the conversation?

(a) The woman uses the computer too often.

(b) The man has lots of work to do on the computer.

(c) The man is unlikely to change his habits.

(d) The woman had been sick because of a computer.

이 대화에서 추측할 수 있는 것은?

(a) 여자는 컴퓨터를 너무 자주 사용한다.

(b) 남자는 컴퓨터로 할 일이 많다.

(c) 남자는 습관을 바꿀 것 같지 않다.

(d) 여자는 컴퓨터 때문에 병이 난 적이 있었다.

해설 남자가 컴퓨터 앞에서 너무 많은 시간을 보낸다고 생각하는 여자와 그렇지 않다고 여기는 남자와의 대화이다. 여자는 그것이 건강에 좋지 않기 때문에 자제를 권하지만, 남자는 그게 방해가 되기는커녕, 오히려 긴장 완화에 도움이 된다고 주장하고 있다. 이것으로 볼 때, 남자는 자신의 습관을 바꾸려는 태도를 전혀 보이지 않고 있기 때문에, 정답은 (c)가 된다.

함정 (b) 남자가 직장에서 컴퓨터를 이용하기는 하지만, 그것으로 컴퓨터로 할 일이 많다고 유추할 수는 없다.

어휘 in front of ~의 앞에 | healthy 건강한, 건강에 좋은 | in addition to ~에 더하여, ~일뿐 아니라, ~외에 또 | at work 직장에서, 일하는 | bother ~을 귀찮게 하다, ~에게 폐를 끼치다 | unwind 긴장을 풀다, 편한 마음을 갖게 하다 | convince 확신시키다, 납득시키다 | be unlikely to ~할 것 같지 않다

6   Detail

M: Today I want to talk about something that has had a great impact on Washington State art. Washington's large yet quiet forests, abundant lakes, heavy rains and wide foggy sea coast has developed a theme of loneliness and solitude in many art forms. Dave Tobey is a famous Washington modern artist who has painted dark, forbidding themes of pain and suffering. Dale Chihuly is likewise internationally known for his drooping, sad glassworks. Although the two artists work in very different fields, it is clear what has affected both men's styles.

M: 오늘, 저는 워싱턴 주의 예술에 커다란 영향을 미친 것에 대해 말하려 합니다. 워싱턴의 커다랗지만 고요한 숲, 많은 호수, 많은 비와 안개가 넓게 퍼져 있는 해안은 많은 형태의 예술에서 외로움과 고독이라는 주제로 발전되었습니다. Dave Tobey는 고통과 시련이라는 어둡고, 음침한 주제를 그리는 워싱턴의 유명한 현대 예술가입니다. Dale Chihuly도 마찬가지로 의도적으로 늘어지고 슬픈 유리공예품으로 국제적으로 알려져 있습니

다. 이 두 예술가는 서로 전혀 다른 분야에서 활동하지만, 무엇이 그 두 사람 모두의 스타일에 영향을 미쳤는지는 분명합니다.

Q What has affected the artists' styles?

(a) the environment

(b) development of the city

(c) individualized society

(d) various fields of art

무엇이 그 예술가들의 스타일에 영향을 미쳤는가?

(a) 환경

(b) 도시의 발달

(c) 개인화된 사회

(d) 예술의 다양한 분야

해설 워싱턴의 자연 환경이 예술가들에게 미친 영향을 다루는 강의이다. 숲, 호수, 비와 안개 등이 외로움과 고독을 주제로 예술 활동을 하게 했는데, 그 예로 화가와 유리공예 작가를 들고 있다. 환경이 두 사람 모두의 스타일에 영향을 미쳤다는 것이므로, (a)가 정답이다.

어휘 impact 충돌, 영향 | forest 숲 | abundant 풍부한, 많은
foggy 안개가 자욱한 | solitude 고독
forbidding 기분 나쁜, 무서운 | theme 주제 |
droop 축 늘어지다, 처지다 | glasswork 유리공예

7

M: Welcome aboard the USS Garvin. This is a Class 7 destroyer built domestically in 1997 at Norfolk, Virginia. The ship has state-of-the-art weapons, including the most advanced command and control combat management equipment in the world. The Minerva radar and fire-control system it has enables the ship to engage over 200 land, air, sea and underwater targets at once. It thus has the weapons' capability to fight an entire enemy fleet on its own. The ship also has 2 helicopters for reconnaissance, antisubmarine operations, or search and rescue missions. Today, we are open to the public. You are free to look around selected areas of the ship and ask any questions you have. Thank you.

M: USS Garvin에 탑승하신 것을 환영합니다. 여기는 1997년 국내 버지니아 노르포크에서 건조(建造)된 Class 7 구축함입니다. 이 선박은 세계에서 가장 진보적인 명령 및 통제 전투 운영 장비를 포함하여, 가장 최신식 무기들을 보유하고 있습니다. 이 함대가 보유한 미네르바 레이더 및 사격 통제 시스템은 동시에 200발 이상의 육해공 및 수중 목표물을 상대로 한 교전을 가능케 합니다. 요컨대 이 함대는 자체적으로 적의 전체 함대와

대항할 무기 능력을 보유하고 있습니다. 이 함대는 또한 정찰, 대잠수함 작전, 또는 수색 구조 임무를 위한 2대의 헬기를 탑재하고 있습니다. 오늘 우리는 일반인들에게 함대를 공개합니다. 함대의 공개된 부분을 자유롭게 살펴보시고, 궁금한 사항이 있으면 질문하시기 바랍니다. 감사합니다.

Q What is the speaker mainly doing in the announcement?

(a) receiving visitors on a warship

(b) giving commands to sailors at sea

(c) describing war exhibits in a museum

(d) explaining the history of a fleet

화자가 이 공지에서 주로 하고 있는 것은?

(a) 군함 방문객 환영

(b) 해상 선원들에게 명령 전달

(c) 박물관에서 전쟁 관련 전시품 설명

(d) 함대의 역사 설명

해설 Class 7 구축함을 일반 공개하여, 보러 온 방문객들을 맞이하는 내용의 이야기이다. 구축함의 특징을 설명하고 자유롭게 둘러보도록 권하고 있으므로 정답은 (a)이다.

함정 일반 방문객들의 이해를 돕기 위해 Class 7 구축함의 특징을 설명하는 것이지 함대의 역사를 설명하는 것이 목적이 아니므로 (d)는 답이 될 수 없다. 또한 해상 선원들(b)이나 박물관(d)에 대해서는 언급되지 않았다.

어휘 destroyer 구축함, 파괴자
domestically 국내에서, 국내 문제에 관해서
state-of-the-art 첨단 기술을 사용한, 최신식의
combat 전투, 투쟁 | management 관리, 처리, 감독
equipment 장비 | fire-control system 사격 통제 시스템
engage (적군과) 교전하다, (군대를) 교전시키다 | fleet 함대, 선박
reconnaissance 정찰(대) | antisubmarine 대(對)잠수함의
search 수색 | rescue 구조

---

8 Detail

W: Oh no, have you heard the weather forecast?

M: No, what did it say?

W: There'll be heavy snow this evening. That means it's going to be freezing at night.

M: You'd better bundle up.

W: I will just take this jacket with me.

M: And try not to be late. You know we have a dinner appointment at 7 with Jenny's teacher.

W: I know. I will try to come as soon as possible.

M: I mean there might be heavy traffic after work. Last time when it was raining hard, it took you more than an hour to get home, remember?

W: Yeah, we were supposed to go to a friend's house for dinner, but we couldn't make it because I was late. I'll try to leave the office as soon as my boss leaves.

M: Call me if you can't make it on time. I can't make Ms. Johnson wait at the restaurant for a long time.

W: 아, 이럴 수가, 일기예보 들었어요?

M: 아니, 뭐라고 했는데요?

W: 오늘 저녁에 눈이 많이 온대요. 그 말은 밤에는 날씨가 엄청 추워질 거라는 뜻이죠.

M: 당신은 따뜻하게 껴입는 게 좋겠어요.

W: 이 재킷을 가져가면 될 거예요.

M: 그리고 늦지 않도록 해요. 당신도 알다시피, Jenny의 선생님과 7시에 저녁 약속이 있잖아요.

W: 알아요. 가능하면 빨리 오도록 할게요.

M: 퇴근시간에 길이 막힐 수도 있다는 거예요. 지난번에 비가 많이 왔을 때, 집에 오는 데 1시간 이상 걸린 거 기억나죠?

W: 그래요, 친구네 집에 저녁 먹으러 가기로 했었는데, 내가 너무 늦어서 못 갔잖아요. 사장님이 퇴근하면 바로 사무실에서 나올 게요.

M: 시간을 맞출 수 없으면 전화해요. Johnson 선생님이 식당에서 오래 동안 기다리게 할 수는 없죠.

Q What is the man worried about?

(a) being late for the appointment

(b) cold weather at night

(c) meeting Jenny's teacher

(d) visiting a friend's house

남자는 무엇을 걱정하고 있는가?

(a) 약속에 늦는 것

(b) 밤의 추운 날씨

(c) Jenny의 선생님을 만나는 것

(d) 친구의 집을 방문하는 것

해설 밤에 눈이 내린다는 일기예보를 듣고 대화하는 내용이다. 남자는 여자에게 따뜻하게 입고 저녁에 약속이 있으니 늦지 말라고 당부하고 있다. 폭설로 인해 길이 막힐 수 있고 선생님을 기다리게 할 수 없다는 말로 보아 남자가 걱정하고 있는 것은 (a)이다.

함정 (c) Jenny의 선생님을 만나는 것 자체를 걱정하고 있는 것은 아니다.

어휘 **weather forecast** 일기예보 | **heavy snow** 큰 눈, 폭설 | **freezing** 어는, 몹시 추운 | **bundle up** 따뜻하게 옷을 껴 입다 |

---

heavy traffic 극심한 교통량 | **get home** 귀가하다 | **be supposed to** ~하기로 되어 있다 | **make it** 약속을 지키다, 해내다

9

W: In my career as business educator, I have seen some dramatic changes in business education. In the past 5 years, for example, we've introduced Web business courses, incorporated new business models and inserted trendy corporate valuations and analyses into the curriculum. We also take business ethics courses, although the concept of ethics has not gained the importance it deserves. If current reports are true, it seems that business graduates are more interested in getting course credits than acquiring moral standards! One only has to open the daily papers to read about tales of CEOs being arrested for accounting fraud, stock manipulation, embezzlement, or other ethical lapses. One of the most infamous of these was the case of the company Enron.

W: 기업 교육자인 저는 업무상 기업 교육에 있어 몇 가지 중대한 변화를 목격해왔습니다. 예를 들어, 지난 5년간 우리는 웹 사업 강좌를 도입했으며, 새로운 회사 모델을 만들었고, 요즘에 유행하고 있는 기업 평가와 분석을 커리큘럼에 집어넣었습니다. 윤리 개념이 그 중대성을 제대로 인정받지 못함에도 불구하고, 우리는 또한 (커리큘럼에) 기업 윤리 과정을 포함시켰습니다. 현재 보도되는 내용들이 사실이라면, 경영학 과정을 졸업한 사람들은 도덕적 기준을 습득하는 것보다 학점을 따는 것에 보다 많은 관심이 있는 것으로 보입니다. 누구나 신문을 펼치면 회계 부정, 주가 조작, 횡령, 또는 기타 도덕적 타락으로 체포되는 최고경영자들에 관한 얘기를 읽게 됩니다. 그들 중 가장 악명 높은 것은 Enron 사에 관한 사건입니다.

Q What will the speaker probably talk about next?

(a) the importance of leadership in business

(b) a specific example of unethical practices

(c) the issue of falling standards in business education

(d) course credits needed for a business degree

화자가 다음에 무엇에 대해 말할 것 같은가?

(a) 기업에서의 리더십의 중요성

(b) 비윤리적인 행위의 구체적인 예

(c) 기업 교육에서의 도덕적 규범 하락과 관련한 문제

(d) 경영학 학위에 필요한 이수 학점

해설 기업 교육자인 화자는 기업 윤리를 등한시하는 현 세태를 비판하면서 신문에 보도되는 기업 경영자들의 여러 가지 부정행위들에 대해 언급하고 있다. 마지막 문장에 가장 악명 높은 회사에 대한 언급이 있으므로, 다음에

이어질 내용은 그 회사에 대한 구체적인 사례라고 짐작할 수 있다. 따라서 정답은 (b)이다. 이어서 나올 내용에 대한 문제일 경우, 뒷부분의 내용을 주의해서 들어야 한다.

어휘 incorporate 짜 넣다, 만들다, (회사를) 법인 조직으로 만들다 | insert 끼워 넣다, 삽입하다 | valuation 평가, 사정 | analysis 분석 (pl. analyses) | ethics 윤리학, 도덕론 | deserve ~을 받을 만하다, ~의 가치가 있다 | credit 학점 | accounting 회계 | fraud 사기, 기만 | stock manipulation 주가 조작 | embezzlement 횡령, 착복 | lapse 잘못, 실수, 타락

10

W: Today, I'll continue with French colonialism, one of the most important elements in French history. From the 16th century forward, France dedicated much of its military strength to <u>acquiring possessions overseas and quelling rebellion in its colonies</u>. Its colonial decline began in the early 1950s with a failed attempt to overcome a Vietnamese nationalist or communist movement. The French suffered <u>a humiliating defeat and surrender</u> to the Vietnamese forces in the northern part of the country, after <u>being surrounded and shelled</u> for an extended period. Trouble continued through that decade, with France losing the last of its major colonies, Algeria, as the decade closed. Despite this, several former French colonies, especially those in Africa, <u>occasionally expect to receive military assistance</u> from France.

W: 오늘은 프랑스 역사에서 가장 중요한 요소 중의 하나라고 할 수 있는 프랑스 식민주의에 대해 계속하겠습니다. 16세기 이후, 프랑스는 해외로부터 부를 취득하고 식민지의 폭동을 진압하는 데 군사적 힘을 쏟았습니다. 프랑스의 식민지 쇠퇴는 1950년대 초 베트남 민족주의자, 혹은 공산주의자 활동을 저지하려는 시도가 실패로 돌아가면서 시작되었습니다. 프랑스 사람들은 장기간 포위된 상태로 포격을 받은 후, 패배의 치욕을 겪으며 베트남 북부에서 베트남군에 항복하였습니다. 그 십년간 어려움은 지속되었고 프랑스는 그 십년이 끝날 즈음에 마지막 주요 식민지였던 알제리까지 잃었습니다. 그럼에도 불구하고 몇몇 이전의 프랑스 식민지 국가들, 특히 아프리카 내 식민국들은 때때로 프랑스로부터 군사적 도움을 받기를 기대하고 있습니다.

Q Which is correct according to the lecture?

(a) France turned to colonialism before the 16th century.

(b) French colonies sometimes rebelled against French authorities.

(c) France won a military campaign in Vietnam in the early 1950s.

(d) French colonies were ruled by armies comprised of natives.

강의에 따르면 다음 중 옳은 것은?

(a) 프랑스는 16세기 이전에 식민주의로 전향했다.

(b) 프랑스 식민지 국가들은 때때로 프랑스 당국에 반란을 일으켰다.

(c) 프랑스는 1950년대 초 베트남에서 일어난 군사 작전에서 승리했다.

(d) 프랑스 식민지 국가들은 토착민들로 구성된 군대에 의해 지배되었다.

해설 프랑스 식민주의의 쇠퇴에 관한 강의이다. 16세기 이후 시작된 프랑스 식민주의는 무력으로 식민지의 반란군을 진압하고 재산을 착취하였으나, 1950년 베트남 공산주의자에게 패함으로써 그 막을 내렸다는 내용의 강의이다. 따라서 강의의 내용과 일치하는 것은 (b)이다.

함정 (a) 프랑스가 식민주의로 전향한 것은 16세기 이후이며, (c) 1950년대 초 베트남에서 일어난 전쟁에서 패하면서 식민주의가 끝나게 되었다.

어휘 colonialism 식민주의 | dedicate A to B B에 A를 바치다 | possession 재산, 부 | quell 억누르다, 진압하다 | rebellion 반란, 폭동 | colonial 식민지의 | decline 쇠퇴, 하락 | attempt 시도 | communist 공산주의 | movement 활동, 운동 | humiliating 치욕이 되는, 굴욕적인 | defeat 패배 | surrender 항복 | shell 포격하다 | extended 장기간에 걸친

LISTENING REVIEW

A

1. habitat	2. hostility
3. sober	4. abundant
5. droop	6. cuddle
7. embezzle	8. unwind
9. destroyer	10. solitude
11. state-of-the-art	12. encroach
13. fraud	14. populism
15. humiliating	16. reconnaissance

1. the natural environment in which an animal or plant normally lives or grows

2. unfriendly or aggressive behavior towards people or ideas

3. not drunk

4. present in large quantities

5. to hang or lean downwards with no strength or firmness

6. to put your arms around someone and hold them close as a way of showing your affection

7. to take and use money of someone's organization or company illegally for one's own purposes

8. to relax after you have done something that makes you tense or tired

9. a small, heavily armed warship

10. the state of being alone, especially when this is peaceful and pleasant

11. being the best available because it has been made using the most modern techniques and technology

12. to spread and take over more and more of a place

13. the crime of gaining money or financial benefits by a trick or lying

14. political activities or ideas that claim to promote the interests and opinions of ordinary people

15. embarrassing you and making you feel ashamed and stupid

16. the activity of obtaining military information about a place by sending soldiers or planes there, or by the use of satellites

B

1. a	2. a	3. a	4. b	5. b

1. 적어도 전화해서 알려 줄 수 있었잖아요.

   (a) At least you could have called to let me know.

   (b) At most you must have called to let me know.

2. 함대의 공개된 부분을 자유롭게 둘러보세요.

   (a) You are free to look around selected areas of the ship.

   (b) Don't hesitate to select areas you would like to check on the ship.

3. 프랑스는 해외에서 부를 취득하는 데 군사적 힘을 쏟았다.

   (a) France dedicated much of its military strength to acquiring possessions overseas.

   (b) The French suffered a humiliating defeat and surrender overseas.

4. 윤리 개념이 그 중대성을 제대로 인정받지 못해 왔다.

   (a) The importance of ethics didn't deserve the value it has gained.

   (b) The concept of ethics has not gained the importance it deserves.

5. 세금 인상이 부유층에 돌아가지 않고, 실제로는 중산층에게 돌아갈 것이다.

   (a) The tax increase would create an immense tax burden for both upper and middle-income citizens.

   (b) The tax increase, instead of falling on the wealthy, would in truth fall mainly on the middle class.

C

1. The one who got promoted kept on calling.

2. It is clear what has affected both men's styles.

3. The system it has enables the ship to engage over 200 land targets.

4. I can't make Ms. Johnson wait at the restaurant for a long time.

5. Spending so much time in front of the computer may not be healthy for you.

1. the one / kept on calling / who got promoted

2. both men's styles / what has affected / it is clear

3. it has / the system / enables the ship to engage over 200 land targets

4. Ms. Johnson / wait at the restaurant for a long time / I can't make

5. in front of the computer / spending so much time / may not be healthy for you

D

1. a	2. b	3. a	4. a	5. b

1. These turtles may become extinct one day.

   (a) These turtles are on the verge of extinction.

   (b) These turtles are one of the oldest species on Earth.

2. Because I didn't know, I could not do anything to kill them.

   (a) If I knew, I could do something to kill them.

   (b) If I had known, I could have done something to kill them.

3. His co-worker didn't let anybody go early.

   (a) His co-worker kept on insisting everybody stay late.

   (b) His co-worker took everybody out for drinks.

4. Babies can distinguish humans from other objects.

   **(a) Babies' reaction to human faces is different from
   their reaction to inanimate objects.**

   (b) Babies try to react differently to any objects and hold
   them.

5. The UN will reduce the number of peacekeepers in
   Yugoslavia.

   (a) The countries had supplied most of the troops to the
   UN peacekeeping forces in Yugoslavia.

   **(b) The UN will call back some of its peacekeeping
   personnel in Yugoslavia.**

VOCABULARY PREVIEW

01. conclusive 결정적인, 확실한

02. substantial 실질적인

03. fake-looking 가짜처럼 보이는

04. kidney 신장

05. transplant 이식

06. prognosis 예후

07. magnificent 장대한, 굉장한

08. prominent 저명한, 탁월한

09. intimate 깊은, 심오한

10. glimpse 일별, 힐끗 봄

11. delve into ~을 탐구하다

12. aptly 적절히, 교묘히

13. glamorize 낭만적으로 다루다, 미화하다

14. conceive 생각하다, 고안하다

15. venue 장소, 현장

16. mingle 어울리다, 섞이다

17. acclaim 갈채하다, 환호하다

18. span (짧은) 기간, 거리

19. marvel 놀라운 일, 경이로움

20. by leaps and bounds 급속도로

21. obese 살찐, 뚱뚱한

22. console 위로하다

23. compelling 강력한, 감탄하지 않을 수 없는

24. custody 구류

GUIDED LISTENING

1	1. a	2. a	2	1. d	2. a
3	1. c	2. c	4	1. c	2. c

1 Conversation

W: Do you know Derek?

M: The guy <u>who wears a ponytail</u> and <u>stays next to the bakery</u>?

W: Yeah. He wants to join us for our hiking trip.

M: Sounds strange! I've never seen him talking to anybody. What did you say to him?

W: Well, I told him that <u>I'd ask everybody and get back to him</u>. What do you think?

M: Is everybody okay with it?

W: No, actually nobody liked <u>the idea of taking him along</u>. I just don't understand why.

M: Well, I heard that <u>he has a bad temper</u> and <u>that's why he doesn't get along with people</u>.

W: Maybe that's the reason he's always alone.

W: Derek을 알아?

M: 꽁지머리를 하고 빵집 옆에 사는 애?

W: 그래. 걔가 우리랑 하이킹 가고 싶대.

M: 이상하네! 나는 걔가 누구한테 말 거는 것을 본 적이 없어. 그래서 너는 걔한테 뭐라고 했어?

W: 음, 모두에게 물어 보고 대답하겠다고 했지. 어떻게 생각해?

M: 모두 괜찮대?

W: 아니, 사실 아무도 걔랑 같이 간다는 생각을 좋아하지 않더라. 왜 그런지 모르겠어.

M: 음, 걔는 성격이 안 좋아서 사람들과 잘 지내지 못한다고 들었어.

W: 아마도 그게 걔가 항상 혼자인 이유인가 봐.

Comprehension

1 What does NOT match the information in the conversation?

(a) They have never met Derek before.

(b) Derek is known to have a bad temper.

(c) The man and the woman are going hiking.

(d) The man does not have a good opinion of Derek.

이 대화의 내용과 일치하지 않는 것은?

(a) 그들은 Derek을 전에 만난 적이 없다.

(b) Derek은 성격이 나쁘다고 알려졌다.

(c) 남자와 여자는 하이킹을 갈 것이다.

(d) 남자는 Derek에 대해 좋은 의견을 가지고 있지 않다.

해설 하이킹을 함께 가자고 했던 Derek이라는 아이에 관한 대화이다. 남자와 여자는 다른 사람들과 하이킹을 갈 것인데, 남자나 여자 모두 그와 함께 가는 것을 탐탁지 않게 생각하고 있다. (b), (c), (d)는 모두 대화의 내

용과 일치하나, (a)는 Derek이 여자에게 하이킹에 같이 가자고 했던 것으로 보아, 일치하지 않는다는 것을 알 수 있다.

Inference II

2   What can be inferred about the man?

(a) He is not comfortable with Derek.

(b) He doesn't know who Derek is.

(c) He doesn't want others to join.

(d) He is not familiar with the other friends.

남자에 대해 추론할 수 있는 것은?

(a) Derek을 별로 마음에 들어 하지 않는다.

(b) Derek이 누구인지 알지 못한다.

(c) 다른 사람들이 끼는 것을 원하지 않는다.

(d) 다른 친구들과 친하지 않다.

해설 남자는 소문을 들어 Derek에 대한 좋지 않은 견해를 가지고 있으므로 (a)가 정답이다.

함정 (b) 남자는 Derek과 친하지는 않지만 누구인지는 알고 있다. (c)와 (d)는 알 수 없는 내용이다.

어휘 ponytail 포니테일(뒤에서 묶어 아래로 드리운 머리)
take along ~을 가지고[데리고] 가다 | familiar 친한, 익숙한

2 Conversation

W: Can you believe this? There's another photo of Bigfoot in the newspaper. They're <u>trying to trace its source</u>.

M: Let me see. This one looks like a real picture.

W: Don't you think it could just be <u>a man in some gorilla suit</u>?

M: Not likely. The report also says that they've found <u>some hair samples</u>.

W: The results of the hair samples are never conclusive. Don't you remember the mammoth case? They <u>couldn't tell to whom or what those hairs belonged</u>.

M: You're right, but I'm sure this time they'll be able to find <u>something substantial</u>.

W: But they <u>don't have any proof</u> that Bigfoot exists, except for some fake-looking photographs and some odd hair samples.

M: Well, there are people who say that they have seen Bigfoot.

W: I don't believe those jerks. They might have seen

some ordinary animal in the dark.

W: 이걸 믿을 수 있겠어요? 신문에 Bigfoot 사진이 또 나왔어요. 진원지를 찾고 있대요.

M: 어디 봐요. 이건 진짜 사진 같네요.

W: 고릴라 복장을 한 남자일 것 같다고 생각하지 않으세요?

M: 그런 것 같지는 않은데요. 그 기사에는 털 샘플도 발견했다고 되어 있어요.

W: 털 샘플의 결과는 절대 결정적이지 않아요. 매머드의 경우가 기억나지 않으세요? 그 털들이 누구에게 또는 무엇에 속했던 것인지 알 수 없었잖아요.

M: 맞아요. 하지만 이번에는 뭔가 실제적인 것들을 알아낼 수 있을 거예요.

W: 하지만 가짜 같아 보이는 사진들과 단편적인 몇몇 털 샘플 말고는 Bigfoot이 존재한다는 어떤 증거도 없어요.

M: 음, Bigfoot을 보았다고 말하는 사람들도 있어요.

W: 그런 바보들 말은 믿지 않아요. 아마 어둠 속에서 어떤 평범한 동물을 봤을 거예요.

Comprehension

1   Which of the following is correct according to the conversation?

(a) The man and other people have seen Bigfoot.

(b) The woman thinks the photos are real.

(c) The hair samples belong to Bigfoot.

(d) The woman thinks there is lack of proof.

이 대화에 따르면 다음 중 옳은 것은?

(a) 남자와 다른 사람은 Bigfoot을 본 적이 있다.

(b) 여자는 사진이 진짜일 거라고 생각한다.

(c) 털 샘플은 Bigfoot의 것이다.

(d) 여자는 증거가 부족하다고 생각한다.

해설 숲속에 사는 크고 이상한 괴물이라고 알려진 Bigfoot에 관한 대화이다. 남자는 Bigfoot이 존재할 수도 있다고 믿는 반면, 여자는 그렇지 않을 거라고 이야기하고 있다. 누군가 고릴라 복장을 한 사진일 수도 있고 주변에서 발견된 털 샘플이 누구의 것인지는 아직 밝혀지지 않아서, 여자는 믿을 수 없다고 생각하므로 (d)가 정답이다.

Inference II

2   What can be inferred from the conversation?

(a) They have seen the photo of Bigfoot before.

(b) They have some proof that Bigfoot exists.

(c) The man thinks that gorilla suits are too widely available.

(d) The woman believes that the hair samples prove

Bigfoot's existence.

이 대화에서 추론할 수 있는 것은?

(a) 그들은 전에도 Bigfoot의 사진을 본 적이 있다.

(b) 그들은 Bigfoot이 존재한다는 증거를 가지고 있다.

(c) 남자는 고릴라 복장이 너무 널리 사용된다고 생각한다.

(d) 여자는 털 샘플이 Bigfoot의 존재를 증명하는 것이라고 믿는다.

[해설] 남녀의 첫 번째 대화, 신문에 Bigfoot 사진이 또 나왔다는 여자의 말과 이번에는 진짜 같다는 남자의 말로 보아, 그들이 이전에도 Bigfoot의 사진을 본 적이 있다는 것을 추론할 수 있다.

[함정] (d)는 이 대화와 관련 없는 내용이다. 털 샘플이 Bigfoot의 존재를 증명해 줄 것이라고 믿는 사람은 여자가 아니라 남자이므로, (d)는 오답이다.

[어휘] trace 추적하다 | suit 복장 | conclusive 결정적인, 확실한 | mammoth 매머드 | belong to ~에 속하다 | substantial 실질적인 | fake-looking 가짜처럼 보이는 | odd 단편적인, 우연한, 임시의 | jerk 바보, 얼간이 | ordinary 평범한, 보통의

3 Monologue

M: William Wright underwent surgery to receive liver, heart and kidney transplants yesterday, and to everybody's amazement his condition seems to be stable. His condition was initially critical but has now dramatically improved. He is being taken care of in the intensive care unit of Boston General Hospital. All three organs of Mr. Wright were diseased and had to be removed. The surgery went on for about 16 hours and 20 minutes. The doctor who headed the surgical team that performed the surgery said that the coming few days will be important in terms of overall prognosis. Considering the present condition of Mr. Wright, the doctors are hopeful for his complete recovery. Mr. Wright is expected to remain in the intensive care unit for another week.

M: William Wright는 어제 간, 심장과 신장 이식 수술을 받았고, 모든 사람들이 놀랍게도 그의 상태는 안정되어 보입니다. 처음에는 그의 상태가 위험했지만, 지금은 극적으로 호전되었습니다. 그는 Boston General Hospital의 중환자실에서 치료를 받고 있습니다. Wright 씨의 3가지 장기 모두는 병이 들어서 제거해야 했습니다. 수술은 약 16시간 20분 동안 계속되었습니다. 이 수술을 행했던 수술 팀 팀장 의사는 앞으로 며칠이 전반적인 예후에 중요할 것이라고 말했습니다. Wright 씨의 현재 상태를 고려해 보면, 의사들은 그의 완벽한 회복에 희망적입니다. Wright 씨는 중환자실에서 일주일 더 치료를 받을 예정입니다.

Comprehension

1 Which is correct about William Wright?

(a) He doesn't have heart surgery.

(b) He has been in critical condition for a week.

(c) He's in stable condition presently.

(d) His surgery was finished within an hour.

William Wright에 대해 다음 중 옳은 것은?

(a) 그는 심장 수술을 받지 않았다.

(b) 그는 일주일 동안 위험한 상태이다.

(c) 그는 현재 안정된 상태이다.

(d) 그의 수술은 한 시간 안에 끝났다.

[해설] 3개의 장기 이식 수술을 받은 William Wright에 관한 내용이다. 16시간 이상 수술을 받았고, 처음에는 위험했지만 지금은 안정된 상태여서 회복이 희망적이다. 그러므로 옳은 것은 (c)이다.

[함정] 처음에는 위험했다는 내용은 있지만, 일주일 동안이라는 언급은 없으므로 (b)는 오답이다.

Inference II

2 What can be inferred from the news?

(a) William will be given permission to leave the hospital after a week.

(b) The doctors are hesitant to announce the positive result.

(c) William will need a great deal of care for a certain period of time.

(d) It was the biggest surgery that the team has performed.

이 뉴스에서 추론할 수 있는 것은?

(a) William은 일주일 후에 퇴원이 허락될 것이다.

(b) 의료진은 긍정적인 결과를 발표하기 꺼리고 있다.

(c) William은 일정 기간 동안 집중 치료가 필요하다.

(d) 그것이 그 팀이 수술했던 가장 큰 대수술이었다.

[해설] 마지막 문장 Mr. Wright is expected to remain in the intensive care unit for another week.(Wright씨는 일주일 더 집중 치료를 받을 예정입니다.)에서 (c)의 내용을 추론할 수 있다.

[함정] (a) William은 일주일 간 집중 치료를 받을 것이다. (b) 의료진은 긍정적인 결과에 희망적임을 발표하고 있다. (d)에 관한 내용은 알 수 없다.

[어휘] surgery 수술 | liver 간 | kidney 신장 | transplant 이식 | stable 안정된 | initially 처음에는 | take care of ~을 돌보다, 보살피다 | intensive care unit 중환자실, 집중 치료부 병동 | organ 기관, 장기 | prognosis 예후

4 Monologue

W: Kings or "pharaohs" in ancient Egypt used to be buried in impressive funeral masks. An example worth citing is that of Tutankhamen's. Tutankhamen was a teenage pharaoh, who died when he was just 18 years of age. He was buried in a grand funeral mask which was made out of solid gold. In addition to the gold, it also contained the best treasures of Egypt available at that time. His funeral mask looked magnificent, and well represented the artistry of Egypt in earlier times. Tutankhamen's tomb was first opened in 1922, many centuries after he was buried. There is evidence to indicate the era of Egyptian history to which he belonged. But, there is no mention of Tutankhamen in Egyptian writings, suggesting that he may have not been a very prominent figure in his times.

W: 고대 이집트의 왕, 즉 "파라오"는 인상적인 장례식용 마스크를 쓰고 묻히곤 했습니다. 예로 들 만한 것은 투탕카멘의 마스크입니다. 투탕카멘은 10대 때 왕이 되었는데, 겨우 18세에 사망하였습니다. 그는 순금으로 만들어진 웅대한 장례식용 황금마스크를 쓰고 묻혔습니다. 금 외에도, 그 시대에 있을 수 있는 이집트의 가장 좋은 보물들로 장식되어 있었습니다. 그의 장례식용 황금마스크는 장엄해 보이는데, 고대 이집트의 예술성을 잘 보여 주고 있습니다. 투탕카멘의 무덤은 1922년에 처음 공개되었는데, 그것은 그가 묻힌 후 많은 세기가 흐른 뒤였습니다. 거기에는 그가 속했던 이집트 역사의 시대를 가르쳐 주는 증거가 있습니다. 그러나 이집트 기록들에는 투탕카멘에 대한 언급이 없는데, 이는 그가 그의 시대에 매우 탁월한 인물은 아니었을지 모른다는 점을 제시하는 것입니다.

Comprehension

1 Which is correct about Tutankhamen, according to the lecture?

(a) He was known for his long life.

(b) He was one of the most influential kings.

(c) His achievements were not documented.

(d) His tomb was found outside a pyramid.

이 강의에 따르면, 투탕카멘에 대해 옳은 것은?

(a) 그는 장수한 것으로 유명하다.

(b) 그는 가장 영향력 있는 왕들 중 하나였다.

(c) 그의 업적은 기록되어 있지 않았다.

(d) 그의 무덤은 피라미드 밖에서 발견되었다.

해설 투탕카멘 무덤에 관한 강의이다. 투탕카멘은 10대 때 왕이 되어, 18세에 요절한 왕이었는데, 20세기 초에 그 피라미드가 발견되어 공개되었다. 투탕카멘은 장례식용 황금마스크를 쓰고 묻혀 있었지만, 이집트 기록에는 투탕카멘에 관한 자료가 없는 것으로 보아, 탁월한 왕은 아니었을지

모른다고 했다. 그러므로 투탕카멘에 대해 옳은 것은 (c)이다.

Detail

2 What can we learn from the treasures in the tomb?

(a) his age of death

(b) how prominent he was

(c) the era he lived in

(d) his artistic taste

무덤에서 발견된 보물들로 우리는 무엇을 알 수 있는가?

(a) 그가 죽은 나이

(b) 그가 얼마나 탁월했는지

(c) 그가 살았던 시대

(d) 그의 미적 취향

해설 중간 부분의 There is evidence to indicate the era of Egyptian history to which he belonged.(거기에는 그가 속했던 이집트 역사의 시대를 가르쳐 주는 증거가 있습니다.)로 보아, 그가 살았던 시대를 알 수 있으므로 (c)가 정답이다.

어휘 **pharaoh** (고대 이집트의) 왕, 파라오 | **funeral** 장례식의 | **cite** 인용하다 | **Tutankhamen** 투탕카멘 (기원전 14세기 이집트 제 18왕조의 젊은 왕; 1922년에 그 분묘가 발견되었음.) | **grand** 웅대한, 장엄한 | **be made out of** ~으로 만들어지다 | **solid gold** 순금 | **in addition to** ~외에도 | **magnificent** 장대한, 굉장한 | **artistry** 예술적 기교(수완) | **era** 시대, 시기 | **prominent** 저명한, 탁월한 | **figure** 인물

PRACTICAL LISTENING

1. b	2. a	3. d	4. b	5. c
6. d	7. d	8. b	9. d	10. b

1 Comprehension

M: Today's lecture deals with one of the greatest figures in French Literature, Michel De Montagne. His essays during the Renaissance provided intimate glimpses into his own life and delved deep into his feelings. He wrote of his failing memory, his scorn of man's thirst for fame and his wish to detach himself from all things worldly. Even as he wrote about himself, Montagne was in fact chronicling all mankind. His true genius lies in this achievement.

M: 오늘 강의에서는 프랑스 문학의 거성 중 하나인 Michel De

Montagne를 다루겠습니다. 르네상스 시대에 쓴 그의 에세이는 그의 삶을 깊게 엿볼 수 있으며, 그의 정서를 깊게 탐구했습니다. 그는 자신의 쇠락해가는 기억력, 명성을 갈구하는 인간에 대한 냉소, 세속으로부터 벗어나고 싶은 자신의 소망을 글로 썼습니다. 비록 자신에 대한 이야기였지만, Montagne는 사실 모든 인류에 대해 기술한 것이었습니다. 그의 진정한 천재성은 이러한 성과에 있습니다.

Q Which is correct about Montagne according to the lecture?

(a) His sense of detachment kept him from pursuing fame.

(b) His largely autobiographical writing aptly captured human nature.

(c) He glamorized himself in order to comment on humanity.

(d) He detailed common people's everyday lives with great accuracy.

강의에 따르면 Montagne에 관해 옳은 것은?

(a) 그는 초연함 때문에 명성을 추구하지 않았다.

(b) 그의 광범위한 자서전적 글은 인간의 본성을 적절히 파악했다.

(c) 인간성에 대해 이야기하기 위해 자신을 미화했다.

(d) 그는 보통 사람들의 일상생활을 아주 정확히 묘사했다.

해설 프랑스 작가 Michel De Montagne에 대한 강의 내용이다. 마지막 두 번째 문장에서 화자는 작가가 자신의 얘기를 썼지만, 자신뿐만 아니라 인류 자체에 대한 성찰이 담겨 있다고 말하고 있다. 따라서 (b)가 정답이다.

함정 (a) 결국 명성을 갈구하는 인간을 냉소했다는 내용이 자신에게도 해당하는 것임을 알아야 한다. 본문 내용에서는 작가 자신의 삶과 정서를 에세이에 잘 드러냈다고 했으므로, 이 에세이에서 자신을 미화했다고 보기 어렵다. 따라서 (c)와 (d)는 오답이다.

어휘 intimate 깊은, 심오한 | glimpse 일별, 힐끗 봄 | delve into ~을 탐구하다 | failing 약해 가는 | scorn 경멸, 냉소 | detach oneself from ~로부터 이탈하다, 떨어지다 | chronicle 연대순으로 기록하다 | aptly 적절히, 교묘히 | glamorize 낭만적으로 다루다, 미화하다 | detachment 분리, 초연함 | with accuracy 정확하게

2

M: I think we should get a second car now.

W: Yes. The office is quite far. Going by car would give us more flexibility. But I'm not sure if we can afford it.

M: How about getting a loan?

W: The interest rate for the loan will be really high. I don't think we can afford that.

M: How about buying a used car?

W: Buying a used car wouldn't solve the problem completely. You know those reliable used cars are still expensive, and we will still need some money.

M: We can draw our savings out. How about that?

W: Maybe. But what about the cost of insurance and gas?

M: Well, if we get a small car, we could manage those costs.

W: Fine, let's go ahead with it.

M: 차를 한 대 더 사야 할 것 같은데.

W: 응, 사무실이 너무 멀어서, 차로 가는 게 더 많은 융통성을 가져다 줄 거야. 그런데 그걸 살 만한 여유가 될지 모르겠네.

M: 대출 받는 건 어때?

W: 대출 이자율이 상당히 높을 거야. 그걸 감당할 여유가 없을 것 같아.

M: 중고차를 사는 건 어때?

W: 중고차를 산다고 해서 문제가 완전히 해결되는 것은 아니야. 너도 알잖아, 믿을 만한 중고차는 그래도 비싸기 때문에, 돈이 좀 필요할 거야.

M: 적금을 좀 뺄 수도 있잖아. 어떻게 생각해?

W: 그럴 수도 있지. 하지만 근데 보험료랑 기름값은 어쩌지?

M: 음, 경차를 산다면 그 비용을 어떻게든 꾸려나갈 수 있을 거야.

W: 좋아, 그럼 그렇게 추진하자.

Q What are the man and woman mainly discussing?

(a) whether they can buy a second car or not

(b) how highly-priced cars are

(c) what kind of car they will buy

(d) where they will get a loan from

여자와 남자는 주로 무슨 이야기를 하고 있는가?

(a) 차를 한 대 더 살지 말지

(b) 차가 얼마나 비싼지

(c) 어떤 모델의 차를 살 것인지

(d) 어디서 대출을 받을지

해설 사무실이 너무 멀어서 차를 한 대 더 사야 하는데, 그럴 만한 여유가 되는지에 대해 이야기하고 있다. 대출은 받지 않고 적금을 빼서, 소형차를 사면 유지비가 줄어들고 감당해낼 수 있겠다는 결론에 도달했다. 따라서 정답은 (a)가 된다.

어휘 second 두 번째의, 또 하나의, 추가의 | flexibility 유연성, 융통성 | afford ~할 여유가 있다 | loan 대출, 융자 | insurance 보험 |

manage 어떻게든 ~하다, ~을 경영하다, 꾸려나가다 |
go ahead with ~을 진행하다, 자, 어서 ~하세요 |
highly-priced 고가의, 비싼

3

W: As founders of the United Film Festival, we are proud to see it enter its 20th year. We <u>look back with pride on its beginnings</u> and look forward to its great future. We're proud to say that many young directors <u>found the first major screenings of their movies</u> here, such as Ming Li Pao, who released his first film, "Shades of Autumn" at the festival, and later became one of the greatest directors in the world. The festival was conceived as a platform to bring together Western and Eastern cultures <u>through the common medium of film</u>. It is one of the best venues for directors, actors, and producers from two different cultures <u>to mix and mingle</u>. We never imagined it would become an <u>internationally acclaimed</u> event <u>in such a short span of time</u>.

- -

W: United 영화제의 창시자로서 우리는 영화제가 20주년이 된 것을 자랑스럽게 생각합니다. 우리는 영화제가 시작했을 때를 자부심을 가지고 돌아보고 또한 커다란 미래를 기대합니다. 우리는 많은 젊은 영화감독들의 첫 작품이 이곳에서 상영되었다는 것을 자랑스럽게 얘기할 수 있습니다. 예를 들어 Ming Li Pao 감독의 첫 영화 '가을의 그림자'는 이 영화제에서 상영되었는데, 나중에 그는 세계적인 감독이 되었습니다. 본 영화제는 동서양 문화를 영화라는 공동 매개체로 이어보자는 취지로 계획되었습니다. 서로 다른 두 문화의 감독, 배우, 제작자들이 섞이고 어울릴 수 있는 곳이 바로 우리 영화제입니다. 우리는 이렇게 짧은 기간 내에 국제적인 명성과 갈채를 받는 영화제가 되리라고는 상상조차 할 수 없었습니다.

Q What can be inferred about the festival?

(a) It launches new film-makers.

(b) It helped its founders earn international fame.

(c) It is dedicated to preserving Western cultural identity.

(d) It features both Western and Asian films.

이 행사에 대해 추론할 수 있는 것은?

(a) 새로운 영화 제작사를 출범시킨다.

(b) 창시자들이 국제적인 명성을 얻게 하였다.

(c) 서양 문화 정체성을 지키도록 헌신하고 있다.

(d) 서양과 동양의 영화를 모두 다룬다.

해설 20주년이 된 영화제 소개이다. 이 영화제가 동서양을 잇는 국제 가교 역할을 한다는 점에서 서양과 동양의 모든 영화들을 소개한다는 것을 추론

할 수 있다.

함정 영화 제작사가 아니라 영화 감독의 진출에 대해 말하고 있으므로 (a)는 오답이며, (b)는 언급되지 않았다. (c)는 반대되는 말인데, 정체성을 지키기보다는 서로 다른 두 문화의 감독, 제작자, 배우들이 섞이고 어울리는 장으로서의 영화제가 언급되고 있다.

어휘 founder 창시자 | look forward to ~을 기대하다, 기다리다 |
release 개봉하다, 공개하다 | conceive 생각하다, 고안하다 |
venue 장소, 현장 | mingle 어울리다, 섞이다 |
acclaim 갈채하다, 환호하다 | span (짧은) 기간, 거리

4

W: Oh, tomorrow is <u>the deadline to submit this article</u>! I hate deadlines.

M: But as a journalist <u>you can't avoid them</u>.

W: If I'd had few more hours, <u>I could have written it much better</u>.

M: It's not only you, all journalists feel the need for more time.

W: Do you also think that way?

M: Yes. I <u>get quite stressed out</u> working under deadlines.

W: I'm surprised to know that. I mean you always look relaxed and seem to have a lot of time.

M: Do I? Well, that's not true at all. <u>I work my head off</u> when I have to.

- -

W: 아, 내일이 기사 제출 마감일이네! 마감은 정말 싫어.

M: 하지만 기자가 그걸 피할 순 없지.

W: 시간이 조금만 더 있었어도, 훨씬 더 잘 쓸 수 있었을 텐데.

M: 너만 그런 게 아냐. 모든 기자들이 시간이 더 필요하다고 느껴.

W: 너도 그렇게 생각하니?

M: 응. 마감에 쫓기면서 일해서 나도 정말 스트레스 받는다고.

W: 그렇다니 정말 놀랍네. 내 말은, 너는 항상 느긋하고 시간이 많은 것처럼 보이거든.

M: 내가? 음, 그건 전혀 사실이 아니야. 급할 때는 진짜 정신없이 일한다고.

Q What is mainly being discussed?

(a) the deadline of the article

(b) the burden of meeting deadlines

(c) the scope of journalism

(d) the man's career as a journalist

주로 무엇이 이야기되고 있는가?

(a) 기사 마감일

(b) 기사 마감을 맞추는 부담감

(c) 언론의 영역

(d) 기자로서의 남자 직업

해설 기사 마감일에 대해 두 사람이 어떻게 느끼고 있는지에 관한 대화이다. 여자는 '마감이 정말 싫다.(I hate deadlines.)'고 하면서, 마감에 대한 스트레스를 직접적으로 표현하고 있으며, 남자도 역시 마감에 쫓겨 가면서 일해서 정말 스트레스 받는다고 말하고 있다. 따라서 두 사람은 마감이 얼마나 많은 부담감과 스트레스를 주는지에 대해 서로 이야기하고 있으므로, 정답은 (b)이다. 나머지 (c)와 (d)는 언급되지 않았다.

함정 내일로 닥쳐온 기사 마감 때문에 여자가 괴로워하고 있는 장면으로 대화가 시작되고 있으며, 남자도 역시 그것으로 인해 많이 스트레스를 받는다고 말하고 있다. 따라서 두 사람은 '기사 마감일 자체에 대해서 이야기하고 있는 것이 아니라, 그것이 주는 부담감이나 스트레스에 대해서 서로 이야기하고 있는 것이므로, (a)는 정답이 아니다.

어휘 deadline 원고 마감 시간, 마감 시한 | submit ~을 제출하다 |
journalist 기자, 언론인 |
stressed out 스트레스로 지친, 스트레스가 쌓인 | relaxed 느긋한 |
work one's head off 뼈 빠지게 일하다, 몰두해서 일하다 |
burden 짐, 의무, 부담, 피로움 | scope 범위, 영역

방 한 편에서 로봇을 지휘하는 것을 볼 수 있습니다. 환상적인 볼거리가 될 것입니다. 자 바로 지금부터 보실까요?

Q What is mainly being introduced here?

(a) surgeons endorsing technology

(b) Paris as a leader in medical science

(c) the latest robot-assisted surgery

(d) the risks in remote control surgery

여기서 주로 소개되고 있는 것은 무엇인가?

(a) 의사들이 보증하는 기술

(b) 의료계에서 선두적인 파리

(c) 최신 로봇이 돕는 수술

(d) 원격 조정 수술의 위험성

해설 기술의 발달로 인한 로봇이 참여하고 집도의가 조정하는 수술 과정에 대한 설명이 주를 이루고 있으므로 정답은 (c)이다.

어휘 marvel 놀라운 일, 경이로움 |
by leaps and bounds 급속도로 | advance 진척, 향상 |
chief surgeon 집도의 | fascinating 놀라운 |
endorse 보증하다, (어음 따위에) 배서하다 | assist 돕다

5

W: Welcome to TechWatch, where we show you scientific marvels from around the world. This week's edition of TechWatch takes you to Europe as we bring you the latest in medical technology. As we know, that's a field growing by leaps and bounds — with new advances that allow doctors to treat patients more effectively and safer than ever. Through the use of these technologies, medicine is being truly revolutionized on several levels. First, we go to Paris to watch a robot helping with an open heart surgery. The chief surgeon is not at the operating table for this procedure. Instead you can watch him directing it from the far side of the room by using a remote control device. It promises to be a fascinating spectacle. Let's watch right now!

W: 전 세계 과학의 경이로움을 보여 줄 TechWatch에 오신 것을 환영합니다. 이번 주 TechWatch에서는 유럽의 최신 의료 기술을 보여 드릴까 합니다. 우리가 알고 있듯이 이 분야는 새로운 기술의 증진으로 인하여 의사들로 하여금 이전의 어느 때보다 더 효과적이고 안전하게 환자들을 치료할 수 있게 하며 급속도록 발전하고 있습니다. 이러한 기술을 이용함으로써 의학은 몇몇 단계를 비약적으로 뛰어넘고 있습니다. 우선 우리는 심장 절개 수술을 돕는 로봇을 보기위해 파리로 갈 것입니다. 집도의는 이 수술 과정에 함께 하지 않습니다. 대신 집도의가 원격 조정기를 이용하여 수술

6

M: If your child has a serious obesity problem, it's time to begin establishing healthy eating habits. Waiting could have terrible health consequences. Obese children are prone to a wide variety of illnesses, including heart disease and diabetes. It's important to establish healthy habits and proper weight management to avoid that. Don't overemphasize physical appearance, though, because that rarely works. Indeed, it could sometimes cause the opposite to happen, with a child who is depressed about his appearance eating more to console himself. Instead, enforce a regular routine of balanced eating and a schedule of physical exercise to boost weight loss. Most importantly, you need to avoid bad eating habits so they do not ruin your child's health. Make sure that you cook healthy meals at home for the child. Set a positive example, too by eating right yourself.

M: 만약 당신의 아이가 심각한 비만 문제를 안고 있다면, 이제는 건강한 식습관을 쌓아나가야 할 때입니다. 마냥 기다리기만 한다면 더욱 심각한 결과를 초래할 것입니다. 비만 아이들은 심장병 및 당뇨 등의 다양한 질병을 앓기 쉽습니다. 이러한 문제점들을 피하기 위하여 건강 습관과 적정한 체중 관리를 하는 것이 중요합니다. 효과가 거의 없으니 신체적인 외모를

너무 강조하지는 마세요. 사실 외모에 너무 스트레스를 받는 아이들은 스스로를 위로하기 위하여 더 많이 먹는 반대의 결과를 초래하기도 합니다. 대신 규칙적이고 균형 잡힌 식습관과 체중 감량을 활성화시키기 위한 운동 시간표를 시행해 보세요. 가장 중요한 점은 당신 스스로 나쁜 식습관을 피함으로써 아이들 건강을 해치지 않는 것입니다. 아이를 위하여 건강한 음식을 요리하는 것을 잊지 마세요. 또한 스스로 바른 식습관을 통하여 긍정적인 예가 되어 보세요.

Q What is the main topic of the talk?

(a) what behaviors parents should avoid

(b) which diets are unsuitable for young children

(c) why young children become overweight

(d) how parents can help overweight children

이 이야기의 주요 화제는 무엇인가?

(a) 어떤 행동을 부모들이 피해야 하는지

(b) 어떤 식습관이 아이들에게 적합하지 않는지

(c) 왜 어린아이들이 비만이 되는지

(d) 과체중인 아이들을 부모가 어떻게 도울 수 있는지

해설 자녀들의 비만을 해소하기 위한 부모들의 행동 지침을 제시하고 있다. 첫 문장에 담화의 주제가 잘 드러나 있다. 비만인 아이들은 질병에 걸릴 확률이 크므로, 건강한 식습관과 적절한 체중 관리를 해 주어야 한다는 내용이다. 따라서 정답은 (d)이다.

함정 부모들이 먼저 나쁜 식습관을 피해야 한다는 언급이 있지만, 이는 단순히 부모들이 피해야 하는 행동을 이야기하려는 것은 아니므로 (a)는 오답이다.

어휘 obesity 비만 | consequence 결과 | obese 살찐, 뚱뚱한 | be prone to ~하는 경향이 있다 | diabetes 당뇨 | rarely 거의 ~하지 않는 | console 위로하다 | enforce 집행하다, 강요하다 | boost 끌어올리다, 증대시키다 | ruin 망치다 | positive 긍정적인

7 Comprehension

M: There are so many people on the platform. What's the matter?

W: I'm not sure. I think the subway is late for some reason.

M: Was there an accident on the line?

W: That's quite possible. At least they should <u>inform us of what's happening</u>, though.

M: Yeah, how long can we <u>keep waiting like this</u>?

W: I bet it'll take some time. I don't think we should wait here <u>without knowing when the subway is going to arrive</u>. Why don't we take a taxi?

M: Well, <u>that'd be better than waiting here</u>. But what about <u>the fare we paid</u>?

W: I'm sure we can get our money back.

M: Well, let's just go find out.

M: 플랫폼에 사람들이 너무 많은데. 무슨 일이지?

W: 모르겠어. 지하철이 무슨 이유로 늦어지나 봐.

M: 선로에 사고가 있었나?

W: 그럴 가능성이 높아. 적어도 무슨 일이 일어났는지는 알려줘야 할 텐데.

M: 맞아, 이렇게 얼마나 계속 기다려야 하지?

W: 분명히 시간이 좀 걸릴 거야. 전철이 언제 올지도 모르면서 여기서 기다리면 안 될 것 같아. 택시를 탈까?

M: 음, 여기서 기다리는 것보다 그게 낫겠어. 이미 낸 전철비는 어쩌지?

W: 분명히 다시 돌려받을 수 있을 거야.

M: 음, 일단 가서 알아보자.

Q Which is correct according to the conversation?

(a) The subway train arrived late at the station.

(b) The subway train had an accident.

(c) The man does not want to wait for a taxi.

(d) The woman is unsure why the subway train is late.

대화에 따르면 옳은 것은?

(a) 지하철이 역에 늦게 도착했다.

(b) 지하철에 사고가 있었다.

(c) 남자는 택시를 기다리는 것은 원하지 않는다.

(d) 여자는 왜 지하철이 지연되는지 모른다.

해설 지하철을 기다리면서 두 사람이 나누는 대화이다. 플랫폼에 사람들이 너무 많이 모여 있는 광경을 보고, 선로에 무슨 사고라도 난 것이 아닌가 하고 추측만 하고 있으며, 안내 방송도 나오지 않고 있기 때문에, 지하철이 왜 지연되는지에 대해 전혀 모르고 있다. 따라서 정답은 (d)이다.

함정 지하철이 역에 늦게 도착한 것이 아니라, 도착이 지연되고 있기 때문에 (a)는 옳지 않으며, 지하철에서 사고가 났을지도 모른다고 추측만 하고 있는 것이기 때문에 (b)도 오답이다. 또한 언제까지 마냥 지하철을 기다리는 것보다 택시 타는 것이 낫겠다고 말하는 것으로 보아 (c)는 틀린 설명이다.

어휘 for some reason 어떠한 이유로 | at least 적어도 | inform A of B A에게 B를 알리다, 통지하다 | keep -ing 계속해서 ~하다 | I bet 틀림없이 ~이다 | fare 운임, 요금 | unsure 확신이 없는, 불안한, 모르는

8

W: Elaine's Jewelry owes a great deal to Frank Parks,

who helped <u>make this store what it is today</u>. His window displays have been as scintillating and compelling as any artist's. For 40 years, these displays, numbering over 7,000, <u>have set the standard for other jewelry shops</u> in town. He has always known just <u>how to arrange jewelry for a stunning effect</u> in any window, making them true works of art that have made it onto the pages of <u>an endless line of fashion and culture magazines</u> like *USA Style* and *Milan Elegance*. Today we, the employees of Elaine's, honor him as he retires. Here's to Frank. It's safe to say that <u>we wouldn't be where we are today</u> without his contribution to our store over the decades.

W: Elaine's Jewelry는 오늘날 우리가 이 자리에 있게 도와 준 Frank Parks에게 큰 빚을 졌습니다. 그의 윈도우 전시는 어떤 예술가의 작품만큼 뛰어나고 압도적이었습니다. 40년 동안 약 7,000여 번의 윈도우 전시들이 도시에 있는 다른 보석 가게에 전시 표준을 마련했습니다. Frank Parks는 *USA Style*과 *Milan Elegance* 같은 패션 문화 잡지에 끝없이 홍보될 정도로 진정한 예술 작품인 보석들을 어떻게 전시하는 것이 윈도우 전시에서 가장 뛰어난 효과를 발휘할 수 있는가를 항상 알고 있었습니다. 오늘 우리 직원들은 은퇴하는 그에게 경의를 표합니다. Frank Parks에게 건배. 수십 년 동안 우리 보석 가게에 그의 공헌이 없었다면 오늘의 우리 Elaine도 없었다고 말해도 과언이 아닐 것입니다.

Q What is the speaker mainly doing in the talk?

(a) introducing an artist's new work

(b) paying tribute to an employee

(c) announcing an honor won by an employee

(d) telling colleagues to complete a window display

....

이 이야기에서 화자는 주로 무엇을 하고 있는가?

(a) 한 예술가의 새로운 작품 소개하기

(b) 고용인에게 찬사를 표하기

(c) 고용인에 의해 수여된 훈장을 공표하기

(d) 동료들에게 윈도우 전시를 완성하라고 말하기

해설 Elaine's Jewelry를 위해 40년 동안 일한 Frank Parks의 은퇴를 축하하며 감사하는 내용이다. 그의 업적들을 나열하며 그의 은퇴에 경의를 표하고 있으므로 고용인에게 찬사를 표하고 있음을 알 수 있다. 그러므로 (b)가 정답이다.

어휘 jewelry 보석(류) | scintillating 번쩍이는, 재치가 넘치는 | compelling 강력한, 감탄하지 않을 수 없는 | stunning effect 뛰어난 효과 | retire 은퇴하다 | Here's to ~에게 건배.(~에게 행운이 있기를) | It's safe to say that ~라 해도 괜찮다, 과언이 아니다 | contribution 공헌 | colleague 동료

---

9 Comprehension

M: Towns in the North American colonies of the 15th century usually appointed constables <u>to uphold the peace</u>. Constables earned no salary and had no uniform. <u>Nor were they exempt from their regular jobs</u> while doing their duty. These men were never very popular, since their jobs entailed reporting neighbors' behavior to the courts, arresting criminal offenders and being responsible for their <u>custody until trial</u>. Constables were usually chosen because they had <u>a detailed knowledge of the citizens</u> of a town and their activities. Constables rarely had to <u>do any serious investigative work</u>. Knowing the "town bad guys" and the activities they engaged in, they could usually quickly <u>catch a perpetrator</u> within days or even hours of a crime. On the downside, it also meant that they were <u>perpetually nosy</u>, always asking about the goings-on of the innocent as well.

M: 15세기 미국 식민지 마을들은 평화를 지키기 위하여 일반적으로 보안관을 임명했습니다. 보안관은 무급으로 제복조차 없었다. 또한 보안관 임무를 수행하면서 그들의 본업도 가져야 했죠. 또한 그들은 이웃들을 감시하여 법원에 보고하고 범죄자들을 잡아야 했으며 이들이 재판에 송부될 때까지 구류에 대한 책임을 지는 등의 이유로 그다지 인기가 없었습니다. 보안관들은 마을의 시민들과 그들의 행동에 대하여 상세한 지식을 가지고 있다는 이유로 선택되어졌습니다. 그들이 어떤 심각한 수사 업무를 해야 하는 경우는 거의 없었습니다. "마을의 악당들"을 잘 알고 그들의 행동 반경을 잘 이해하고 있어서, 보안관들은 범죄자들을 수일 혹은 수 시간 내에 잡기도 했죠. 부정적인 측면에서 볼 때, 보안관들은 언제나 캐물어야 하고 결백한 사람들에게도 일어나고 있는 일들에 대해 항상 질문해야 했습니다.

Q What is correct about the constable's position according to the lecture?

(a) It involved giving up regular work.

(b) People appointed to it enjoyed high status.

(c) People often volunteered for it.

(d) It entailed operating as an informant.

....

이 강의에 따르면 보안관 지위에 대해 옳은 것은?

(a) 본업을 포기해야 했다.

(b) 임명된 사람들은 높은 지위를 누렸다.

(c) 사람들은 종종 자원하기도 하였다.

(d) 정보원으로서 일해야 하기도 했다.

해설 15세기 보안관 제도에 대한 설명이다. 보안관은 마을 사람들이 동네를 잘 알고 있는 사람을 지명하여 뽑는다고 되어 있다. 보수도 제복도 없어서 본업을 가지고 있어야 했으며, 이웃을 감시하고 범인을 잡고 여러 책임을 져야 해서 인기가 없었다고 했다. 또한 여러 가지 일들을 캐고 다녀야

했다는 마지막 말로 보아, (d)가 정답임을 알 수 있다.

오답 초창기 보안관은 본업이 따로 있었다고 했으므로 (a)는 답이 될 수 없고, (b)와 (c)는 언급되지 않았다.

어휘 appoint 지명하다, 임명하다 | constable 보안관, 치안관, 경관 | uphold 지키다 | exempt 면제된 | entail ~을 필요로 하다, 수반하다 | arrest 체포하다 | offender 범죄자, 위반자 | custody 구류 | trial 재판 | perpetrator 범죄자, 가해자 | downside 부정적인 면 | perpetually 끊임없이 | nosy 캐묻기 좋아하는 | informant 정보 제공자, 밀고자

10 Comprehension

M: What happened to the new credit card <u>you applied for</u>? Did you get it?

W: No, I didn't.

M: Why? Did you <u>fail to submit any document</u>?

W: No. <u>You wouldn't believe this</u>. They found my credit history to be too short. It should be a minimum of six months. I didn't know that I have to have a credit history.

M: Well, I think <u>they will issue your card</u> if you get somebody to co-sign.

W: Well, I thought about that, but they don't allow it. I mean if I don't get a credit card, how am I going to ever have a history? I would have understood <u>if I had a bad credit record</u>.

M: Maybe you should try some other banks. They might be less rigid. Once you get one and use it for several months, then you will have your history.

W: You're right. I definitely need a credit card so that I don't have to go to an ATM <u>every time I run out of cash</u>.

M: 새로 신청한 신용카드 어떻게 됐어? 받았니?

W: 아니.

M: 왜? 무슨 서류라도 제출하지 못한 거야?

W: 아니, 알 수 없는 일이 있었어. 내 신용 기록이 너무 짧대. 최소 6개월이어야 한다고. 난 신용 기록이 있어야 한다고 생각해 보지도 못했어.

M: 음. 연대 보증인으로 서명할 사람이 있으면 발급해 줄 것 같은데.

W: 음. 나도 그렇게 생각했는데, 은행에서 안 된대. 그러니까 내가 신용카드를 받지 못하면, 언제 그 기록을 쌓을 수가 있는 거지? 오히려 안 좋은 신용 기록이 있다면, 이해하겠어.

M: 다른 은행에 가서 해 봐야겠다. 그쪽은 좀 덜 엄격할지도 몰라. 하나 발급받아서 몇 달 쓰고 나면, 기록을 갖게 되는 거겠지.

W: 네 말이 맞아. 현금이 떨어질 때마다 ATM을 찾지 않으려면, 나는 신

용카드가 꼭 필요해.

Q Which is correct about the woman according to the conversation?

(a) Her credit card limit has been exceeded.

(b) Her credit card application was rejected.

(c) She turned down a credit card offer.

(d) She has a bad credit record for not paying off her bills.

대화에 따르면 여자에 대한 설명으로 옳은 것은?

(a) 그녀의 신용카드 한도액이 초과되었다.

(b) 그녀의 신용카드 신청이 거절되었다.

(c) 그녀는 신용카드 제안을 거절했다.

(d) 그녀는 대금을 지불하지 않아서 안 좋은 신용기록을 가지고 있다.

해설 여자가 새로 신청한 신용카드에 대한 두 사람의 대화이다. 여자는 은행에서 새 신용카드를 신청했으나, 그녀의 신용기록(credit history)이 너무 짧고 연대 보증인을 세우는 것도 허락되지 않아서, 신청이 거부되었다. 따라서 정답은 (b)이다.

오답 여자가 신용카드 제안을 거절한 것이 아니라, 은행으로부터 거절당한 것이므로 (c)는 오답이다.

어휘 apply for 신청하다, 지원하다 | fail to ~하지 못하다(않다) | submit 제출하다, 제시하다 | document 서류, 문서 | co-sign 공동 서명하다, 연대 보증인으로 서명하다 | rigid 엄격한, 완고한 | ATM 현금 자동 지급기(automated-teller machine) | run out of ~을 다 쓰다, ~이 다 떨어지다

LISTENING REVIEW

A

1. obese	2. exempt
3. kidney	4. custody
5. artistry	6. constable
7. prognosis	8. perpetrator
9. console	10. chronicle
11. glamorize	12. mingle
13. transplant	14. detachment
15. delve	16. scintillating

1. extremely fat

2. free from a particular rule, duty, or obligation

3. the organs in your body that take waste matter from your blood and send it out of your body as urine

4. the state of being arrested and being kept in prison until someone can be tried in a court

5. the creative skill of an artist, writer, actor, or musician

6. an official who helps keep the peace in a town

7. an estimate of the future of someone or something, especially about whether a patient will recover from an illness

8. someone who perpetrates a crime or any other immoral or harmful act

9. to try to make someone who is unhappy about something feel more cheerful

10. to write about a series of events or show them in the order in which they happened

11. to make something look or seem more attractive than it really is, especially in a film, book, or program

12. to become mixed together but are usually still recognizable

13. a medical operation in which a part of a person's body is replaced because it is diseased

14. the feeling that you have of not being personally involved in something or of having no emotional interest in it

15. to try to discover new information about something

16. very lively and interesting

B

1. b	2. a	3. b	4. b	5. b

1. 그것이 그가 사람들과 잘 지내지 못하는 이유이다.

   (a) That's because he is not familiar with people.

   (b) That's why he doesn't get along with people.

2. 내가 신용 기록이 있어야 한다는 것을 몰랐어.

   (a) I didn't know that I have to have a credit history.

   (b) I didn't know that I don't have a credit history.

3. 비만 아이들은 다양한 질병을 앓기 쉽습니다.

   (a) Obese children are likely to avoid bad eating habits.

   (b) Obese children are prone to a wide variety of illnesses.

4. 또한 임무를 수행하면서, 그들은 본업을 안 가질 수도 없었다.

   (a) Also, they had to give up their regular works for their duty.

   (b) Nor were they exempt from their regular jobs while doing their duty.

5. 그의 공헌이 없었다면 오늘의 우리도 없었을 것이다.

   (a) He owes a great deal to us who made this store what it is today.

   (b) We wouldn't be where we are today without his contribution.

C

1. Nobody liked the idea of taking him along.

2. We are proud to see it enter its 20th year.

3. They couldn't tell to whom or what those hairs belonged.

4. Going by car would give us more flexibility.

5. At least they should inform us of what's happening.

1. nobody / of taking him along / liked the idea

2. we are proud / enter its 20th year / to see it

3. to whom or what / those hairs belonged / they couldn't tell

4. would give / going by car / us more flexibility

5. they should inform us / of what's happening / at least

D

1. a	2. b	3. a	4. b	5. b

1. Some people say they seemed to see Bigfoot.

   (a) There are people who say that they have seen Bigfoot.

   (b) What some people really saw is Bigfoot.

2. The Constable's position entailed operating as an informant.

   (a) Constables rarely had to do any serious investigative work.

   (b) Constables' jobs entailed reporting neighbors' behavior to the courts.

3. The festival features both Western and Asian cultures.

   (a) The festival is a platform to bring together Western and Eastern cultures.

   (b) The festival is dedicated to preserving Western cultural identity.

4. Mr. Wright will need a great deal of care for a week.

   (a) Mr. Wright has been taken care of in the intensive care unit for a week.

   (b) Mr. Wright is expected to remain in the intensive care unit for another week.

5. Tutankhamen's achievement was not documented in history.

   (a) There is evidence to indicate the era to which Tutankhamen belonged.

   (b) There is no mention of Tutankhamen's works in Egyptian writings.

CHAPTER 05 RELATIONSHIP OF IDEAS

VOCABULARY PREVIEW

01. avenue 대로, 수단, 방법
02. wire some money 돈을 송금하다
03. starve to death 굶어 죽다
04. reputation 명성
05. implementation 이행, 수행
06. boost 증가시키다, 높이다
07. tusk (코끼리 따위의) 엄니
08. dominance 우월함, 지배
09. herd 무리, 떼
10. herbivorous 초식성의
11. fossil 화석
12. brutal 잔인한
13. relatively 비교적
14. emir (이슬람 국가의) 수장, 족장
15. emissary 사자, 밀사
16. ratification 비준
17. treaty 조약, 협약
18. stretch ~을 펴다, 한껏 사용하다
19. kind of stifling 다소 갑갑한
20. tablet 정제, 알약
21. congestion 혼잡, 붐빔
22. impending 절박한
23. restoration 회복, 복구
24. shunt 옆으로 돌리다, 회피하다

GUIDED LISTENING

| **1** 1. a | 2. d | **2** 1. d | 2. b |
| **3** 1. c | 2. a | **4** 1. c | 2. c |

1 Conversation

M: Yesterday I saw this movie "Amazing Man" <u>starring a superhero</u> and about his exciting adventures.

W: Is it the movie that <u>got the international award</u>?

M: Yes. Have you seen the movie?

W: Yeah. It was <u>amazingly good</u>.

M: Uh... I think it could have been better, if the computer-generated imagery was used less often. It looked more <u>like a cartoon</u> than a movie.

W: No, I felt the effects were good. Well, have you seen the movie "Dark Night?" It is one of the old superhero movies <u>without those effects</u>. I mean many famous actors and actress starred in the movie. And <u>the creative storyline was awesome</u>. But I didn't feel it was very good.

M: I've seen it. You're right. <u>It was not appealing at all</u>.

W: Right. I think the technology has really <u>opened up a new avenue</u> for creativity.

M: Yeah. I hope we get to see more such films in the future.

M: 어제 나는 슈퍼 히어로와 흥미진진한 모험이 있는 "Amazing Man" 이라는 영화를 봤어.

W: 국제 영화상을 탄 그 영화 말이지?

M: 그래. 그 영화 봤어?

W: 응. 정말로 좋더라.

M: 어... 특수 효과가 아주 조금만 더 적었더라면, 더 좋았을 것 같아. 영화라기보다는 만화 같잖아.

W: 아니, 나는 좋았다고 생각해. 음, "Dark Night" 이라는 영화 봤어? 특수 효과가 사용되지 않은 예전의 슈퍼 히어로 영화 중 하나지. 유명한 배우들이 그 영화에 나와. 그리고 줄거리도 훌륭하지. 하지만 그다지 좋지 않았어.

M: 나도 봤어. 네 말이 맞아. 전혀 재미있지 않더라.

W: 거봐. 기술이 창조적인 영화의 정말 새로운 장을 연 거야.

M: 그래. 앞으로 그런 영화를 더 많이 보면 좋겠다.

Relationship of Ideas

1 What comparison do the speakers make between two movies?

(a) the use of special effects

(b) the appearance of famous stars

(c) the creativity of storyline

(d) the availability of films

화자들은 두 영화에 대해 무엇을 비교하고 있는가?

(a) 특수 효과의 사용

(b) 유명한 스타의 출연

(c) 줄거리의 독창성

(d) 영화의 입수 가능성

해설 컴퓨터 특수 효과가 쓰인 영화에 관한 대화이다. "Amazing Man"이라는 영화가 좋았지만, 특수 효과가 조금만 덜 사용되면 더 좋았을 것 같다는 남자의 말에, 여자는 그렇지 않다고 반박하고 있다. 배우와 줄거리가 모두 좋은 "Dark Night"이라는 영화는 특수 효과가 사용되지 않아 좋지 않았다는 데에 둘 다 동의하고 있다. 그러므로 이 대화는 컴퓨터 특수 효과 사용에 대한 것임을 알 수 있다.

Inference II

2   What can be inferred from the conversation?

(a) The woman does not like superheroes.

(b) The man does not like computer effects in movies.

(c) The man is interested in making movies.

(d) The woman likes to see movies with computer effects.

이 대화에서 추론할 수 있는 것은 무엇인가?

(a) 여자는 슈퍼 히어로를 좋아하지 않는다.

(b) 남자는 영화의 컴퓨터 효과를 좋아하지 않는다.

(c) 남자는 영화를 제작하는 데 관심이 있다.

(d) 여자는 컴퓨터 효과가 있는 영화를 보는 것을 좋아한다.

해설 남자가 영화 "Amazing Man"에 특수 효과가 조금만 덜 사용되면 더 좋았을 것이라고 말하자, 여자는 "Dark Night"이라는 영화는 특수 효과가 사용되지 않아 좋지 않았고 예를 들면서 반박하고 있다. 여기서 여자는 컴퓨터 효과가 사용된 영화를 좋아한다는 것을 알 수 있으므로 정답은 (d)이다.

함정 "특수 효과가 아주 조금만 더 적었더라면, 더 좋았을 것 같아."라는 남자의 말을 (b) 남자가 컴퓨터 효과를 좋아하지 않는다고 말할 수는 없다는 데에 유의한다.

어휘 star 주연하다 | superhero 슈퍼 히어로, 초능력을 가진 영웅 | cartoon 만화 | awesome 최고의, 멋진 | appealing 매력적인, 흥미를 끄는 | avenue 수단, 방법 | special effect 특수 효과

2 Conversation

W: Are you going to the food court, Sam?

M: Yes, I'm going to have lunch. Could I get you something?

W: Yeah. Please get me a hotdog. I'm too busy to go out.

M: Sure. But you'll have to wait for an hour or so. I've got a few odd jobs to take care of while I'm out.

W: Really? What're you going to be doing?

M: Well, I have to go to the bank. My sister asked me to wire some money for her audition fee which has to be paid in 15 minutes, or else she will have to wait another 3 months.

W: I see. Is there any other place you have to go?

M: I will have to drop by the library. But it won't take that long since I just need to return this book that I borrowed a week ago. It is due at noon. They charge $5 on all late returns.

W: All right.

M: On my way back I'll stop to have lunch at a food court and get the hotdog for you.

W: Just don't make me starve to death.

W: Sam, 푸드코트에 갈 건가요?

M: 네, 점심을 먹으려고요. 뭐 좀 사다 줄까요?

W: 예, 핫도그 하나 사다 주세요. 나가기에는 너무 바쁘네요.

M: 그러죠. 하지만, 한 시간 정도 기다려야 해요. 나가는 김에 몇몇 잡일들을 할 게 있어요.

W: 그래요? 뭘 하러 갈 건데요?

M: 음, 은행에 가야 해요. 여동생이 돈을 좀 부쳐 달라고 했거든요. 오디션 비용을 15분 내로 내야 한대요, 그렇지 못하면 석 달을 더 기다려야 할 거예요.

W: 알겠어요. 가야 할 다른 곳들은 또 어디예요?

M: 도서관에 잠깐 들러야 해요. 하지만 일주일 전에 빌린 책만 반납하면 되니까, 그다지 오래 걸리지는 않을 거예요. 오늘 정오가 대출 기한이거든요. 반납을 늦게 하면 5달러를 청구할 거예요.

W: 알겠어요.

M: 돌아오는 길에 푸드코트에 들러서 점심을 먹고 핫도그를 살게요.

W: 배고파 죽게 만들지만 않아 줘요.

Relationship of Ideas

1   In what order will he take care of the jobs?

(a) from the most private to the least private

(b) from the most time taking to the least time taking

(c) from the most difficult to the least difficult

(d) from the most urgent to the least urgent

남자가 어떤 순서로 일을 처리할 것인가?

(a) 가장 사적인 것에서 가장 덜 사적인 것으로

(b) 시간이 가장 많이 걸리는 것에서 가장 적게 걸리는 것으로

(c) 가장 어려운 것에서 가장 덜 어려운 것으로

(d) 가장 급한 것에서 가장 덜 급한 것으로

해설 점심을 먹으러 나가는 남자에게 여자가 점심을 사다 줄 것을 요청했다. 남자는 할 일이 좀 있어서 1시간 정도 걸릴 것이라고 말했다. 남자가 할 일은 15분 내로 여동생에게 송금을 해야 하고, 정오까지 반납해야 하는 도서를 반납하고, 점심을 먹고, 여자를 위해 핫도그를 사올 것이다. 남자는 가장 급한 것부터 하고 덜 급한 것을 나중에 할 것이므로 (d)가 정답이다.

Inference I

2   What can be inferred about the speakers?

(a) The woman is not going to wait for him.

(b) The man is going to have lunch alone.

(c) The woman is freer than the man.

(d) The man is going to withdraw some money.

화자들에 관해 추론할 수 있는 것은?

(a) 여자는 남자를 기다리지 않을 것이다.

(b) 남자는 점심을 혼자 먹을 것이다.

(c) 여자는 남자보다 더 한가하다.

(d) 남자는 돈을 인출할 것이다.

해설 남자는 볼일을 보고 점심을 먹고 나서, 여자를 위해 핫도그를 사올 것이므로 (b) 혼자 점심을 먹을 것이다.

함정 (a) 배고파 죽게 만들지만 말아 달라는 여자의 말로 보아 여자는 남자가 사오는 점심을 기다릴 것이다. (c) 여자는 바빠서 점심 먹으러 나갈 시간이 없다고 했다. (d) 남자는 돈을 인출하는 것이 아니라, 여동생에게 송금할 것이다.

어휘 too ~ to …하기에는 너무 ~하다 |
odd 여분의, 나머지의, 단편적인 | wire some money 돈을 송금하다 |
fee 요금, 수수료 | or else 그렇지 않으면 | drop by ~에 들르다 |
due 마감 기한인 | charge 청구하다 | starve to death 굶어 죽다 |
urgent 급한, 긴박한 | withdraw (돈을) 인출하다

3   Monologue

M: Many of you may be concerned about the time, cost and investment we are putting into training the managers preparing to work overseas. The company has signed new contracts with overseas clients which are very important when it comes to financial benefits and growth. Managers working with these clients need special training. I would suggest that you consider the financial aspects when a manager loses an overseas client because of lack of training. It is a huge loss for the company because our reputation is worsened and we also lose the customer. This cost is much more than what we spend on the training of the managers. I am sure we all can understand what the implementation of this method could bring.

M: 여러분들 대부분은 해외에서 일할 수 있도록 관리자들을 준비시키는 데에 우리가 제공하고 있는 시간, 비용과 투자에 대해 염려하실 것입니다. 회사는 재정상의 이익과 성장 면에서 매우 중요한 해외 고객들과 새로운 계약을 체결하였습니다. 이러한 고객들과 일하는 관리자들은 특별한 훈련이 필요합니다. 한 관리자가 훈련 부족으로 해외 고객을 잃게 될 때 재정적인 면에 대해 생각해 볼 것을 부탁드리는 바입니다. 우리의 명성이 떨어지고 고객을 잃게 되기 때문에 회사의 손실은 막대할 것입니다. 이때 들어가게 될 비용이 관리자 훈련에 쓰이는 것보다 훨씬 더 많습니다. 이 방법을 따르는 것이 어떤 이익을 가져올지 우리 모두 이해할 것이라 확신합니다.

Relationship of Ideas

1   What comparison does the speaker make between training and not training the managers?

(a) chance of success abroad

(b) length of employment

(c) amount of loss and gain

(d) degree of satisfactory service

관리자를 훈련시키는 것과 훈련시키지 않는 것에 대해 화자가 비교하고 있는 것은?

(a) 해외에서 성공 확률

(b) 고용 기간

(c) 손실과 이득의 비용

(d) 만족스러운 서비스의 정도

해설 해외 고객들과 일하는 회사의 관리자들에게 특별 훈련을 시켜야 한다는 내용이다. 훈련에는 비용이 들지만, 훈련 부족으로 문제가 생기면 고객을 잃을 뿐 아니라, 회사의 명성에도 흠집이 생길 것이라고 말하고 있다. 그러므로 매니저를 훈련시키는 것과 훈련시키지 않는 것에 대해 화자가 비교하고 있는 것은 (c) 손실과 이득의 비용이다.

Inference II

2   What can be inferred from the talk?

(a) Training methods will boost a company's reputation.

(b) There have been serious financial losses.

(c) The speaker is going overseas soon.

(d) The previous training was not effective for managers.

이 담화에서 추론할 수 있는 것은 무엇인가?

(a) 훈련이 회사의 명성을 높일 것이다.

(b) 심각한 재정적 손실이 있었다.

(c) 화자는 곧 해외로 갈 것이다.

(d) 이전의 훈련은 관리자들에게 효과적이지 않다.

해설 훈련 부족으로 문제가 생기면 고객을 잃을 뿐 아니라, 회사의 명성에도 흠집이 생길 것이라고 말하고 있으므로 훈련이 회사의 명성을 높일 것이라는 (a)가 정답이다.

함정 이미 심각한 재정적 손실이 있었다는 언급은 아니므로, (b)는 오답이다.

어휘 investment 투자 | overseas 해외에서 | aspect 국면, 양상 | reputation 명성 | worsen 악화하다, 악화시키다 | implementation 이행, 수행 | boost 증가시키다, 높이다

4 Monologue

M: Mastodons were huge, hairy, elephant-like animals that lived between 10,000 and 4 million years ago. They had long tusks and trunks like elephants, but their tusks were bigger than those of modern-day elephants. Scientists suggest that large tusks in Mastodons were used to protect their territories and prove dominance in their herds, similar to the other herbivorous tusked species. Fossil evidence obtained in the American Northeast shows that Mastodons over the age of twenty fought violently with each other during spring and summer, probably for mating rights. The brutal fights caused severe damage and internal injuries, which is apparent in mastodon fossils. The fossils obtained from a Midwestern site reveal relatively less damage to the tusk. It is quite possible that due to hunting, Mastodons decreased in numbers, thereby decreasing the competition among the herd.

M: 마스토돈은 1만 년에서 4백만 년 전에 살았던 거대하고 털이 많은 코끼리를 닮은 동물입니다. 마스토돈은 코끼리 같은 긴 엄니와 코를 가지고 있지만, 그 엄니는 현대의 코끼리의 것보다 더 컸습니다. 과학자들은 다른 초식성의 엄니를 가진 종들과 비슷하게, 마스토돈의 큰 엄니도 그들의 영역을 지키고 그들 무리에서 우월함을 증명해 보이는 데에 사용되었다고 말합니다. 아메리카 북동부에서 발견된 화석의 증거는 20살이 넘는 마스토돈이 봄과 여름에 서로 격렬하게 싸웠다는 것을 보여 주는데, 아마도 짝짓기 권리를 위한 것이었을 것입니다. 그 잔인한 싸움은 심각한 상해와 내상을 입혔고, 그것은 마스토돈의 화석에서 분명하게 보입니다. 중서부 지역에서 발견된 화석은 엄니에 비교적 더 적은 상처가 있습니다. 그것은 사냥으로 인해 마스토돈의 수가 감소해서 무리 속에서의 경쟁이 줄었기 때문인 것 같습니다.

Relationship of Ideas

1 Which best explains the relationship between damaged tusks of Mastodons and its population?

(a) Severely damaged tusks mean the number of Mastodons decreased.

(b) Less damaged tusks mean the number of Mastodons increased.

(c) Severely damaged tusks mean there were a lot of Mastodons.

(d) Less damaged tusks mean there was much competition among Mastodons.

다친 마스토돈의 엄니와 그 개체수 사이의 관련을 가장 잘 설명한 것은?

(a) 심하게 다친 엄니는 마스토돈의 수가 감소했다는 것을 의미한다.

(b) 덜 다친 엄니는 마스토돈의 수가 증가했다는 것을 의미한다.

(c) 심하게 다친 엄니는 마스토돈이 많았다는 것을 의미한다.

(d) 덜 다친 엄니는 마스토돈 사이에 경쟁이 많았다는 것을 의미한다.

해설 화석은 그들이 서로 격렬하게 싸웠다는 것을 보여 주는데, 중서부 지역에서 발견된 화석에 상처가 더 적은 것은 사냥으로 인해 마스토돈의 수가 감소했기 때문이라고 말하고 있다. 그러므로 심하게 다친 엄니는 마스토돈이 많았다는 것을 의미한다는 내용의 (c)가 정답이다.

Main Topic

2 What is the main topic of the talk?

(a) the function of elephants' tusks

(b) elephants and their violent behavior

(c) Mastodons' tusk usage

(d) mating rituals among elephants and Mastodons

이 담화의 주된 화제는 무엇인가?

(a) 코끼리 엄니의 기능

(b) 코끼리와 그들의 폭력적인 행동

(c) 마스토돈 엄니의 용도

(d) 코끼리와 마스토돈의 짝짓기 의식

해설 마스토돈은 코끼리와 비슷한 동물로, 그들의 엄니는 자신의 영역을 지키고 무리 중에서 우월함을 보여 주는 용도로 사용되었다고 한다. 그러므로 이 담화의 화제는 (c)임을 알 수 있다.

함정 이 담화는 코끼리에 관한 것이 아니라 코끼리와 비슷한 마스토돈이라는 동물에 관한 것임에 유의한다.

어휘 Mastodon 마스토돈 (코끼리 비슷한 고대 생물) | hairy 털이 많은, 텁수룩한 | tusk (코끼리 따위의) 엄니 | trunk (코끼리의) 코 | be used to ~하는 데에 사용되다 | territory 영토, 영역 | dominance 우월함, 지배 | herd 무리, 떼 | similar to ~과 비슷한 | herbivorous 초식성의 | fossil 화석 | mating 짝짓기, 교미 | brutal 잔인한 | internal 내부의, 깊은 | reveal 드러내다, 나타내다 | relatively 비교적 | competition 경쟁 | function 기능 | usage 용법, 용도 | ritual 의식, 제식

1

M: Monday's auction, <u>featuring a silver dollar</u> dated 1805 and <u>issued as a special gift</u> to the Emir of Yemen, was expected to receive record-breaking bids of almost three million dollars. The silver dollar was <u>secretly carried to the Middle East</u> by an emissary of U.S. president Andrew Jackson as a present for the Emir <u>following the ratification of a new trade treaty</u>. The coin has special value because it <u>symbolizes the first real political contact</u> between the young United States of America and a nation in the Middle East. Thus, prior to bidding opening, most analysts expected it would ultimately <u>fetch a high price</u>. To the surprise of many, however, the silver dollar remained unsold after bids failed to meet the reserve price. The coin may be put on auction sometime again when conditions are more favorable.

M: 1805년도에 발행되어 예멘의 수장에게 선물된 1달러짜리 은화가 월요 경매에 부쳐질 예정이며 약 300만 달러에 달하는 가격으로 기존의 기록을 갱신할 것으로 예상되었습니다. 그 1달러짜리 은화는 새로운 무역 조약의 비준 후 그 수장에게 선물로 주기 위해 미국 대통령 Andrew Jackson이 보낸 밀사에 의해 비밀스럽게 중동으로 전달되었습니다. 이 동전의 가치는 특별한데 그 이유는 바로 신생국인 미국과 중동 국가의 첫 번째 정치적인 조약을 상징하기 때문입니다. 그러므로 오늘 경매가 열리기 전 대부분의 분석가들은 높은 가격으로 낙찰될 것이라고 예상하였습니다. 그러나 놀랍게도 최저 경매 가격에 미치지 못하여 경매가 유찰되어, 이 동전은 팔리지 못했습니다. 그 동전은 상황이 좀 더 좋아지면 다시 경매에 부쳐질 예정입니다.

Q What is the news report mainly about?

(a) the value of an antique silver dollar

(b) rare coins discovered in the Middle East

(c) the auctioning of a special silver dollar

(d) a gift planned for the Emir of Yemen

이 뉴스는 주로 무엇에 관한 것인가?

(a) 오래된 1달러짜리 은화의 가치

(b) 중동에서 발견된 희귀 동전

(c) 특별한 1달러짜리 은화의 경매

(d) 예멘 수장을 위해 계획된 선물

해설 미국과 중동 국가와의 첫 번째 조약을 기념하여 미국이 예멘 수장에게 선물했던 1달러짜리 은화가 경매에 부쳐졌었다는 기사이다. 높은 경매가를 예상했던 전문가들의 예측과는 달리 유찰되었다는 내용이므로, (c)가 정답이다.

어휘 silver dollar 1달러짜리 은화 | issue 발행하다 | emir (이슬람 국가들의) 수장, 족장 | bid 입찰가 | emissary 사자, 밀사 | ratification 비준 | treaty 조약, 협약 | analyst 분석 전문가 | fetch 가져오다, (~가격에) 팔리다 | meet 충족시키다 | reserve price 경매 최저 가격 | favorable 유리한, 알맞은

2 Relationship of Ideas

M: Your new apartment is quite spacious. <u>It must have cost you a fortune.</u>

W: Well, I had to <u>stretch my finances to buy it</u>. I <u>got a small loan</u>, too.

M: Oh, do you think it was wise to spend money that way?

W: It's my dream apartment, so I don't mind <u>spending a bit extra for it</u>.

M: I thought your previous place was not that bad.

W: Yeah, it was very close to my office and clean. But it was kind of stifling.

M: But can you <u>afford the maintenance</u>?

W: That's exactly what I mean by dream apartment. It doesn't cost much for the maintenance. The apartment is huge but new, so it costs less. Remember? For the maintenance in the previous apartment, I had to <u>sacrifice a few of my activities</u>.

M: I see your point.

M: 새 아파트가 상당히 넓구나. 분명히 돈이 많이 들었겠다.

W: 아파트를 사느라 무리하게 돈을 조달해야만 했어. 대출도 좀 받았고.

M: 그렇게 돈을 쓰는 게 현명했다고 생각하니?

W: 내가 꿈에 그리던 아파트라서, 약간 추가로 돈을 더 쓰는 건 괜찮아.

M: 이전 집도 그렇게 나쁘지는 않았던 것 같은데.

W: 그래, 사무실하고 굉장히 가까웠고 깨끗했지. 하지만 좀 갑갑했어.

M: 그런데 관리비는 낼 수 있겠어?

W: 그게 바로 내가 꿈꾸던 아파트라는 얘기야. 관리비가 많이 들지 않아. 아파트는 크고 새 것이어서, 비용이 덜 드나봐. 기억해? 이전 아파트 관리비 때문에, 나는 하고 싶은 것들을 단념해야 했잖아.

M: 무슨 말인지 알겠다.

Q What comparison does the woman make between the

previous and the new apartments?

(a) the size and maintenance

(b) the price and size

(c) the distance to the office and cleanness

(d) the maintenance and distance to the office

여자가 이전 아파트와 새 아파트의 무엇을 비교하고 있는가?

(a) 크기와 관리비

(b) 가격과 크기

(c) 사무실까지의 거리와 청결

(d) 관리비와 사무실까지의 거리

해설 여자가 구입한 넓은 아파트에 관한 대화이다. 돈이 많이 들었지만, 여자는 아주 만족해하고 있다. 이전의 아파트도 나쁘지 않았다는 남자의 말에, 여자는 이전의 아파트는 사무실하고 가깝고 깨끗하기는 했지만 답답했다고 했다. 그에 비해 새로운 아파트는 크고 새 아파트여서 관리비가 적게 든다고 말하고 있으므로, 여자는 크기와 관리비에 대해 말하고 있는 것이다.

함정 새 아파트가 더 비싸기는 하지만, 가격을 비교하고 있지는 않으며, 이전 아파트가 사무실에서 가깝기는 했지만, 여자에게는 그것도 비교 대상이 되지 않는다.

어휘 spacious 넓은 | must have p.p. ~였음에 틀림없다 | fortune 재산, 거금, 큰돈 | stretch ~을 펴다, 한껏 사용하다 | finance 금융거래, 재정, 자금조달 | loan 대부, 대출, 융자 | mind (-ing) ~하는 것을 싫어하다, 걱정하다 | previous 이전의 | kind of stifling 다소 갑갑한 | afford ~할 수 있다, 여유가 있다 | maintenance 유지, 관리 | sacrifice ~을 희생하다, 바치다, 단념하다

3

W: Mr. Baylor, here's your prescription.

M: Thank you. When should I take these?

W: It's <u>written on the label</u>. You should <u>take a tablet after breakfast and dinner</u>.

M: It says here that I will have to take these for a week. Is that right?

W: Yeah, you'll have to <u>come in for a checkup after that</u>, as your doctor <u>recommended</u>.

M: So, <u>will the prescription be changed then</u>?

W: It depends on your doctor.

M: Okay. <u>How much will that be</u>? Oh, do I pay here?

W: You can <u>pay at the cashier on the way out</u>. It is $9.75 total.

M: Thank you.

W: Baylor씨, 여기 처방약입니다.

M: 고맙습니다. 이걸 언제 먹어야 하나요?

W: 라벨에 쓰여 있어요. 아침과 저녁 식사 후 한 알씩 드시면 됩니다.

M: 일주일 동안 복용해야 한다고 여기 쓰여 있네요. 맞나요?

W: 네, 의사가 권해드린 대로, 다 드신 후에 오셔서 검진을 받으셔야 합니다.

M: 그럼 그때는 처방이 바뀌나요?

W: 그건 의사선생님이 결정하실 겁니다.

M: 좋습니다. 얼마죠? 아, 여기서 내면 되나요?

W: 출구에 있는 출납원에게 내시면 됩니다. 총 9.75달러입니다.

M: 감사합니다.

Q Which is correct about Mr. Baylor according to the conversation?

(a) He has to come in for a checkup after a month.

(b) He must take a tablet after every meal.

(c) He needs to take two tablets a day.

(d) He needs to change his old prescription.

대화에 따르면 Baylor씨에 대한 설명으로 옳은 것은?

(a) 한 달 후에 검진을 받으러 와야 한다.

(b) 식사 후마다 한 알씩 먹어야 한다.

(c) 하루에 약알을 두 개씩 먹어야 한다.

(d) 이전의 처방을 바꿔야 한다.

해설 처방약에 관한 두 사람의 대화이다. 남자는 여자가 건네준 처방약을 일주일 동안 아침과 저녁 식사 후 한 알씩 복용한 후, 다시 병원에 와서 진단을 받아야 한다. 아침 저녁으로 복용해야 하므로 하루에 두 알이 옳다. 따라서 정답은 (c)이다.

함정 이전의 처방(old prescription)을 바꿔야 할지 말아야 할지는 일주일 후 건강검진을 받고, 의사가 다시 결정할 사항이므로 (d)는 오답이다.

어휘 prescription 처방, 처방약 | tablet 정제, 알약 | come in for ~을 받다 | checkup 점검, 정밀검사, 건강진단 | recommend 추천하다, 권하다, 충고하다 | depend on ~에 달려 있다

4 Relationship of Ideas

W: Attention, passengers. Orient Air <u>flight 445</u> from Cape Town <u>bound for</u> Bangkok is now boarding. Please listen carefully <u>for the boarding instructions</u> before moving toward the entrance gate — this will serve <u>to smooth the entire boarding procedure</u>. Passengers booked in First Class, <u>requiring assistance</u> or traveling with children are asked to board right now. We'll open boarding to passengers in Rows 34 through

54 in a few minutes. We request that you remain seated until that time. You will be asked to show your boarding pass <u>upon arrival at the gate</u>. You cannot enter the plane <u>until your row is called</u>, but you may enter the aircraft any time after that. If you have any questions about your seating, please ask the gate staff. Thank you; we will begin boarding now.

W: 탑승객에게 알립니다. 케이프타운에서 방콕으로 가는 오리엔트 항공 445기가 탑승을 시작합니다. 탑승구로 가시기 전 탑승 안내를 잘 들어 주십시오. 이는 전체 탑승 과정을 보다 용이하게 만들어 줄 것입니다. 일등석 탑승객들과 도움이 필요하신 분들, 아이를 동반하신 분들은 지금 바로 탑승해 주십시오. 곧이어 34열에서 54열의 탑승객들 탑승을 시작할 예정입니다. 그 외 탑승객들은 자리에서 기다려 주십시오. 입구에 도착하면 탑승권을 보여 주셔야 합니다. 좌석 열 번호가 불리기 전에는 탑승하실 수 없지만, 그 이후에는 언제든지 답승할 수 있습니다. 만약 좌석에 대하여 질문이 있으시다면 탑승구 직원에게 질문해 주세요. 감사합니다. 지금부터 탑승을 시작하겠습니다.

Q Which of the following is NOT mentioned as a process of boarding?

(a) to proceed to the gate

(b) to present a boarding pass

(c) to wait until the row is allowed to proceed

(d) to get the row confirmed by gate staff

탑승 절차로 언급되지 않은 것은?

(a) 탑승구로 오기

(b) 탑승권 제시하기

(c) 열 번호가 들어가게 될 때까지 기다리기

(d) 탑승구 직원에게 열 번호 확인받기

해설 탑승 안내방송이다. 먼저 안내방송을 듣고 탑승구로 와서, 일등석과 도움이 필요한 고객, 아이가 있는 고객이 먼저 탑승하고, 호명되는 열 순서대로 탑승해야 한다. 열 번호가 불릴 때까지 기다렸다가, 탑승구에 오면 탑승권을 보여 줘야 한다. 마지막으로 질문이 있으면 탑승구 직원에게 하면 된다고 한다. 이것으로 보아, (d)는 언급되지 않은 내용임을 알 수 있다.

어휘 passenger 승객 | bound for ~행인, ~를 향한 | board 탑승하다 | move toward ~를 향해 움직이다 | smooth 매끄럽게 하다, 수월하게 하다

5

M: June 14th is National Carpool Day! As responsible British citizens, show your concern for the environment and <u>the increasing congestion</u> on our roads by sharing a car with family, friends, or colleagues. The more cars <u>that we share</u>, the fewer total cars we'll have on the roads. That means that we'll have a cleaner Britain and <u>ultimately a cleaner world</u> for everyone. National Carpool Day is a way that every citizen can join this effort. <u>Carpooling is also less stressful</u> — <u>let others take over the responsibility</u> of driving for a while! We're certain that once you carpool, you'll understand its lower price, ease and environmental benefits — and continue with it. Register at www.carpool.org to find other passengers traveling on your route and to know more about events <u>scheduled for this special date</u>.

M: 6월 14일은 전국 카풀 데이입니다. 책임있는 영국 시민으로서의 환경과 증가하는 도로 정체에 대한 당신의 관심을 가족, 친구, 동료들과 차를 함께 타는 것으로써 보여 주세요. 더 많은 차를 공유할수록, 도로에는 차량이 줄어들 것입니다. 그것은 우리가 더 깨끗한 영국, 나아가 모든 이들을 위한 더 깨끗한 세계를 가질 수 있다는 것을 의미합니다. 전국 카풀 데이는 모든 시민이 이러한 노력에 동참할 수 있는 한 가지 방법입니다. 카풀은 또한 스트레스를 줄여 줍니다. 잠시만이라도 다른 이에게 차를 운전하는 책임을 떠넘기세요! 우리는 확신합니다. 한번만 카풀을 이용해 보면, 낮은 가격과 편리함과 자연 보호의 이점을 이해할 것이라는 것을, 그리고 계속 이용하게 되리라는 점을. www.carpool.org에서 등록해서 같은 길을 이용하는 사람들을 찾으세요. 그리고 전국 카풀 데이와 관련된 특별한 행사 스케줄도 알 수 있습니다.

Q What is the advertisement mainly about?

(a) a national holiday in Britain

(b) a nationwide carpooling day

(c) a special carpooling service

(d) a new public transport system

이 광고는 주로 무엇에 대한 것인가?

(a) 영국의 국경일

(b) 전국적인 카풀 데이

(c) 특별한 카풀 서비스

(d) 새로운 대중교통 시스템

해설 영국의 전국 카풀 데이에 대한 안내이다. 몇몇 사람이 차를 함께 타는 카풀 데이를 지정해서 더 많은 사람들이 카풀 제도를 이용하게 하려는 국가적 차원의 광고이다. 비용이 덜 들고, 환경에 이롭다는 장점을 설명하면서 설득하고 있는 내용이다. 그러므로 정답은 (b)이다.

어휘 responsible 책임감 있는 | congestion 혼잡, 붐빔 | colleague 동료 | take over 인계받다, 떠맡다 | for a while 잠시 동안 | route 도로, 노선 | public transport 대중교통

6

W: A modern infrastructure is crucial to economic prosperity. We need modern roads and rail systems and ports to make sure that goods can <u>move into, out of, and around the country smoothly</u>. When infrastructure is lacking, billions of dollars are wasted as cars, trucks, trains, and ships <u>suffer needless breakdowns</u>, <u>get into accidents</u> — or <u>wait endlessly</u> in various lines or traffic jams. Yet, the infrastructure in our country is aging and we don't seem to be doing much to either maintain or replace it. We have only <u>the apathy of our politicians to blame</u>. After all, there is nothing politically exciting about maintaining a road system. Years of poor funding and a nationwide neglect of maintenance have left the country's transportation systems <u>incapable of handling any further stress</u>. In terms of impending infrastructure failure, America's older cities are like volcanoes waiting to erupt.

W: 현대 사회 기반시설은 경제 성장에 중요합니다. 우리는 국내외 화물 운송을 원활하게 하기 위하여 현대적인 도로, 철도, 항구가 필요합니다. 사회 기간시설이 부족하면 차, 트럭, 기차, 배 등이 불필요한 고장을 겪고 사고가 일어나거나 교통 혼잡으로 끊임없이 기다리는 등의 수십억 달러에 달하는 손실을 겪게 될 것입니다. 그러나 우리나라의 기간시설들은 오래되었고, 우리는 그것들을 유지하거나 대체하기 위한 시설 확충에 대하여 별로 준비하고 있지 않은 듯합니다. 우리는 무관심한 정치인들을 비난할 뿐입니다. 결국 이런 도로 시스템을 관리하는 데에 어떠한 정치적인 흥미 역시 없는 것입니다. 수년간 지속되어온 부족한 자금 확보와 정비에 대한 국가적인 무관심이 국가의 교통 시스템을 미래에 발생할 수 있는 어떤 문제에 대해서도 대체할 수 없게 만들었습니다. 절박한 사회 기간시설의 실패에 있어서, 미국의 오래된 도시들은 폭발하기를 기다리는 화산과 같습니다.

Q What is the speech mainly about?

(a) a review of American maintenance systems today

(b) paying for infrastructure restoration in older American cities

(c) American cities at risk from possible volcanic eruptions

(d) the threat of infrastructure failures in old American cities

이 연설의 주로 무엇에 관한 것인가?

(a) 오늘날 미국 시설 관리 시스템에 대한 논평

(b) 오래된 미국 도시들의 사회 기간시설 재정비를 위한 재정적 지원

(c) 화산 폭발의 가능성으로 위험에 처해 있는 미국 도시들

(d) 오래된 미국 도시들에서 사회 기반구조 실패의 위협

해설 사회 기간시설의 문제에 대하여 정치가들의 무관심과 자금운용 부족이 주제이다. 화자는 오래된 미국 도시들의 사회 기간시설 확충을 위한 관심과 자금이 필요하다고 역설하고 있다. 그러므로 정답은 (b)이다.

함정 (a)와 (d)는 언급되었으나 전체의 주제가 되기에는 한정적이며, 사회 기간시설의 재건에 실패한 오래된 도시들을 폭발 직전에 화산에 비유한 말은 왜곡하여 해석한 (c)는 답이 될 수 없다.

어휘 infrastructure 기간시설 | crucial 주요한 | prosperity 번창, 융성 | goods 화물, 상품 | breakdown 고장, 파손, 붕괴, 와해 | apathy 무관심 | neglect 경시, 간과, 소홀함 | incapable of ~할 수 없게 하는 | in terms of ~에 관하여, ~의 점에서 (보아) | impending 절박한 | erupt 폭발하다 | restoration 회복, 복구

7

M: Jane, what's the status of the financial report I asked you to do?

W: Well, I'm almost <u>done with it</u>.

M: I requested that report a week ago.

W: I'm really sorry for that, but I was busy with the reports <u>for the annual conference</u>, assigned by Mr. Ford. I didn't even have much time <u>to collect the data I need for your report</u>.

M: So when can I expect it?

W: I think I can have it done in about two hours <u>provided I'm not called into any other meetings</u>.

M: It's almost time to leave. Why don't you just <u>let me have it</u> tomorrow morning?

W: That will give me some time to review before I give it to you. Thanks.

M: Well, I'm sorry that <u>I forgot you were busy with another important thing</u>.

W: That's okay.

M: Jane, 내가 부탁했던 회계 보고서 상황은 어떤가요?

W: 음, 거의 다 마쳤습니다.

M: 일주일 전에 부탁한 보고서예요.

W: 정말 죄송하지만, Ford 씨가 부탁했던 연례회의 보고서 때문에 바빴어요. 보고서에 필요한 데이터를 모을 시간조차 충분하지 않았어요.

M: 그럼 언제면 될까요?

W: 다른 회의에 불려가지 않는다면, 2시간쯤 후면 될 수 있을 거예요.

M: 거의 퇴근할 시간이네요. 내일 아침에 내가 받는 건 어때요?

W: 그러면 드리기 전에 검토할 시간이 좀 되겠네요. 감사합니다.

M: 음, 당신이 다른 중요한 일로 바쁘다는 것을 잊고 있어서 미안해요.

W: 괜찮습니다.

Q What can be inferred about the woman from the conversation?

(a) She does not want to attend a meeting.

(b) She is usually late in her submissions.

(c) She has no experience in preparing reports.

(d) She doesn't get work from just one person.

대화에서 여자에 대해 추측할 수 있는 것은?

(a) 회의에 참석하길 원하지 않는다.

(b) 주로 늦게 제출한다.

(c) 보고서 작성 경험이 없다.

(d) 한 사람에게 업무지시를 받지는 않는다.

해설 여자는 연례회 보고서 때문에 남자가 일주일 전에 부탁한 회계보고서를 아직 다 마치지 못한 상태이며, 2시간 정도면 될 거라고 하면서도, 다른 회의에 불려갈 가능성을 배제하지 않고 있다. 즉, 여자는 이 남자뿐 아니라, 다른 사람들로부터 여러 가지 회의 업무를 요청받고 있다는 것을 짐작할 수 있으므로, 정답은 (d)이다.

어휘 status 지위, 신분, 상태 | financial 재정의, 회계의 | be busy with ~로 바쁘다 | annual 일년의, 해마다의 | provided 만일 ~라면 | submission 제출, 제안, 복종

8 Relationship of Ideas

W: Welcome to Sydney Visitors Bureau. How can I help you?

M: I just arrived from California and would like to reserve a hotel room.

W: Would you like to stay in the city or in the suburbs?

M: Well, I'm here for a conference and would like some place near Einstein Hall in the city.

W: In that case you have a choice between the Le Carte and the Continental. You can get a room that has a great night view in the Le Carte since most of the rooms are facing downtown.

M: What about the other hotel?

W: You have less chance of getting a room with a nice night view.

M: I see. I bet the Le Carte is more expensive.

W: Well, the hotel bill in the Le Carte is a little higher but the breakfast and sauna are provided free of charge. Meanwhile, the Continental is cheaper but you will have to pay the breakfast and sauna.

M: I'll take the Le Carte for two nights.

W: Sure. I'll make the reservation.

W: 시드니 관광청에 오신 걸 환영합니다. 어떻게 도와 드릴까요?

M: 캘리포니아에서 방금 도착했는데요, 호텔 객실을 예약하고 싶어요.

W: 시내가 좋으세요, 교외가 좋으세요?

M: 음, 회의 때문에 온 거라서, 시내의 아인슈타인 홀과 가까운 곳이 좋겠어요.

W: 그렇다면 르카르트와 콘티넨탈 호텔 중에서 선택하실 수 있습니다. 르카르트 호텔은 거의 모든 객실이 시내를 마주하고 있어서 야경이 좋은 객실을 얻을 수 있어요.

M: 다른 호텔을 어때요?

W: 야경이 좋은 객실을 얻을 가능성이 더 적죠.

M: 알겠습니다. 그럼 르카르트가 틀림없이 더 비싸겠군요.

W: 음, 르카르트 호텔 비용이 약간 더 높지만, 조식과 사우나가 무료로 제공됩니다. 반면에 콘티넨탈은 더 저렴하지만 조식과 사우나를 하시려면 비용을 내야 하실 거에요.

M: 르카르트에서 이틀 밤을 할게요.

W: 알겠습니다. 그럼 예약하겠습니다.

Q What comparison does the woman make between the Le Carte and the Continental?

(a) the size of the rooms with night views and the price

(b) the number of rooms available and the bill

(c) the availability of rooms with a night view and the cost

(d) the distance to the city and the prices of the rooms

여자가 르카르트와 콘티넨탈의 무엇을 비교하고 있는가?

(a) 야경을 볼 수 있는 객실의 크기와 가격

(b) 이용 가능한 객실 수와 비용

(c) 야경을 볼 수 있는 객실의 가능성과 비용

(d) 시내까지의 거리와 객실의 가격

해설 캘리포니아에서 회의차 시드니에 온 남자가 시드니 관광청에서 도시 근처의 호텔방 예약을 하는 대화이다. 관광청 직원인 여자는 르카르트와 콘티넨탈이라는 두 호텔을 소개하고 있다. 르카르트에서는 멋진 야경을 볼 수 있을 가능성이 더 많으며, 약간 더 비싸기는 하지만 조식과 사우나가 포함된 가격이라고 말하고 있으므로 정답은 (c)이다.

함정 (a) 객실의 크기에 대한 언급은 없다. (b) 여자는 먼저 야경에 대해 비교하고 있다. (d) 도시에서의 거리는 둘 다 가까울 것이다.

어휘 bureau (관청의) 국, 안내소 | reserve 예약하다 | suburbs 근교, 교외 | in that case 그 경우는, 그렇다면 | night view 야경 | free of charge 무료로 | make a reservation 예약하다

9

M: Do certain types of music really make you smarter?

This has been <u>a recurring question in pop psychology</u> and talk shows. I'm now going to speak about this <u>ongoing debate among educational psychologists</u> regarding the influence of certain music on intelligence. Many commentators have suggested that classical music makes one smarter. Some mothers or even pregnant women have taken to playing classical music <u>in the hopes of raising their children's IQs</u>. Two recent studies <u>challenge previous research claims</u> that listening to a Schubert sonata will make you smarter. They say that audio inputs of classical music before an IQ test will not <u>significantly improve its outcome</u>. This finding overturns an influential 1992 study which claimed that subjects gained up to 10 IQ points, although temporarily, after listening to Schubert. The earlier study had generated an entire industry for soundtracks leading to so-called <u>mind enhancement</u>.

M: 어떤 특정한 음악이 정말로 여러분을 더욱 똑똑하게 만들까요? 이것은 팝 심리학과 토크 쇼에서 계속 반복되는 질문입니다. 저는 지금부터 특정한 음악이 지적능력에 미치는 영향에 관하여 교육 심리학자들 사이에서의 계속되고 있는 논쟁에 대하여 말하고자 합니다. 많은 논평가들이 말하기를 클래식 음악이 사람을 더 똑똑하게 만든다고 말합니다. 일부 어머니들이나 심지어 임신한 여성들도 자식들의 IQ를 높이고자 하는 희망으로 클래식 음악을 틀어 놓죠. 최근 발표된 두 가지 연구는 슈베르트 소나타를 들으면 더욱 똑똑해 진다는 이전 연구 결과에 반기를 들고 있습니다. 그 연구들은 IQ 테스트 이전에 클래식 음악을 듣는다고 해서, 그 결과가 눈에 뜨일 만큼 향상되는 것은 아니라고 합니다. 이러한 결과는 피실험자들이 비록 일시적이었지만 Schubert의 소나타를 들은 뒤 아이큐가 10점 향상되었다는 1992년의 영향력 있는 연구 결과와 반대되는 것입니다. 이 이전의 연구 결과를 바탕으로 정신 강화라 일컬어지는 음악 산업이 형성되기도 했었습니다.

Q What is called into question by the speaker?

(a) the link between IQ and musical talent

(b) the subjects used in a renowned 1992 study

(c) the possible impact of music on intelligence

(d) the strategies of mind-enhancing recordings

화자에 의해 제기되고 있는 문제는 무엇인가?

(a) IQ와 음악적 재능의 관계

(b) 저명한 1992년 연구에 사용되었던 피실험자들

(c) 음악이 지적능력에 미칠 수 있는 영향

(d) 정신 강화 음악의 전략

해설 음악이 지능에 미치는 영향에 관한 내용이다. 1992년의 연구 결과 클래식 음악이 지능을 높인다고 두루 알려졌지만, 최근 발표된 두 가지 연구 결과는 그 이전의 연구 결과를 번복하는 것이라는 내용이다. 그러므로

화자가 제시하고 있는 문제는 (c)이다.

어휘 recurring 되풀이하는, 계속 나타나는 | psychology 심리학 | ongoing 계속되고 있는 | debate 토론, 논쟁 | regarding ~에 관한 | intelligence 지능, 지성 | commentator 논평가 | pregnant 임신한 | recent 최근의 | previous 이전의 | outcome 결과 | overturn 뒤집어엎다, 전복시키다 | subject (실험의) 대상자, 피실험자 | temporarily 일시적으로, 임시로 | enhancement 강화, 증진

10 Relationship of Ideas

W: Of all the things we need to understand <u>if we are to function effectively</u> in this world, we think our feelings are the easiest to comprehend. This, sadly, is not the case. Many people in fact <u>ignore their feelings</u> to such an extent that they consequently don't know how to deal with them. Often they <u>suppress or ignore them</u>. The truth is that being <u>sensitive to one's own feelings</u> is a basic part of understanding oneself and the world around one. <u>Feelings are not the antithesis of logic</u>, but its complement. If something seems right logically, but our feelings object to it, we shouldn't just shunt our feelings aside. They may be sending us <u>vital information that we need</u> to make the correct decisions in our lives. The phrase "listen to your heart" has more than a bit of wisdom in it.

W: 세상을 효과적으로 살아가는 데 있어 우리가 이해해야 하는 것들 중에, 우리는 우리의 감정이 가장 이해하기 쉬운 것이라고 생각합니다. 그러나 슬프게도 그것은 그렇지 않습니다. 사실 많은 사람들이 어느 정도는 스스로의 감정을 무시하기 때문에, 그 결과 사람들은 감정을 어떻게 다루어야 하는지 잘 모릅니다. 종종 사람들은 그들의 감정을 억누르거나 무시합니다. 사실은 자기 자신의 감정에 대하여 민감한 것이 바로 그들 스스로와 그들 주위의 세상을 이해하는 데에 있어 기본이 됩니다. 감정은 논리의 반대편에 있는 것이 아니라 논리를 보완해 주는 것입니다. 만약 어떤 것이 논리적으로는 맞지만 우리의 감정이 반대한다면, 우리는 이 감정을 회피해서는 안 됩니다. 감정은 우리 인생에 있어서 올바른 결정을 내릴 수 있도록 절대적으로 필요한 정보를 제공하는 것일지도 모릅니다. '당신의 마음에 귀 기울이세요'라는 문구는 작은 지혜라기보다 더 많은 것을 내포하고 있습니다.

Q Which of the following best describes the relationship between feeling and logic?

(a) disturbances of decision making

(b) basic qualities that should complement each other

(c) two basic things necessary when decision making

(d) disturbing quality and useful quality

감정과 논리 사이의 관계를 가장 잘 묘사한 것은?

(a) 의사결정의 혼란

(b) 서로 보완이 되는 기본적 성질

(c) 의사결정시 필요한 두 가지 기본적인 것들

(d) 방해가 되는 것과 유용한 것

해설 사람들이 흔히 논리를 중요시하고 감정을 억누르는 경향이 있는데, 감정은 스스로와 세상에 대해 더 알게 하고 절대적인 암시일 수 있다는 것이 화자의 주장이다. 올바른 결정을 내리기 위해서는 논리와 감정 둘 다 중요하다고 역설하고 있다. 즉, 감정은 논리를 거스르는 것이 아니라, 상호보완적이라고 말하고 있으므로, (b)가 정답이다.

어휘 function 기능하다, 역할하다 | effectively 효과적으로 | comprehend 이해하다 | to such an extent 어느 정도로는 | suppress 억누르다 | antithesis 정반대, 대조 | logic 논리 | complement 보충, 보완 | object to ~에 반대하다 | shunt 옆으로 돌리다, 회피하다 | vital 생명의, 절대적으로 필요한 | disturbance 혼란, 방해

LISTENING REVIEW

A

1. pregnant	2. withdraw
3. congestion	4. avenue
5. stifling	6. trunk
7. starve	8. antithesis
9. emir	10. impending
11. tusks	12. disturbance
13. herbivorous	14. apathy
15. emissary	16. suppress

1. having a baby or babies developing in her body

2. to take money out of a bank account

3. the state of being extremely crowded and blocked with traffic or people

4. a way of getting something done

5. so intense that it makes you feel uncomfortable

6. a very long nose that an elephant uses to lift food and water to its mouth

7. to suffer greatly from lack of food which sometimes leads to their death

8. exact opposite of something

9. a Muslim ruler

10. going to happen very soon

11. two very long, curved, pointed teeth of an elephant or wild boar

12. upsetting or disorganizing something which was previously in a calm and well-ordered state

13. of an animal that only eats plants

14. the feeling of not seeming to be interested in or enthusiastic about anything

15. a representative sent by one government or leader to another

16. to prevent an activity from continuing, by using force or making it illegal

B

1. a	2. a	3. a	4. b	5. b

1. 당신이 다른 중요한 일로 바쁘다는 것을 잊고 있었어요.

(a) I forgot you were busy with another important thing.

(b) I forgot you had to do an important thing at the time.

2. 감정은 논리의 반대편에 있는 것이 아니라 논리를 보완해 주는 것입니다.

(a) Feelings are not the antithesis of logic, but its complement.

(b) Being sensitive to our own feelings is basic to understanding logic.

3. 야경이 좋은 객실을 얻을 가능성이 더 적죠.

(a) You have less chance of getting a room with a nice night view.

(b) You can never get a room that has a great night view.

4. 많은 논평가들이 말하기를 클래식 음악이 사람을 더 똑똑하게 만든다고 말합니다.

(a) Many pregnant women have taken to playing classical music for their children's IQs.

(b) Many commentators have suggested that classical music makes one smarter.

5. 우리가 더 많은 차를 나눠 탈수록, 도로에는 차량이 더 줄어들 것입니다.

(a) We'll have fewer total cars on the roads when we share fewer cars.

(b) The more cars that we share, the fewer total cars we'll have on the roads.

C

1. You can get a room that has a great night view.
2. I saw this movie "Amazing Man" starring a superhero.
3. Managers working with these clients need special training.
4. We have only the apathy of our politicians to blame.
5. I didn't even have much time to collect the data I need for your report.

1. that has a great night view / you can get / a room
2. this movie "Amazing Man" / starring a superhero / I saw
3. need special training / working with these clients / managers
4. the apathy of our politicians / to blame / we have only
5. I need for your report / to collect the data / I didn't even have much time

D

1. a	2. b	3. b	4. b	5. a

1. You need to take two tablets a day.
   (a) You should take a tablet after breakfast and dinner.
   (b) You must take a tablet after every meal.

2. You can enter the plane after your row is called.
   (a) You may enter the plane at any time.
   (b) You cannot enter the plane until your row is called.

3. It will take only a few minutes as I just have to return this book.
   (a) It will take a few minutes for me to borrow this book.
   (b) It won't take that long since I just need to return this book.

4. This cost is much less, if we spend money on the training of the managers.
   (a) The manager gains an overseas client despite the lack of training.
   (b) This cost is much more than what we spend on the training of the managers.

5. Relatively less damaged tusks indicate that Mastodons decreased in numbers.
   (a) Severely damaged tusks mean there were a lot of Mastodons.
   (b) Severely damaged tusks mean the number of Mastodons decreased.

CHAPTER 06 INFERENCE I

VOCABULARY PREVIEW

01. big-budget 큰 자본을 들인
02. gadget 장치, 도구
03. sophisticated 복잡한
04. calamity 재해, 재난
05. mishap 불행한 일, 불운
06. landslide 산사태
07. exceptional 특별히 뛰어난, 비범한
08. goaltending (스포츠의) 골 수비, 골 방어
09. indicative ~을 나타내는, ~의 표시인
10. oppression 억압, 중압감
11. stick to ~을 고수하다, ~에 달라붙다
12. glucose 포도당
13. inadequate 불충분한
14. vital 절대로 필요한, 중요한
15. swap 교환하다, 바꾸다
16. subjective 주관적인
17. passive 수동적인
18. seamlessly 이음매 없이, 구분 없이
19. waddle 비틀거리다, 뒤뚱거리다
20. inevitable 피할 수 없는
21. behold 보다
22. eatery 간이식당
23. agile 기민한, 날쌘
24. clumsy 서투른, 솜씨 없는

GUIDED LISTENING

1	1. a	2. b	2	1. c	2. d
3	1. c	2. d	4	1. a	2. b

1 Conversation

M: <u>You have with us this evening</u> the superstar of the year, Miss Nina Forest! How have you been doing, Nina?

W: Fine, George. Thank you.

M: Currently you are <u>working on a very big-budget film</u>, *The Seasons*. Would you like to tell us something about that?

W: Yeah, the movie is an emotional drama and I'm playing <u>the lead role of a woman</u> caught between two families. And for the first time I'm sharing the screen with the legendary Tom McKenzie.

M: How is it, working with such an experienced actor?

W: Oh, I'm so lucky to be working with him. There is so much to learn from him.

M: We heard that the movie is <u>being shot in locales</u> around Hong Kong. Do you like the place?

W: Well, Hong Kong is a beautiful city; however, I found it to be too warm. You know where I grew up, right? I mean I'm from Maine. Anyways, it took me some time to adjust to it. Overall, it was great fun, though!

M: Well, we wish you the best for <u>the upcoming release of the movie</u>. Thank you for coming to the show.

M: 오늘 저녁 올해의 슈퍼스타 Miss Nina Forest와 함께 하시고 계십니다! 어떻게 지내셨나요, Nina?

W: 잘 지냈어요, George. 감사합니다.

M: 요새 막대한 제작비가 투입된 영화, 'The Seasons' 를 찍고 있다고 들었습니다. 그것에 관해 조금만 말씀해 주시겠어요?

W: 네, 그 영화는 감성영화인데, 저는 두 가족과 얽힌 주연 여배우역을 맡고 있어요. 그리고 처음으로 저는 전설적인 Tom McKenzie와 함께 영화에 출연하고 있어요.

M: 그렇게 노련한 배우와 함께 일하는 것은 어떻죠?

W: 아, 그와 함께 일하게 된 것은 정말 행운이에요. 그에게서는 배울 게 아주 많거든요.

M: 영화가 홍콩 근처에서 현지 촬영되고 있다고 들었어요. 거기가 마음에 드나요?

W: 음, 홍콩은 아름다운 도시이지만, 너무 덥더라고요. 제가 어디에서 자랐는지 아시죠? 그러니까 저는 메인 주 출신이잖아요. 어쨌든 거기 적응하는 데에는 시간이 좀 걸렸어요. 하지만 전반적으로는 아주 좋았어요!

M: 음, 곧 개봉될 영화가 홍행에 성공하시길 바랄게요. 나와 주셔서 감사드립니다.

Inference I

1   What can be inferred about the actress?

   (a) She is used to cold weather.

   (b) She became successful through this film.

   (c) She likes the weather of Hong Kong.

   (d) She does not feel comfortable working with Tom.

여배우에 대해 추론할 수 있는 것은?

(a) 그녀는 추운 날씨에 익숙하다.

(b) 그녀는 이번 영화를 통해 성공했다.

(c) 그녀는 홍콩의 날씨를 좋아한다.

(d) 그녀는 Tom과 함께 일하는 것이 불편하다.

해설 남자가 진행하는 토크쇼에 영화배우인 여자가 나와서 나누는 대화이다. 초반에 함께 출연하는 경험 많은 남자배우에 관한 언급에 이어 현지 촬영 중인 홍콩에 대한 내용이 나온다. 여자는 추운 지역인 메인 주 출신이기 때문에, 더운 홍콩 날씨에 적응하는 데에 시간이 걸렸다. 그러므로 여자에 대해 추론할 수 있는 것은 (a)이다.

함정 (b) 영화는 아직 개봉하지 않았고, (c) 홍콩의 날씨가 그녀에게는 너무 더웠으며, (d) Tom에게서는 많은 것을 배웠다고 했다.

Comprehension

2   Which of the following is correct according to the interview?

   (a) Nina is working with a legendary movie director.

   (b) The setting for the movie is an Asian city.

   (c) The movie was released a couple of days ago.

   (d) Nina was brought up in two families.

인터뷰에 따르면 다음 중 옳은 것은?

(a) Nina는 전설적인 영화 감독과 일하고 있다.

(b) 영화의 배경은 아시아의 한 도시이다.

(c) 영화는 며칠 전에 개봉되었다.

(d) Nina는 두 가족 사이에서 성장했다.

해설 홍콩에서 현지 촬영 중이라고 했으므로, (b)의 내용이 옳다. (a) 감독에 대한 이야기는 언급되지 않았고, (c) 영화는 아직 개봉하지 않았다. 또한 (d) 두 가족과 사이에서 성장한 것은 여배우가 아니라, 영화 속 설정임에 유의한다.

어휘 currently 현재, 지금 | big-budget 큰 자본을 들인 | for the first time 처음으로 | legendary 전설적인 | locale 현장, 장소 | Maine 메인 주(미국 북동쪽에 있는 주) | adjust to ~에 적응하다, 순응하다 | overall 전반적으로, 총체적으로

2 Conversation

M: I'm going to the bookstore. <u>Want to come along?</u>

W: Sure. Are you looking for a specific book?

M: Yeah. There was a program on TV about a fiction writer, who usually writes about <u>his vision of the future</u>. What they showed on TV was quite interesting.

W: You mean a science fiction story <u>set in the future</u>? I can guess what it's going to be about: robots, machinery, and gadgets.

M: Well, the book is quite different. It imagines a future without describing any sophisticated machinery or hi-tech computers. It's <u>all about human beings and humanity</u>.

W: Sounds interesting! Does the book deal with <u>natural calamities</u> or <u>man-made mishaps</u> occurring in the future?

M: Yes. That's what makes the book so exciting.

W: In that case, I might be interested in reading it after you finish it.

M: 서점에 갈 건데, 같이 갈래?

W: 그래. 뭐 특별하게 찾는 책이 있니?

M: 어. 한 소설가에 대한 TV 프로그램이 있었는데, 그는 항상 미래에 대해 상상하여 글을 쓴대. TV에 방영된 것이 정말 재미있었어.

W: 미래 배경의 공상과학소설 말하는 거야? 그럼 로봇, 기계류, 장치에 관한 거겠다.

M: 음, 이 책은 정말 달라. 복잡한 기계나 첨단 컴퓨터에 대한 언급 없이 미래를 상상한대. 전적으로 인류와 인류애에 관한 것이지.

W: 재미있겠다! 그 책은 미래에 일어날 자연 재해나 인간으로 인한 재난을 다루는 거야?

M: 응. 그게 그 책을 그렇게 재미있게 만드는 거지.

W: 그렇다면, 네가 다 읽은 후에, 나도 읽어야겠다.

Inference I

1   What can be inferred about the speakers?

   (a) Both of them will buy the book.

   (b) The man has read the book before.

   (c) The woman is not going to buy the book.

   (d) The woman is not interested in fiction.

화자들에 대해 추측할 수 있는 것은?

(a) 둘 다 그 책을 살 것이다.

(b) 남자는 전에 그 책을 읽었다.

(c) 여자는 그 책을 사지 않을 것이다.

(d) 여자는 소설에 관심이 없다.

해설 TV에서 소개되었던 미래에 관한 소설에 대한 대화이다. 남자는 TV를 보고 그 책을 사려고 서점에 가려고 한다. 단순한 공상과학 소설이 아니라 인류와 인류애에 관한 소설이어서, 남자가 다 읽은 후에 여자도 읽겠다고 하고 있다.(I might be interested in reading it after you finish it.) 남자가 다 읽은 후에 읽겠다고 하는 것으로 보아, 여자는 책을 사지 않을 것임을 추측할 수 있다.

Comprehension

2 What could NOT be the source of the fictional future mentioned in the book?

(a) a nuclear war

(b) a massive landslide

(c) a sudden ice age

(d) sophisticated robots

이 책에서 언급된 공상 미래의 내용이 아닐 수 있는 것은 무엇인가?

(a) 핵전쟁

(b) 심한 산사태

(c) 갑작스러운 빙하기

(d) 복잡한 로봇

해설 로봇, 기계류, 장치 등에 관한 내용이 아니라, 전적으로 인류와 인류애에 관한 것으로 자연 재해나 인간으로 인한 재난을 다룬다고 했다. 그러므로 이 책에 나오지 않을 법한 것은 (d)이다.

함정 (b)와 (c)는 자연 재해, (a)는 인간으로 인한 재난이다.

어휘 fiction 소설, 허구 | machinery 기계류 | gadget 장치, 도구 | sophisticated 복잡한 | humanity 인간성, 인류애 | calamity 재해, 재난 | man-made 인간이 만든, 인조의 | mishap 불행한 일, 불운 | nuclear 핵의 | massive 대량의 | landslide 산사태 | ice age 빙하기

3 Monologue

W: Today was the last day of the World Soccer Championship. <u>The final match between Brazil and France</u>, played in Stevens Outdoor Stadium, was another important match that <u>kept the spectators watching</u> every moment of the game. France won the match, despite the fact that Brazil was stronger, with many well-known players. Worth mentioning was <u>the exceptional goaltending</u> of Darius Brown, who did not <u>let the opponents get</u> even a single goal. France is proud of winning the title <u>for the second time in a row</u>. With Darius Brown on the team, France is hopeful of

winning an Olympic gold medal as well. The Olympic games will be held in September, two months from now.

W: 오늘은 세계 축구대회의 마지막 날이었습니다. 브라질과 프랑스의 결승전이 Stevens 실외 경기장에서 열렸는데, 관중들로 하여금 경기의 순간 순간을 놓치지 않게 했던 중요한 경기였습니다. 브라질이 더 강하고 유명한 선수들이 많음에도 불구하고, 프랑스가 우승을 차지했습니다. 언급할 만한 것은 빼어난 수비수 Darius Brown인데, 그는 상대 선수들에게 단 한 골도 허용하지 않았습니다. 프랑스는 2년 연속 우승을 차지한 것을 자랑스러워합니다. 대표팀의 Darius Brown와 함께, 프랑스는 올림픽 금메달도 차지할 수 있기를 바라고 있습니다. 올림픽 게임은 지금부터 두 달 뒤인 9월에 개최될 것입니다.

Inference I

1 What can be inferred about the World Soccer Championship?

(a) The Brazilian team was weaker than people thought.

(b) The Brazilian team lacked good players.

(c) France won because of outstanding defense.

(d) France won because of its strong teamwork.

세계 축구대회에 관해 추론할 수 있는 것은 무엇인가?

(a) 사람들이 생각했던 것보다 브라질 팀은 더 약했다.

(b) 브라질 팀은 훌륭한 선수가 부족했다.

(c) 프랑스는 뛰어난 수비 때문에 승리했다.

(d) 프랑스는 강한 팀워크 때문에 승리했다.

해설 브라질이 축구를 더 잘하고 좋은 선수가 많았음에도 불구하고, 프랑스가 우승했다는 소식이다. 우승의 영광은 뛰어난 수비수 Darius Brown의 공이라고 언급하고 있다. 그러므로 (c)가 정답이다.

함정 (a) 브라질 팀에 대한 사람들의 기대는 언급되지 않았고, 브라질은 강한 팀이었지만 프랑스의 수비력 때문에 우승하지 못했다. (d) 프랑스의 팀워크가 강했는지 어땠는지에 대한 언급은 없다.

Inference I

2 What can be inferred about Darius Brown?

(a) He scored many goals in the championship.

(b) He was not recognized much before the championship.

(c) He won the championship twice in a row.

(d) He will be playing at the Olympic games.

Darius Brown에 대해 추측할 수 있는 것은 무엇인가?

(a) 그는 대회에서 많은 득점을 했다.

(b) 그는 그 대회 이전에는 그다지 알려지지 않았었다.

(c) 그는 연속해서 두 번 우승했다.

(d) 그는 올림픽 경기에도 출전할 것이다.

[해설] 결승전을 프랑스의 우승으로 이끈 것은 뛰어난 수비수 Darius Brown 때문이며, 이 선수 때문에 앞으로 있을 올림픽에서도 금메달 획득에 희망적이라고 되어 있다. 그러므로 그는 올림픽 경기에도 출전할 것임을 알 수 있다.

[함정] (b)는 전혀 알 수 없는 내용이며, (c) 프랑스가 두 번 연속 승리하기는 했으나, 이전 결승에도 Darius Brown이 수비수였는지는 언급되지 않았다.

[어휘] spectator 관중 despite ~에도 불구하고
mention 언급하다 exceptional 특별히 뛰어난, 비범한
goaltending (스포츠의) 골 방어, 골 수비
opponent (경기 · 논쟁 따위의) 적, 상대
in a row 일렬로, 연속적으로 outstanding 눈에 띄는, 현저한
defense 수비, 방어

4 Monologue

W: High school dances in the 1950s were called sock hops because the dances were performed without shoes. This <u>phenomenon of not wearing shoes</u> was indicative of the changing cultural practices at the time. High school dances, during those days, used to be held on gyms' basketball courts — which were <u>usually made of wood</u>. Before <u>the popularity of rock and roll music</u>, the dances were of a slow, smooth nature and were performed <u>with leather-soled shoes on</u>. However, leather-soled shoes were <u>a misfit with</u> rock and roll music: active rock music dancing could damage wooden floors. Gradually, the leather-soled dress shoe <u>went out of fashion</u>. High school dances were still called sock hops for a while even though the kids were dancing with their casual shoes on.

W: 1950년대 고등학교 댄스는, 그 춤이 신발을 신지 않고 추는 것이었기 때문에 sock hops라고 불렸습니다. 신발을 신지 않는 이러한 현상은 그 시대의 변하고 있는 문화 풍습을 나타내는 것이었습니다. 그 시대의 고등학교 댄스는 체육관의 농구 코트에서 열리곤 했는데, 농구 코트는 대개 나무로 만들어져 있었습니다. 로큰롤 뮤직이 대중화되기 전에, 춤은 느리고 부드러웠으며 바닥이 가죽으로 된 신발을 신고 추었습니다. 하지만 바닥이 가죽으로 된 신발은 로큰롤 뮤직과는 맞지 않았는데, 활기찬 록 뮤직 댄스가 나무 바닥을 손상시켰기 때문입니다. 점차적으로, 바닥이 가죽으로 된 정장용 구두는 유행하지 않게 되었습니다. 아이들이 캐주얼 슈즈를 신고 춤을 추게 되었는데도 불구하고, 고등학교 댄스는 여전히 한동안은 sock hops라고 불렸습니다.

Inference I

1 What can be inferred about the term sock hops?

(a) The term lost currency after a while.

(b) The term was coined by high school students.

(c) The term was used by a variety of people.

(d) The term represents rock and roll music.

sock hops라는 용어에 대해 추론할 수 있는 것은?

(a) 그 용어는 얼마 후에 사용되지 않게 되었다.

(b) 그 용어는 고등학교 학생들에 의해 만들어졌다.

(c) 그 용어는 다양한 사람들에 의해 사용되었다.

(d) 그 용어는 로큰롤 뮤직을 상징한다.

[해설] 1950년대 고등학생들이 추던 춤에 대한 내용이다. 로큰롤이 유행하기 전에는 바닥이 가죽으로 된 신발을 신고 춤을 출 수 있었지만, 로큰롤은 격해서 나무 바닥을 손상시켰기 때문에 신발을 벗고 양말만 신고 춤을 추게 되어 sock hops라는 춤 이름이 생겼다는 것이다. 다른 캐주얼 슈즈를 신고 춤을 추게 된 다음에도 한동안은 sock hops라고 불렸다는 마지막 문장에서 얼마 후에는 그 용어가 사용되지 않았음을 알 수 있다.

[함정] (d) 거친 로큰롤 음악 때문에 sock hops라는 춤 이름이 생기기는 했지만, 그 용어가 로큰롤 뮤직을 상징한다고 볼 수는 없다.

Relationship of Ideas

2 What are the causes for the emergence of sock hops?

(a) the oppression of high schools and the students' desire for freedom

(b) a change in trendy music and the wooden courts

(c) the acceptance and popularity of new dancing fashion

(d) the unpopularity and decline of leather-soled shoes

sock hops가 출현하게 된 동기는 무엇인가?

(a) 고등학교의 중압감과 자유에의 갈망

(b) 유행 음악의 변화와 나무로 된 코트

(c) 새로운 춤 유행의 수용과 인기

(d) 바닥이 가죽으로 된 신발의 비인기와 쇠퇴

[해설] 느린 음악에 맞추어 춤을 출 때는 고무바닥 신발이 괜찮았으나, 로큰롤이 유행하면서 고무바닥 신발이 춤추는 장소의 나무 바닥을 손상시키게 되어 신발을 벗고 춤을 추게 되었기 때문에, 그 시절의 춤이 sock hops라 불렸다는 내용이다. 그러므로 sock hops가 출현하게 된 동기는 (b) 유행 음악의 변화와 나무로 된 코트라고 할 수 있다.

[어휘] phenomenon 현상 indicative ~을 나타내는, ~의 표시인
used to ~하고는 했다
leather-soled shoes 바닥이 가죽으로 된 신발
misfit 부적합, 맞지 않는 것 out of fashion 유행이 지난

term 용어, 말 | currency 통용, 유통 |
represent 대표하다, 상징하다 | oppression 억압, 중압감 |
trendy 유행하는

1. b	2. c	3. b	4. b	5. d
6. d	7. c	8. c	9. a	10. d

1 Inference I

M: I've started doubting myself. Did I do the right thing by starting my own business?

W: Yes, indeed. Why would you think otherwise?

M: There's no money coming in. I'm even unable to repay the loan I took out to start the business.

W: Don't worry. Once your business is up and running, money will eventually flow in.

M: I don't know. I wouldn't be worried about these things if I stuck to the company I worked for. Plus, I didn't have to take out the loan that burdens me the most these days.

W: Well, true, but you wouldn't be enjoying the flexible working hours. You always complained that you didn't have time for yourself since you had to go to work very early almost every day.

M: Yeah, but everything's going very slowly at the moment and doesn't seem to be picking up.

W: It will. You need to have patience to wait for long-term results.

M: 내 자신이 의심스러워지기 시작했어요. 개인사업을 시작한 게 옳은 일이었을까요?

W: 네, 물론이죠. 왜 아닐 거라고 생각하죠?

M: 들어오는 돈이 없어요. 사업 시작하려고 빌린 대출금도 못 갚고 있어요.

W: 걱정하지 마세요. 일단 사업이 자리를 잡고 일이 순조롭게 진행되면, 돈은 결국 흘러 들어올 거예요.

M: 모르겠어요. 다니던 회사에서 계속 붙어있었다면, 이런 것들에 대해 걱정하지 않았을 텐데 말이에요. 게다가, 요즘 나를 심하게 짓누르는 대출도 받지 않아도 되었을 테고요.

W: 음, 그래요, 하지만 그랬으면 탄력적인 근무 시간을 가지지 못했을 거예요. 당신은 거의 매일 너무 일찍 출근해야 했어서, 자신을 위한 시간이 없다고 항상 불평했잖아요.

M: 네, 그런데 지금은 모든 게 너무 더디기만 하고 좋아질 것 같지가 않아요.

W: 좋아질 거예요. 장기적인 성과를 기다릴 수 있는 인내심을 가져야 해요.

Q What can be inferred about the man?

(a) He had been successful in his previous company.

(b) He is regretting having started his business.

(c) He wants the woman to help him with the business.

(d) He is thinking of closing his own business.

남자에 대해 추론할 수 있는 것은?

(a) 이전 회사에서 성공했다.

(b) 그의 사업을 시작한 것을 후회하고 있다.

(c) 여자가 자기 사업을 도와주기 바란다.

(d) 자기 사업을 접는 것에 대해 생각하고 있다.

해설 개인 사업을 시작한 뒤로, 돈도 잘 벌리지 않고 대출금도 못 갚고 있는 안 좋은 상황에 처하자, 자신이 괜히 사업을 벌인 게 아닌가 하고 후회하고 있는 남자에게 여자는 걱정하지 말고 장기적으로 결실을 맛볼 수 있게 될 것이라고 위로하고 있다. 그러므로 남자에 대해 추측할 수 있는 것은 (b)이다.

함정 (a) 이전 회사에 다녔으면, 이런 걱정은 하지 않아도 될 것이라는 남자의 말은 있지만, 이전 회사에서 성공했었는지는 알 수 없다. (d) 남자는 자기 사업을 벌인 것에 후회하고는 있지만, 접는 것을 고려하고 있는지는 알 수 없다.

어휘 even ~조차도, ~마저 | eventually 결국에는 |
flow in 흘러 들어오다 | stick to ~을 고수하다, ~에 달라붙다 |
take out a loan 빚을 내다, 대출 받다 |
burden ~에게 짐을 지우다, ~을 괴롭히다 |
flexible 탄력적인, 융통성이 있는 | at the moment 바로 지금 |
pick up (장사 따위가) 잘되다 | patience 참을성 |
long-term 장기적인

2

M: Today I've come to talk to you about diabetes, more specifically Type-2 diabetes, the most common kind. Type-2 occurs when the body is unable to absorb insulin. Insulin is a hormone that is vital to the body. It is necessary to transfer sugar or glucose from our food into the body's cells so as to provide them with energy. So when insulin is absent or is inadequate, glucose is not absorbed by cells. This leads to a rise in blood sugar levels. A person with this condition is a Type-2 diabetic. If not detected in time, or left untreated, diabetes can seriously affect the brain, nerves, heart and other critical parts of the body. Type-2 diabetes can most easily be treated by proper diet and exercise, <u>particularly in its early stages</u>.

M: 저는 오늘 여러분에게 당뇨병, 보다 정확하게는 당뇨병의 가장 일반적인 종류인 Type-2 당뇨병에 대해 말씀드리기 위해 여기 왔습니다. Type-2 당뇨병은 몸이 인슐린을 흡수하지 못하는 경우 생겨납니다. 인슐린은 신체에 대단히 중요한 호르몬입니다. 인슐린은 음식물에 들어있는 당분이나 포도당을 우리 몸속 세포로 날라 에너지를 공급하는 데 필요합니다. 따라서 인슐린이 결핍되거나 (그 양이) 충분치 못하면 세포가 포도당을 흡수하지 못하게 됩니다. 그렇게 되면 혈당 수치가 높아지는 결과를 초래합니다. 이런 상태에 있는 사람이 Type-2 당뇨병 환자입니다. 제때 (병세를) 발견하지 못하거나 치료받지 않은 상태로 방치할 경우 당뇨병은 뇌, 신경 조직, 심장, 그리고 신체의 다른 중요 부위에 심각한 영향을 미칠 수 있습니다. Type-2 당뇨병은 적절한 식이요법과 운동으로 대부분 쉽게 치료될 수 있습니다. 특히 초기 단계에서라면 말입니다.

Q   Which is correct according to the lecture?

(a) Insulin impedes the absorption of glucose.

(b) Insulin causes blood sugar levels to go up.

(c) High blood sugar levels can damage nerves.

(d) Type-2 diabetes is rarer than Type-1.

이 강의에 따르면 옳은 것은?

(a) 인슐린은 포도당 흡수를 방해한다.

(b) 인슐린은 혈당 수치 상승의 원인이다.

(c) 높은 혈당 수치는 신경에 손상을 줄 수 있다.

(d) Type-2 당뇨병은 Type-1 당뇨병보다 희귀하다.

해설 당뇨병 중에서도 가장 일반적인 종류인 Type-2 당뇨병에 대한 내용이다. 인슐린을 제대로 흡수하지 못하면 혈당 수치가 상승하면서 당뇨병이 발생하며, 이는 뇌, 신경 조직, 심장, 그리고 신체의 다른 중요 부위에 심각한 손상을 초래할 수 있다고 했으므로 정답은 (c)이다.

함정 (a)와 (b)는 내용과 상반되는 진술이다. (d) Type-2가 나왔으므로 Type-1에 대한 언급이 있었을 거라고 지레짐작하기 쉽다. 그러나 전체 문맥상 오직 Type-2 당뇨병과 그 원인에 대해 집중적으로 말하고 있음을 알수 있다.

어휘 **diabetes** 당뇨병 **absorb** 흡수하다
insulin 인슐린(췌장에서 분비되는 단백질 호르몬; 당뇨병 치료제)
transfer 옮기다, 건네다 **glucose** 포도당 **cell** 세포
absent 없는, 결여된 **inadequate** 불충분한
diabetic 당뇨병 환자, 당뇨병의

3

W: What are your plans for summer vacation?

M: I'm going to Egypt.

W: Wow, it will be really nice. I heard Egypt has many historical places. What are you going to do there?

M: I plan to go sightseeing and visit all the Pyramids.

W: <u>How long are you staying there</u>?

M: For five days.

W: And you think you can <u>visit all the Pyramids in five days</u>?

M: I know there are a lot of things to see, but if you find out <u>how packed my schedule is</u>, you will understand.

W: I think a vacation <u>should be relaxing</u>. If I were you, I wouldn't be very excited.

M: It's not like I can go to Egypt every vacation. <u>I don't want to miss anything</u> when I have a chance.

W: Well, I hope you have a wonderful time there. Gee, I wish I could go somewhere for my vacation.

M: <u>You could, if you saved enough</u>.

W: I will have to try to do that before my next vacation.

W: 여름휴가 계획이 뭐야?

M: 이집트에 갈 거야.

W: 와. 정말 좋겠다. 이집트에는 역사적인 곳이 많다고 들었는데. 거기서 뭐 할 거야?

M: 관광도 하고 피라미드에 다 가 볼 작정이야.

W: 거기에서 얼마나 묵을 건데?

M: 5일 동안.

W: 5일이면 피라미드를 다 돌아볼 수 있을 거라고 생각해?

M: 볼 것이 많다는 것은 알지만, 내 일정표가 얼마나 빡빡한지 알게 되면, 이해할 거야.

W: 휴가는 좀 여유가 있어야 하는데. 내가 너라면 그렇게 신나지만은 않을 거야.

M: 휴가 때마다 이집트에 갈 수는 없잖아. 기회가 있을 때, 아무것도 놓치고 싶지 않아.

W: 음. 거기에서 좋은 시간을 보내길 바랄게. 이런. 나도 휴가 때 어디를 좀 다녀와야 할 텐데.

M: 돈을 충분히 모았다면 갈 수 있겠지.

W: 음. 다음 휴가 때 한번 시도해 봐야겠다.

Q   Which is correct according to the conversation?

(a) The man is going to go to Egypt next vacation.

(b) The man's schedule in Egypt is very tight.

(c) The woman has been to Egypt once before.

(d) The woman has saved enough money for a

vacation.

대화에 따르면 옳은 것은?

(a) 남자는 다음 휴가 때 이집트에 갈 것이다.

(b) 이집트에서의 남자의 일정은 매우 빠듯하다.

(c) 여자는 전에 이집트에 가 본 적이 있다.

(d) 여자는 휴가를 위해 돈을 충분히 저축했다.

[해설] 여름휴가 계획에 대한 두 사람의 대화이다. 남자는 5일 동안 이집트에서 관광도 하고 피라미드에도 다 가 볼 계획이라고 한다. 5일 동안 피라미드를 다 돌아볼 수 있겠느냐는 여자의 질문에, 남자는 자기 일정이 얼마나 빠듯한지 알게 되면 이해할 수 있을 거라고 답하고 있다. 그러므로 이 대화와 일치하는 것은 (b)이다.

[함정] (a) 남자는 다음 휴가가 아니라 이번 휴가에 이집트를 여행할 것이다. (c) 여자가 이집트에 가 봤는지에 대한 언급은 없다. (d) 다음 휴가 때나 어딘가 가야 한다는 여자의 마지막 말로 보아, 여자는 돈을 충분히 저축하지 않았음을 알 수 있다.

[어휘] **historical** 역사의, 역사적인 | **go sightseeing** 관광을 가다 | **packed** 꽉 찬, 빽빽한 | **relaxing** 여유 있는

4

W: I have an important announcement to make before completing this class. Your <u>final oral testing period</u> is scheduled for next week. I have posted a blank schedule on my office door. By 9:00 a.m. this Friday morning, you are required to write your name <u>in a time slot in that schedule</u>, to show when you'd like to be tested. It is vital that <u>you submit it by the due date</u>. If you want to get the slot of your choice, I suggest picking one early. I will not allow any student to take another student's slot, <u>nor allow students to swap slots</u> once they have posted. My suggestion to you is that if you know the slot you want, <u>sign up for it as soon as you leave this class</u>. Also, please check the class webpage for instructions regarding your final assignment.

W: 수업을 마치기 전에 중요하게 할 공지사항이 있습니다. 여러분의 기말 구술시험 기간이 다음 주로 정해졌습니다. 내 사무실 문에 빈 일정표를 붙여 두었습니다. 이번 금요일 오전 9시까지, 그 일정표의 비어 있는 시간에 여러분의 이름을 써서 시험을 치르고 싶은 때를 알려주세요. 정해진 날짜 안에 적어야 하는 것이 중요합니다. 원하는 시간에 시험을 보길 원한다면, 빨리 골라야 하는 것이죠. 어떤 학생도 다른 학생의 시간에 시험을 치를 수 없으며, 정해진 시간표를 학생들끼리 바꾸는 것도 허용되지 않을 것입니다. 여러분에게 내가 할 수 있는 제안은 원하는 시간이 있다면 이 수업이 끝나자마자 신청하라는 것입니다. 또한 기말 과제에 대한 안내 사항은 웹페이지에서 확인하세요.

Q What should students do before the end of the week?

(a) take the final oral test

(b) select a time to be tested

(c) decide on an assignment topic

(d) hand in their final assignment

이번 주가 끝나기 전 학생들이 해야 할 일은?

(a) 기말 구술시험을 치르기

(b) 시험 칠 시간 정하기

(c) 과제의 토픽 정하기

(d) 기말 과제 제출하기

[해설] 기말 구술시험에 대해 알려 주는 내용이다. 시험 기간은 다음 주로, 이번 주 금요일 오전까지 사무실 문 앞에 붙여 둔 시간표에 각자 시험을 보고 싶은 시간을 정해 놓으라는 것이다. 그러므로 이번 주가 끝나기 전 학생들이 해야 할 일은 (b)이다.

[어휘] **complete** 완성하다, 마치다 | **oral** 구술의, 입의 | **post** 게시하다, 공시하다 | **vital** 절대로 필요한, 지극히 중요한 | **due date** 마감 날짜 | **swap** 교환하다, 바꾸다 | **assignment** 과제, 숙제 | **hand in** ~을 제출하다

5 Inference I

M: Like a true modernist, Virginia Woolf approached reality differently. When she described <u>subjective experiences</u>, she sought to make them authentic, hold them up as being relative and show how they were constantly changing. Her characters were not "flat," with <u>steady, constant emotions</u>. They were constantly changing, constantly reflecting on where they were, where they had been, and where they were going. Reading Woolf, the reader <u>goes right into the minds of the characters</u>, and so moves beyond being a passive observer. Her novel *Mrs. Dalloway* is a fine expression of the style referred to as stream-of-consciousness, with its rich texture <u>comprising the thoughts and dreams of her characters</u>. The narrative <u>moves seamlessly</u> between the conscious and the unconscious, the real and the fantastic and from memory to the present moment.

M: 진정한 모더니스트처럼 Virginia Woolf는 현실을 다르게 접근하였습니다. 주관적인 경험들을 묘사할 때 그녀는 그 경험들을 실질적으로 표현하려고 했고, 관련성을 유지하려고 하였으며 어떻게 끊임없이 변하는지 보여 주려고 했습니다. 그녀의 주인공들은 한결같고 지속적인 감정을 가진 "평면적인" 인물들이 아니었습니다. 그들은 끊임없이 변화하여, 자기가 어디에 있는지, 어디에 있었는지, 그리고 어디에 있을 것인지에 대하여 계속

적으로 되돌아보는 인물들이었죠. 독자들은 Woolf의 소설을 읽을 때, 수동적인 관찰자에서 벗어나, 등장인물의 마음으로 바로 들어가게 됩니다. 그녀의 소설 「Mrs. Dalloway」는 의식의 흐름이라고 일컬어지는 그녀의 특색을 잘 보여 주는 작품으로, 인물들의 생각과 꿈으로 이루어진 훌륭한 구성으로 짜여져 있습니다. 이야기는 의식과 무의식, 현실과 환상, 그리고 기억에서 현재 순간으로 구분 없이 넘나듭니다.

Q What can be inferred about the novel *Mrs. Dalloway* from the lecture?

(a) Its characters tend to resemble Woolf herself.

(b) Woolf's personal consciousness is absent from it.

(c) It reveals Woolf's awareness of contemporary philosophy.

(d) The story deals with the past and memory of its characters.

이 강의에서 소설 「Mrs. Dalloway」에 대해 추론할 수 있는 것은?

(a) 주인공들이 Woolf 자신과 닮아 있는 경향이 있다.

(b) Woolf의 개인적인 의식이 여기에 결여되어 있다.

(c) 현대 철학에 대한 Woolf의 인식을 보여준다.

(d) 이야기는 주인공의 과거와 기억을 다루고 있다.

해설 Virginia Woolf에 관한 강의이다. 의식의 흐름이라는 기법으로 유명한 소설 「Mrs. Dalloway」에 대해 언급하고 있다. 그 소설은 인물들의 생각과 꿈으로 이루어져 있으며, 과거와 현재를 넘나들고 있다고 했으므로 주인공의 과거와 기억을 다루고 있다는 것을 알 수 있다. 그러므로 (d)가 정답이다.

함정 Virginia Woolf가 주관적인 경험을 묘사했다는 언급은 있지만 주인공들이 작가 자신과 닮았다는 말은 없으므로 (a)는 답이 아니며, (b)와 (c)는 언급되어 있지 않다.

어휘 subjective 주관적인 character 등장인물 flat 평면적인
steady 꾸준한 passive 수동적인 observer 관찰자
referred to as ~이라고 일컬어지는
stream-of-consciousness 의식의 흐름 texture 조직, 구성
seamlessly 이음매 없이, 구분 없이

6

M: I will be ready in 5 minutes. What about you?

W: I've just finished packing everything. I'm ready.

M: Please check if there is anything you should do before we leave.

W: Oh, I just remembered. We haven't paid this month's rent yet.

M: But last Sunday you told me that you'd pay it.

W: Yeah. I was supposed to pay the rent that day, but

we had to visit your mother.

M: Oh, yes, I remember, she was ill and we became very busy helping her.

W: And after that I forgot to pay the rent. What should we do now? Should we just visit the landlord now and pay?

M: I think we should wire the money first and call her to explain this situation.

W: That would be better.

M: 5분만 있으면 준비될 거예요. 당신은 어때요?

W: 방금 짐을 다 쌌어요. 준비되었어요.

M: 떠나기 전에 해야 할 일이 있는지 확인해 봐요.

W: 아, 지금 생각났어요. 우리 아직 이번 달 임대료를 지불하지 않았어요.

M: 지난 일요일에 냈다고 했잖아요.

W: 네, 그날 내기로 되어 있었는데, 당신 어머니한테 가야 했잖아요.

M: 아 그래요, 기억나요, 어머니가 아프셔서 도와드리느라 무척 바빴었죠.

W: 그런 다음 임대료 내는 것을 깜빡했어요. 이제 어떡하죠? 지금 주인에게 가서 내야 할까요?

M: 먼저 돈을 송금하고 전화해서 상황을 설명해야 할 것 같아요.

W: 그게 좋겠네요.

Q Which is correct according to the conversation?

(a) They forgot to pay the man's mother's medical bills.

(b) They are going to visit the landlord soon.

(c) They didn't know the rent was to be paid on Sunday.

(d) They are going to send the rent to the landlord.

대화에 따르면 옳은 것은?

(a) 그들은 남자 어머니의 의료비 지불을 잊어버렸다.

(b) 곧 집주인을 방문할 것이다.

(c) 임대료 지불이 일요일이라는 것을 알지 못했다.

(d) 그들은 집주인에게 임대료를 보낼 것이다.

해설 미처 지불하지 못한 임대료에 관해 두 사람이 나누는 대화이다. 지난 일요일에 임대료를 내기로 되어 있었는데, 그 날 남자의 어머니가 아파서 도와드리느라 무척 바빴기 때문에, 깜빡 잊고 그냥 지나가 버렸다. 곧 떠나야 하는 상황이어서 먼저 임대료를 송금하고 전화로 설명하기로 했으므로, 정답은 (d)이다.

어휘 rent 임대(료) be supposed to ~하기로 되어 있다
landlord 집주인 wire (돈을) 송금하다 medical bill 의료비

7

W: On today's outing we're going to see humpback whales, named <u>on account of their oval-shaped backs</u>. They are largely black, <u>with distinctive white throats</u> and long wing-shaped flippers. They are a sight to behold as they break the surface of the water and <u>expel water through their blowholes</u> before diving deep again. As they generally swim close to the shore, whalers once found it easy to target them, causing <u>a drastic decline</u> in their numbers. It was once feared that the whales would be made extinct through excessive hunting, and only the concern of environmentalists and legal action <u>prevented this from happening</u>. A law prohibiting the hunting of humpbacks, passed in 1972, has since helped them recover. It is unclear, however, whether we will ever see humpbacks return to the large populations which once dotted the American coasts.

W: 오늘 소풍에서 우리는 혹등고래를 보러 가는데, 그 고래는 굽은 등 모양 때문에 그런 이름이 붙여졌습니다. 주로 검지만 목 부분이 눈에 띄게 하얗고 지느러미는 긴 날개 모양을 하고 있습니다. 이 고래들은 다시 깊이 잠수하기 전에, 수면 위로 올라와 물 뿜는 구멍으로 물을 분사하기 때문에 볼거리입니다. 혹등고래들은 일반적으로 해안가 근처에서 헤엄치기 때문에 한때 고래잡이들의 쉬운 목표물이 되었으며 이로 인해 그 수가 급격히 줄어들었습니다. 한때는 과도한 사냥으로 멸종하는 것이 아닌가 하는 우려도 있었지만 환경보호론자들의 우려와 법적 조치로 이런 일이 생기는 것을 막을 수 있었습니다. 1972년 통과된 혹등고래 사냥 금지 법안이 이 이후로 그들의 회복을 도왔습니다. 그러나 한때 미국 해안가를 수놓았던 이 혹등고래들의 수가 다시 원상복구 될 것인지는 미지수입니다.

Q Which is correct about humpbacks according to the talk?

(a) They have short flippers.

(b) They continue to dwindle in number.

(c) They are protected by law.

(d) They are mainly white in color.

이 이야기에 따르면 혹등고래에 대해 옳은 것은?

(a) 지느러미가 짧다.

(b) 수가 계속 줄어들고 있다.

(c) 법에 의해 보호된다.

(d) 주로 하얀 색이다.

해설 혹등고래에 관한 이야기이다. 혹등고래는 주로 검고 목 부분은 하얗고 지느러미는 긴 날개 모양이다. 해안에서 자주 볼 수 있었던 혹등고래가 사냥으로 멸종의 위기에 처했었지만, 1972년 사냥 금지 법안으로 보호되어 그 수가 다시 회복되고 있다고 했다. 그러므로 정답은 (c)이다.

함정 혹등고래의 지느러미는 길고 날개 모양을 하고 있다고 했으므로 (a)는 잘못된 내용이다. 1972년 통과된 법안으로 혹등고래 사냥이 불법화되었고 그 수가 줄어드는 것을 막을 수 있었다는 내용으로 보아 (b) 또한 오답이다. 혹등고래의 색은 대부분 검다고 하였으므로 (d)도 답이 될 수 없다.

어휘 outing 소풍 | humpback whale 혹등고래 | oval-shaped 타원형의 | distinctive 독특한, 분명한 | throat 목 | flipper 지느러미 모양의 발 | behold 보다 | surface 표면 | expel 내뿜다 | blowhole (고래의) 분수 구멍 | drastic 급격한, 과격한 | extinct 멸종된, 절멸한 | dwindle 줄다, 적어지다

8 Inference I

W: This pizza place is too crowded. Can we go somewhere else?

M: But <u>we've just got here</u>. We will have to wait anywhere we go around this time.

W: I know, but I don't like standing and waiting like this. And the line is not getting shorter. I'm starving.

M: Fine, do you know any other place?

W: Yeah, there's <u>an eatery just around the corner</u>.

M: What do they serve there? <u>Is it a fast food outlet</u>?

W: Yes. They have <u>all varieties of fast food served quickly</u>.

M: I thought that you wanted to have pizza.

W: Not any more.

M: Okay, let's have lunch there. We can't waste any more time searching for other places.

W: I know. And I have no more energy to move around.

M: Let's <u>grab something quickly</u> and go back to the office.

W: 이 피자집 너무 붐빈다. 다른 데로 갈까?

M: 근데 우린 방금 왔잖아. 이 시간에는 어딜 가도 다 기다려야 할 거야.

W: 알아, 하지만 이렇게 서서 기다리기는 싫어. 그리고 줄은 짧아지지도 않잖아. 나는 배고프다고.

M: 좋아, 다른 데 아는 곳 있어?

W: 응, 저 모퉁이를 돌면 바로 간이식당이 하나 있어.

M: 거기서 뭘 파는데? 패스트푸드점이야?

W: 응, 각종 패스트푸드가 빨리 나와.

M: 나는 네가 피자를 먹고 싶어 하는 줄 알았는데

W: 이제는 아니야.

M: 좋아, 거기서 점심을 먹자. 다른 곳을 찾느라 시간을 더 이상 낭비할

수는 없지.

W: 알아. 그리고 나는 돌아다닐 힘도 없어.

M: 뭔가 빨리 먹고 사무실로 돌아가자.

Q What can be inferred about the man?

(a) He wanted to have some pizza for lunch.

(b) He does not enjoy fast food very much.

(c) He does not mind what he eats for lunch.

(d) He is irritated with the woman.

남자에 대해 추측할 수 있는 것은?

(a) 점심으로 피자를 먹고 싶어 했다.

(b) 패스트푸드를 그다지 좋아하지 않는다.

(c) 점심으로 뭘 먹든 개의치 않는다.

(d) 여자에게 짜증이 나 있다.

해설 여자가 먹고 싶어 해서 두 사람이 찾아간 피자집이 사람들로 너무 붐비자, 다른 곳을 가기로 한다. 여자가 근처에 있는 패스트푸드점에서 음식이 빨리 나온다고 하자, 남자는 다른 곳을 찾아 헤매느니 그냥 그곳에서 먹는 게 낫겠다고 말하고 있다. 남자는 점심으로 무엇을 먹을지에 대해 별로 상관하지 않고 있으므로, 정답은 (c)이다.

함정 I thought that you wanted to have pizza.(나는 네가 피자를 먹고 싶어 하는 줄 알았는데.)라는 남자의 말로 보아, 원래 피자를 먹고 싶어 했던 것은 남자가 아니라 여자이다.

어휘 crowded 붐비는, 혼잡한 starve 굶주리다, 배고프다 eatery 간이식당 outlet 소매점, 판매점 variety 변화, 다양성 search for ~을 찾다

9

M: Of the numerous unique animal species on Earth, many can be found in the tropical rain forests of Northern Queensland in Australia. One of them is the Tree Kangaroo which, true to its name, lives high up in the trees and feeds on leaves and fruit. By living there high above the ground, it avoids ground-based predators and also is able to feed on higher-hanging foods that it would be unable to reach from the ground. As in all nature, however, there are the inevitable trade-offs. The Tree Kangaroo is fascinatingly agile as it moves among the treetops, but is quite clumsy on the ground, waddling around back and forth uncertainly. The Tree Kangaroo looks more like a small bear with a long tail than a kangaroo, but the two kangaroo species actually have the same ancestors.

M: 호주 퀸즈랜드 북부의 열대우림에서는 지구상에 존재하는 다양한 희

귀동물들을 볼 수 있습니다. 그 중 하나가 나무 캥거루로 그 이름처럼 나무의 높은 곳에 지내며 나뭇잎과 과일을 먹고 삽니다. 땅보다 높은 곳에서 살기 때문에 땅에 사는 포식동물들을 피하며 땅에서는 딸 수 없는 높은 곳에 달려 있는 음식을 먹을 수 있습니다. 그러나 자연이 다 그렇듯이 어쩔 수 없는 대가가 있습니다. 나무 캥거루는 나무 꼭대기 사이를 지나다닐 만큼 민첩하지만, 땅에서는 불안하게 앞뒤로 뒤뚱거리며 아주 서툽니다. 나무 캥거루는 캥거루보다는 긴 꼬리를 가진 작은 곰과 비슷한 모양이지만, 사실은 두 캥거루 종은 조상이 같습니다.

Q Which is correct about Tree Kangaroos according to the lecture?

(a) They resemble small bears.

(b) They live mainly on the forest floor.

(c) They move swiftly on the ground.

(d) They have short and thick tails.

이 강의에 따르면 나무 캥거루에 대한 설명으로 옳은 것은?

(a) 작은 곰을 닮았다.

(b) 숲 바닥에서 산다.

(c) 땅에서 민첩하게 움직인다.

(d) 짧고 굵은 꼬리를 가지고 있다.

해설 나무 캥거루에 관한 강의이다. 이름 그대로 나무 꼭대기에 사는 이 캥거루는 땅에서 걷는 것에는 서툴다고 하였으며, 긴 꼬리를 가진 작은 곰과 닮았다고 했다. 그러므로 정답은 (a)이다.

함정 나무 캥거루는 나무의 높은 곳에 지내므로 (b)는 오답이다. (c)의 언급과 달리 나무 캥거루는 나무 꼭대기 사이를 지나다닐 만큼 민첩하지만 땅에서는 불안정하게 뒤뚱거리며 서툴다고 했다. 나무 캥거루가 긴 꼬리를 가진 작은 곰과 비슷한 모양이라는 것으로 보아 (d)와 달리 나무 캥거루의 꼬리는 길다는 것을 알 수 있다.

어휘 numerous 다수의, 많은 unique 독특한 species 종, 종류 feed on ~을 먹고 살다 predator 육식동물 inevitable 피할 수 없는 trade-offs 타협점, (교섭에서의) 교환 조건 agile 기민한, 날쌘 clumsy 서투른, 솜씨 없는 waddle 비틀거리다, 뒤뚱거리다 back and forth 앞뒤로 uncertainly 불안정하게

10 Inference I

W: I've called this meeting of executives to make an important announcement. You all know that our airline's operating costs have shot up over the last two quarters, primarily because of fuel costs which continue to rise. During this same time, our revenues have dropped. The result of this has been that our profit margins have been squeezed. We have to change this situation before things become truly serious and <u>our corporation is put into jeopardy</u>. At yesterday's board meeting we decided that we would start offering low-cost flights to attract more customers. It is something we've wanted to do for a long time. Our new service will be called "BudJet" and we plan to launch it across the nation. "BudJet" will offer no free services on flights — even meals and beverages will be charged to customers. All luggage <u>carried onto the plane or stowed</u> will also be charged.

W: 중요한 발표를 하기 위하여 중역 회의를 소집하였습니다. 여러분도 모두 알다시피, 우리 항공 운행 비용이 지난 2분기 동안 급등했는데, 주로 계속되는 유가 인상으로 인한 것입니다. 같은 기간 동안, 수익은 떨어졌습니다. 그 결과 우리 이윤은 거의 남지 않았습니다. 우리는 상황이 더욱 심각해지기 전에, 그리고 회사가 더 이상의 위험에 직면하기 전에 이러한 상황을 변화시켜야 합니다. 어제의 이사회에서 우리는 더 많은 고객을 끌기 위한 저가 항공을 시작하기로 결정했습니다. 오래 전부터 하려고 했던 것입니다. 우리의 새로운 서비스는 '버젯'이라고 불릴 것이며 전국에 걸쳐 실시할 예정입니다. '버젯'은 항공기 내에서 음식과 음료를 포함하여 어떠한 무료 서비스도 제공하지 않을 것이며 이 모든 것은 유료로 제공될 것입니다. 비행기에 가지고 타든 화물로 부치든 모든 짐들 역시 비용이 청구될 것입니다.

Q   What can be inferred about the airline from the talk?

(a) It has long considered changing its name.

(b) It will reduce the number of its aircraft.

(c) It will operate new routes outside the nation.

(d) It seeks to benefit from a higher volume of customers.

이 이야기에서 볼 때 항공사에 대해 무엇을 추측할 수 있나?

(a) 명칭 바꾸는 것을 오랫동안 고려해 왔다.

(b) 항공기 숫자를 줄일 것이다

(c) 국외 신규 항로를 운행할 것이다

(d) 더 많은 고객을 끌어들여 이윤을 창출할 것이다.

해설 유가가 높아짐에 따라 비용은 늘고 수입이 줄고 있는 항공사가 마련한 대책에 관한 내용이다. 저가 항공을 보급하여 더 많은 고객을 끌어들임으로써 이윤을 내기로 결정했다는 내용이다. 따라서 정답은 (d)이다.

함정 (a) 명칭 바꾸는 것이 아니라 저가 항공 사업을 오랫동안 고려해 왔다는 내용이다.

어휘 executive 중역, 간부, 경영진 | shoot up 하늘 높이 치솟다, (물가가) 급등하다 | quarter 4분의 1, (1년의) 사분기 | revenue 수익, 수입 | profit margin 이윤 마진 | squeeze 짜내다 | jeopardy 위험 | attract 끌다, ~의 마음을 끌다 | beverage 음료 | charge 부담시키다, 청구하다 | luggage 화물 | stow 싣다, 실어 넣다

LISTENING REVIEW

A

1. spectator	2. gadget
3. outing	4. glucose
5. oval-shaped	6. eatery
7. mishap	8. predator
9. subjective	10. waddle
11. swap	12. calamity
13. flipper	14. seamlessly
15. agile	16. dwindle

1. someone who watches something, especially a sporting event

2. a small machine or device which does something useful

3. a short enjoyable trip, usually with a group of people, away from your home, school, or place of work

4. a type of sugar that gives you energy

5. being like a circle but is wider in one direction than the other

6. a place where you can buy and eat food

7. an unfortunate but not very serious event that happens to someone

8. an animal that kills and eats other animals

9. based on personal opinions and feelings rather than on facts

10. to walk with short, quick steps, swinging slightly from side to side

11. to give something to someone and receive a different thing in exchange

12. an event that causes a great deal of damage, destruction, or personal distress

13. the two or four flat limbs which a sea creature uses for swimming

14. having no breaks or gaps in something or which continues without stopping

15. moving quickly and easily

16. to become smaller, weaker, or less in number

B

1. b	2. b	3. b	4. a	5. b

1. 임대료는 그날 내기로 되어 있었다.

   (a) I'm sure that the rent was paid that day.

   (b) I was supposed to pay the rent that day.

2. 고등학교 댄스는 여전히 한동안은 sock hops라고 불렸다.

   (a) The term sock hops represents high school dances at the time.

   (b) High school dances were still called sock hops for a while.

3. 그것은 음식물에 들어 있는 당분이나 포도당을 우리 몸속 세포로 나르는 데에 필요하다.

   (a) It is a hormone that is a vital sugar or glucose to the body.

   (b) It is necessary to transfer sugar or glucose from our food into the body's cells.

4. 혹등고래들의 수가 다시 원상복구 되는 것을 볼 수 있을 것인지는 미지수이다.

   (a) It is unclear whether we will ever see humpbacks return to the large populations.

   (b) It is uncertain that humpbacks continue to dwindle in number.

5. 독자들은 Woolf의 소설을 읽을 때, 등장인물의 마음으로 바로 들어가게 된다.

   (a) The character's mind goes right into the reader while reading woolf novel.

   (b) Reading Woolf, the reader goes right into the minds of the characters.

C

  1. I found it to be too warm.

  2. I thought that you wanted to have pizza.

  3. What they showed on TV was quite interesting.

  4. I didn't have to take out the loan that burdens me the most these days.

  5. One of them is the Tree Kangaroo which lives high up in the trees.

1. it / I found / to be too warm

2. pizza / I thought / that you wanted to have

3. quite interesting / what they showed on TV / was

4. I didn't have to / that burdens me the most these days /

take out the loan

5. which lives high up in the trees / one of them / is the Tree Kangaroo

D

  1. b   **2. a**   **3. b**   **4. a**   **5. b**

1. The brain, nerves, and heart can be damaged by diabetes.

   (a) Diabetes can most easily be treated by proper diet and exercise.

   (b) Diabetes can seriously affect the brain, nerves, and heart.

2. Humpbacks are protected by law to prevent their extinction.

   (a) A law prohibiting the hunting of humpbacks has helped them recover.

   (b) Humpbacks could be made extinct through excessive hunting.

3. The opponents didn't get a single goal because of the exceptional goaltender.

   (a) The opponents did not let the exceptional goaltender prevent a single goal.

   (b) The exceptional goaltender did not let the opponents get even a single goal.

4. We have decided to benefit from a higher volume of customers by offering low-cost flights.

   (a) We will start offering low-cost flights to attract more customers.

   (b) We have to change this situation before things become truly serious.

5. You have to write your name in a blank of the schedule before the end of the week.

   (a) You are required to swap time slots of the schedule by this Friday.

   (b) By this Friday, you are required to write your name in a time slot in that schedule.

VOCABULARY PREVIEW

01. censor 검열하다, 검열하여 삭제하다
02. snatch 앗아가다
03. perspective 견해, 시야
04. offend ~의 감정을 상하게 하다
05. prevalent 널리 보급된, 우세한
06. patrol 순찰하다
07. drastic 급격한, 격렬한
08. take the initiative 솔선하다
09. personnel 전직원, 인원
10. reportedly 보도에 의하면
11. gender-neutral 남녀 구별이 없는
12. counterpart 상대방, 짝의 한 쪽
13. endorse 보증하다, (어음 따위에) 배서하다
14. accuse 고발하다, 고소하다
15. pharmaceutical 제약의
16. willful 계획적인, 고의의
17. attic 다락방
18. untidiness 지저분함
19. tribe 부족
20. barbaric 미개한, 야만인 같은
21. sanction 인가하다, 규정을 설정하다
22. feasibly 실행할 수 있도록, 그럴 듯하게
23. pictograph 상형문자
24. juxtapose 병렬하다, 병치하다

GUIDED LISTENING

1	1. a	2. c	**2**	1. b	2. a
3	1. b	2. b	**4**	1. a	2. c

1 Conversation

M: Are you a fan of James Bond?

W: Well, no. Why do you ask?

M: Have you seen his latest movie *Secret Underwater*?

W: No. Actually I don't like those kinds of movies filled with action and unreal gadgets.

M: Yeah, those movies don't really turn me on either. But I heard it is quite different from typical Bond movies.

W: Oh, really? What is it about?

M: The movie is about a national treasure hunt, but doesn't have those action-packed scenes. It's all about strategy.

W: Oh, that wouldn't be that bad.

M: So what do you say?

W: Let's see if there are seats available.

M: James Bond를 좋아하니?

W: 음, 아니. 왜 물어?

M: 그의 최신 영화 "Secret Underwater"를 봤니?

W: 아니. 사실 나는 액션과 비현실적인 기계 장치들로 가득한 그런 종류의 영화는 좋아하지 않아.

M: 맞아, 나도 그런 영화들에 흥미를 못 느껴. 하지만 이 영화는 전형적인 Bond 영화와는 차원이 다르다고 들었어.

W: 아, 그래? 뭐에 관한 건데?

M: 그 영화는 국보를 찾아내는 것이지만, 액션이 난무한 장면은 없어. 완전히 전략적이지.

W: 그다지 나쁘지 않을 것 같은데?

M: 어떻게 할까?

M: 좌석이 있는지 알아보자.

Inference II

1 What can be inferred from the conversation?

(a) They both are not interested in violent movies.

(b) The man has seen the movie recently.

(c) The new Bond movie will be released soon.

(d) The woman likes action movies.

이 대화에서 추론할 수 있는 것은 무엇인가?

(a) 그들은 둘 다 폭력 영화에 관심이 없다.

(b) 남자는 최근에 그 영화를 봤다.

(c) 새로운 Bond 영화가 곧 개봉될 것이다.

(d) 여자는 액션 영화를 좋아한다.

해설 영화관에 어떤 영화를 볼지 고르고 있는 대화이다. 남자나 여자 모두 액션이나 기계 장치가 많은 영화는 좋아하지 않는다는 데에 동의하고 있으므로 (a)가 정답이다.

함정 (b) 둘 다 그 영화를 보지 않았으며, (c) 새로운 Bond 영화는 이미 개봉 중이다.

Detail

2   What are the speakers doing in the conversation?

(a) asking what kinds of movies each other likes

(b) exchanging opinions about Bond movies

(c) deciding which movie to watch

(d) talking about what the movie was like

대화에서 화자들이 하고 있는 것은 무엇인가?

(a) 어떤 종류의 영화를 좋아하는지에 대해 묻기

(b) Bond 영화에 대한 의견 나누기

(c) 어떤 영화를 볼지 결정하기

(d) 영화가 어땠는지 이야기하기

해설 남자나 여자 모두 액션이나 장치가 많은 영화는 좋아하지 않지만, 이번 James Bond의 최신 영화는 이전 영화들과는 다르다고 하면서, 그 영화의 좌석이 있는지 알아보자고 말하고 있다. 영화관에 어떤 영화를 볼지 고르고 있는 대화이므로 (c)가 정답이다.

함정 (a) 마지막 대화를 놓치면, 단순히 어떤 종류의 영화의 좋아하는지에 대한 대화라고 착각할 수 있으므로 유의한다.

어휘 latest 최신의, 최근의   gadget 기계 장치   typical 전형적인 strategy 전략, 작전

2 Conversation

M: Stella, can you manage to go to the concert alone?

W: Why? Aren't you coming?

M: I've got a terrible toothache. Luckily, I have an appointment with my dentist in the evening.

W: Oh no. Why don't you go home and take a rest?

M: I can't afford to do that now. I have some important clients coming over in the afternoon; I need to see them.

W: Okay, I understand. Can I get you some medicine for your pain?

M: Thanks, I've already taken a pill. That's why I'm able to talk now.

W: Good. As soon as I finish my work, I'll leave for the concert.

M: Stella, 콘서트에 혼자 갈 수 있겠어요?

W: 왜요? 당신은 못 가나요?

M: 치통이 심해요. 다행스럽게도, 오늘밤에 치과 예약이 되었거든요.

W: 저런. 집에 가서 쉬지 그래요?

M: 지금은 그럴 여유가 없어요. 오후에 중요한 손님이 오시로 되어 있거든요. 그들을 만나야 해요.

W: 좋아요, 이해해요. 치통 약을 좀 드릴까요?

M: 고맙지만, 이미 한 알 먹었어요. 그래서 지금 말이라도 할 수 있는 거죠.

W: 다행이네요. 저는 일을 마치는 대로, 콘서트 보러 갈게요.

Inference II

1   What can be inferred from the conversation?

(a) Neither of them will go to the concert.

(b) The man's toothache is severe.

(c) The woman will get a refund for the tickets.

(d) Today is the last day of the concert.

이 대화에서 추론할 수 있는 것은?

(a) 그들은 둘 다 콘서트에 가지 않을 것이다.

(b) 남자의 치통이 심하다.

(c) 여자는 티켓을 환불받을 것이다.

(d) 오늘은 콘서트의 마지막 날이다.

해설 남자의 치통 때문에 약속했던 콘서트에 갈 수 없다는 대화이다. 남자는 치통이 심해 저녁에 치과에 예약을 해서, 콘서트에 갈 수 없겠다고 여자에게 말하고 있다. 그러므로 남자의 치통이 심하다는 (b)가 정답이다.

함정 여자 혼자 콘서트에 가겠다는 내용이 있으므로 (a)와 (c)는 옳지 않다.

Comprehension

2   Which is correct according to the conversation?

(a) The man made an appointment at the dental clinic.

(b) The man postponed the meeting until the afternoon.

(c) They will go to the concert after work.

(d) The woman is expecting some clients in the afternoon.

이 대화에 따르면 옳은 것은?

(a) 남자는 치과 예약을 했다.

(b) 남자는 회의를 오후까지 미루었다.

(c) 여자와 남자는 퇴근 후에 콘서트에 갈 것이다.

(d) 여자는 오후에 만날 고객들을 기다리고 있다.

해설 남자는 치통이 있어서 저녁에 치과 예약을 했기 때문에, 콘서트에 갈 수 없다. 집에 가서 쉬라는 여자의 말에 오후에 중요한 손님이 오기로 되어

있어서 그럴 수 없다는 내용도 있다. 그러므로 (a)가 정답이다.

함정 회의가 있어서 손님을 기다리고 있는 것은 남자이다. 그러므로 (b)와 (d)는 옳지 않다.

어휘 have an appointment 예약하다, 약속하다 |
dentist 치과의사 | take a rest 쉬다

3 Monologue

M: Democracy is all about the right to freedom of expression. <u>Censoring literature</u>, in other words, is like snatching away one's basic human rights. By censoring certain literature, we are limiting a writer's <u>free flow of thoughts</u> and disrespecting his or her talent. We are also restricting ourselves <u>to a narrowed way of thinking</u> rather than broadening our perspectives. Content which may be offending to one person may not be offending to another. Therefore, <u>it should be left to the reader</u> to decide which content is suitable for him or her. Moreover, teachers who teach literature <u>not only describe literary styles</u> but also connect literature to prevalent social attitudes. If we censor their content, we refuse to learn and <u>acknowledge social trends</u>.

M: 민주주의란 표현의 자유를 위한 권리를 뜻합니다. 문학을 검열하는 것은 다른 말로 하면 인간의 기본적인 권리를 빼앗는 것과 같습니다. 어떤 문학을 검열함으로써, 우리는 작가의 자유로운 사고 흐름을 제한하게 되고, 그 사람의 재능을 무시하게 됩니다. 또한 우리의 시야를 넓히는 것이 아니라, 우리 스스로를 편협한 사고방식으로 제한하게 될 것입니다. 어떤 한 사람에게 거슬릴지 모르는 내용이 다른 사람에게는 그렇지 않을 수 있습니다. 그러므로 자신에게 어떤 내용이 맞는지는 독자가 결정하도록 남겨져야 합니다. 더욱이, 문학을 가르치는 교사들은 문학 스타일만 묘사할 것이 아니라 문학을 널리 보급되어 있는 사회적 태도와 연결시켜 줘야 합니다. 우리가 내용을 검열한다면, 사회적 추세를 배우고 알게 되는 것을 거부하는 것입니다.

Inference II

1   What can be inferred from the talk?

(a) Censorship for young people is necessary in some sense.

(b) Censorship is not beneficial for writers and readers.

(c) All democracies around the world censor sometimes.

(d) Teachers should have the right to censor literature for their students.

이 이야기에서 추론할 수 있는 것은 무엇인가?

(a) 젊은 사람들을 위해 문학을 검열하는 것이 어떤 면에서는 필요하다.

(b) 문학의 검열은 작가나 독자에게 이롭지 않다.

(c) 전 세계의 모든 민주주의 국가들이 때때로 검열을 한다.

(d) 교사들은 학생들을 위해 문학을 검열한 권리가 있어야 한다.

해설 문학 검열에 관한 내용이다. 문학을 검열하는 것은 인간의 권리를 빼앗고 작가들을 무시하는 행위이며, 이로써 독자들의 사고마저 제한해서 편협하게 만든다고 했다. 그러므로 문학의 검열은 작가나 독자에게 이롭지 않다는 (b)가 정답임을 알 수 있다.

함정 화자는 검열이 필요하지 않다는 의견을 피력하고 있으므로, (a), (c), (d) 모두 정답이 아니다.

Relationship of Ideas

2   What are the two reasons that support the speaker's opinion on censorship?

(a) It interferes with our thoughts and confuses our perspectives.

(b) It violates the right to express ourselves and limits our thought.

(c) It is disrespectful of the writers and restricts their creativity.

(d) It violates the right to read and limits the development of literature.

문학 검열에 대한 화자의 의견을 뒷받침하는 두 가지 이유는?

(a) 검열은 우리의 사고를 방해하고 시야를 혼란스럽게 한다.

(b) 검열은 표현의 자유에 위배되고 우리의 사고를 제한한다.

(c) 검열은 작가를 경시하는 것이며 그들의 창의력을 제한한다.

(d) 검열은 읽을 권리에 위배되고 문학 발전을 제한한다.

해설 문학을 검열하는 것은 인간의 기본 권리를 빼앗는 것이며, 시야를 제한해서 사고를 편협하게 한다는 주장이다. 문학은 검열되어서는 안 된다는 주장을 하기 위해 화자는, 문학 검열은 표현의 자유에 위배되고 우리의 사고를 제한한다고 말하고 있으므로, (b)가 정답이다.

어휘 democracy 민주주의 | right 권리 |
censor 검열하다, 검열하여 삭제하다 | snatch 앗아가다 | flow 흐름 |
disrespect 경시하다, 무시하다 | restrict 제한하다, 한정하다 |
broaden 넓히다, 확장하다 | perspective 견해, 시야 |
content 내용 | offend ~의 감정을 상하게 하다, 불쾌하게 하다 |
prevalent 널리 보급된, 우세한 | trend 경향, 추세

4 Monologue

W: Dealing with the increasing crime rate is <u>a topic of endless debate</u>. I must point out some surprising facts about it. Many crime <u>prevention programs</u> are being managed by the people themselves, including individuals, business groups and communities. It is quite astonishing to know that the public police force is <u>three times smaller than private police forces</u>. Many business groups have hired private security forces for their safety. Many citizens have <u>formed volunteer groups</u> that patrol the city when required. As a result, there has been <u>a drastic fall in the crime rate</u> in the city. These examples indicate the level of awareness and sense of responsibility among common citizens.

W: 늘어나고 있는 범죄율에 대처하는 일은 끊임없는 논쟁거리입니다. 그것에 관한 몇몇 놀라운 사실을 지적해야겠습니다. 많은 범죄 예방 프로그램들이 개인들, 기업과 지역 공동체를 포함한 사람들 스스로에 의해 이루어지고 있습니다. 경찰 공권력이 사설 보안 인력보다 3배 적다는 것을 알게 된 것은 상당히 놀라운 일입니다. 많은 기업들이 그들의 안전을 위해 사설 경비인력을 고용하고 있습니다. 많은 시민들이 필요할 때 도시를 순찰하는 자원봉사 단체를 조직하였습니다. 그 결과, 도시 범죄율이 급격히 하락하였습니다. 이러한 실례들은 일반 시민들 사이의 의식과 책임감의 수준을 보여 주는 것입니다.

Inference II

1 What can be inferred from the speech?

(a) Citizens are taking their own initiatives to prevent crime.

(b) People consider the police useless.

(c) Private security firms are replacing public police.

(d) Public police departments need more personnel.

이 연설에서 추론할 수 있는 것은 무엇인가?
(a) 시민들이 범죄를 예방하기 위해 솔선수범하고 있다.
(b) 사람들은 경찰이 쓸모가 없다고 생각한다.
(c) 사설 경비업체들이 경찰 병력을 대신하고 있다.
(d) 경찰부서는 더 많은 인원을 필요로 한다.

해설 늘어나고 있는 범죄율에 대처하기 위해 시민들이 직접 나서고 있다는 내용이다. 개인들과 기업들의 노력으로 범죄율이 극적으로 떨어지게 되었다는 언급도 있다. 특히 Many citizens have formed volunteer groups that patrol the city when required.(많은 시민들이 필요할 때 도시를 순찰하는 자원봉사 단체를 조직하였습니다.)에서 (a)의 내용을 추측할 수 있다.

함정 (b) 경찰이 쓸모가 없다거나 (c) 사설 경비업체들이 경찰 병력을 대신하고 있다는 내용은 너무 확대 해석한 것으로 답이 될 수 없다.

Comprehension

2 Which of the following is correct according to the speech?

(a) The crime rate has been increasing recently.

(b) Security forces hired by many businesses patrol the city.

(c) Many people volunteer to patrol the city when necessary.

(d) The number of public police officers has decreased.

이 연설에 따르면 옳은 것은?
(a) 최근 범죄율이 증가했다.
(b) 많은 기업에 의해 고용된 경비업체가 도시를 순찰한다.
(c) 필요하면 많은 사람들이 자원하여 도시를 순찰한다.
(d) 공공 경찰관들의 수가 줄었다.

해설 1번 문제와 마찬가지로 Many citizens have formed volunteer groups that patrol the city when required.(많은 시민들이 필요할 때 도시를 순찰하는 자원봉사 단체를 조직하였습니다.)에서 (c)의 내용이 옳다는 것을 알 수 있다.

어휘 deal with ~을 다루다, ~에 대처하다   debate 토론, 논쟁
prevention 예방   security 보안, 안전
volunteer 자원봉사자, 지원자   patrol 순찰하다
drastic 급격한, 격렬한   awareness 인지도
take the initiative 솔선하다   personnel 전직원, 인원

PRACTICAL LISTENING

1. a	2. c	3. b	4. d	5. a
6. c	7. b	8. d	9. a	10. d

1

M: An official from China's space program announced last night that the nation's first team of female astronauts will <u>leave on a space mission</u> before 2010. They will join their male colleagues as mission commanders and flight engineers. The chief of the space program has reportedly said that four female astronauts will be sent on the mission. China's air force has already <u>selected thirty five female pilots</u> to be given training as astronauts. China has <u>made a determined effort</u> to ensure that its space program is <u>gender-neutral</u>, and that women astronauts <u>have as many opportunities as their male counterparts</u>. Nevertheless, South Korea remains the only nation so far whose first astronaut was a woman.

M: 어젯밤 중국 우주 프로그램 관계자는 2010년 전에 우주 미션을 위하여 첫 여성 우주비행사 팀이 출발할 것이라고 발표했습니다. 그들은 미션 사령관과 비행 기술자 등으로 남자 비행사들과 함께 할 것입니다. 보도에 따르면, 이 우주 프로그램의 지휘자가 네 명의 여성 우주비행사를 보낼 것이라고 했다고 합니다. 중국 공군은 이미 35명의 여성 파일럿을 우주비행사로 훈련시키고 있다고 합니다. 중국은 우주 프로그램이 남녀에게 모두 균등한 기회가 될 것을 보장하기 위해 확고한 노력을 기울이고 있으며, 여성 우주비행사들이 남자 비행사들처럼 많은 기회를 보장받도록 노력하고 있습니다. 그렇지만 한국은 지금까지 첫 우주 비행사가 여성이었다는 기록을 가진 유일한 나라입니다.

Q Which is correct according to the news report?

(a) **China plans to send women into space by 2010.**

(b) China has trained thirty five male pilots to be astronauts.

(c) China's next space program has fewer women than South Korea's.

(d) China's air force gives more advanced training to female astronauts.

이 뉴스에 따르면 옳은 것은?

ⓐ 중국은 2010년까지 여성을 우주에 보낼 계획이다.

ⓑ 중국은 35명의 남성 비행사를 우주비행사가 되기 위해 훈련시킨다.

ⓒ 중국의 다음 우주 프로그램은 한국보다 여성이 적다.

ⓓ 중국 공군은 여성 우주비행사에게 더 고급 훈련을 시킨다.

해설 중국이 우주비행사에 여성을 참여시키려고 노력한다는 뉴스이다. 현재 훈련 중인 35명의 여성들 가운데 4명의 여자 우주비행사들을 선정하여 2010년 전에 남자 비행사들과 함께 내보내려고 한다는 내용이다. 한국의 첫 우주비행사는 여성이었다는 언급으로 뉴스를 마무리하고 있다. 그러므로 옳은 것은 (a)이다.

함정 중국 공군은 이미 35명의 여성 파일럿을 우주 비행사로 훈련시키고 있다고 하므로 (b)는 옳지 않다. (c)와 (d)의 내용은 언급되지 않았다.

어휘 colleague 동료 | commander 지휘관, 사령관 | reportedly 보도에 따르면, 들리는 바에 의하면 | determined 확실한, 결심한, 단호한 | ensure 확실시하다 | gender-neutral 남녀 구별이 없는, 남녀에게 균등한 | counterpart 상대방, 짝의 한 쪽 | nevertheless 그럼에도 불구하고, 그렇지만

2 Inference II

M: I feel so tired.

W: Maybe because it is the first day of the workshop.

M: Maybe. I'd better get some sleep before any night activities.

W: Yeah. I think I'm going to get some shut-eye for a while, too.

M: You can have the bed. I'll sleep on the couch.

W: Thanks. By the way, are you going to keep the fan running while you sleep?

M: Yes. Why not?

W: Keeping a fan on while sleeping can make you sick.

M: I've never heard that before. If it is an air conditioner, it might not be that healthy, but it's a fan.

W: I heard it spreads dust, increasing your risk of getting sick.

M: Well, I've been doing this since childhood and have never had any problem.

W: You mean you've never had any problem yet. You know it's always good to be on the safe side.

M: Well, I guess turning off the fan wouldn't hurt me, either.

M: 나 너무 피곤해.

W: 아마 오늘이 연수 첫 날이라 그럴 거야.

M: 그럴지도 모르겠다. 야간 활동 전에 잠깐 자두는 게 좋겠어.

W: 그래. 나도 잠깐 눈을 붙여야겠어.

M: 네가 침대에서 자도 돼. 나는 소파에서 잘게.

W: 고마워. 그런데 잘 때 선풍기를 계속 틀어 놓을 거니?

M: 응, 안 돼?

W: 잘 때 틀어 놓으면 병이 날 수 있어.

M: 그런 말은 들어 본 적 없는데. 에어컨이라면 건강에 그다지 좋지 않겠지만, 선풍기인 걸 뭐.

W: 선풍기는 먼지를 퍼뜨려서 병에 걸릴 위험성을 높이는 거래.

M: 글쎄, 난 어렸을 때부터 그래 왔는데, 아무 문제 없었거든.

W: 아직은 아무 문제가 없었다는 거잖아. 항상 조심하는 게 좋은 거잖아.

M: 음, 선풍기를 꺼도 내가 병이 나지는 않을 테니까.

Q What can be inferred from the conversation?

(a) They have a habit of keeping a fan on while sleeping.

(b) They agree that keeping a fan on is bad for their health.

(c) **They are not going to use a fan while sleeping.**

(d) They prefer fans to air conditioners.

이 대화에서 추측할 수 있는 것은?

(a) 그들은 잘 때 선풍기를 켜놓는 습관이 있다.

(b) 그들은 선풍기를 켜두는 것이 건강에 나쁘다는 데에 동의한다.

(c) 그들은 잘 때 선풍기를 사용하지 않을 것이다.

(d) 그들은 에어컨보다 선풍기를 좋아한다.

해설 선풍기를 켜놓고 자는 남자와 끄고 자는 여자가 나누는 대화이다. 잘 때 늘 선풍기를 켜놓고 자는 습관을 가진 남자에게 여자는 선풍기가 더러운 먼지를 공기 중에 퍼뜨려서 병에 걸릴 수 있기 때문에 조심해야 한다고 충고하고 있다. 선풍기를 켜놓고 자는 습관을 가진 남자는 지금까지는 아무 문제가 없었지만, 끄고 자도 아무 문제 없을 것이므로 선풍기를 끄기로 한다. 그러므로 (c)가 정답이다.

함정 (a) 잘 때 선풍기를 켜놓는 습관은 남자에게만 있다. (b) 남자는 선풍기를 켜두는 것이 건강에 나쁘다는 데에 동의한 것이 아니라, 꺼두어도 괜찮다는 데에만 동의했다. (d)에 관한 언급은 없다.

어휘 get some sleep 조금 자두다

get some shut-eye 눈을 붙이다, 잠깐 자다 couch 침상, 소파

keep ~ -ing ~을 계속 …하게 하다 fan 선풍기

spread 퍼뜨리다, 뿌리다, 퍼지게 하다 dust 먼지

be on the safe side 조심하다, 신중을 기하다 turn off 끄다

prefer A to B B보다 A를 더 좋아하다

3

W: Leading baseball player Patrick Henry is being sued by a consumer rights group for misrepresenting facts about the weight loss pills he endorsed. The group has <u>accused</u> Henry <u>of making false claims</u> about the effectiveness of Eazy Diet pills, manufactured by the Glindia Pharmaceutical Company. Independent research has repeatedly shown that pills like Eazy Diet <u>have little impact on weight loss</u>. Glindia is accused of knowing this fact, and yet marketing the pills as useful anyway — a form of <u>advertising fraud</u>. Henry, who is on a 4-year contract with Glindia, <u>denies willful wrongdoing</u>. He says that Glindia told him repeatedly that the pills were effective in losing weight. Henry admits, however, that he never used the pills himself, <u>contrary to what he stated</u> in his ads.

W: 일류 아구선수 Patrick Henry가 한 소비자 권리 단체에 의하여 그가 홍보했던 체중 감량 알약에 대한 거짓 사실 때문에 고소되었습니다. 그 단체는 Henry가 글린디아 제약회사에서 제조된 이지 다이어트 알약의 효과에 대하여 거짓 정보를 제공했다고 고소했습니다. 독자적인 연구 결과가 끊임없이 주장하듯 이지 다이어트 같은 약은 체중 감소에 큰 효과가 없다고 합니다. 글린디아는 이 사실을 알면서도 광고 사기 형태로 이 약이 좋다고 홍보했기 때문에 고소되었습니다. 글린디아와 4년간의 계약을 체결한 Henry는 자신의 의지와 상관없는 잘못이라고 이야기합니다. 그는 글린디

아가 반복적으로 그에게 약이 살을 빼는 데 효과가 있다고 말했다고 합니다. 그러나 Henry는 그가 광고에서 이야기했던 것처럼 직접 그 약을 복용한 적은 없다고 인정하고 있습니다.

Q Which of the following is true according to the news report?

(a) Eazy Diet pills can actually cause people to gain weight.

(b) Henry maintains he was unaware they were ineffective.

(c) Glindia received bad publicity over similar harmful drugs.

(d) Researchers used outdated methods to test their effectiveness.

이 뉴스 기사에 따르면 다음 중 사실인 것은?

(a) 이지 다이어트 알약은 실제로는 체중증가를 가져온다.

(b) Henry는 그것이 효과가 없다는 것을 알지 못했다고 주장한다.

(c) 글린디아는 이와 비슷한 유해 약품을 제조한 것으로 악명 높다.

(d) 연구진은 그 효과를 시험하는 데 구식 방법을 사용했다.

해설 일류 아구선수 Patrick Henry가 홍보한 체중 감량 약품이 효과가 없어서, 고소되었다는 뉴스이다. 그가 홍보에서 말했던 것처럼 직접 복용하지는 않았지만, 제약회사에서 그에게 말한 것처럼 체중 감량에는 효과가 있을 거라고 생각하고 광고했다고 하므로, 정답은 (b)이다.

함정 (a) 이지 다이어트 알약은 체중 감량에는 효과가 없지만, 실제로 체중 증가를 가져오는지는 알 수 없다. (c) 글린디아가 이전에 이와 비슷한 유해 약품을 제조했는지에 대한 언급은 없다. (d) 실험에 오래된 방법을 사용했다는 언급은 없다.

어휘 sue 고소하다, 소송을 제기하다

misrepresent 잘못 전하다, 거짓 전하다 pill 알약

endorse 보증하다, (어음 따위에) 배서하다

accuse 고발하다, 고소하다 manufacture 제조하다

pharmaceutical 제약의

have little impact on ~에 거의 영향을 미치지 않다 fraud 사기

willful 계획적인, 고의의 admit 인정하다

contrary to ~와는 반대로 outdated 낡은, 시대에 뒤진

4

W: I'd like to <u>enroll in Spanish 301</u>, please.

M: Which section would you like to join?

W: The 8:30 class, please.

M: I'm sorry, it's already full. You can enroll in the 10:30.

W: That's not possible. I have another class at the

same time.

M: <u>What is the name of the class</u>?

W: English Literature 302.

M: English Literature 302? Let me see. Well, <u>there is a session for</u> English Literature 302 at 8:30. Why don't you take it in the morning and take Spanish at 10:30?

W: Can I do that?

M: <u>Let me check if you can register</u>. I'm really sorry. English Literature 302 at 8:30 is also full.

W: <u>I really need these classes</u>. They are important for my graduation.

M: <u>It'd be better</u> if you spoke to the course supervisor. He may be able to help you.

W: Okay, thank you. I'll do that.

W: 스페인어 301을 등록하고 싶어요.

M: 어떤 반에 들어가고 싶으세요?

W: 8시 30분 거요.

M: 죄송하지만, 이미 다 찼네요. 10시 30분 수업은 등록할 수 있습니다.

W: 그럴 수 없어요. 같은 시간에 다른 수업이 있거든요.

M: 그 수업명이 뭔가요?

W: 영문학 302요.

M: 영문학 302요? 제가 좀 볼게요. 음, 영미 문학 302는 8시 30분 수업이 있네요. 아침에 그 수업을 듣고 10시 30분에는 스페인어를 듣는 게 어때요?

W: 그럴 수 있을까요?

M: 등록할 수 있는지 확인해 볼게요. 죄송해요. 8시 30분 영문학 302도 다 찼군요.

W: 저는 그 수업이 꼭 필요해요. 졸업에 중요한 과목이거든요.

M: 과목담당 교수님과 이야기해 보는 게 좋을 것 같군요. 그 분이 도와줄 수 있을지도 몰라요.

W: 네, 고맙습니다. 그렇게 할게요.

Q Which is correct according to the conversation?

(a) The woman wants to take either English or Spanish.

(b) The woman will be graduating next semester.

(c) The man advises the woman to drop one of the classes.

(d) The man can't help the woman when the class is full.

이 대화에 따르면 옳은 것은?

(a) 여자는 영어나 스페인어를 듣고 싶어 한다.

(b) 여자는 다음 학기에 졸업할 것이다.

(c) 남자는 여자에게 한 가지 수업을 취소하라고 조언한다.

(d) 남자는 수업 인원이 다 차서 여자를 도와줄 수 없다.

해설 스페인어 301 수강 신청을 놓고 두 사람이 나누는 대화이다. 여자는 8시30분 수업을 등록하고 싶어 하지만, 그 시간에는 이미 인원이 다 찬 관계로, 남자는 10시30분 수업을 권하고 있다. 하지만 여자는 그 시간에 다른 수업이 있다. 어떻게든 여자를 도와 주려고 노력했지만, 정원이 다 차서 도와줄 수 없다. 과목담당 교수님과 이야기해 보는 게 좋겠다는 남자의 말로 보아, (d)의 내용을 알 수 있다.

함정 (a) 여자는 영문학과 스페인어를 둘 다 듣고 싶어 한다. (b) 여자가 언제 졸업할 것인지에 대한 언급은 없다.

어휘 enroll in ~에 등록하다 graduation 졸업
supervisor 감독(자), 관리자, 지도주임 semester 학기

5

M: I'm really grateful that you <u>offered to help me</u>.

W: Hey, you're always welcome. Moreover, <u>all the things in your dad's attic</u> are so interesting.

M: Yeah, he used to collect anything that had unusual colors or shapes.

W: He must be a very creative person.

M: Yeah, but it will take us a long time <u>to clean up all of these things</u>.

W: I can't wait to open these things and look into the contents.

M: Well, let's move <u>all of these downstairs</u> and then we can open them one by one.

W: Okay, should we take these boxes first?

M: Well, let's take those cabinets; they <u>seem to be quite heavy</u>.

M: 나를 도와주겠다고 해서 정말 고마워.

W: 언제든지 환영이야. 더군다나 너희 아빠 다락방에 있는 모든 것들이 정말 흥미로워.

M: 응, 아버지는 색상이나 모양이 특이한 거면 뭐든지 수집하셨어.

W: 틀림없이 무척 창의적인 분이실 거야.

M: 그래, 하지만 이것들을 모두 치우려면 시간이 오래 걸릴 거야.

W: 빨리 이것들을 열어서 내용물을 보고 싶어.

M: 자, 이것들을 다 아래층으로 옮긴 다음에 하나씩 열어 보자.

W: 알았어, 먼저 이 상자들을 가져가는 게 좋을까?

M: 음, 저 캐비닛을 가져가자. 꽤 무거워 보이는데 말이야.

Q What is the conversation mainly about?

(a) the cleaning up of the attic

(b) the untidiness of the attic

(c) the contents of the boxes

(d) the work of the man's father

이 대화는 주로 무엇에 관한 내용인가?

(a) 다락방 치우기

(b) 다락방의 지저분함

(c) 상자 속의 내용물

(d) 남자 아버지의 일

해설 여자는 남자를 도와 남자 아버지의 다락방을 말끔히 치우려고 하고 있다. 그곳에 있는 흥미를 끄는 내용물들을 여자가 보고 싶어 하자, 남자는 물건들을 아래층으로 다 옮긴 후에 하나씩 열어 보자면서 캐비닛부터 옮기려고 하고 있다. 따라서 정답은 (a)이다.

함정 상자 속 내용물을 여자가 몹시 궁금해하기는 하지만, 짐을 다 옮기고 나중에 열어보자는 것에서 대화가 그쳤기 때문에, 그 내용물이 대화의 주제가 되지는 못한다. 따라서 (c)는 오답이다.

어휘 grateful 고맙게 여기는, 감사하는 | moreover 게다가, 더구나 | attic 다락방 | used to ~하곤 했다. 이전에는 ~이었다 | can't wait to ~하는 것을 기다릴 수 없다 | contents 속에 든 것, 내용물, 목차 | downstairs 아래층에(으로) | one by one 하나씩, 차례로 | cabinet 수납장, 진열장 | untidiness 지저분함

6 Inference II

M: The Aztecs are said to have had one of the most advanced cultures among ancient South American tribes, but we must remember that these advances were largely borrowed. The Aztecs were a people who easily absorbed the best elements of foreign cultures, and this was a decided strength for them. For centuries, they remained barbaric nomads limited to northern Mexico, where they struggled to survive. In the 12th century they migrated to central Mexico and built their capital city. From then on, they began to adopt the advanced ways of existing cultures and expand their power through conquest. The dominant position they made for themselves by the 14th century was entirely through this policy of absorption and acquisition.

M: 아즈텍 문명은 고대 남아메리카 부족 중에서 가장 발전된 문명이었다고 일컬어지지만, 이러한 선진 문명들 대부분이 빌려온 것이었다는 사실을 기억해야 합니다. 아즈텍 사람들은 외국 문물을 쉽게 받아들이는 사람들로서 이 점이 그들에게 확실히 강점이 되었습니다. 수세기 동안 그들은 야만 유목민으로 북 멕시코에 남아 생존하기 위해 애썼습니다. 12세기 그들은

중앙 멕시코로 이주해 왔고 그들의 수도를 세웠습니다. 그때부터 그들은 이미 존재하던 문화로부터 선진기술을 받아들여 그들의 힘을 정복을 통해 넓혀가기 시작했습니다. 그들이 14세기까지 이룩한 우세한 지배 위치는 전반적으로 그들의 흡수와 습득 정책에 의거한 것이었습니다.

Q What can be inferred from the lecture?

(a) The Aztecs taught their skills to neighboring tribes.

(b) The Aztecs were pervasive and powerful even as nomads.

(c) The Aztecs were not leaders in cultural innovation.

(d) The Aztecs moved to central Mexico to cultivate crops.

강의를 통해 추론할 수 있는 것은?

(a) 아즈텍 사람들은 이웃 부족에게 그들의 기술을 가르쳤다.

(b) 아즈텍 사람들은 유목민일 때도 잘 널리 퍼져 있었고 힘이 있었다.

(c) 아즈텍 사람들은 문화 혁신에 있어서 리더가 아니었다.

(d) 아즈텍 사람들은 농작물 경작을 위해 중앙 멕시코로 이주했다.

해설 아즈텍의 문명에 관한 강의이다. 흔히 가장 진보된 문명이라고 알고 있지만, 거의 대부분 외국에서 받아들인 문명이었다는 내용이다. 오랫동안 북 멕시코에만 살던 유목민이었는데, 12세기에 중앙 멕시코로 이주해서 수도를 세웠으며, 주변 국가들을 정복했다는 내용이다. 그러므로 정답은 (c)이다.

함정 (a) 아즈텍 사람들은 이웃 부족에게서 문화를 받아들였으며, (b) 유목민으로서 제한된 장소에 살고 있었다. (d) 또한 멕시코로 이주해서 수도를 세웠다.

어휘 advanced 진보한, 앞선 | tribe 부족 | absorb 흡수하다 | barbaric 미개한, 야만인 같은 | nomad 유목민 | survive 살아남다 | migrate 이주하다 | adopt 채택하다, 채용하다 | expand 확장하다 | conquest 정복 | dominant 우세한, 지배적인 | absorption 흡수, 병합 | acquisition 습득, 획득 | pervasive 널리 퍼져 있는 | innovation 쇄신, 혁명 | cultivate 경작하다

7

W: Students, let me remind you that Web for Democracy in Asia, or WFDA, is meeting this week. You probably didn't know this, but the WFDA was launched in 1997 at a conference of Internet news organizations in Singapore. Its aim was to promote independent Web journalism, human rights and democratic participation throughout the Asian region. The WFDA maintains that democracy in the modern era is dependent on mass participation, and the Web is ideal for that. Online gatherings and discussions, political movements, <u>voter awareness campaigns</u>, and other activities help grow democracy across the Pacific and Indian Oceans. I hope you will all make time <u>to attend the forum</u>, because it combines your interest <u>in new electronic media</u> with your passion for democracy.

W: 학생 여러분, 아시아 지역 민주주의를 위한 웹, 줄여서 WFDA의 미팅이 이번 주 개최됨을 다시 한 번 상기시켜 드리겠습니다. 여러분들은 아마 모르셨겠지만, WFDA는 1997년 싱가포르 인터넷 뉴스 단체들의 회담에서 처음 출범했습니다. WFDA의 목표는 아시아 전 지역에 독자적인 웹 저널리즘, 인권, 민주주의 참여 등을 활성화하는 것입니다. WFDA는, 현대에 있어 민주주의는 대중의 참여에 의존하고 있고 웹이 이러한 점에 있어 이상적인 것이라고 주장합니다. 온라인을 통한 모임이나 토론, 정치적 행보, 유권자 인식 캠페인 및 기타 활동들이 태평양과 인도양 전역의 민주주의를 성장시키는 데 도움이 됩니다. 저는 여러분들 모두 시간을 내서 이번 포럼에 참여하시기를 바랍니다. 왜냐하면 이 포럼이 민주주의에 대한 여러분의 열정과 함께 새로운 전자 미디어에 대한 여러분의 관심을 잘 조합시키는 것이기 때문입니다.

Q Which is correct according to the announcement?

(a) The WFDA receives little support outside Asia.

(b) Internet news organizations founded the WFDA.

(c) The WFDA is a website run from Singapore.

(d) The WFDA is hosting a conference in India.

이 공지에 따르면 사실인 것은?

(a) WFDA는 아시아 외의 지역에서는 거의 지지를 받지 못하고 있다.

(b) 인터넷 뉴스 단체들이 WFDA를 창설했다.

(c) WFDA는 싱가포르에서 운영되는 웹사이트이다.

(d) WFDA는 인도에서 회담을 개최한다.

[해설] WFDA, 즉 아시아 지역 민주주의를 위한 웹 모임 참여를 권하는 내용의 공지이다. WFDA는 1997년 싱가포르 내 인터넷 뉴스 단체들에 의해 창설되었으며, 미디어를 통해 태평양과 인도양 전역의 민주주의를 성장시키는 데에 도움이 되고 있으므로 정답은 (b)이다.

[함정] (a)의 내용은 공지사항만으로는 알 수 없는 사항이다. (c) WFDA는 웹사이트가 아니라 싱가포르 인터넷 뉴스 단체들의 모임이라는 데에 유의한다. (d)의 내용은 언급된 바 없다.

[어휘] **democracy** 민주주의 | **launch** 착수하다, 진출시키다 | **organization** 조직, 구성, 단체 | **promote** 활성화하다, 진행시키다 | **participation** 참여, 관여 | **region** 지역 | **maintain** 주장하다, 지지하다 | **be dependent on** ~에 의존하다 | **mass** 대중, 다수 | **gathering** 모임 | **voter** 유권자 | **awareness** 인식, 깨달음 | **combine** 결합하다, 화합하다 | **passion** 열정

8 Inference II

M: Hi, I would like to meet Mr. Kingsley. <u>I'm his attorney</u>.

W: Well, he's in a company meeting. Did you make an appointment?

M: No, but I want to speak to him urgently.

W: I'm sorry, sir. <u>We can't disturb</u> Mr. Kingsley now.

M: Okay, when will the meeting be over?

W: It may take about an hour or so. Would you like to wait here?

M: <u>I can't wait that long</u> since I have an appointment with another client in 30 minutes. Well, can you just <u>go in for a second</u> and give him these papers? I'm sure he will understand. And I will wait here <u>since he might want to see me now</u>.

W: All right.

M: Oh, let me just write something on the paper.

W: Sure. Take your time.

M: If he can't come out, please tell him that I will call him later <u>to arrange a meeting tomorrow</u>. Thanks a lot.

W: No problem.

M: 안녕하세요. Kingsley씨를 만나고 싶어요. 저는 그의 변호사입니다.

W: 지금 회의 중입니다. 약속을 하셨나요?

M: 아니요, 하지만 급하게 할 말이 있습니다.

W: 죄송합니다. 지금은 Kingsley씨를 방해할 수 없어요.

M: 그래요, 회의가 언제 끝날까요?

W: 1시간 정도 걸릴 거예요. 여기서 기다리시겠어요?

M: 30분 후에 다른 고객과 약속이 있어서 그렇게 오래 기다릴 수는 없어요. 음, 잠깐 들어가셔서 이 서류만 전해 주시겠어요? 그도 이해할 거예요. 그러면 그가 지금 저를 만나고 싶어 할지도 모르니 여기서 기다릴게요.

W: 좋습니다.

M: 아, 서류에 잠깐 뭐 좀 쓸게요.

W: 그러세요. 천천히 하세요.

M: 그가 나올 수 없다면, 내일 약속을 정하기 위해 제가 이따가 전화하겠다고 말해 주세요. 정말 고맙습니다.

W: 아니에요.

Q What can be inferred from the conversation?

(a) The attorney will meet Mr. Kingsley immediately.

(b) Mr. Kingsley doesn't like being interrupted during a meeting.

(c) The man is one of Mr. Kingsley's several attorneys.

(d) The attorney thinks Mr. Kingsley will see him now if it's urgent.

대화에서 추론할 수 있는 것은?

(a) 변호사는 Kingsley씨를 즉각 만날 것이다.

(b) Kingsley씨는 회의 동안 방해받는 것을 좋아하지 않는다.

(c) 남자는 Kingsley씨의 몇몇 변호사들 중 한 명이다.

(d) 급한 일이라면 Kingsley씨가 바로 그를 만날 것이라고 변호사는 생각한다.

해설 Kingsley씨의 변호사인 남자는 급한 일로 그를 만나고자 하지만, 지금 회의 중인 관계로 바로 만날 수 없다고 여자는 말하고 있다. 회의가 약 1시간 정도 걸릴 거라는 여자의 말에, 남자는 서류만 전해 주면, 급한 일이라는 것을 알게 되어 Kingsley씨가 그를 만나러 나올지도 모른다고 말하고 있으므로 정답은(d)이다.

함정 (a) Kingsley씨가 급한 사항이라고 생각해야만 곧 만나게 될 것이다. (b) Kingsley씨가 회의 동안 방해받는 것을 좋아하는지 좋아하지 않는지는 알 수 없다.

어휘 attorney 변호사 | make an appointment 선약하다 | urgently 다급하게 | disturb 방해하다 | be over 끝나다 | arrange 정하다, 준비하다 | immediately 즉시 | interrupt 방해하다

9

M: There's much more to be done about the world climate issue than just negotiating agreements. International agreements like the Kyoto Treaty are meaningless until the major polluters of the world like North America, Japan, and Europe make substantial cuts in their greenhouse gas emissions. These treaties also need empowered international monitors who can sanction polluters no matter where they are. Most importantly, major polluting countries must instill a strong sense of civic duty in their citizens and corporations. In the end, this is what will reduce pollution, since monitors cannot feasibly visit every factory within a large country. Treaties and agreements amount to nothing more than legal and technical grandstanding, and achieve very little in concrete terms — unless polluting countries truly move to enforce them.

M: 협상을 진행하는 것을 넘어서 세계 기후 문제와 관련하여 처리되어야 할 것들이 아주 많이 있습니다. 교토 의정서 같은 국제 조약은 주요 오염국, 북미나 일본과 유럽 등이 그들의 온실 가스 방출을 실질적으로 줄이지 않는 이상 별 의미가 없습니다. 이러한 조약들은 어디에 있든지간에 오염국들에게 규제를 가할 수 있는 강력한 국제 감시단들이 필요합니다. 가장

중요한 것은 주요 오염국들이 그들의 시민들과 기업들에게 강력한 시민의 의무감을 심어 주어야 한다는 것입니다. 결국, 이런 방법이 오염을 줄일 것입니다. 감시단들이 큰 국가 안의 모든 공장을 일일이 방문하지 못하기 때문입니다. 조약과 협약은 법적이고 기술적으로 유리한 입지를 얻으려는 것이나 매한가지이며, 구체적인 조항들도 거의 성취하지 못할 것입니다. 오염 발생국들이 진정으로 그것들을 집행하지 못한다면 말이죠.

Q What is the speaker's view of present international climate negotiations?

(a) They are of no value and produce insubstantial results.

(b) They create more discord than peace among nations.

(c) They pressure major polluters to make overnight changes.

(d) They are of interest only to climate experts.

현재 국제 기후 협상에 대한 화자의 관점은?

(a) 가치가 없고 미미한 결과만을 도출한다.

(b) 국가간 평화보다는 알력을 초래한다.

(c) 하룻밤에 변화하라고 주요 오염국들을 압박한다.

(d) 단지 기후 전문가들만 관심을 가진다.

해설 세계 기후 문제에 관한 연설이다. 기후에 관한 여러 국제적인 협약들이 있기는 하지만, 거의 효과가 없다고 역설하고 있다. 효과가 있으려면, 강력한 감시원단을 두어, 오염국들로 하여금 자국의 국민들과 기업들에 제재를 가하게 해야 한다고 주장하고 있다. 화자는 현재 협약들의 비효율성과 영향을 미치지 못한다고 비판하고 있으므로 정답은 (a)이다.

어휘 negotiate 협상하다, 협의하다 | substantial 실질적인, 주요한 | greenhouse gas 온실 가스 | emission 방출 | empowered 권한을 가진 | sanction 인가하다, 규정을 설정하다 | instill 주입시키다, 조금씩 가르치다 | feasibly 실행할 수 있도록, 그럴듯하게 | amount to ~이나 매한가지이다, 결국 ~이 되다 | grandstanding 유리한 입지를 얻으려는 행동 | concrete 구체적인 | term 조건, 조항 | enforce 강요하다, 집행하다 | of no value 가치가 없는 | discord 불일치, 알력

10 Inference II

W: You all know that the Egyptians began using pictographs as a means to represent concrete objects, most commonly for the purpose of trade. These pictographs were one of the earliest forms of human communication, and made ancient Egypt quite advanced compared to earlier civilizations which lacked a written language of any type. Today I will tell you about the more complex pictography that the Egyptians' pictographs <u>evolved into</u>. In this system, they juxtaposed existing pictographs <u>to represent intangible things or ideas</u>. For example, if they wanted to refer to the human soul, the custom was to draw an eagle above a man's head. This shows that Egyptian pictographs were sophisticated enough <u>to deal with philosophical concepts</u>, not just physical acts and items.

....

W: 여러분은 모두 이집트인들이 구체적인 대상을 표현하기 위한 수단으로 상형문자를 사용하기 시작했다는 것을 알고 계실 것입니다. 특히 일반적으로는 거래의 목적으로 사용되었죠. 이 상형문자들은 역사상 가장 초기 의사 소통 형태 가운데 하나였으며, 이로써 이집트는 어떤 형태든 문자 언어를 갖지 못한 그 이전의 문명들에 비해 상당히 진보한 문명이 될 수 있었습니다. 오늘은 이집트인들이 발전시킨 보다 복잡한 상형문자에 관해 말씀 드리겠습니다. 이 시스템에서 이집트인들은 손으로 만질 수 없는 사물이나 개념을 표현할 수 있도록 기존의 상형문자들을 병치해서 사용했습니다. 예를 들어, 인간의 영혼을 표현하고 싶을 때는 사람의 머리 위에 독수리를 그려 넣는 식이었습니다. 이는 이집트의 상형문자들이 단지 물리적인 행동이나 물체들뿐만 아니라 철학적인 개념들을 표현할 만큼 충분히 정교해졌음을 보여 줍니다.

Q　What can be inferred from the lecture?

(a) Pictographs from ancient Egypt can be confusing.

(b) Pictography is an inherently rigid system of writing.

(c) Egyptian writing has remained the same since ancient times.

(d) Egyptian pictographs represented more than just real objects.

....

이 강의에서 추론할 수 있는 것은?

(a) 고대 이집트의 상형문자는 혼란스러울 수 있다.

(b) 상형문자는 원래부터 있던 견고한 문자 시스템이다.

(c) 이집트 문자는 고대 이후와 다름없이 똑같다.

(d) 이집트 상형문자는 실제 사물 이상의 것을 표현했다.

해설 이집트인들이 사용한 상형문자의 진보성에 대한 강의이다. 강의를 통해 강사는 이집트 문자가 물리적인 행동이나 물체뿐만 아니라 철학적인 개념들까지 표현할 정도로 정교했다고 했으므로 정답은 (d)이다.

함정 (a) 이집트 상형문자는 다른 문명에 비해 정교했다고 했지 혼동을 초래한다고는 하지 않았다. 이집트 상형문자는 계속 발전했다고 했으므로 (b)와 (c)는 오답이다.

어휘 pictograph 상형문자 | represent 나타내다 | concrete 구체적인 | object 대상, 물체 | trade 거래, 교환 | advanced 진보한, 진보적인 | lack ~이 없다, 모자라다 | evolve 발달시키다 | juxtapose 병렬하다, 병치하다 |

intangible 손으로 만질 수 없는 |
sophisticated 정교한, 매우 복잡한

LISTENING REVIEW

A

1. patrol	2. enroll
3. attic	4. censor
5. interrupt	6. pharmaceutical
7. intangible	8. barbaric
9. couch	10. evolve
11. counterpart	12. instill
13. sophisticated	14. nomad
15. negotiate	16. juxtapose

1. to move around an area or building in order to make sure that there is no trouble there

2. officially to join and pay a fee for an institution or on a course

3. a room at the top of a house just below the roof

4. officially to examine letters or the media and cut out any information that is regarded as secret

5. to stop a process or activity for a period of time

6. connected with the industrial production of medicine

7. abstract or hard to define or measure

8. extremely cruel or uncivilized

9. a long, comfortable seat for two or three people

10. gradually to change and develop into different forms

11. another person or thing that has a similar function or position in a different place

12. to make someone think or feel an idea or feeling, especially over a period of time

13. more advanced or complex than others

14. a member of a group of people who travel from place to place rather than living in one place all the time

15. to talk about a problem or a situation in order to solve the problem or complete the arrangement

16. to place two contrasting objects, images, or ideas together or describe them together, so that the differences between them are emphasized

B

1.a	2. a	3. b	4. b	5. b

1. 그들은 이미 존재하던 문화로부터 선진기술을 받아들이기 시작했다.

   (a) They began to adopt the advanced ways of existing cultures.

   (b) They were leaders in existing cultural innovation.

2. 훨씬 더 많은 것들이 세계 기후 문제와 관련하여 처리되어야 한다.

   (a) There's much more to be done about the world climate issue.

   (b) There are much more that we cannot do about the world climate problem.

3. 감시단들이 큰 국가 안의 모든 공장을 일일이 방문할 수 있을 것 같지 않다.

   (a) These treaties also need empowered monitors who can sanction polluters.

   (b) Monitors cannot feasibly visit every factory within a large country.

4. 이집트의 상형문자는 철학적인 개념들을 표현할 만큼 충분히 정교했다.

   (a) The Egyptians began using pictographs as a means to represent concrete objects.

   (b) Egyptian pictographs were sophisticated enough to deal with philosophical concepts.

5. 그린디아는 이 사실을 알면서도 이 약이 좋다고 홍보했기 때문에 고소되었다.

   (a) Glindia accused him of making false claims about the effectiveness of the pills.

   (b) Glindia is accused of knowing this fact, and yet marketing the pills as useful anyway.

C

1. Let me remind you that the WFDA is meeting this week.

2. Keeping a fan on while sleeping can make you sick.

3. He used to collect anything that had unusual colors or shapes.

4. I have some important clients coming over in the afternoon.

5. Glindia told him repeatedly that the pills were effective in losing weight.

1. that the WFDA is meeting this week / remind you / let me

2. you sick / can make/ keeping a fan on while sleeping

3. collect anything / he used to / that had unusual colors or shapes

4. some important clients / I have / coming over in the afternoon

5. that the pills were effective / in losing weight / Glindia told him repeatedly

D

1. b	2. b	3. a	4. a	5. b

1. The Aztecs moved to central Mexico to build their capital city.

   (a) The Aztecs remained barbaric nomads limited to northern Mexico.

   (b) The Aztecs migrated to central Mexico and built their capital city.

2. Many people volunteer to patrol the city when necessary.

   (a) Security forces hired by many businesses patrol the city when required.

   (b) Many citizens have formed volunteer groups that patrol the city when required.

3. Internet news organizations founded the WFDA.

   (a) The WFDA was launched at a conference of Internet news organizations.

   (b) The WFDA maintains that we should found Internet news organizations.

4. China plans to send women into space by 2010.

   (a) China's first team of female astronauts will leave on a space mission before 2010.

   (b) China's air force will give more advanced training to female astronauts by 2010.

5. Censoring certain literature is disrespectful of the writers and restricts their creativity.

   (a) Censoring literature, in other words, is like snatching away one's basic human rights.

   (b) By censoring certain literature, we are limiting a writer's free flow of thoughts and disrespecting his or her talent.

CHAPTER 08 STANCE / FUNCTION

VOCABULARY PREVIEW

01. puerile 철없는, 미숙한
02. skeptical 의심쩍은
03. manageable 처리할 수 있는
04. dispose of ~을 처분하다
05. constitute 구성하다
06. satellite 위성
07. discard 버리다, 폐기하다
08. collide 충돌하다
09. inflict (타격 · 상처 · 고통 따위를) 주다, 입히다
10. artificial 인공의
11. striking 놀라운
12. hazard 위험
13. urine 소변
14. lead 납
15. mercury 수은
16. pesticide 살충제
17. brood 곰곰이 생각하다
18. merciless 무자비한, 냉혹한
19. glow 타오르는 듯한 밝음
20. weary 피로한, 지쳐 있는
21. desolation 쓸쓸함, 황폐함
22. synopsis 개요, 개관
23. subdue 정복하다, 진압시키다
24. predecessor 전임자, 이전에 있었던 것

GUIDED LISTENING

1	1. a	2. b	2	1. c	2. d
3	1. c	2. c	4	1. b	2. d

1 Conversation

W: Hey, your shirt has got a big rip. What happened?

M: It's all due to my alarm clock.

W: Did the alarm clock rip your shirt? Sounds ridiculous!

M: Oh no. The alarm clock didn't ring on time this morning, so I got up too late! I quickly took my clothes from the drawer, dressed myself and rushed to the subway.

W: But then who tore your shirt?

M: Well, it was in the subway that I noticed that people were staring at me. So I took a look down and found a big rip in my shirt. As I was already running late, I decided to go ahead to the office.

W: That rip is quite obvious; why don't you get a shirt from a nearby store?

M: That's a good idea. I'll get it right now before other people find me dressed like this.

W: Good! Go ahead, but don't take too much time.

W: 이봐요, 셔츠가 많이 찢어졌어요. 무슨 일 있었어요?

M: 이게 다 내 알람시계 때문이에요.

W: 알람시계가 셔츠를 찢었다고요? 엉뚱하군요!

M: 아, 아니에요. 오늘 아침에 알람시계가 제대로 울리지 않아서, 늦게 일어났거든요! 서랍에서 서둘러 옷을 꺼내 입으면서 전철을 타러 달렸죠.

W: 그런데 그때 누군가 당신 셔츠를 찢었나요?

M: 음, 사람들이 저를 쳐다본다는 것을 알아챈 것은 전철에서였어요. 그래서 내려다보니 셔츠가 많이 찢어져 있더라고요. 이미 늦었기 때문에, 그냥 사무실로 가야겠다고 결정했죠.

W: 찢어진 게 너무 분명하게 보여요. 가까운 상점에 가서 셔츠를 사지 그래요?

M: 좋은 생각이군요. 사람들이 이렇게 입은 저를 보기 전에, 지금 바로 가야겠어요.

W: 그래요! 어서 가세요, 하지만 너무 오래 걸리지는 마세요.

Function

1 Why does the man say he noticed the rip in the subway?

(a) to imply that he is not sure how the shirt got the rip

(b) to explain where he got the rip on his shirt

(c) to emphasize how embarrassed he was in the morning

(d) to explain how the shirt got ripped in the subway

전철에서 찢어진 것을 알게 되었다고 남자가 말하는 이유는 무엇인가?

(a) 셔츠가 어떻게 찢어졌는지 확실하게 알 수 없다는 것을 암시하려고

(b) 셔츠의 어디가 찢어졌는지 설명하려고

(c) 아침에 그가 얼마나 민망했는지 설명하려고

(d) 어떻게 전철에서 셔츠가 찢어졌는지 설명하려고

해설 남자의 찢어진 셔츠에 관한 대화이다. 남자는 자명종이 제 시간에 울리지 않아 늦게 일어나서 부랴부랴 나오느라 옷이 찢어진 줄 몰랐다. 전철에서 사람들이 자기를 쳐다봐서 알게 되었다는 것은 셔츠가 어떻게 찢어진 것인지 정확하게는 모르겠다는 것을 말하기 위해서이므로 정답은 (a)이다.

합정 전철에서 옷이 찢어진 것을 알고는 민망했겠지만, 민망함을 설명하려는 대화는 아니라는 데에 주의한다.

Comprehension

2 Which of the following is correct according to the conversation?

(a) The man's clock stopped this morning.

(b) The woman noticed the rip as soon as she saw him.

(c) The man doesn't know where the store is.

(d) The woman thinks the man is ridiculous.

대화에 따르면 다음 중 옳은 것은?

(a) 남자의 시계는 오늘 아침에 멈추었다.

(b) 여자는 남자를 보자마자 셔츠가 찢어진 것을 알아챘다.

(c) 남자는 가게가 어디에 있는지 모른다.

(d) 여자는 남자가 엉뚱하다고 생각한다.

해설 이미 회사에 늦었는데, 사무실의 다른 사람들이 보기 전에 가게에 가서 옷을 사 입으라는 대화로 보아, 여자는 남자의 셔츠가 찢어진 것을 바로 알아챘음을 알 수 있다. 따라서 정답은 (b)이다.

합정 (a) 남자의 시계는 멈춘 것이 아니라, 제 시간에 울리지 않았다. (d) 여자는 엉뚱하다고 말한 것은 알람시계가 남자의 셔츠를 찢었다고 말한 대목에서이다. 남자 자체가 엉뚱하다고 생각하는 것은 아니다.

어휘 rip 쪼개다, 찢다, 찢음 | due to ~ 때문에 | ridiculous 어리석은, 우스운, 엉뚱한 | drawer 서랍 | rush to ~로 돌진하다 | stare at ~를 쳐다보다 | obvious 분명해 보이는, 확실하게 보이는

2 Conversation

M: Hey, there's a piece of mail for you. It says that you've won a million dollars! Do you think it's real?

W: It could be. Give it to me.

M: I thought you'd tell me to throw it out. Do you believe in this stuff?

W: Well, yes. I know people who have really won prizes.

M: I can't believe that. Do they want you to do something to win the prize?

W: Not exactly; however, you'd need to subscribe to a few magazines first.

M: Now, I see why you've built up a big pile of magazines. I don't want you to subscribe to any more of them!

W: Don't tell me that nobody else reads the magazines. I'm sure dad and mom do.

M: I'm just going to throw out all of your mail and magazines if you don't listen to me.

M: 얘야, 너에게 온 우편물이 있구나. 네가 백만 달러에 당첨되었다고 하는데! 진짜라고 생각하니?

W: 그럴 수도 있죠. 줘 보세요.

M: 나는 네가 그걸 버리라고 할 줄 알았는데. 이걸 믿는 거니?

W: 음, 네. 정말로 당첨된 사람들이 있는 걸요.

M: 나는 믿을 수가 없구나. 상금을 타기 위해 네가 무엇을 해야 하니?

W: 꼭 그런 건 아니지만, 먼저 몇몇 잡지들을 정기구독해야 해요.

M: 이제야, 잡지를 왜 그렇게 많이 쌓아 두었는지 알겠구나. 더 이상 잡지를 정기구독하지 않았으면 좋겠구나!

W: 아무도 잡지를 읽지 않는다고는 말씀하지 마세요. 아빠 엄마도 보시잖아요.

M: 내 말을 듣지 않으면, 내가 너의 모든 메일과 잡지들을 다 내다 버리겠다.

Stance

1 Which describes the sequence of emotions that the man undergoes?

(a) irritated ➡ curious ➡ skeptical

(b) irritated ➡ skeptical ➡ curious

(c) skeptical ➡ curious ➡ irritated

(d) curious ➡ irritated ➡ skeptical

남자가 느낀 감정의 변화로 적절한 것은?

(a) 화가 난 ➡ 캐묻는 ➡ 의심하는

(b) 화가 난 ➡ 의심하는 ➡ 캐묻는

(c) 의심하는 ➡ 캐묻는 ➡ 화가 난

(d) 캐묻는 ➡ 화가 난 ➡ 의심하는

해설 상금을 받기 위해 딸아이가 많은 잡지들을 정기구독한 것에 대한 대화이다. 아빠는 처음에는 의심쩍어서 이것저것 묻다가 사실을 알게 되어 화를 내고 있는 것이므로, 남자의 심경 변화로는 (c)가 가장 적절하다.

Detail

2 What does the woman have to do to win the prize?

(a) build up a big pile of magazines

(b) read as many magazines as possible

(c) subscribe the magazines at least for a year

(d) invest money in subscribing to the magazines

여자가 상을 타기 위해 해야 하는 것은 무엇인가?

(a) 잡지 더미 쌓기

(b) 가능한 한 많은 잡지 읽기

(c) 적어도 1년 동안 잡지 구독하기

(d) 잡지 구독에 비용 투자하기

해설 상금을 타기 위해 네가 무엇을 해야 하느냐는 남자의 질문에 you'd need to subscribe to a few magazines first (먼저 몇몇 잡지들을 정기구독해야 해요)라는 답변에서 정답을 알 수 있다. 상금을 타기 위해서는 잡지를 정기구독해야 하므로 정답은 (d)이다.

어휘 throw ~ out ~을 버리다 | subscribe 정기구독하다 | irritated 화가 난 | curious 호기심이 있는, 캐묻는 | skeptical 의심하는

3 Monologue

W: Pollution on Earth is quite manageable but trash in space is difficult to dispose of. Space trash is constituted of pieces of satellites or other objects sent to space that have broken into pieces, fallen off larger spaceships or satellites or been discarded in space for some reason. Space trash is a result of the 4,000 satellites that have been launched over the last 60 years. There are around 13,000 such objects being tracked by NASA, while countless others are too small to be tracked. Although sometimes small, space trash travels at very high speeds and is potentially dangerous if it collides with any other thing in space. The government and private agencies are trying to find a solution to space trash, because every time a space shuttle comes back from its mission, it usually has had damage inflicted on it by space trash.

W: 지구 오염은 그래도 처리하기 쉽지만, 우주의 쓰레기는 처분하기 어렵습니다. 우주 쓰레기는 우주로 보내져서, 부서졌거나 큰 우주선이나 위성에서 떨어져 나갔거나 어떤 이유로 우주에 폐기된 위성이나 다른 물체들의 파편으로 구성되어 있습니다. 우주 쓰레기는 지난 60년 넘게 발사되어 왔던 위성 4,000대의 결과입니다. 나사에 의해 추적된 그러한 물체들은 13,000개 정도 되지만, 수없이 많은 다른 것들은 너무 작아서 추적할 수도 없습니다. 때로는 그것이 작을지라도, 우주 쓰레기는 매우 빠른 속도로 움직여서 우주의 다른 물체와 충돌하게 되면, 위험할 수 있습니다. 정부와 사설 기관이 우주 쓰레기에 대해 걱정하고 있는데, 우주 왕복선이 임무를 마치고 돌아올 때마다 우주 쓰레기에 의해 피해를 입게 될 수 있기 때문입니다.

Stance

1 What can be inferred about the speaker?

(a) She is very concerned about pollution on Earth that is not disposable.

(b) She anguishes over the damage caused by space trash

(c) She is worried about the consequence that space trash can bring.

(d) She is optimistic about the missions to dispose of space trash.

화자에 대하여 추론할 수 있는 것은?

(a) 화자는 처분할 수 없는 지구의 오염에 대하여 많이 걱정한다.

(b) 화자는 우주 쓰레기가 일으킨 손상에 대해 괴로워한다.

(c) 화자는 우주 쓰레기가 가져올 수 있는 결과에 대해 걱정한다.

(d) 화자는 우주 쓰레기를 처분하는 임무에 대해 낙관적이다.

해설 우주 쓰레기에 관한 내용이다. 우주 쓰레기는 우주선이나 위성의 파편으로, 아주 작은 것일지라도 그 속도 때문에 위험할 수 있다고 언급하고 있다. 화자는 우주 쓰레기에 대해 걱정하고 있으므로 정답은 (c)이다.

함정 아직 우주 쓰레기가 어떤 손해를 일으킨 것은 아니므로 (b)는 오답이다.

Inference I

2 What does the speaker imply about space trash?

(a) It is formed by spaceship emissions.

(b) It is made of relatively harmless objects in space.

(c) It is harder to manage than pollution on Earth.

(d) It sometimes destroys human life.

화자가 우주 쓰레기에 대해 암시하는 것은 무엇인가?

(a) 우주선 발사에 의해 형성된다.

(b) 우주에서 상대적으로 무해한 물체로 구성되어 있다.

(c) 지구 오염보다 다루기 더 어렵다.

(d) 때로는 인간의 생활을 파괴한다.

해설 우주 쓰레기에 관한 내용이다. 우주 쓰레기는 지구 쓰레기보다 처리하기 어려우며 위험할 수 있다고 언급하고 있다. 그러므로 정답은 (c)이다.

4　Monologue

M: An average American has about 27 different <u>artificial chemicals</u> in his or her body — this striking fact was reported on Thursday by U.S. health researchers. This report is the first scientific evidence of the fact that Americans have measurable levels of artificial chemicals in their bodies which may be <u>harmful over the long term</u>. The researchers revealed that, although the artificial chemicals do not <u>pose any immediate health hazard</u>, their impact on the human body could be harmful if they remain in the body for a long time. Americans' <u>exposure to harmful chemicals</u> such as pollutants may be a possible cause of this finding. As a part of the research, 5,600 people were tested in 12 U.S. regions. The results indicated the presence of 27 different artificial chemicals <u>in the blood and urine</u> of the study participants. Among them were <u>industrial lead and mercury</u>, tobacco smoke and pesticides. Researchers say that more information is necessary to understand <u>the long-term effects</u> of these chemicals.

M: 일반적인 미국 사람은 몸속에 27가지의 인공 화학물질이 있습니다. 이 놀라운 사실은 목요일 미국 보건부 연구진에 의해 보고되었습니다. 이 보고는 미국인들이 장기간에 걸쳐 해로울 수 있는 인공 화학물질을 측정 가능할 정도로 몸속에 가지고 있다는 사실의 첫 번째 과학적 증거입니다. 연구진은 그 인공 화학물질이 당장은 건강을 위협하지 않을지라도, 그것들이 오랫동안 신체에 남아 있으면, 신체에 미치는 영향은 해로울 수 있다는 것을 밝혀냈습니다. 오염물질 같은 해로운 화학물질에 미국 사람들이 노출되어 있는 것이 이 연구 결과의 원인일 수 있습니다. 그 연구의 일환으로, 5,600명의 사람들이 미국 12개 지역에서 검사를 받았습니다. 그 결과, 연구 참가자들의 혈액과 소변에서 27가지의 다른 인공 화학물질이 있다는 것이 밝혀진 것입니다. 그것들 중에는 산업용 납, 수은, 담배 연기와 살충제도 있었습니다. 연구진은 이 화학물질의 장기적인 영향을 이해하려면 더 많은 정보가 필요하다고 말합니다.

Function

1　Why does the speaker say that more information is necessary to understand the long-term effects?

(a) to imply that there is no concrete evidence that the chemicals are harmful

(b) to show the researchers are not sure what diseases the chemicals may cause

(c) to explain the research was important and it needs to be continued

(d) to point out the research was incomplete and has not proved anything yet

장기적인 영향을 이해하려면 더 많은 정보가 필요하다고 화자가 말한 이유는?

(a) 그 화학물질들이 해롭다는 구체적인 증거가 없다는 것을 암시하기 위해

(b) 그 화학물질들이 어떤 질병을 일으킬지 연구진이 확신하지 못한다는 것을 보여 주기 위해

(c) 그 연구가 중요했다는 것과 계속되어야 한다는 점을 설명하기 위해

(d) 그 연구가 완성되지 않아서 아직 아무것도 증명하지 못했다는 것을 지적하기 위해

해설 미국 사람의 몸에서 여러 가지 인공 화학물질이 검출되었다는 내용이다. 당장은 건강을 위협하지 않더라도 장기적으로 건강에 해로울 수 있다고 밝혀졌다고 말한 다음, 마지막 문장에서 더 많은 정보가 필요하다고 했다. 더 많은 연구가 필요한 이유는 어떻게 해로울지에 대한 연구가 더 이루어져야 한다는 의미이므로 정답은 (b)이다.

합정 몸에 있는 인공 화학물질이 어떤 질병을 일으킬지는 아직 연구 전이지만, 사람의 몸에 해롭다는 사실은 밝혀진 결과이므로 (a)는 오답이다.

Detail

2　Which is NOT mentioned as a possible reason for the chemicals in the body?

(a) industrial lead

(b) mercury

(c) tobacco smoke

(d) exhaust gas

신체에 있는 화학물질들의 가능한 원인으로 언급되지 않은 것은?

(a) 산업용 납

(b) 수은

(c) 담배 연기

(d) 배기가스

해설 Among them were industrial lead and mercury, tobacco smoke and pesticides.라는 문장에서 몸속에 있는 인공 화학물질로는 산업용 납, 수은, 담배 연기와 살충제가 언급되고 있다. 그러므로 언급되지

않은 것은 (d) 배기가스이다.

어휘 average 평균의, 보통의 | artificial 인공의 | chemicals 화학물질 | striking 놀라운 | measurable 측정할 수 있는 | over the long term 장기간에 걸쳐 | reveal 밝히다, 드러내다 | pose (문제 등을) 제기하다 | hazard 위험 | impact 영향, 충격 | exposure 노출 | pollutant 오염물질 | region 지역 | presence 존재, 현존 | urine 소변 | participant 참여자, 참가자 | lead 납 | mercury 수은 | pesticide 살충제

PRACTICAL LISTENING

1. d	2. a	3. a	4. d	5. c
6. b	7. b	8. d	9. b	10. a

1

W: Today's gallery walk includes a viewing of one of Edward Hopper's best known paintings, titled *Nighthawks*. In it, you will see <u>brooding diners</u> at a 24-hour cafe. They are <u>captured in the merciless glow of</u> strong electric lights. Each of the characters in the painting looks <u>weary and lacking hope</u>. The painting also implies the characters either work during the night, or work so late that it carries them into the night. There is also <u>a slight air of seediness</u> and hopelessness about the characters. The atmosphere in the painting conveys a sense of <u>extreme loneliness and desolation</u>, making it typically modern, and one of Hopper's greatest works. This same mood can be captured in <u>a number of similar works</u> by different artists that we'll be going on to view in just a few moments.

W: 오늘 미술관 관람은 Edward Hopper의 작품 중에서 가장 잘 알려진 "Nighthawks"라는 그림을 포함하고 있습니다. 그 작품에서 여러분은 24시간 카페에 있는 생각에 잠긴 사람들을 볼 것입니다. 그들은 강한 전깃불에 가차 없이 노출되어 선명하게 포착되어 있습니다. 그림 속 각각의 등장인물들은 모두 피곤하고 희망이 없어 보입니다. 그림은 또한 각각의 인물들이 밤에 일하거나 늦게까지 일해서, 그들이 밤에 거기 있다는 것을 보여줍니다. 인물들에 대해 약간 초라하고 무기력한 분위기도 있습니다. 그림의 분위기는 극도의 외로움과 쓸쓸함을 전달하는데, 이는 전형적인 현대 미술 작품의 특징이며, Hopper의 위대한 작품 중 하나로 만들어 주는 것입니다. 다른 예술가들 역시 이와 비슷한 분위기를 작품에 담고 있는데 곧 보시게 될 것입니다.

Q What can be inferred from the talk?

(a) Hopper's *Nighthawks* is the first ever 'modern' work.

(b) Cafes and diners feature prominently in Hopper's paintings.

(c) Hopper's work is fairly unknown and easily misunderstood.

(d) Modern art typically illustrates themes of isolation.

이 이야기에서 추론할 수 있는 것은?

(a) Hopper의 'Nighthawks'는 최초의 '현대적인' 작품이다.

(b) Hopper의 그림에서는 주로 카페와 손님들이 나타난다.

(c) Hopper의 작품은 잘 알려져 있지 않고 잘못 이해되고 있다.

(d) 현대 예술은 전형적으로 고독에 대하여 이야기한다.

해설 Edward Hopper의 'Nighthawks'라는 그림에 대한 설명이다. 늦은 밤이거나 새벽에 카페에 앉아 있는 손님들이 환한 전깃불에 그대로 드러나는 외롭고 쓸쓸한 분위기의 그림으로, 이는 전형적인 현대 작품의 특징이라고 말하고 있으므로 (d)의 내용을 추론할 수 있다.

함정 그림의 전체적인 분위기가 전형적인 현대 그림의 특징을 나타낸다는 말은 있지만 최초라는 언급은 없으므로 (a)는 오답이다. 해당 작품에 카페와 손님들이 소재로 사용되었을 뿐 이 작가의 그림 전체에 대한 말은 아니므로 (b)도 유추될 수 없다. (c)는 언급되지 않았다.

어휘 brood 곰곰이 생각하다 | merciless 무자비한, 냉혹한 | glow 타오르는 듯한 밝음 | weary 피로한, 지쳐 있는 | imply 내포하다, 암시하다 | seediness 초라함, 기분이 좋지 않음 | convey 전달하다, 옮기다 | extreme 극도의 | desolation 쓸쓸함, 황폐함 | feature ~의 특징을 이루다 | prominently 두드러지게

2 Stance

W: Jonathan, why didn't you come to bingo night? We missed you a lot.

M: <u>I got an emergency call</u> from the hospital and had to be there.

W: We have another session next week. Make sure that you come.

M: I don't know about bingo.

W: What do you mean?

M: I mean the game looks simple, but <u>I don't really get it</u>.

W: Well, listen. You know what bingo cards look like, right? <u>Each space in the grid</u> has a number, except for the center square, which is considered filled. The letters B, I, N, G, O are pre-printed above <u>the five vertical columns</u>, with one letter appearing above each column.

M: I know that part.

W: All right. The printed numbers on the card <u>correspond to the following arrangement</u>: 1 to 15 in the B column; 16 to 30 in the I column; 31 to 45 in the N column; 46 to 60 in the G column and 61 to 75 in the O column.

M: This is exactly what I mean. I mean what is the point of the game?

W: It's fun, and if you're lucky, you can win some money, too.

M: I don't want to be sitting there for hours <u>when there is almost no chance of winning</u>. And I don't think it is fun.

W: Come on, Jonathan! Go there once. I'm sure you'll find it interesting.

....

W: Jonathan, 왜 빙고나이트에 오지 않았니? 우린 네가 없어서 정말 섭섭했어.

M: 병원에서 응급 호출이 와서 거기 가 봐야했어.

W: 다음 주에 다른 게임이 있으니까, 꼭 오도록 해.

M: 나는 빙고에 대해서 잘 모르겠어.

W: 무슨 말이야?

M: 게임은 단순해 보이는데, 잘 이해가 되지 않아.

W: 음, 들어 봐. 빙고 카드가 어떻게 생겼는지는 알지? 격자로 된 각각의 공간에 숫자가 있잖아. 가운데 칸은 빼고. 거기는 채워 넣는 거야. B, I, N, G, O라는 글자가 5개의 수직 칸들 위에 미리 인쇄되어 있는데, 각 칸들의 위에 글자가 하나씩 있는 거잖아.

M: 그건 알아.

W: 좋아. 카드의 그 인쇄된 숫자들은 다음과 같이 배열되어야 해. B의 칸에는 1에서 15까지의 숫자, I의 칸에는 16에서 30까지의 숫자, N의 칸에는 31에서 45까지의 숫자, G의 칸에는 46에서 60까지의 숫자, O의 칸에는 61에서 75까지의 숫자.

M: 내가 하려는 말이 바로 이거야. 그래서 게임의 포인트가 뭐라는 건데?

W: 재미지. 그리고 운이 좋으면 돈도 딸 수 있잖아.

M: 나는 승산 가능성도 별로 없는 곳에서 몇 시간이고 그렇게 앉아 있고 싶지 않아. 그리고 재미도 없어.

W: 이봐, Jonathan! 한번만 가 봐. 재미있다는 것을 분명히 알게 될 거야.

Q What does the man think about playing bingo?

(a) It is wasteful.

(b) It is complicated.

(c) It is risky.

(d) It is puerile.

남자는 빙고 게임을 하는 것에 대해 어떻게 생각하는가?

(a) 시간 낭비다.

(b) 복잡하다.

(c) 위험하다.

(d) 철없는 짓이다.

해설 빙고 게임에 관한 대화이다. 빙고가 뭐하는 건지 잘 모르겠다는 남자의 말에 여자는 경기 규칙에 대해 설명하고 있다. 하지만 남자가 이야기하려는 것은 그런 걸 왜 하느냐는 것이었다. 남자의 마지막 대화, 재미도 없고 승산 가능성도 없는 곳에서 몇 시간이고 앉아 있고 싶지 않다는 말에서 남자는 빙고를 시간 낭비라고 생각한다는 것을 알 수 있으므로 (a)가 정답이다.

어휘 emergency 응급, 위급 | grid 격자 (모양) | except for ~을 제외한 | square 네모 칸 | vertical 수직의 | correspond to 대응하다, (~에) 해당하다 | puerile 철없는, 미숙한

3

M: What time is it?

W: Aren't you sleeping? It's one in the morning.

M: So, we will be arriving in Paris <u>in one hour</u>, right?

W: Yeah!

M: Will it be possible <u>to find a hotel that early</u>?

W: There are a few hotels near the airport. I usually stay there <u>during my layovers</u>.

M: They'll be quite expensive, I guess.

W: Yes, they are. But it's okay <u>to stay for a night</u>.

M: Well, if you don't mind, you can come with me to my friend's apartment. He is coming to the airport to pick me up.

W: Seriously? Well...

M: There are many rooms. I'm sure you will find it comfortable. Plus, you don't want <u>to waste your money on a hotel</u>.

W: If your friend allows, I think it is not bad at all.

....

M: 지금 몇 시야?

W: 안 잤어? 새벽 1시야.

M: 그럼, 우리 1시간 있으면, 파리에 도착하겠네?

W: 응!

M: 그렇게 일찍 호텔을 찾을 수 있을까?

W: 공항 근처에 호텔이 몇 군데 있거든. 나는 경유해서 갈 때 주로 거기서 머물러.

M: 꽤 비쌀 것 같은데.

W: 응, 그래. 하지만 하룻밤 지내기에는 괜찮아.

M: 음, 너만 괜찮다면, 내 친구의 아파트로 갈 수 있는데. 그 친구가 나를 데리러 공항에 올 거거든.

W: 정말? 글쎄….

M: 방이 많아. 틀림없이 편안할 거야. 게다가 호텔에 돈을 쓰고 싶지도 않잖아.

W: 네 친구가 괜찮다면, 나도 전혀 나쁘지 않다고 생각해.

Q What are the man and woman mainly discussing?

(a) finding places to stay in Paris

(b) staying in Paris on vacation

(c) landing in Paris late at night

(d) booking seats on a flight to Paris

남자와 여자는 무엇을 주로 이야기하고 있는가?

(a) 파리에서 머무를 곳 찾기

(b) 휴가 때 파리에서 지내기

(c) 밤늦게 파리에 도착하기

(d) 파리행 비행기 좌석 예약하기

해설 새벽에 파리에 도착하게 될 두 사람이 비행기 안에서 나누는 대화이다. 여자가 공항 근처 호텔에서 묵어야겠다는 말에 남자는 괜찮다면 자신의 친구 집으로 가자고 하고 있다. 그러므로 둘이 나누는 대화는 묵을 곳에 관한 것이므로 (a)가 정답이다.

함정 두 사람이 밤늦게 파리에 도착하는 것은 맞지만, 그 늦은 도착이 대화의 화제가 아니라, 그 시간에 찾을 수 있는 호텔에 관해 주로 이야기하고 있는 것이기 때문에 (c)는 오답이다.

어휘 layover (여행할 때의) 도중 하차, 잠깐 머물기 | pick ~ up ~를 데리러 오다 | plus 게다가, 더하여

4

W: Hope you enjoyed our last hour of country music: I know I did! And now, here's the weather in Tampa with me, Susan. Get out your raincoats! It's going to be a wet one today! The forecast indicates partly cloudy skies in the afternoon, followed by heavy showers this evening. We could get up to a half inch of rain by 9:00 p.m. We're going to have a string of hot days following that rain, hotter than usual even for July. Expect a low of 64°F and a high of 88°F tomorrow, with clear skies and dry heat in the morning. A lot of humidity is going to be building by tomorrow afternoon, so you're probably going to feel hot, sticky and miserable. We won't be able to expect cooler weather anytime before the end of the month, I'm afraid.

W: 컨츄리 뮤직의 마지막 시간을 즐기기를 바랍니다. 저는 그랬습니다!

이제 저 Susan과 함께하는 탐파의 기상예보 시간입니다. 우비를 꺼내놓으세요! 오늘은 비가 올 것 같습니다! 부분적으로 오후에는 구름이 보이고 저녁에는 많은 양의 비가 예상됩니다. 저녁 9시까지 0.5인치 정도에 이르는 비가 예상됩니다. 이번 비가 내린 뒤 한 차례 무더운 날씨가 지속될 것이며 보통의 7월보다 더욱 무더운 날씨가 예상됩니다. 내일 최저 기온은 화씨 64도, 최고 기온은 화씨 88도로 예상되며 아침 하늘은 맑고 건조한 더위가 예상됩니다. 내일 오후에는 습기가 많아져서, 아마도 더욱 뜨겁고 끈적거리고 힘들게 느껴질 것 같습니다. 이번 달 말까지 시원한 날을 예상하기는 어려울 듯합니다.

Q Which is correct according to the weather report?

(a) Tampa will have clear skies this evening.

(b) Stormy weather will continue over the next few days.

(c) Temperatures may fall below 60°F tonight.

(d) Humidity is expected tomorrow afternoon.

기상 예보에 대한 설명 중 옳은 것은?

(a) 탐파의 하늘은 오늘 저녁 맑다.

(b) 다음 며칠동안 폭풍이 예상된다.

(c) 기온은 오늘 밤 화씨 60도까지 떨어진다.

(d) 습기가 내일 오후 예상된다.

해설 기상 예보이다. 오늘 저녁에는 비가 온다고 했으며 폭풍에 대한 언급은 없다. 내일은 최저 화씨 64도, 최고 화씨 88도 기온에 아침에는 맑겠으나 오후에는 습기가 많을 것이라고 했다. 그러므로 옳은 것은 (d)이다.

함정 저녁에 많은 양의 비가 예상되므로 (a)는 답이 될 수 없고, 폭풍에 관한 언급이 없으므로 (b)또한 오답이다. (c) 오늘 밤 기온에 대한 언급도 없다.

어휘 raincoat 우비 | up to 최고 ~까지 | string 일련, 한 차례 | humidity 습기, 습도 | sticky 끈적끈적한, 불쾌한

5 Function

M: Your quarterly assignment this time is writing a literature review. Those who have visited my web site recently may already know the process. That is, you will gather all the critical writing that has been done on today's topic, summarize it, and then "critique the critics," so to speak. After that, you will then inject your own analysis of the work. It will be one of your first steps in learning to become a serious and trained person of literature. For this, you will need to refer to articles, books, web sites and other material related to the topic of today's class discussion. You are required to summarize and evaluate each of the works you have consulted. In effect, you will be giving me a synopsis of

<u>all the important literature</u> published on this subject. Please note that the assignment is <u>due on July 9th</u>.

. . . .

M: 이번 분기 과제는 문헌 비평을 쓰는 것입니다. 최근 제 웹사이트를 방문했던 사람은 이미 알고 있을 것입니다. 즉, 이를 테면 오늘 주제와 관련된 모든 비평서를 모으고 요약한 뒤 그 비평에 대한 비평을 써야 하는 것입니다. 그리고 난 뒤 그 연구에 대한 여러분의 개인적인 분석을 추가해야 한다. 이것은 진지하고 훈련된 진정한 문헌가가 되기 위한 첫걸음이 될 것입니다. 이를 위해, 여러분들은 오늘 토론 주제와 관련된 논문, 서적, 웹사이트와 그 외 관련 자료들을 참조할 필요가 있을 것입니다. 여러분이 참고로 한 각 관련서들을 요약하고 평가해야 합니다. 사실상, 본 주제와 관련되어 출판된 주요한 관련 서적들의 개요를 제출하게 됩니다. 본 과제는 7월 9일 까지임을 메모해 두시기를 바랍니다.

Q Why does the professor mention his web site?

(a) to explain why he has opened his web site

(b) to imply that students who visit there have advantages

(c) to indicate where the details of the assignment are

(d) to recommend that the students visit the web site often

. . . .

교수는 자신의 웹사이트를 왜 언급하는가?

(a) 자신의 웹사이트를 왜 개설했는지를 설명하기 위해

(b) 그곳을 방문한 학생들은 이점이 있다는 것을 암시하기 위해

(c) 과제와 관련된 세부사항이 어디에 있는지 알려 주기 위해

(d) 학생들에게 거기 자주 방문하라고 권하기 위해

해설 분기 과제에 대한 설명이다. 교수는 오늘 주어진 주제와 관련된 비평서들을 요약하고 비평해야 하며, 자신의 견해를 써야 한다고 설명하고 있다. 이에 앞서 자신의 웹사이트를 방문했던 학생들은 이미 알고 있을 것이라고 언급했는데, 이는 그곳에 과제에 대한 설명이 있다는 점을 말하려는 것이므로 (c)가 정답이다.

함정 (a), (b), (d)는 교수가 언급한 내용과는 전혀 상관이 없는 부분이다.

어휘 **quarterly** 연 4회의 | **assignment** 과제, 숙제 |
review 비평, 평론 | **critical** 비판적인 | **summarize** 요약하다 |
critique 비평하다 | **critics** 비평, 비판 |
so to speak 말하자면, 이를테면 | **inject** 삽입하다, 도입하다 |
refer to 언급하다, 인용하다 | **related to** ~과 관련된 |
evaluate 평가하다 | **consult** 참고하다, 참조하다 |
synopsis 개요, 개관 | **due** 만기인, 기한인

6

W: Do you remember that there's a marathon this weekend?

M: Yes, how could I forget? I'm <u>participating in it</u>.

W: Are you really serious about it?

M: Of course I am. You know that I've been planning for it for a long time.

W: That's true, but <u>you should not stress your knee</u>. You've just <u>recovered from surgery</u>.

M: My knee is alright now.

W: I think you should reconsider going.

M: I've been running for a couple days for practice. And <u>I'm fit to run</u>.

W: Well, at least, <u>go talk to your doctor</u> before you participate, would you?

M: I already did, and she said <u>I should be fine</u>.

. . . .

W: 이번 주에 마라톤 대회 있는 거 기억하고 있니?

M: 응, 어떻게 잊을 수 있겠어? 내가 참가하는데.

W: 진짜 나갈 거야?

M: 물론이지. 오랫동안 계획해온 거 너도 알잖아.

W: 그건 그렇지만, 네 무릎에 무리를 주면 안 돼. 이제 막 수술에서 회복 했잖아.

M: 무릎은 이제 괜찮아.

W: 다시 생각해 봐야 할 것 같은데.

M: 며칠 동안 연습 삼아 달렸어. 달릴 수 있을 만큼 건강해.

W: 음. 그래도 참가하기 전에 의사와 이야기라도 해봐, 알았지?

W: 벌써 다녀왔는데, 의사 선생님이 괜찮을 거래.

Q Which is correct about the conversation?

(a) The woman does not think the man will win the marathon.

(b) The man's knee was recently operated on.

(c) The man does not want to run the marathon.

(d) The woman is going to participate in the marathon.

. . . .

대화에 대한 설명으로 옳은 것은?

(a) 여자는 남자가 마라톤에서 이기지 못할 것이라고 생각한다.

(b) 남자는 최근에 무릎 수술을 했다.

(c) 남자는 마라톤에서 달리고 싶어 하지 않는다.

(d) 여자는 마라톤에 참여할 것이다.

해설 남자의 마라톤 참가에 관한 두 사람의 대화이다. 남자는 이번 주 마라톤 대회에 참가할 생각으로 들떠있지만, 여자는 수술에서 회복된 지 얼마 안 된 무릎에 무리를 주면 안 되기 때문에 남자가 출전을 재고하길 원하고 있다. 하지만 남자는 의사가 괜찮을 거라고 했다고 말하고 있다. 그러므로 정답은 (b)이다.

어휘 **participate in** ~에 참가하다, 참여하다 |
stress ~에 압력을 가하다 | **knee** 무릎 |

recover (from) ~에서 낫다, 회복하다 | surgery 수술 |
reconsider 재고하다, 다시 생각하다 | fit 적당한, 꼭 맞는, 건강한 |
operate on ~을 수술하다

해설 남자는 여자를 약속 장소에서 이미 30분 동안 기다렸다. 앞으로 15분을 더 기다린 다음에도 오지 않으면, 먼저 갈 것인데, 못 오더라도 꼭 전화해 달라는 내용이다. 지난번에도 헛되이 기다렸었다는 말을 통해, Naomi에 대한 남자의 태도는 (b) 비판적임을 알 수 있다.

어휘 be supposed to ~하기로 되어 있다 |
housewarming party 집들이 파티 | at least 적어도 |
in vain 헛되이, 무익하게 | make it 약속을 지키다, 성공하다

7 Stance

M: Hey Naomi, this is Ben. We were supposed to meet to go to Brian and Nicole's <u>housewarming party</u> on Stratford, remember? I hope you remember. All the guests are <u>supposed to be there by 9:30</u>, but it'll take at least an hour or so to get there from Burlington Avenue. It's 8:00 p.m. and I've been waiting for you on Burlington in front of Dixon's for the past half hour. You should <u>get back to me</u> as soon as you receive this message. If I don't get your call by 8:15, I'll go to the party without you. You <u>kept me waiting in vain</u> last time. I can't wait any longer when you're not calling me. And I don't want to be late for this event because I promised Brian that I'd be there on time. Even if you can't <u>make it to the party</u>, still call me. You could also <u>send a text to</u> my PDA. So, call or text me soon, bye.

M: 안녕 Naomi. Ben이야. 우리 Stratford에 있는 Brian과 Nicole의 집들이 파티에 가기 위해서 만나기로 한 것 기억해? 네가 기억하고 있기를 바란다. 모든 손님들은 9시 30분까지 도착하기로 되어 있는데 Burlington 가에서 적어도 한 시간 조금 더 걸릴 거야. 지금 8시인데, Dixon's 앞 Burlington에서 너를 기다린 지 30분이 지났어. 이 메시지 받는 즉시 연락해 줘. 만약 8시 15분까지 네 연락이 없으면 혼자 파티에 갈 거야. 나는 지난번에도 너를 기다렸었지만 쓸모없는 일이었잖아. 네가 전화하지 않으면, 더 이상은 기다릴 수 없어. 그리고 Brian과 약속시간을 맞추겠다고 약속했기 때문에 늦게 가고 싶지 않아. 만약 네가 파티에 못 올 것 같아도, 그래도 전화해 줘. 내 PDA로 문자 보내도 돼. 전화하거나 문자 해. 안녕.

Q Which best describes the man's attitude towards Naomi?

(a) hostile

(b) critical

(c) amicable

(d) outraged

Naomi에 대한 남자의 태도는?

(a) 적대적인

(b) 비판적인

(c) 호의적인

(d) 격분한

8

W: Sarcoidosis is <u>a disorder of the immune system</u> mainly affecting the lungs, eyes or skin. Generally the patient suffers no more than severe physical discomfort although there are <u>reported cases of serious organ damage</u>, and even death in an estimated 2.8% of patients. There is <u>no known cure</u> for the condition and very few treatment options. Corticosteroids offer slight relief to some patients, but for a majority of them even <u>this is ineffective</u>. Research continues <u>on other potential treatments</u>, but they have yielded nothing positive yet, mainly because we still understand so little about the human immune system. This means that, for the most part, a person with this illness will exist <u>in state of mild to severe discomfort</u> for the remainder of his or her life.

W: 유육종증은 주로 폐, 눈, 피부를 해치는 면역체계 장애이다. 일반적으로 극심한 신체적인 불편함 외에는 다른 고통을 느끼지는 않지만 때때로 장기가 파손되거나 약 2.8%의 환자가 사망에 이르기도 한다. 이 병에 대해 알려진 치료법은 없으며 처치법 역시 매우 한정적이다. 코르티코스테로이드는 일부 환자들에게 약간의 안정을 주지만 대부분의 환자들에게는 효과적이지 않다. 다른 치료법에 대한 연구가 끊임없이 진행되고 있지만 아직까지 별 다른 결과는 없다. 이는 아직 인간의 면역 체계에 대하여 알려진 지식이 거의 없기 때문이다. 즉 대부분 이 병에 걸린 사람은 그들의 남은 여생 동안 약간의 불쾌함 내지는 극심한 불쾌감 상태로 살게 된다는 것을 의미한다.

Q Which is correct about sarcoidosis, according to the lecture?

(a) It causes damage by attacking the body's skin.

(b) Corticosteroids are known to be an effective cure.

(c) About 2.8% of the population is affected by it.

(d) It could prove to be fatal in some cases.

이 강의에 따르면 유육종증에 대한 설명으로 옳은 것은?

(a) 신체의 피부를 공격하여 손상을 일으킨다.

(b) 코르티코스테로이드가 효과적인 치료법으로 알려져 있다.

(c) 인구의 약 2.8%가 이 병에 걸렸다.

(d) 때로는 치명적일 수 있다고 밝혀졌다.

해설 면역체계 장애인 유육종증에 관한 강의이다. 이 질병은 폐, 눈, 피부에 영향을 미치며, 신체적인 불편함 외에는 고통이 거의 없다. 치료법이 거의 없지만, 코르티코스테로이드가 일부 환자들에게는 효과가 있기도 하다. 이 병에 걸리면 대부분 평생 그냥 그 고통을 받아들이며 살 수밖에 없다고 한다. 하지만 때로는 장기 파손되기도 하며 2.80%가 사망에 이르는 질병이다. 그러므로 정답은 (d)이다.

함정 유육종증은 피부를 공격한다기보다는 면역체계 장애라고 했으므로 (a)는 오답이다. 코르티코스테로이드는 일부 환자들에게 야간의 안정을 주지만 대부분의 환자들에게는 효과적이지 않다는 언급으로 보아 (b) 또한 오답이며, 인구의 2.8%가 이 병에 걸리는 것이 아니라 감염된 환자의 약 2.8%의 환자가 사망에 이르기도 한다는 얘기이므로 (c)도 오답이다.

어휘 sarcoidosis [병리] 유육종증(類肉腫症) (림프절·폐·뼈·피부에 육종 같은 것이 생김) | disorder 장애 | immune system 면역체계 | lung 폐 | no more than 단지, 겨우 (only) | severe 극심한, 호된 | discomfort 불쾌, 불편 | organ 기관, 장기 | corticosteroid 코르티코스테로이드 (부신피질 호르몬 및 그 비슷한 화학 물질) | relief 완화, 안정 | potential 가능한 | yield 생기게 하다, (이익 따위를) 가져오다 | remainder 나머지, 잔여

9 Function

M: Where are you from, Angelina?

W: Well, I consider myself a global citizen.

M: Seems that you've travelled a lot, then.

W: I lived in many places. My dad was in the navy.

M: That sounds exciting! You must have lived in many interesting countries.

W: That's true. I enjoyed it a lot but could not make many friends.

M: That's the main disadvantage when you keep moving.

W: You're right. Other than that, everything was great. What about you? Where are you from?

M: I'm from Canada.

W: You know what? I've never been to Canada.

M: That's good. I mean there is at least one country I know better than you.

W: I really wanted to visit some of my best friends in Ottawa. But I never had a chance.

M: That's where I'm from. Well, if you plan to visit your friends there, I really want to invite you to my house.

W: Great!

M: 어디 출신이에요, Angelina?

W: 음, 나는 내 자신을 국제시민이라고 생각해요.

M: 그렇다면 여행을 많이 한 것 같군요.

W: 네, 아버지가 해군이셔서, 여러 곳에서 지냈어요.

M: 흥미롭군요! 틀림없이 재미있는 많은 나라에서 살았겠군요.

W: 맞아요. 참 즐거웠지만 친구들은 많이 사귀지 못했어요.

M: 계속 이사를 다니게 될 때 생기는 가장 큰 손실이죠.

W: 맞아요. 그것 말고는 다 좋았어요. 당신은 어때요? 어디 출신이죠?

M: 저는 캐나다 출신이에요.

W: 그거 알아요? 저는 캐나다에는 가 본 적이 없어요.

M: 잘됐네요. 그러니까 제 말은 적어도 한 나라에 대해서는 제가 당신보다 잘 안다는 거죠.

W: 오타와에 살고 있는 친한 친구들 몇몇을 찾아가고 싶었는데, 기회가 없었어요.

M: 제가 바로 거기 출신이죠. 음, 거기 친구들을 방문할 계획이라면, 우리 집에도 초대하고 싶어요.

W: 좋아요!

Q Why does the woman mention her father?

(a) to imply that he is a very strict person

(b) to explain why she lived in many places

(c) to suggest he liked to travel a lot

(d) to indicate where she is from

여자가 아버지를 언급한 이유는?

(a) 아버지가 매우 엄격한 분이라는 것을 암시하기 위해

(b) 그녀가 많은 장소에서 살았던 이유를 설명하기 위해

(c) 아버지가 여행을 좋아했다는 것은 제시하기 위해

(d) 그녀가 어디 출신인지 설명하기 위해

해설 여자의 아버지가 해군이었기 때문에, 그녀는 많은 나라를 돌아다니면서 살았다는 내용이다. 그러므로 여자가 아버지를 언급한 이유는 그녀가 여러 지역에서 살았던 이유를 설명하기 위한 것이다.

어휘 navy 해군 | make a friend 친구를 사귀다, 친해지다 | disadvantage 불리한 조건, 불편, 손해

10

M: Let's look at some empires of the ancient world. Ancient Greece was a powerful kingdom that was conquered by Macedonia, which was in turn conquered by Rome. This is the general pattern in ancient history: one kingdom wins battles, becomes powerful and establishes an empire. It manages to subdue its neighbors through its military might, and often has a much larger and more powerful economic and cultural system as well. These factors combine to enable it to overcome competitors both large and small. It lasts until another empire comes along that is stronger, bigger and lasts longer. The new empire's military, economic and cultural power is usually stronger than its predecessor. Now, I'm going to tell you about an empire that grew even bigger and mightier than that of Rome.

M: 고대 세계의 몇몇 제국을 살펴봅시다. 고대 그리스는 강력한 왕국이었지만 마케도니아에 의해 정복당했고 이 마케도니아는 로마에 의하여 정복당합니다. 이것이 일반적인 고대 역사의 흐름입니다. 한 왕국이 전쟁에 이겨서 강력해지고 제국을 건설하는 것이죠. 그 왕국은 군사력을 이용해 주변국을 점령하고, 때로는 훨씬 더 크고 강대한 경제와 문화 제도도 쥐게 됩니다. 이러한 요인들이 합쳐져서 크고 작은 경쟁 상대를 이겨나가는 것입니다. 이 왕국보다 더 힘세고 크고 오래 지속할 제국이 나타날 때까지 계속되는 것입니다. 새로운 제국의 군대와 경제 문화력은 보통 이전의 왕국보다 더 강합니다. 지금부터 나는 로마보다 더 크고 강대했던 제국에 대하여 말해 보고자 합니다.

Q   What will the speaker probably do following this talk?

(a) present a powerful empire that lasted for a long time

(b) discuss the empire founded by Rome

(c) point out Greek, Macedonian, and other empires on a map

(d) list the ancient empires by order on a chart

화자가 이 이야기 다음에 할 것으로 보이는 것은?

(a) 오랜 기간 동안 지속했던 강력한 제국 제시하는 것

(b) 로마에 의해 세워진 제국에 대한 토론하는 것

(c) 그리스, 마케도니아와 다른 제국들을 지도에서 찾아보는 것

(d) 차트에 순서대로 고대 제국들을 나열하는 것

해설 고대 제국들에 관한 역사 강의이다. 다음에 나올 내용을 묻는 문제는 뒷부분을 유의하며 들어야 한다. 마지막 문장 I'm going to tell you about an empire that grew bigger and mightier than that of Rome.에서 나타나듯이 로마보다 더 크고 강대했던 제국에 대한 이야기가 뒤따를 것이다.

어휘 in turn 번갈아, 차례차례 | subdue 정복하다, 진압시키다 | might 힘, 세력, 권력 | as well 또한 | overcome 극복하다 | predecessor 전임자, 이전에 있었던 것

LISTENING REVIEW

A

1. might	2. synopsis
3. dispose of	4. puerile
5. pesticide	6. collide
7. subdue	8. exposure
9. disadvantage	10. vertical
11. mercury	12. evaluate
13. discard	14. predecessor
15. brood	16. yield

1. power or strength

2. a summary of a longer piece of writing or work

3. to throw something away

4. silly and childish

5. chemical substance which farmers put on their crops to kill harmful insects

6. to crash into one another

7. to defeat or bring a group of people under control by using force

8. the state of being in a situation where it might affect you

9. a factor which makes someone or something less useful, acceptable, or successful than others

10. standing or pointing straight up

11. a silver-colored liquid metal that is used especially in thermometers and barometers

12. to consider something or someone in order to make a judgment about them, for example about how good or bad they are

13. to get rid of something because you no longer want it or need it

14. the person who had your job before you

15. to think about it a lot, seriously and often unhappily

16. to produce or provide something, for example, a profit, result, or crop

B

1. a	2. b	3. a	4. b	5. b

1. 나는 지난번에도 너를 기다렸었지만 쓸모없는 일이었잖아.

   (a) You kept me waiting in vain last time.

   (b) You must have waited for me in vain last time.

2. 그들은 강한 전깃불에 가차 없이 노출되어 선명하게 포착되어 있다.

   (a) They could capture the cruel heat of frail electric lights.

   (b) They are captured in the merciless glow of strong electric lights.

3. 틀림없이 재미있는 많은 나라에서 살았겠네요.

   (a) You must have lived in many interesting countries.

   (b) You couldn't have lived in various wonderful countries.

4. 우리는 아직 인간의 면역 체계에 대하여 거의 아무것도 이해하고 있지 못하다.

   (a) The human immune system has revealed almost nothing about human beings.

   (b) We still understand so little about the human immune system.

5. 이 왕국보다 더 힘세고 크고 오래 지속할 제국이 나타날 때까지 계속된다.

   (a) It lasts until a much larger and more powerful economic and cultural system appears.

   (b) It lasts until another empire comes along that is stronger, bigger and lasts longer.

C

1. I see why you've built up a big pile of magazines.
2. These factors combine to enable it to overcome competitors.
3. Those who have visited my web site recently may already know.
4. We're going to have a string of hot days following that rain.
5. Americans' exposure to harmful chemicals may be a possible cause of this finding.

1. a big pile of magazines / I see / why you've built up

2. it to overcome competitors / these factors / combine to enable

3. who have visited my web site recently / may already know / those

4. a string of hot days / we're going to have / following that rain

5. may be a possible cause of this finding / to harmful chemicals / Americans' exposure

D

| 1. b | 2. b | 3. a | 4. b | 5. b |

1. Humidity is expected tomorrow afternoon.

   (a) Expect a low of 64°F and a high of 88°F tomorrow afternoon.

   (b) A lot of humidity is going to be building by tomorrow afternoon.

2. I noticed in the subway that people were staring at me.

   (a) I noticed that people were staring at me, as I wasn't in the subway.

   (b) It was in the subway that I noticed that people were staring at me.

3. Space trash is harder to manage than pollution on Earth.

   (a) Pollution on Earth is quite manageable, but trash in space is difficult to dispose of.

   (b) Space trash travels at very high speeds and is potentially dangerous.

4. The researchers are not sure what diseases these chemicals may cause.

   (a) The researchers revealed that their impact on the human body could be harmful for a long time.

   (b) The researchers say that more information is necessary to understand the effects of these chemicals.

5. You will need to give a synopsis and estimate each of the materials you have referred to.

   (a) You will gather all the critical writing that has been done on today's topic and summarize it.

   (b) You are required to summarize and evaluate each of the works you have consulted.

MEMO

MEMO

AIM HIGH LISTENING

청취의 8가지 핵심 Question Types

토플, 텝스 등 각종 청취 테스트의 핵심적인 문제 유형을 면밀히 분석하여 세분하였다. 모든 유형의 청취 시험에 완벽하게 대비할 수 있도록 다양하고도 근본적인 listening skill들을 연습하도록 구성하였다.

다양한 형태 및 주제에 대한 청취

여러 유형의 테스트에서 접할 수 있는 강의, 연구 결과, 방송, 연설 등의 다양한 담화문과, 일상생활에서 일어날 수 있는 실질적인 대화를 청취함으로써 다양한 청취 형태와 주제에 익숙해지도록 하였다.

소리로 익히는 청취 훈련

청취 훈련을 위해서는 눈으로 읽고 손으로 쓰는 훈련보다는 소리를 듣고 익히며 그 표현을 소리로 인식하고, 같은 뜻이나 비슷한 표현 또한 소리로 인식하는 것이 중요하다. 따라서 읽거나 쓰는 것이 아닌, sound로 익히고 sound로 확인하는 다양한 청취 훈련을 하도록 구성하였다.

Guided Listening 훈련

Listening Notes를 통해 청취하는 내용의 핵심 정보를 메모하는 것은 물론 내용의 전체적인 흐름을 머리로 이해하는 훈련이 되도록 하였다. 청취 지문의 전형적인 구조에 익숙해짐으로써 '예측 청취'를 가능케 하여 전반적인 청해 실력을 향상시킬 수 있다.

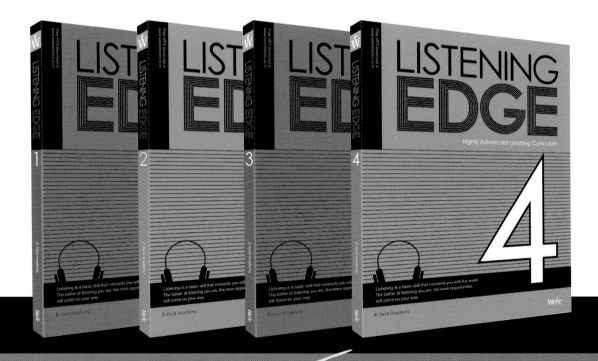